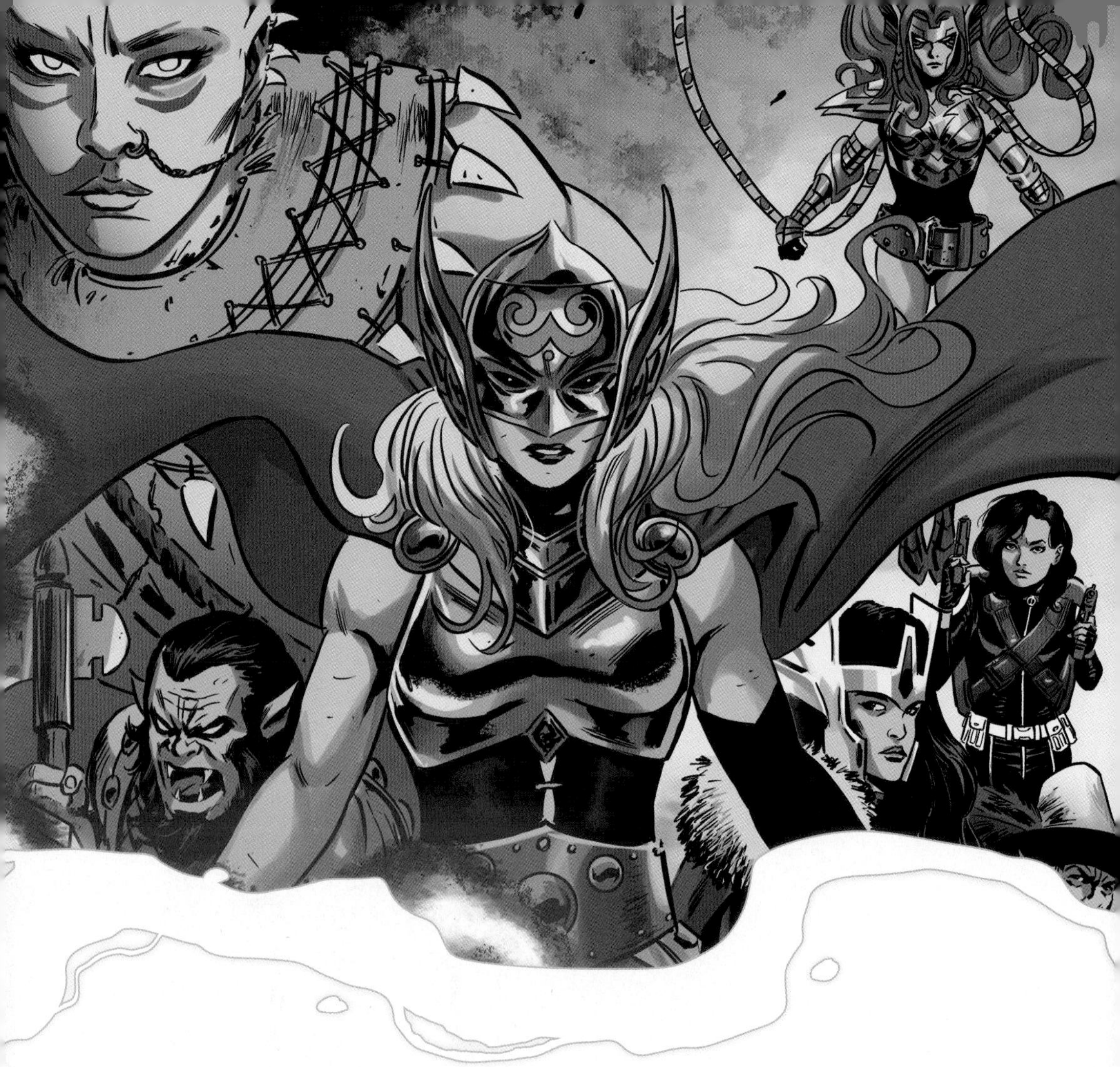

WHEN **DR. JANE FOSTER** LIFTS THE MYSTIC
HAMMER MJOLNIR, SHE IS TRANSFORMED INTO
THE GODDESS OF THUNDER, THE MIGHTY THOR!
HER ENEMIES ARE MANY, AS ASGARD DESCENDS
FURTHER INTO CHAOS AND WAR THREATENS TO SPREAD
THROUGHOUT THE TEN REALMS. YET HER GREATEST
BATTLE WILL BE AGAINST A FAR MORE PERSONAL FOE:
THE CANCER THAT IS KILLING HER MORTAL FORM…

THE WAR OF THE REALMS RAGES ON. MALEKITH,
KING OF THE DARK ELVES, OCCUPIES ALFHEIM, THE REALM
OF THE LIGHT ELVES, AND CONTINUES HIS CAMPAIGN FOR
POWER. HEROES FROM ACROSS THE REALMS HAVE HAD
VARIED SUCCESS, IN HOLDING OFF THE DARK ELF FORCES, BUT
UNLESS THE TIDES TURN SOON, THE WORLD TREE WILL FALL.

ESTRANGED FROM THE POWERS THAT BE IN ASGARD,
THOR HAS TAKEN IT UPON HERSELF TO LIBERATE THE
PEOPLE OF ALFHEIM. BUT, THOUGH GODDESS OF
THUNDER SHE MAY BE, IT THIS IS NOT A TASK
SHE CAN ACCOMPLISH ALONE…

THE MIGHTY THOR

THE ASGARD/SHI'AR WAR

WRITER
JASON AARON

ISSUES #13-14

ARTIST
STEVE EPTING

COLOR ARTIST
FRANK MARTIN

ISSUES #15-19

ARTIST
RUSSELL DAUTERMAN WITH **VALERIO SCHITI** (#19, PP. 11-17 & 19-20)

COLOR ARTIST
MATTHEW WILSON WITH **MAT LOPES** (#19, PP. 11-17 & 19-20)

LETTERER
VC's JOE SABINO

COVER ART
RUSSELL DAUTERMAN & MATTHEW WILSON

ASSISTANT EDITOR
CHARLES BEACHAM

ASSOCIATE EDITOR
SARAH BRUNSTAD

EDITOR
WIL MOSS

COLLECTION EDITOR: **JENNIFER GRÜNWALD**
ASSISTANT EDITOR: **CAITLIN O'CONNELL**
ASSOCIATE MANAGING EDITOR: **KATERI WOODY**
EDITOR, SPECIAL PROJECTS: **MARK D. BEAZLEY**

VP, PRODUCTION & SPECIAL PROJECTS: **JEFF YOUNGQUIST**
SVP PRINT, SALES & MARKETING: **DAVID GABRIEL**
BOOK DESIGNER: **ADAM DEL RE**

EDITOR IN CHIEF: **AXEL ALONSO**
CHIEF CREATIVE OFFICER: **JOE QUESADA**
PRESIDENT: **DAN BUCKLEY**
EXECUTIVE PRODUCER: **ALAN FINE**

THOR CREATED BY **STAN LEE, LARRY LIEBER & JACK KIRBY**

TY THOR VOL. 3: THE ASGARD/SHI'AR WAR. Contains material originally published in magazine form as MIGHTY THOR #13-19. First printing 2017. ISBN# 978-1-302-90308-4. Published by EL WORLDWIDE, INC., a subsidiary of MARVEL ENTERTAINMENT, LLC. OFFICE OF PUBLICATION: 135 West 50th Street, New York, NY 10020. Copyright © 2017 MARVEL No similarity between any names, characters, persons, and/or institutions in this magazine with those of any living or dead person or institution is intended, and any such similarity which may exist is purely coincidental. ed in the U.S.A. DAN BUCKLEY, President, Marvel Entertainment; JOE QUESADA, Chief Creative Officer; TOM BREVOORT, SVP of Publishing; DAVID BOGART, SVP of Business Affairs & Operations, hing & Partnership; C.B. CEBULSKI, VP of Brand Management & Development, Asia; DAVID GABRIEL, SVP of Sales & Marketing, Publishing; JEFF YOUNGQUIST, VP of Production & Special Projects; CARR, Executive Director of Publishing Technology; ALEX MORALES, Director of Publishing Operations; SUSAN CRESPI, Production Manager; STAN LEE, Chairman Emeritus. For information ing advertising in Marvel Comics or on Marvel.com, please contact Vit DeBellis, Integrated Sales Manager, at vdebellis@marvel.com. For Marvel subscription inquiries, please call 888-511-5480. factured between 5/26/2017 and 6/27/2017 by LSC COMMUNICATIONS INC., SALEM, VA, USA.

87654321

13

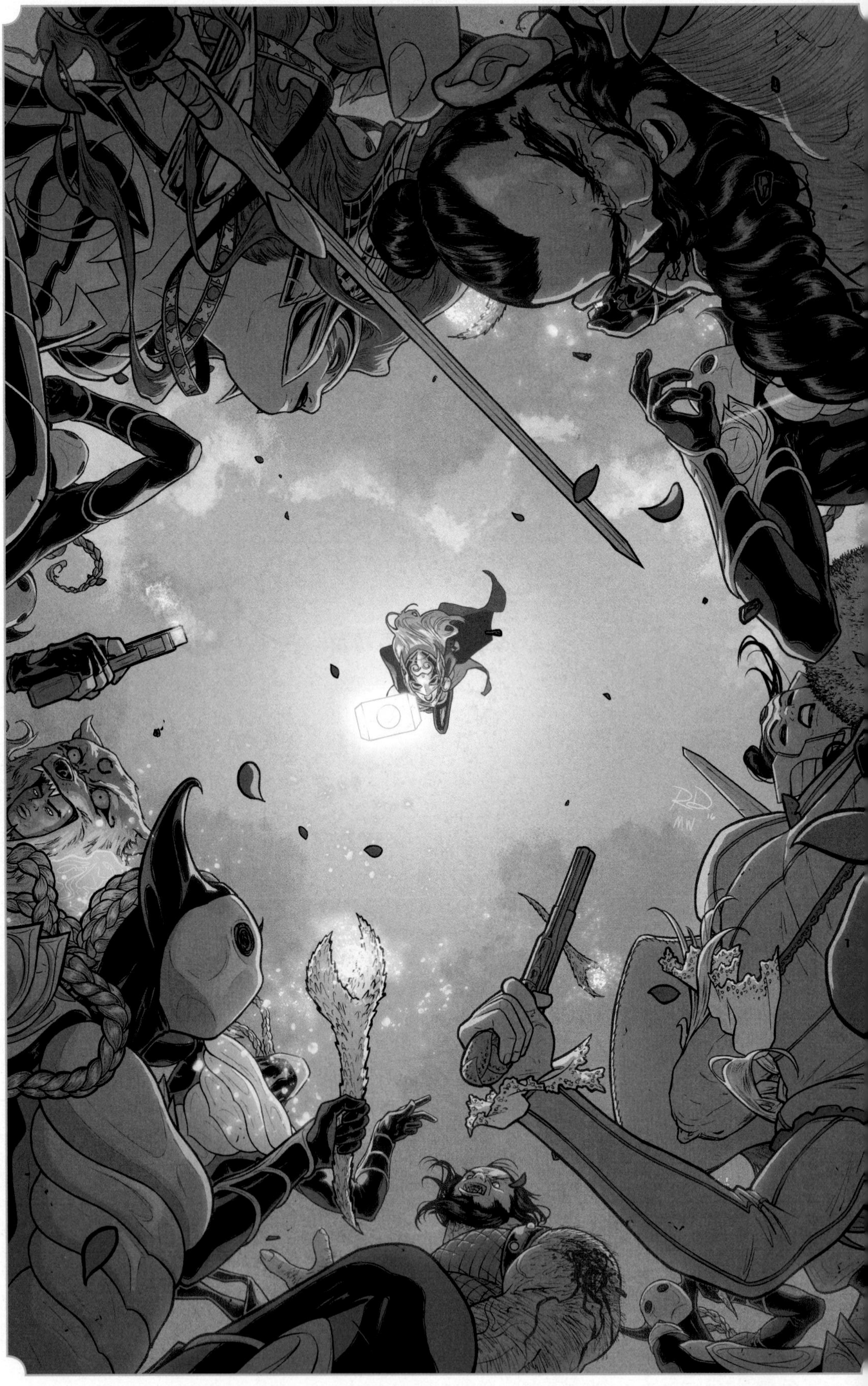

THE LEAGUE OF REALMS RIDES AGAIN

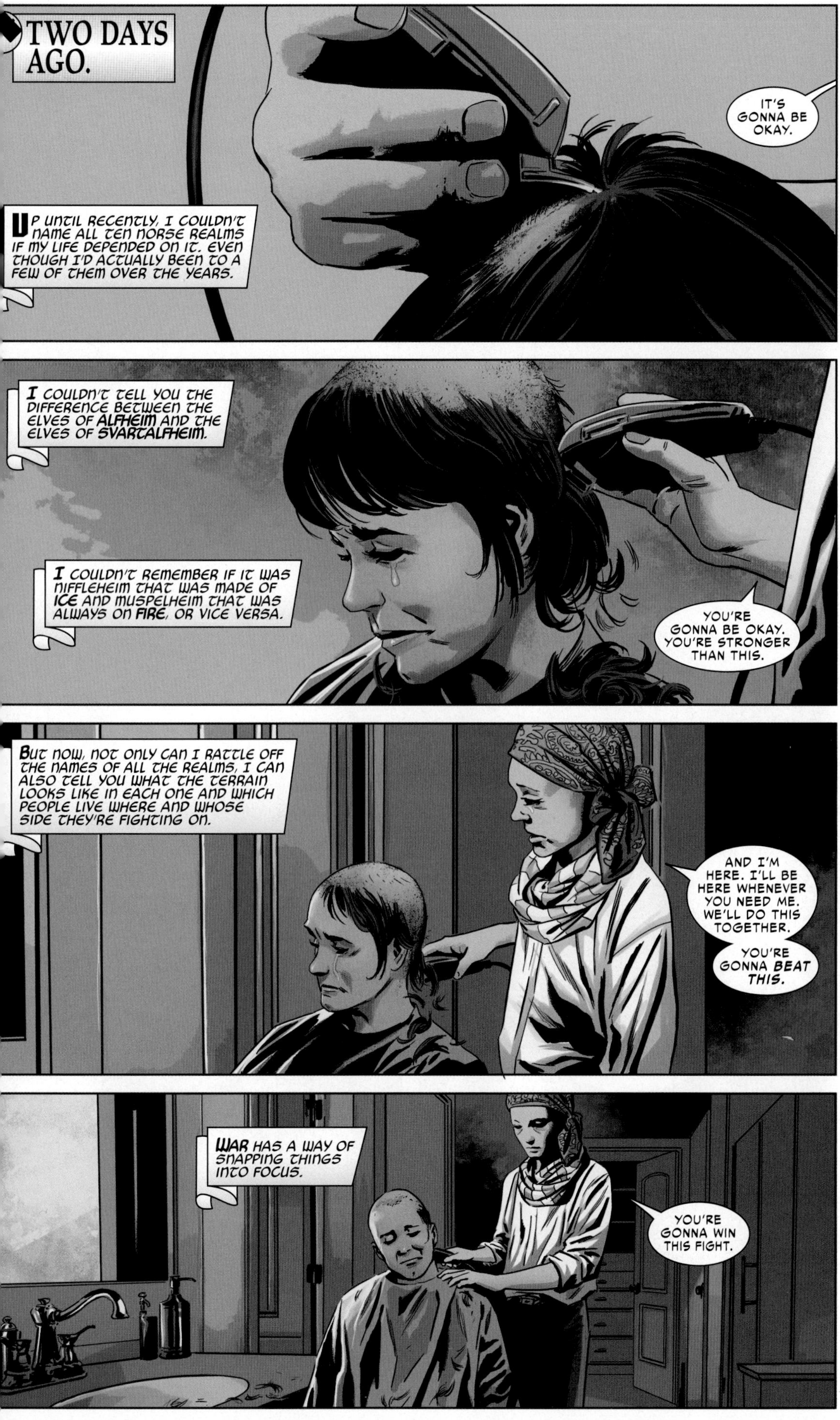
TWO DAYS AGO.
UP UNTIL RECENTLY, I COULDN'T NAME ALL TEN NORSE REALMS IF MY LIFE DEPENDED ON IT. EVEN THOUGH I'D ACTUALLY BEEN TO A FEW OF THEM OVER THE YEARS.
IT'S GONNA BE OKAY.
I COULDN'T TELL YOU THE DIFFERENCE BETWEEN THE ELVES OF ALFHEIM AND THE ELVES OF SVARTALFHEIM.
I COULDN'T REMEMBER IF IT WAS NIFFLEHEIM THAT WAS MADE OF ICE AND MUSPELHEIM THAT WAS ALWAYS ON FIRE, OR VICE VERSA.
YOU'RE GONNA BE OKAY. YOU'RE STRONGER THAN THIS.
BUT NOW, NOT ONLY CAN I RATTLE OFF THE NAMES OF ALL THE REALMS, I CAN ALSO TELL YOU WHAT THE TERRAIN LOOKS LIKE IN EACH ONE AND WHICH PEOPLE LIVE WHERE AND WHOSE SIDE THEY'RE FIGHTING ON.
AND I'M HERE. I'LL BE HERE WHENEVER YOU NEED ME. WE'LL DO THIS TOGETHER.
YOU'RE GONNA BEAT THIS.
WAR HAS A WAY OF SNAPPING THINGS INTO FOCUS.
YOU'RE GONNA WIN THIS FIGHT.

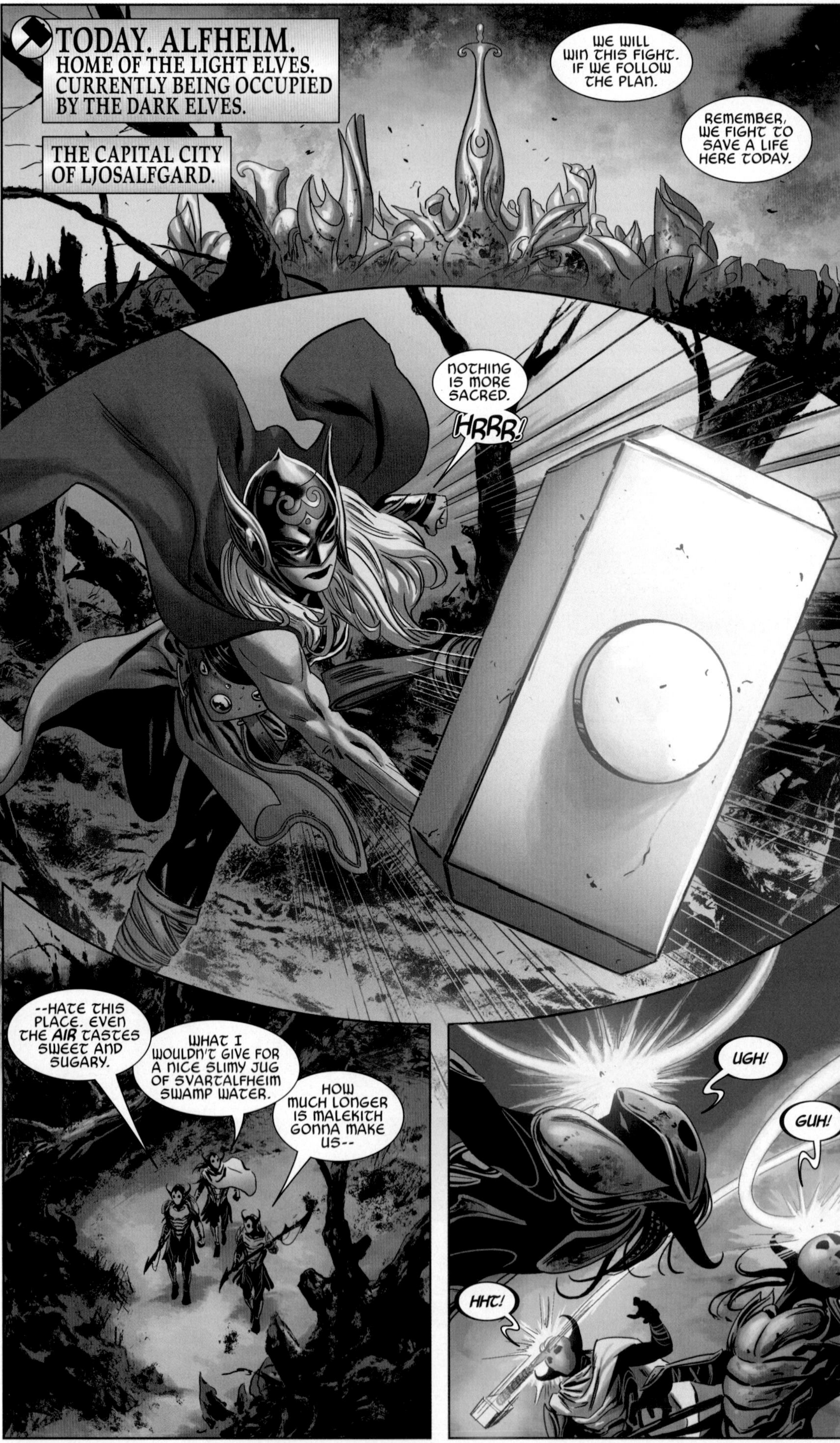
TODAY. ALFHEIM.
HOME OF THE LIGHT ELVES. CURRENTLY BEING OCCUPIED BY THE DARK ELVES.
THE CAPITAL CITY OF LJOSALFGARD.
WE WILL WIN THIS FIGHT. IF WE FOLLOW THE PLAN.
REMEMBER, WE FIGHT TO SAVE A LIFE HERE TODAY.
NOTHING IS MORE SACRED.
HRRR!
--HATE THIS PLACE. EVEN THE AIR TASTES SWEET AND SUGARY.
WHAT I WOULDN'T GIVE FOR A NICE SLIMY JUG OF SVARTALFHEIM SWAMP WATER.
HOW MUCH LONGER IS MALEKITH GONNA MAKE US--
UGH!
GUH!
HHT!

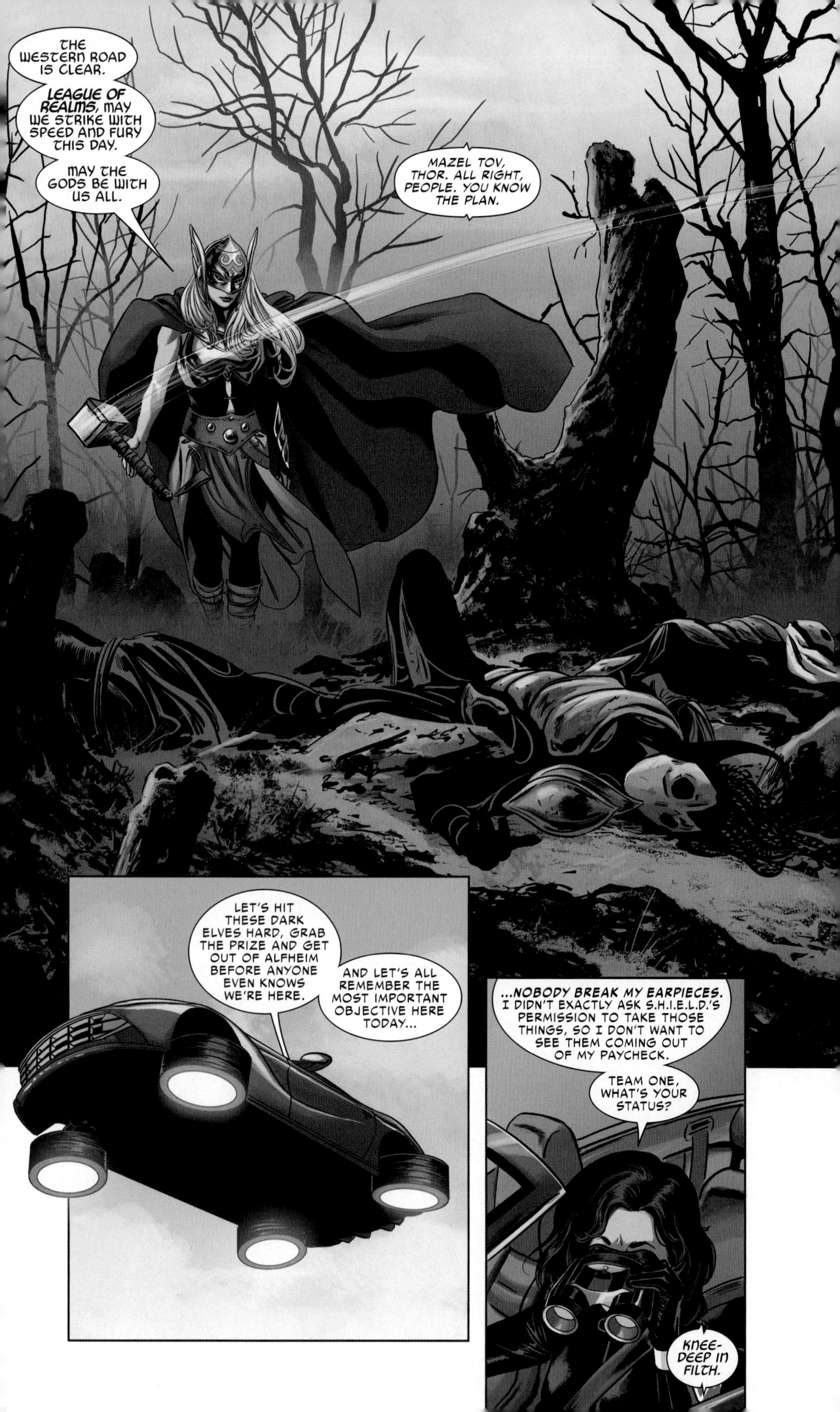

THE WESTERN ROAD IS CLEAR.
LEAGUE OF REALMS, MAY WE STRIKE WITH SPEED AND FURY THIS DAY.
MAY THE GODS BE WITH US ALL.
MAZEL TOV, THOR. ALL RIGHT, PEOPLE. YOU KNOW THE PLAN.
LET'S HIT THESE DARK ELVES HARD, GRAB THE PRIZE AND GET OUT OF ALFHEIM BEFORE ANYONE EVEN KNOWS WE'RE HERE.
AND LET'S ALL REMEMBER THE MOST IMPORTANT OBJECTIVE HERE TODAY...
...NOBODY BREAK MY EARPIECES. I DIDN'T EXACTLY ASK S.H.I.E.L.D.'S PERMISSION TO TAKE THOSE THINGS, SO I DON'T WANT TO SEE THEM COMING OUT OF MY PAYCHECK.
TEAM ONE, WHAT'S YOUR STATUS?
KNEE-DEEP IN FILTH.

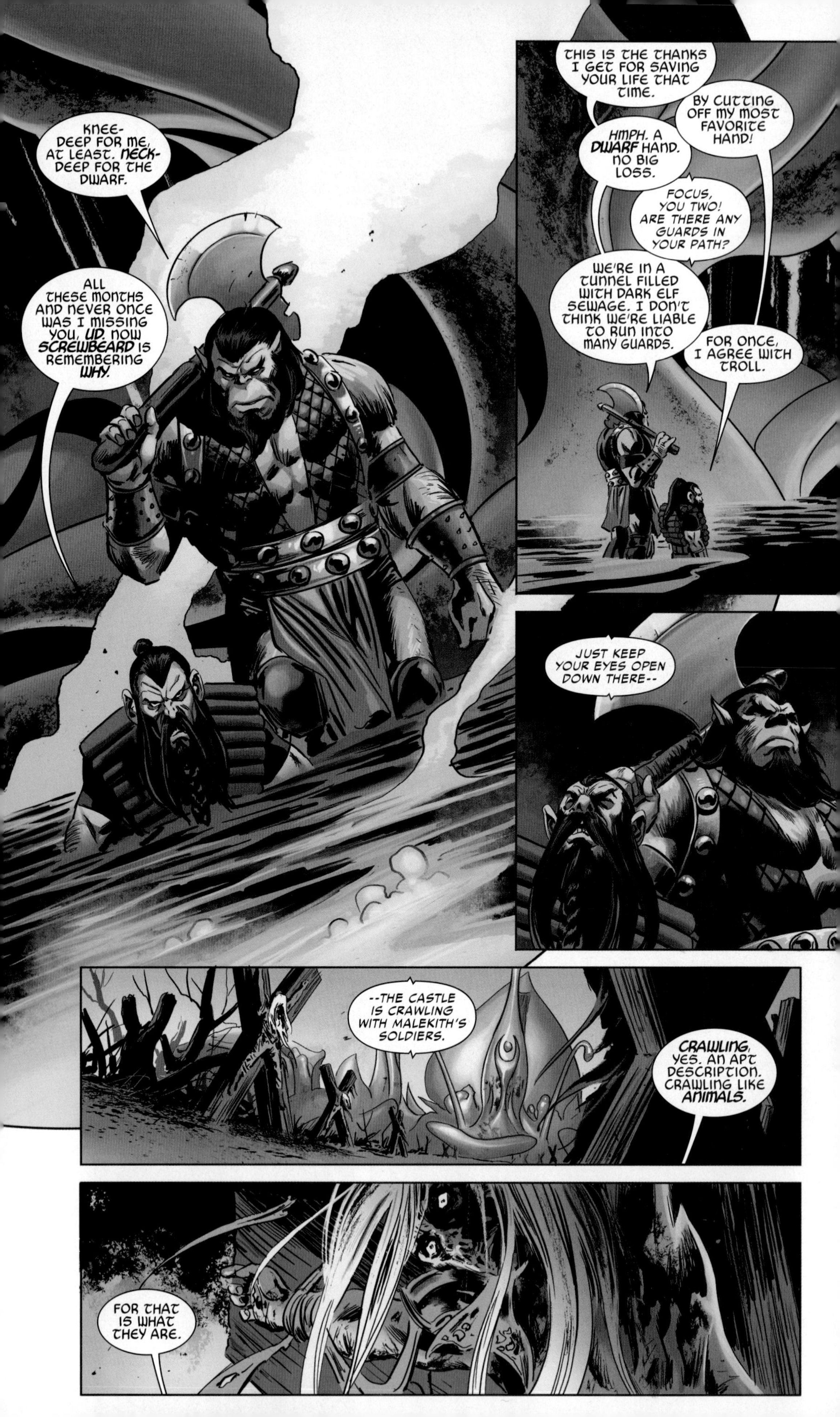
KNEE-DEEP FOR ME, AT LEAST. NECK-DEEP FOR THE DWARF.
ALL THESE MONTHS AND NEVER ONCE WAS I MISSING YOU, UD. NOW SCREWBEARD IS REMEMBERING WHY.
THIS IS THE THANKS I GET FOR SAVING YOUR LIFE THAT TIME.
BY CUTTING OFF MY MOST FAVORITE HAND!
HMPH. A DWARF HAND. NO BIG LOSS.
FOCUS, YOU TWO! ARE THERE ANY GUARDS IN YOUR PATH?
WE'RE IN A TUNNEL FILLED WITH DARK ELF SEWAGE. I DON'T THINK WE'RE LIABLE TO RUN INTO MANY GUARDS.
FOR ONCE, I AGREE WITH TROLL.
JUST KEEP YOUR EYES OPEN DOWN THERE--
--THE CASTLE IS CRAWLING WITH MALEKITH'S SOLDIERS.
CRAWLING, YES. AN APT DESCRIPTION. CRAWLING LIKE ANIMALS.
FOR THAT IS WHAT THEY ARE.

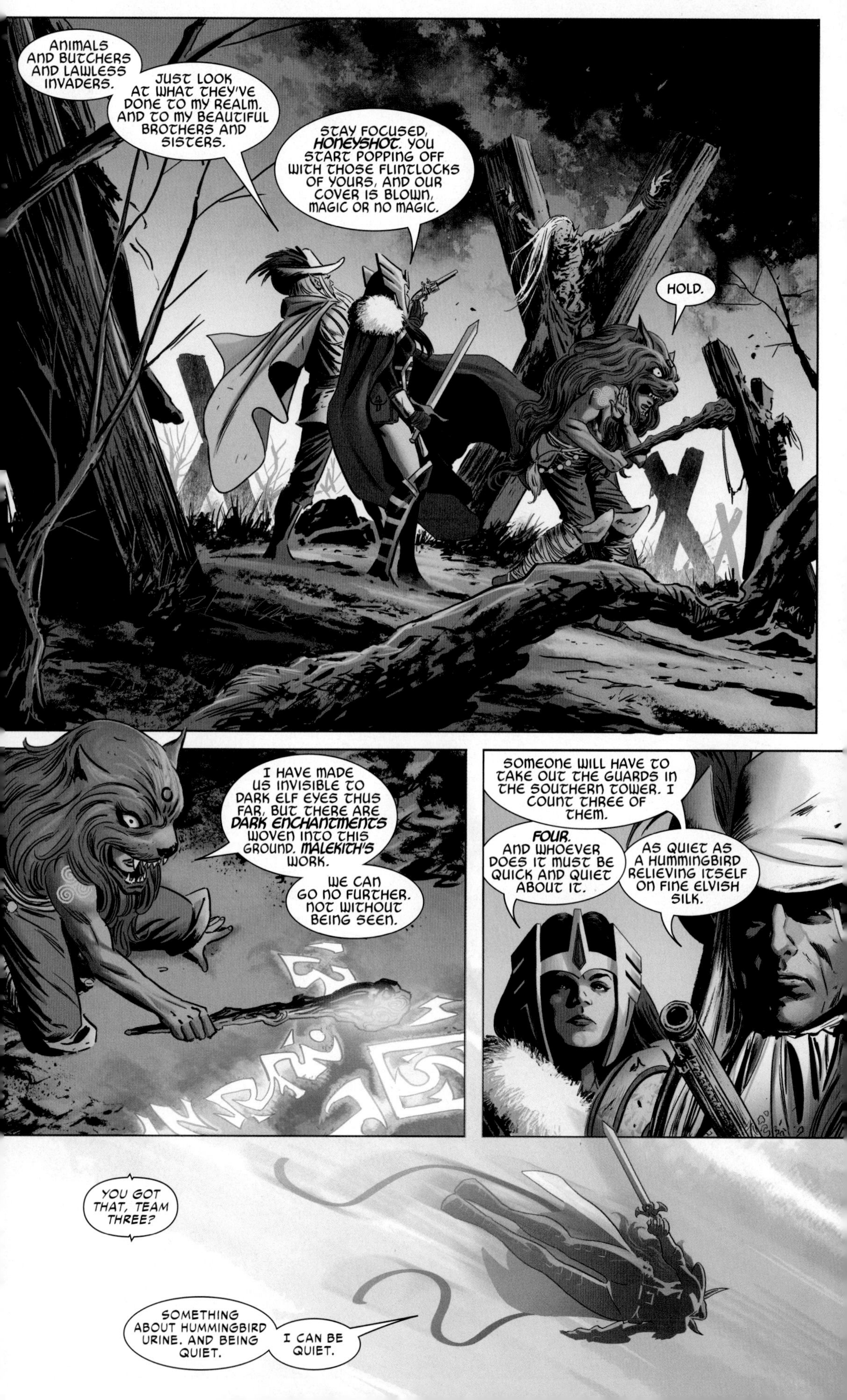
ANIMALS AND BUTCHERS AND LAWLESS INVADERS.
JUST LOOK AT WHAT THEY'VE DONE TO MY REALM. AND TO MY BEAUTIFUL BROTHERS AND SISTERS.
STAY FOCUSED, HONEYSHOT. YOU START POPPING OFF WITH THOSE FLINTLOCKS OF YOURS, AND OUR COVER IS BLOWN, MAGIC OR NO MAGIC.
HOLD.
I HAVE MADE US INVISIBLE TO DARK ELF EYES THUS FAR, BUT THERE ARE DARK ENCHANTMENTS WOVEN INTO THIS GROUND. MALEKITH'S WORK.
WE CAN GO NO FURTHER. NOT WITHOUT BEING SEEN.
SOMEONE WILL HAVE TO TAKE OUT THE GUARDS IN THE SOUTHERN TOWER. I COUNT THREE OF THEM.
FOUR. AND WHOEVER DOES IT MUST BE QUICK AND QUIET ABOUT IT.
AS QUIET AS A HUMMINGBIRD RELIEVING ITSELF ON FINE ELVISH SILK.
YOU GOT THAT, TEAM THREE?
SOMETHING ABOUT HUMMINGBIRD URINE. AND BEING QUIET.
I CAN BE QUIET.

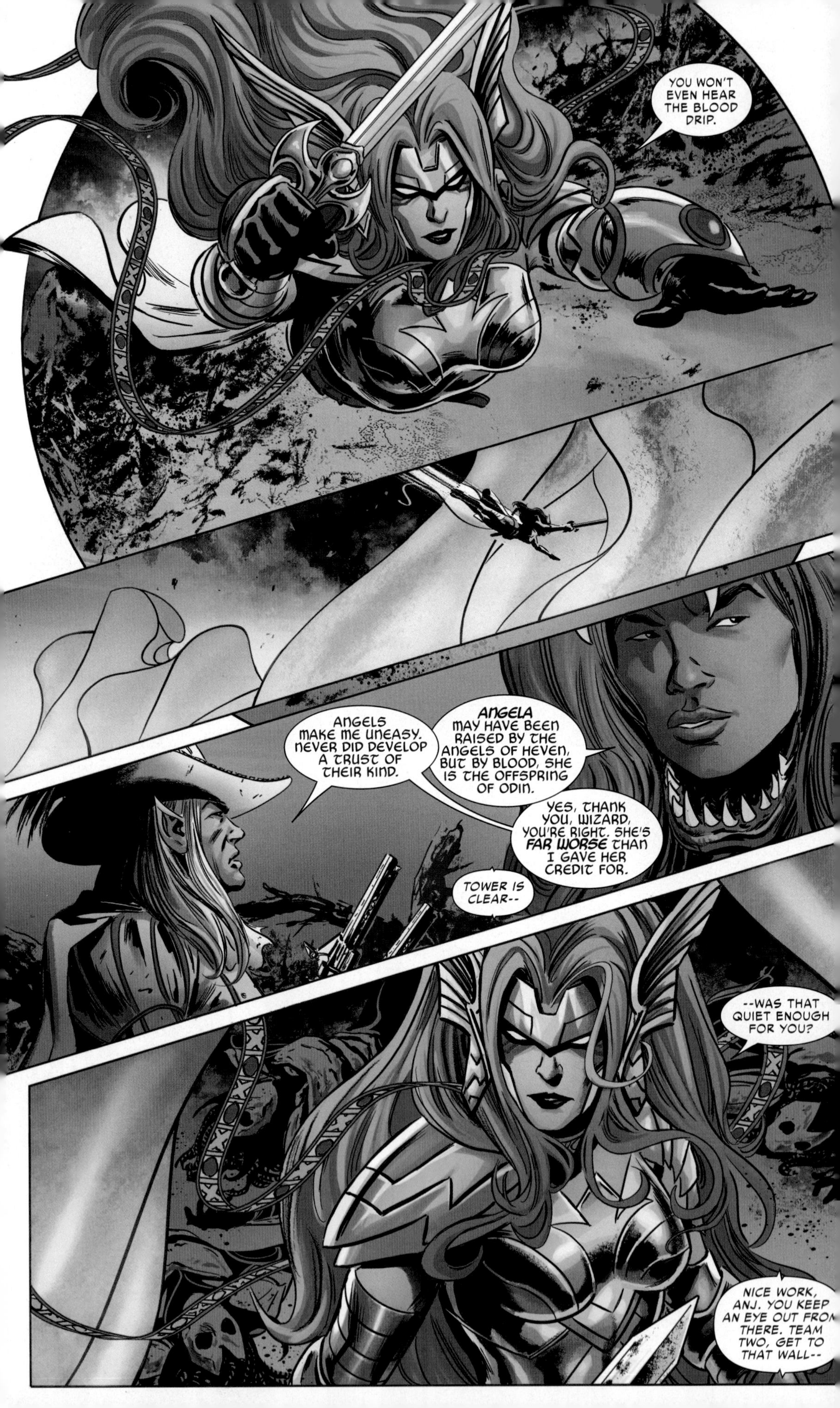
YOU WON'T EVEN HEAR THE BLOOD DRIP.
ANGELS MAKE ME UNEASY. NEVER DID DEVELOP A TRUST OF THEIR KIND.
ANGELA MAY HAVE BEEN RAISED BY THE ANGELS OF HEVEN, BUT BY BLOOD, SHE IS THE OFFSPRING OF ODIN.
YES, THANK YOU, WIZARD, YOU'RE RIGHT. SHE'S FAR WORSE THAN I GAVE HER CREDIT FOR.
TOWER IS CLEAR--
--WAS THAT QUIET ENOUGH FOR YOU?
NICE WORK, ANJ. YOU KEEP AN EYE OUT FROM THERE. TEAM TWO, GET TO THAT WALL--

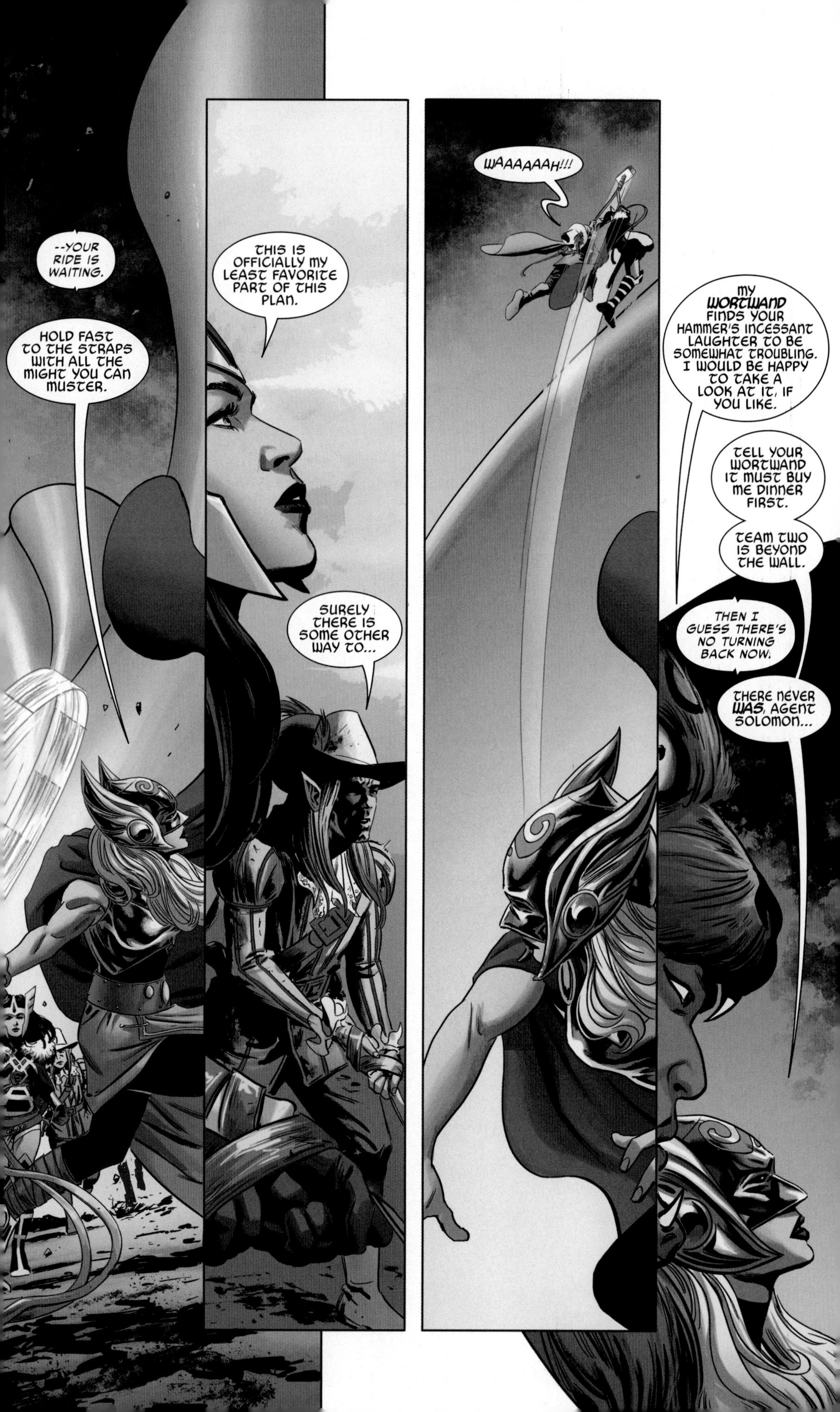
--YOUR RIDE IS WAITING.
HOLD FAST TO THE STRAPS WITH ALL THE MIGHT YOU CAN MUSTER.
THIS IS OFFICIALLY MY LEAST FAVORITE PART OF THIS PLAN.
SURELY THERE IS SOME OTHER WAY TO...
WAAAAAAH!!!
MY WORTWAND FINDS YOUR HAMMER'S INCESSANT LAUGHTER TO BE SOMEWHAT TROUBLING. I WOULD BE HAPPY TO TAKE A LOOK AT IT, IF YOU LIKE.
TELL YOUR WORTWAND IT MUST BUY ME DINNER FIRST.
TEAM TWO IS BEYOND THE WALL.
THEN I GUESS THERE'S NO TURNING BACK NOW.
THERE NEVER WAS, AGENT SOLOMON...

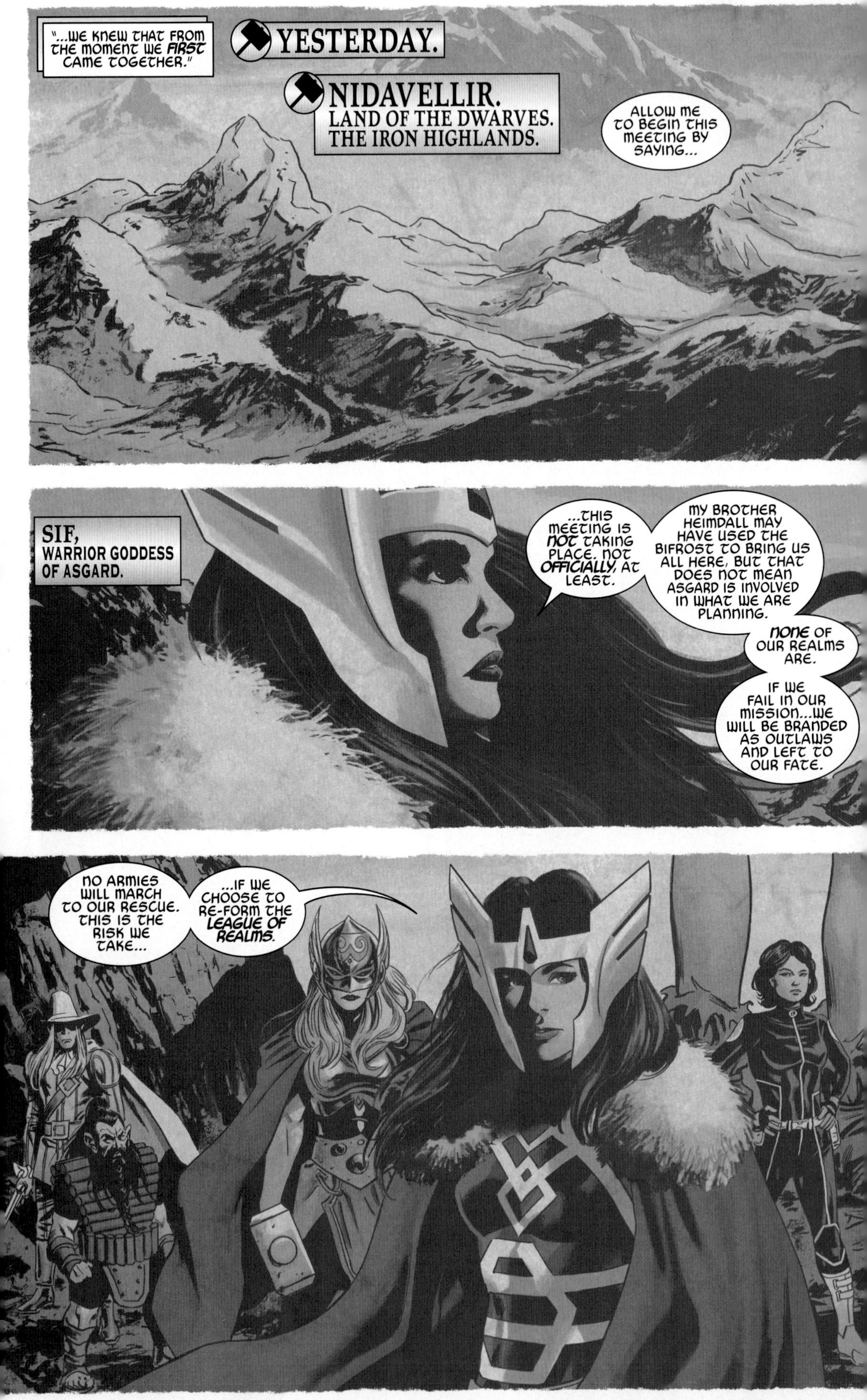

"...WE KNEW THAT FROM THE MOMENT WE FIRST CAME TOGETHER."
YESTERDAY.
NIDAVELLIR. LAND OF THE DWARVES. THE IRON HIGHLANDS.
ALLOW ME TO BEGIN THIS MEETING BY SAYING...
SIF, WARRIOR GODDESS OF ASGARD.
...THIS MEETING IS NOT TAKING PLACE. NOT OFFICIALLY, AT LEAST.
MY BROTHER HEIMDALL MAY HAVE USED THE BIFROST TO BRING US ALL HERE, BUT THAT DOES NOT MEAN ASGARD IS INVOLVED IN WHAT WE ARE PLANNING.
NONE OF OUR REALMS ARE.
IF WE FAIL IN OUR MISSION...WE WILL BE BRANDED AS OUTLAWS AND LEFT TO OUR FATE.
NO ARMIES WILL MARCH TO OUR RESCUE. THIS IS THE RISK WE TAKE...
...IF WE CHOOSE TO RE-FORM THE LEAGUE OF REALMS.

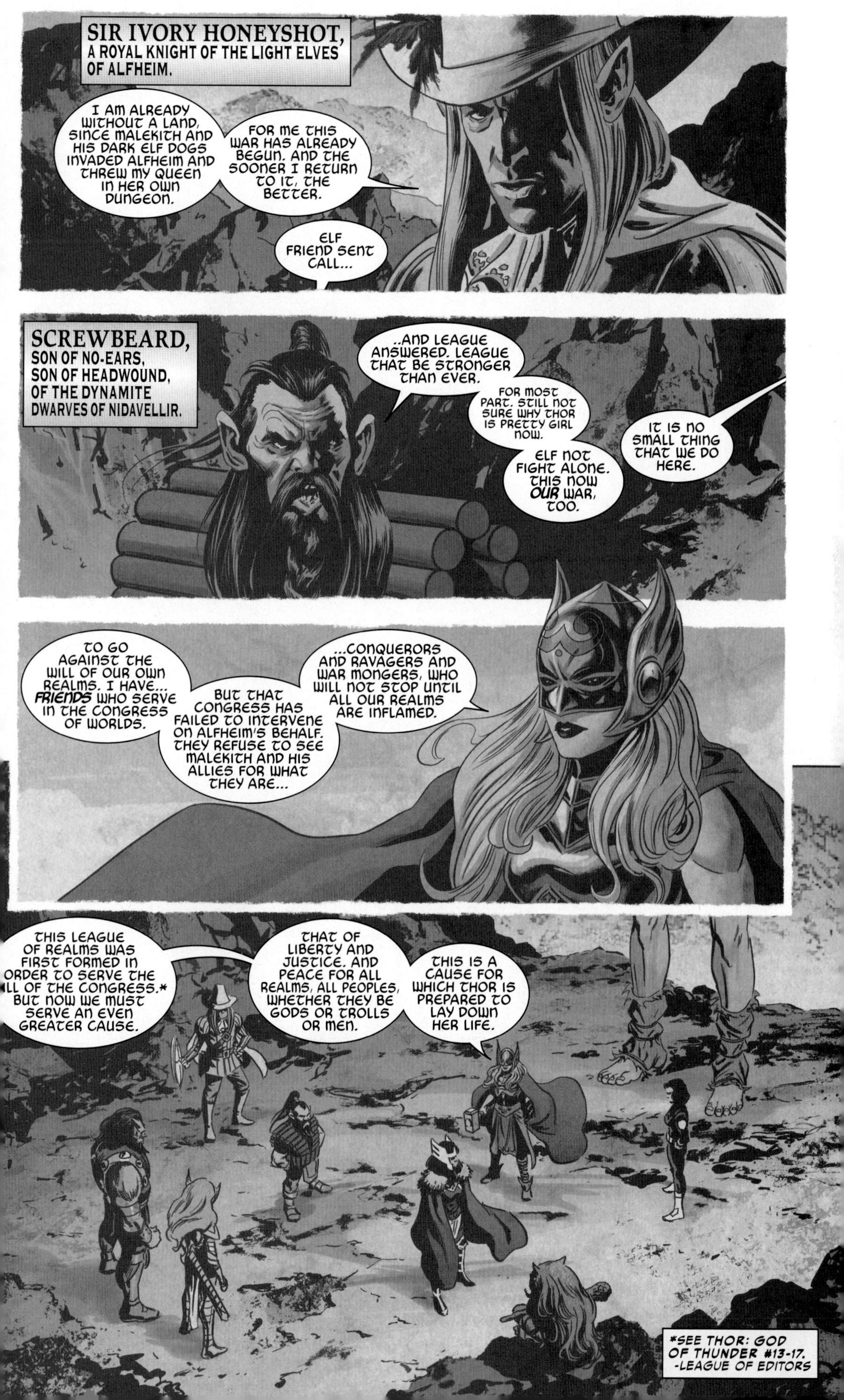
SIR IVORY HONEYSHOT, A ROYAL KNIGHT OF THE LIGHT ELVES OF ALFHEIM.
I AM ALREADY WITHOUT A LAND, SINCE MALEKITH AND HIS DARK ELF DOGS INVADED ALFHEIM AND THREW MY QUEEN IN HER OWN DUNGEON.
FOR ME THIS WAR HAS ALREADY BEGUN. AND THE SOONER I RETURN TO IT, THE BETTER.
ELF FRIEND SENT CALL...
SCREWBEARD, SON OF NO-EARS, SON OF HEADWOUND, OF THE DYNAMITE DWARVES OF NIDAVELLIR.
..AND LEAGUE ANSWERED. LEAGUE THAT BE STRONGER THAN EVER.
FOR MOST PART. STILL NOT SURE WHY THOR IS PRETTY GIRL NOW.
ELF NOT FIGHT ALONE. THIS NOW OUR WAR, TOO.
IT IS NO SMALL THING THAT WE DO HERE.
TO GO AGAINST THE WILL OF OUR OWN REALMS. I HAVE... FRIENDS WHO SERVE IN THE CONGRESS OF WORLDS.
BUT THAT CONGRESS HAS FAILED TO INTERVENE ON ALFHEIM'S BEHALF. THEY REFUSE TO SEE MALEKITH AND HIS ALLIES FOR WHAT THEY ARE...
...CONQUERORS AND RAVAGERS AND WAR MONGERS, WHO WILL NOT STOP UNTIL ALL OUR REALMS ARE INFLAMED.
THIS LEAGUE OF REALMS WAS FIRST FORMED IN ORDER TO SERVE THE LL OF THE CONGRESS.* BUT NOW WE MUST SERVE AN EVEN GREATER CAUSE.
THAT OF LIBERTY AND JUSTICE. AND PEACE FOR ALL REALMS, ALL PEOPLES, WHETHER THEY BE GODS OR TROLLS OR MEN.
THIS IS A CAUSE FOR WHICH THOR IS PREPARED TO LAY DOWN HER LIFE.
*SEE THOR: GOD OF THUNDER #13-17. -LEAGUE OF EDITORS

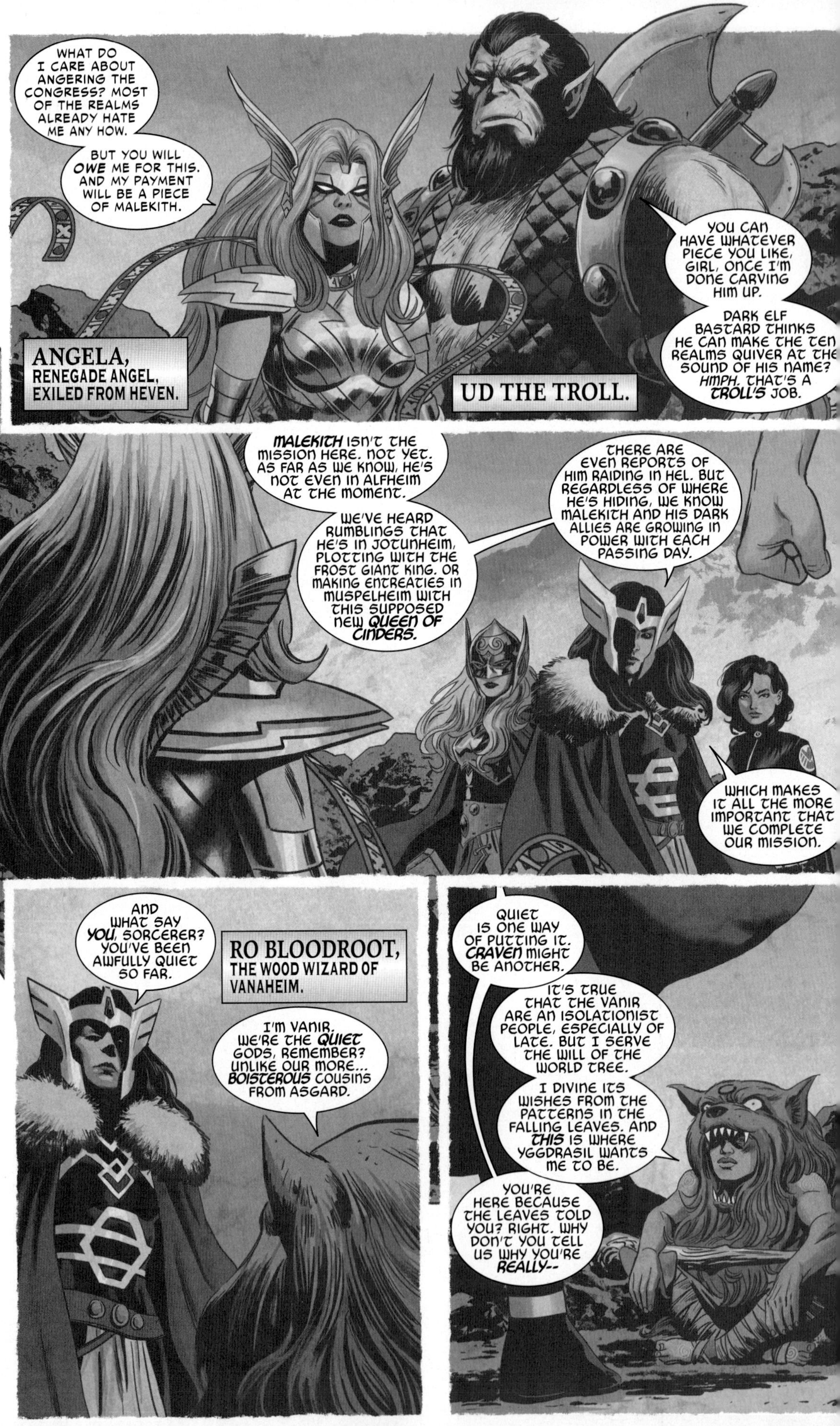
WHAT DO I CARE ABOUT ANGERING THE CONGRESS? MOST OF THE REALMS ALREADY HATE ME ANY HOW.
BUT YOU WILL OWE ME FOR THIS. AND MY PAYMENT WILL BE A PIECE OF MALEKITH.
ANGELA, RENEGADE ANGEL, EXILED FROM HEVEN.
UD THE TROLL.
YOU CAN HAVE WHATEVER PIECE YOU LIKE, GIRL, ONCE I'M DONE CARVING HIM UP.
DARK ELF BASTARD THINKS HE CAN MAKE THE TEN REALMS QUIVER AT THE SOUND OF HIS NAME? HMPH. THAT'S A TROLL'S JOB.
MALEKITH ISN'T THE MISSION HERE. NOT YET. AS FAR AS WE KNOW, HE'S NOT EVEN IN ALFHEIM AT THE MOMENT.
WE'VE HEARD RUMBLINGS THAT HE'S IN JOTUNHEIM, PLOTTING WITH THE FROST GIANT KING. OR MAKING ENTREATIES IN MUSPELHEIM WITH THIS SUPPOSED NEW QUEEN OF CINDERS.
THERE ARE EVEN REPORTS OF HIM RAIDING IN HEL. BUT REGARDLESS OF WHERE HE'S HIDING, WE KNOW MALEKITH AND HIS DARK ALLIES ARE GROWING IN POWER WITH EACH PASSING DAY.
WHICH MAKES IT ALL THE MORE IMPORTANT THAT WE COMPLETE OUR MISSION.
AND WHAT SAY YOU, SORCERER? YOU'VE BEEN AWFULLY QUIET SO FAR.
RO BLOODROOT, THE WOOD WIZARD OF VANAHEIM.
I'M VANIR. WE'RE THE QUIET GODS, REMEMBER? UNLIKE OUR MORE... BOISTEROUS COUSINS FROM ASGARD.
QUIET IS ONE WAY OF PUTTING IT. CRAVEN MIGHT BE ANOTHER.
IT'S TRUE THAT THE VANIR ARE AN ISOLATIONIST PEOPLE, ESPECIALLY OF LATE. BUT I SERVE THE WILL OF THE WORLD TREE.
I DIVINE ITS WISHES FROM THE PATTERNS IN THE FALLING LEAVES. AND THIS IS WHERE YGGDRASIL WANTS ME TO BE.
YOU'RE HERE BECAUSE THE LEAVES TOLD YOU? RIGHT. WHY DON'T YOU TELL US WHY YOU'RE REALLY--

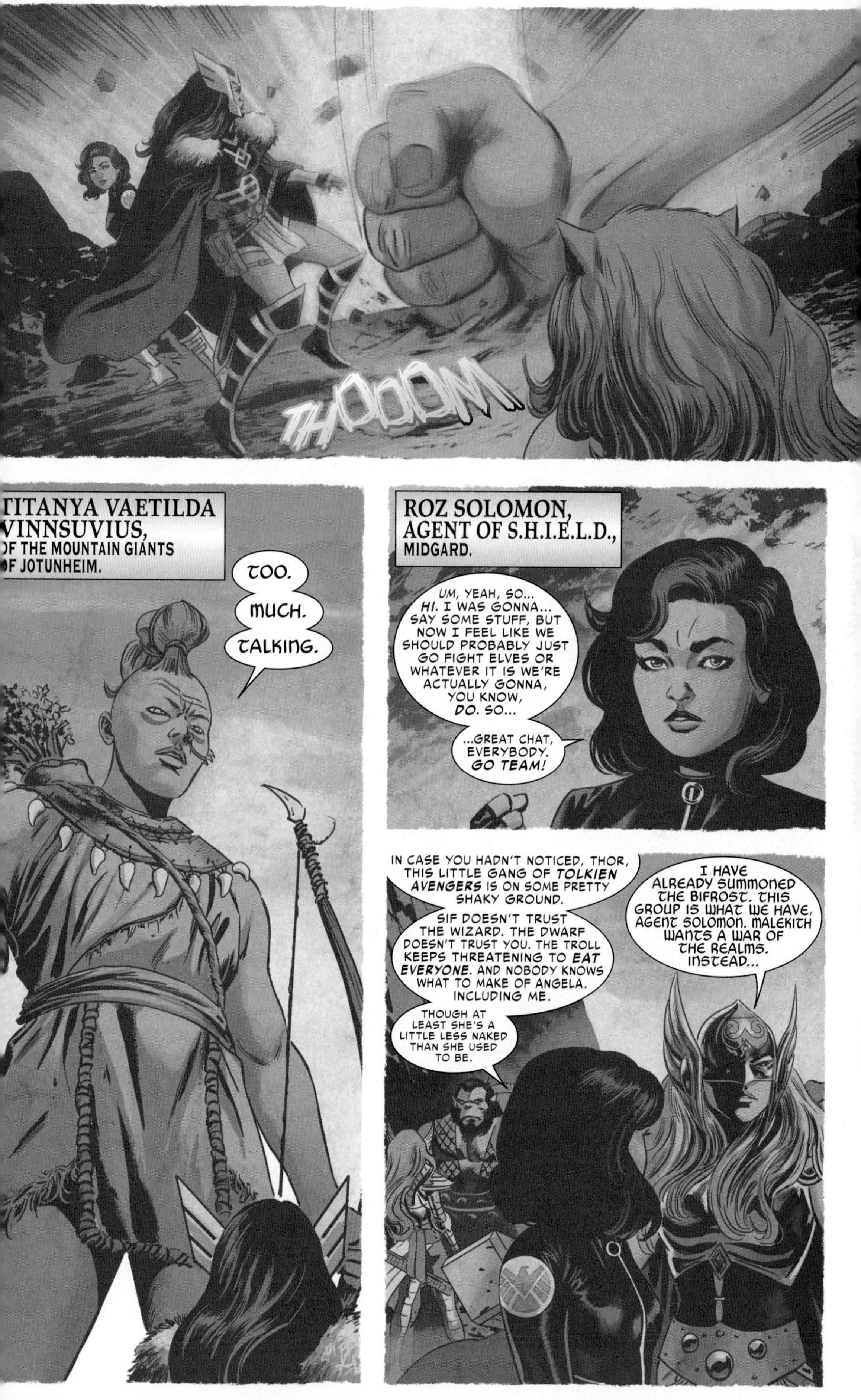
THOOOM
TITANYA VAETILDA VINNSUVIUS, OF THE MOUNTAIN GIANTS OF JOTUNHEIM.
TOO. MUCH. TALKING.
ROZ SOLOMON, AGENT OF S.H.I.E.L.D., MIDGARD.
UM, YEAH, SO... HI. I WAS GONNA... SAY SOME STUFF, BUT NOW I FEEL LIKE WE SHOULD PROBABLY JUST GO FIGHT ELVES OR WHATEVER IT IS WE'RE ACTUALLY GONNA, YOU KNOW, DO. SO...
...GREAT CHAT, EVERYBODY. GO TEAM!
IN CASE YOU HADN'T NOTICED, THOR, THIS LITTLE GANG OF TOLKIEN AVENGERS IS ON SOME PRETTY SHAKY GROUND.
SIF DOESN'T TRUST THE WIZARD. THE DWARF DOESN'T TRUST YOU. THE TROLL KEEPS THREATENING TO EAT EVERYONE. AND NOBODY KNOWS WHAT TO MAKE OF ANGELA. INCLUDING ME.
THOUGH AT LEAST SHE'S A LITTLE LESS NAKED THAN SHE USED TO BE.
I HAVE ALREADY SUMMONED THE BIFROST. THIS GROUP IS WHAT WE HAVE, AGENT SOLOMON. MALEKITH WANTS A WAR OF THE REALMS. INSTEAD...

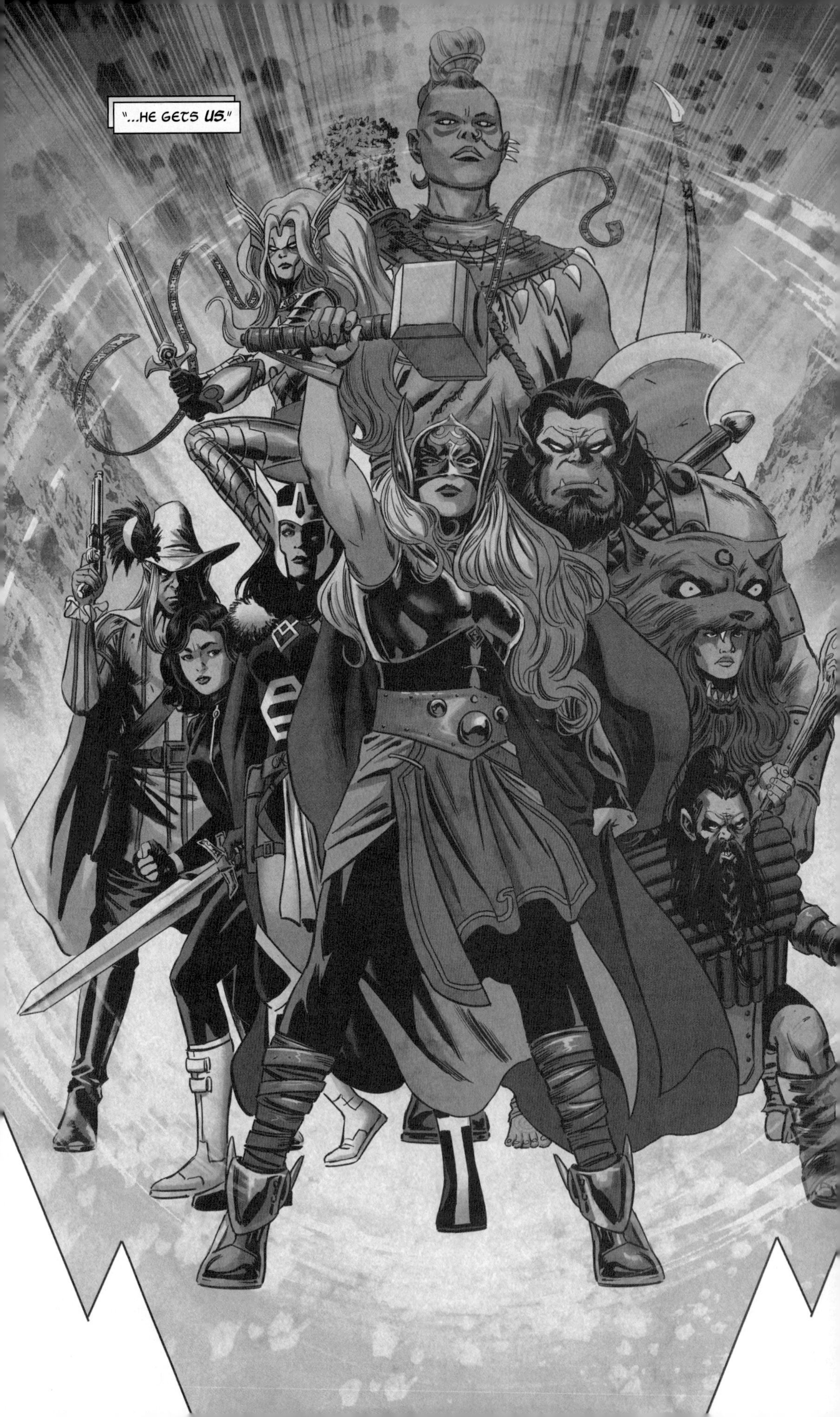
"...HE GETS US."

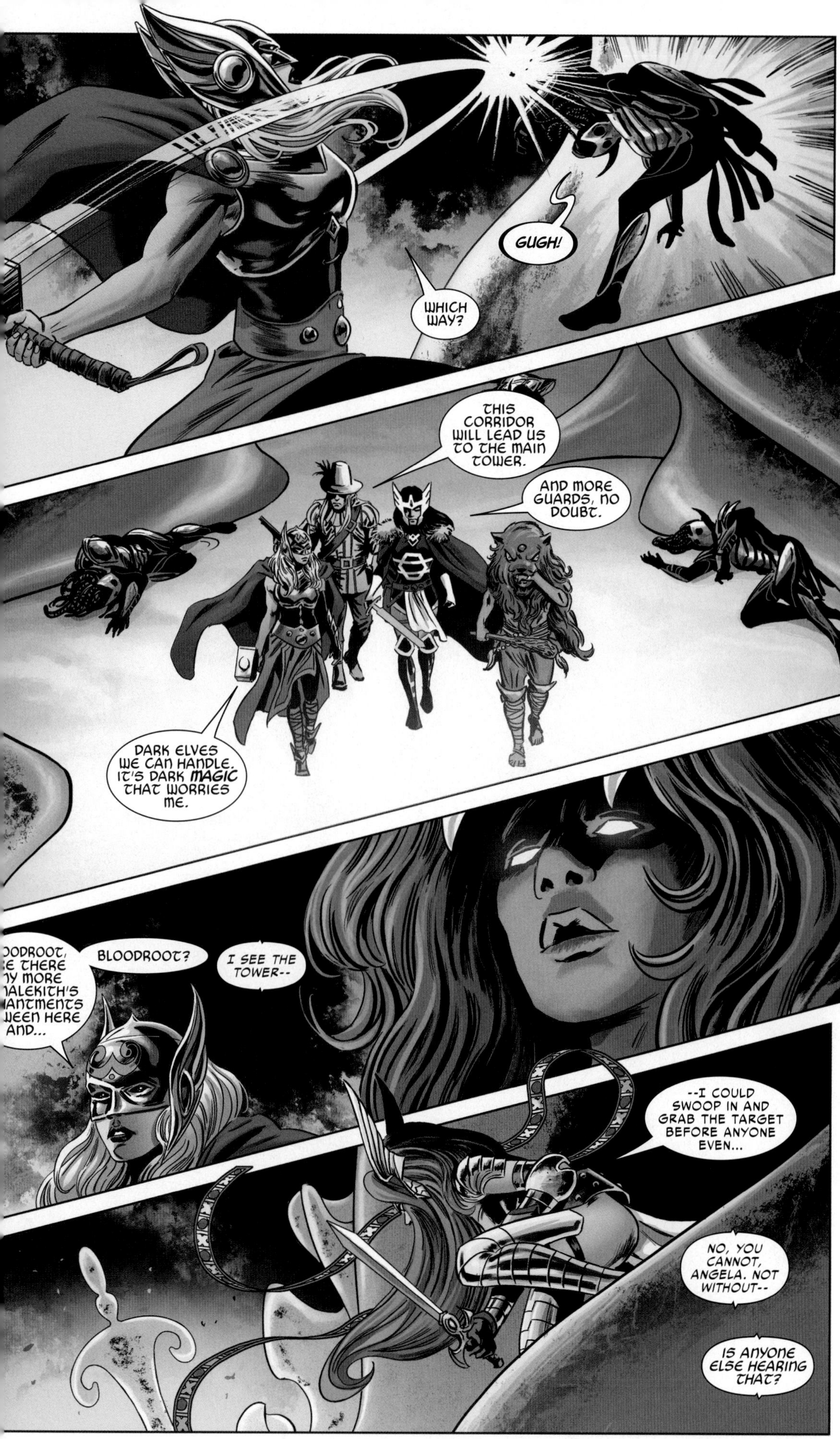
GUGH!
WHICH WAY?
THIS CORRIDOR WILL LEAD US TO THE MAIN TOWER.
AND MORE GUARDS, NO DOUBT.
DARK ELVES WE CAN HANDLE. IT'S DARK **MAGIC** THAT WORRIES ME.
OODROOT, E THERE NY MORE MALEKITH'S NANTMENTS WEEN HERE AND...
BLOODROOT?
I SEE THE TOWER--
--I COULD SWOOP IN AND GRAB THE TARGET BEFORE ANYONE EVEN...
NO, YOU CANNOT, ANGELA. NOT WITHOUT--
IS ANYONE ELSE HEARING THAT?

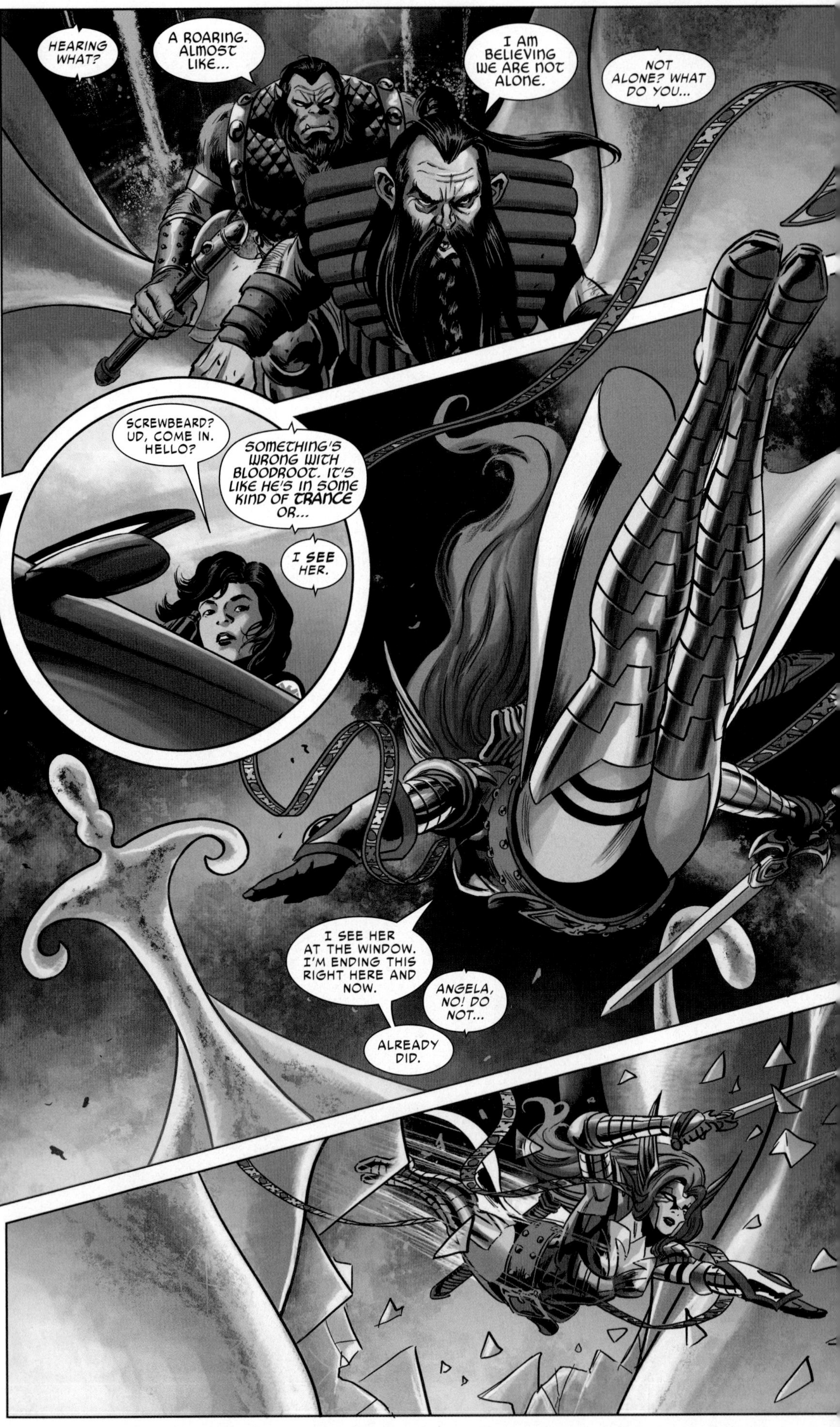
HEARING WHAT?
A ROARING. ALMOST LIKE...
I AM BELIEVING WE ARE NOT ALONE.
NOT ALONE? WHAT DO YOU...
SCREWBEARD? UD, COME IN. HELLO?
SOMETHING'S WRONG WITH BLOODROOT. IT'S LIKE HE'S IN SOME KIND OF TRANCE OR...
I SEE HER.
I SEE HER AT THE WINDOW. I'M ENDING THIS RIGHT HERE AND NOW.
ANGELA, NO! DO NOT...
ALREADY DID.

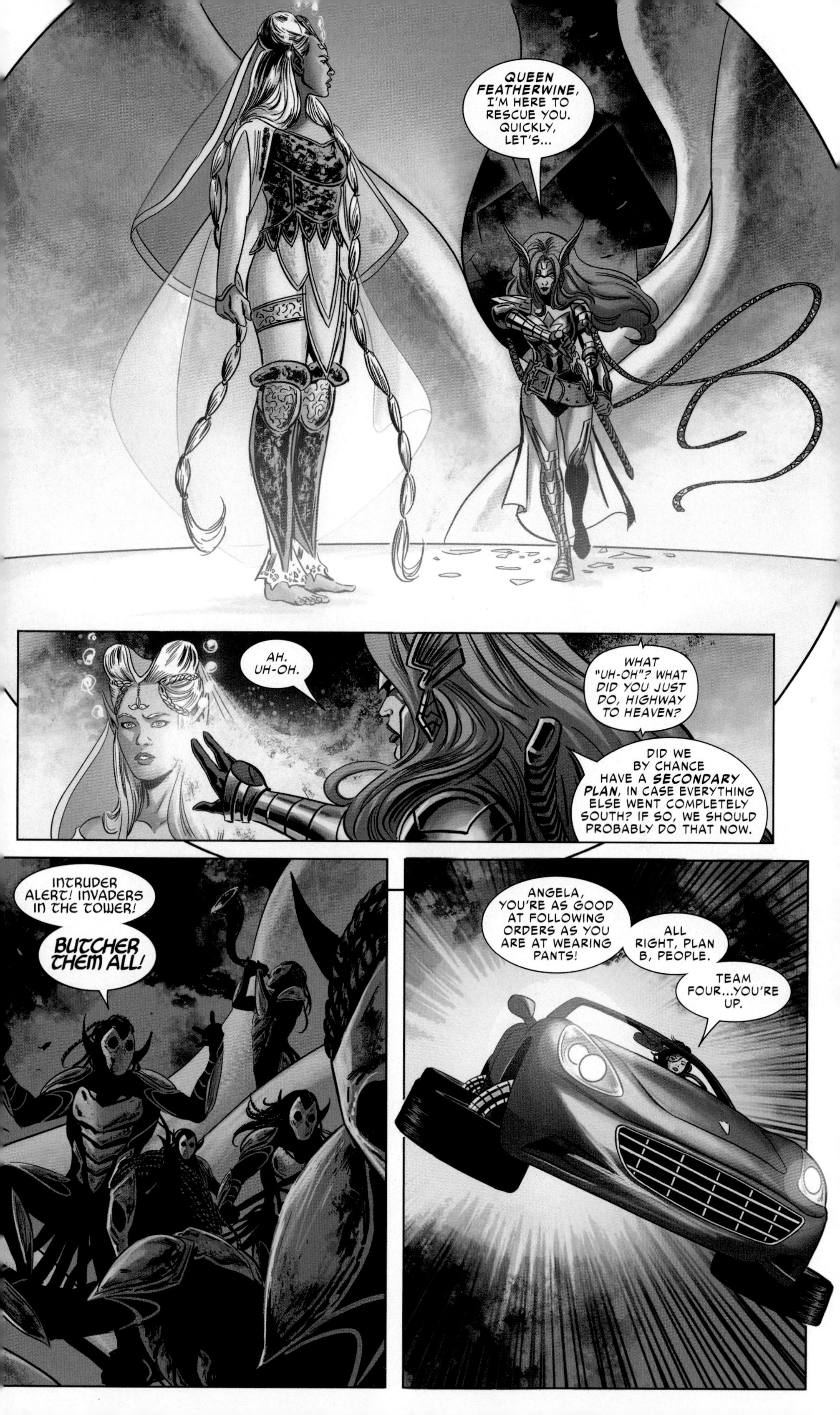

QUEEN FEATHERWINE, I'M HERE TO RESCUE YOU. QUICKLY, LET'S...
AH. UH-OH.
WHAT "UH-OH"? WHAT DID YOU JUST DO, HIGHWAY TO HEAVEN?
DID WE BY CHANCE HAVE A SECONDARY PLAN, IN CASE EVERYTHING ELSE WENT COMPLETELY SOUTH? IF SO, WE SHOULD PROBABLY DO THAT NOW.
INTRUDER ALERT! INVADERS IN THE TOWER!
BUTCHER THEM ALL!
ANGELA, YOU'RE AS GOOD AT FOLLOWING ORDERS AS YOU ARE AT WEARING PANTS!
ALL RIGHT, PLAN B, PEOPLE.
TEAM FOUR...YOU'RE UP.

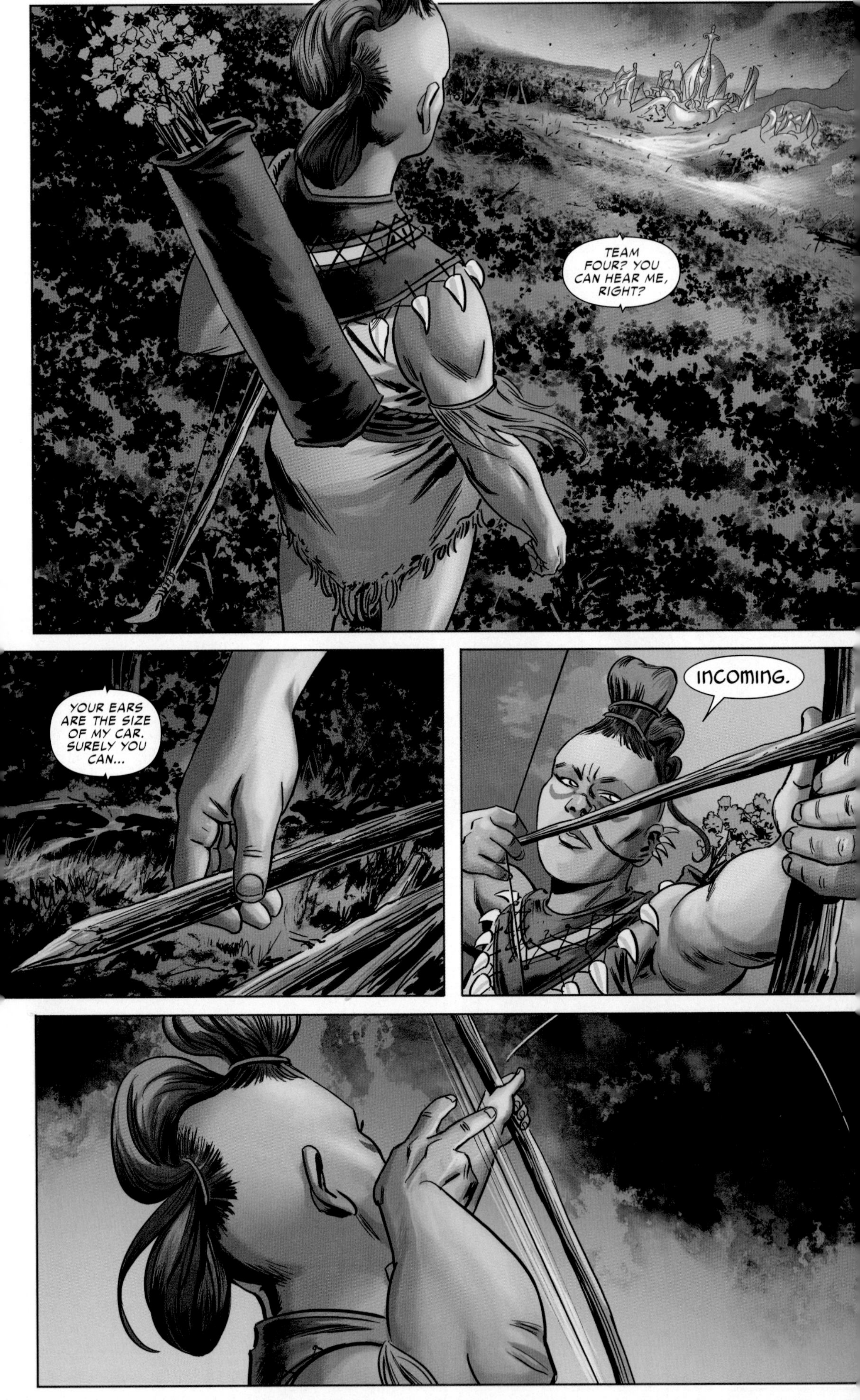
TEAM FOUR? YOU CAN HEAR ME, RIGHT?
YOUR EARS ARE THE SIZE OF MY CAR. SURELY YOU CAN...
INCOMING.

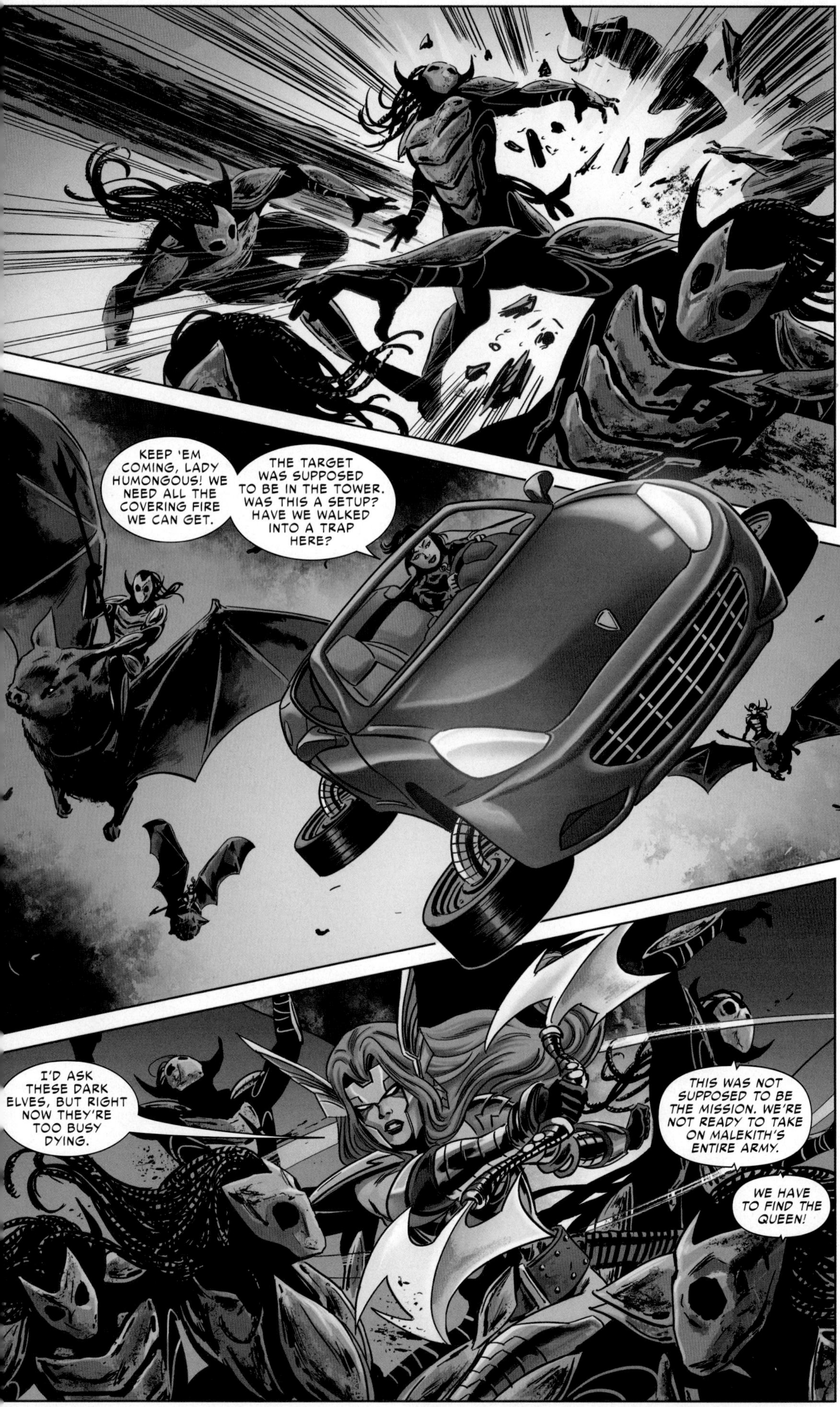
KEEP 'EM COMING, LADY HUMONGOUS! WE NEED ALL THE COVERING FIRE WE CAN GET.
THE TARGET WAS SUPPOSED TO BE IN THE TOWER. WAS THIS A SETUP? HAVE WE WALKED INTO A TRAP HERE?
I'D ASK THESE DARK ELVES, BUT RIGHT NOW THEY'RE TOO BUSY DYING.
THIS WAS NOT SUPPOSED TO BE THE MISSION. WE'RE NOT READY TO TAKE ON MALEKITH'S ENTIRE ARMY.
WE HAVE TO FIND THE QUEEN!

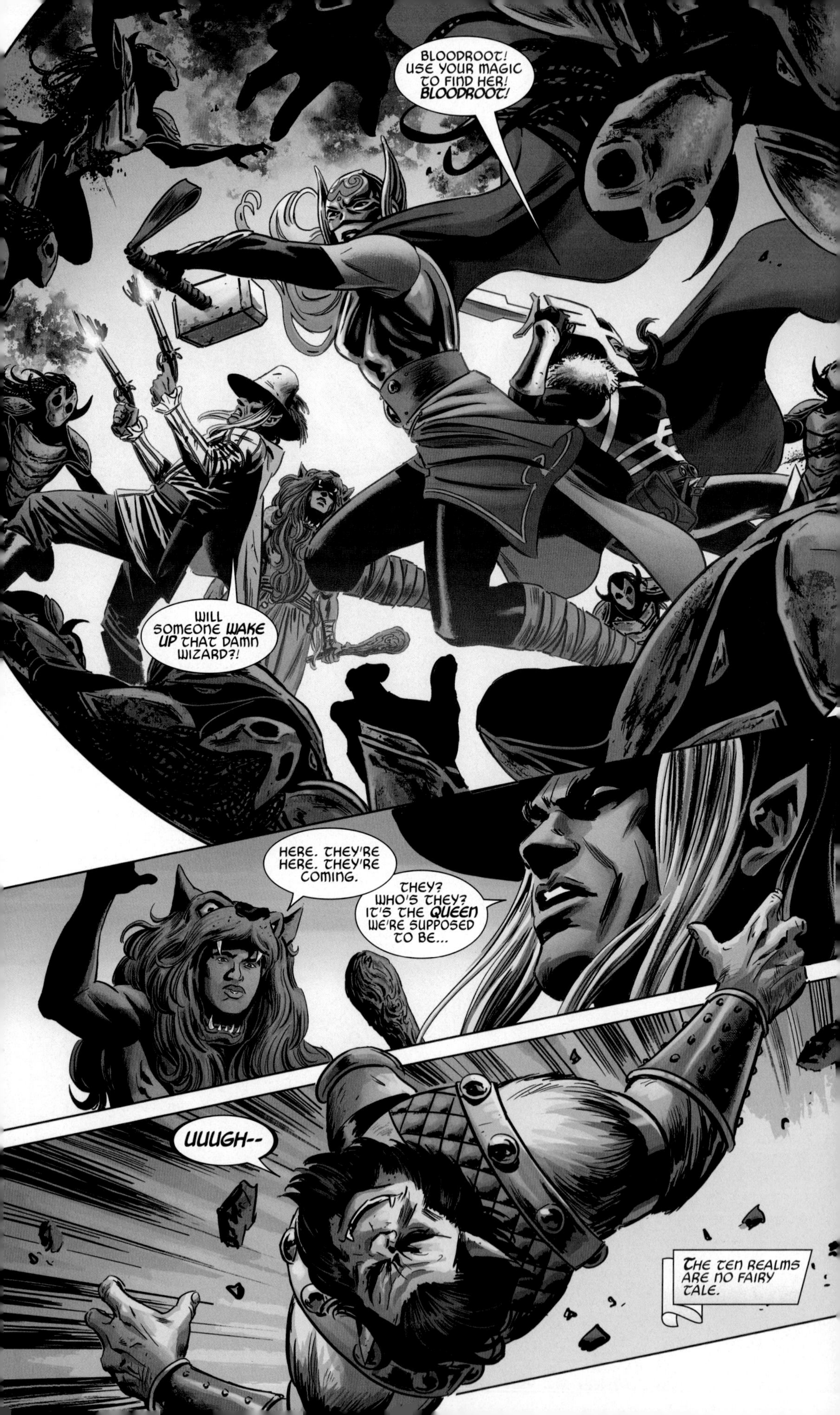
BLOODROOT! USE YOUR MAGIC TO FIND HER! BLOODROOT!
WILL SOMEONE WAKE UP THAT DAMN WIZARD?!
HERE. THEY'RE HERE. THEY'RE COMING.
THEY? WHO'S THEY? IT'S THE QUEEN WE'RE SUPPOSED TO BE...
UUUGH--
THE TEN REALMS ARE NO FAIRY TALE.

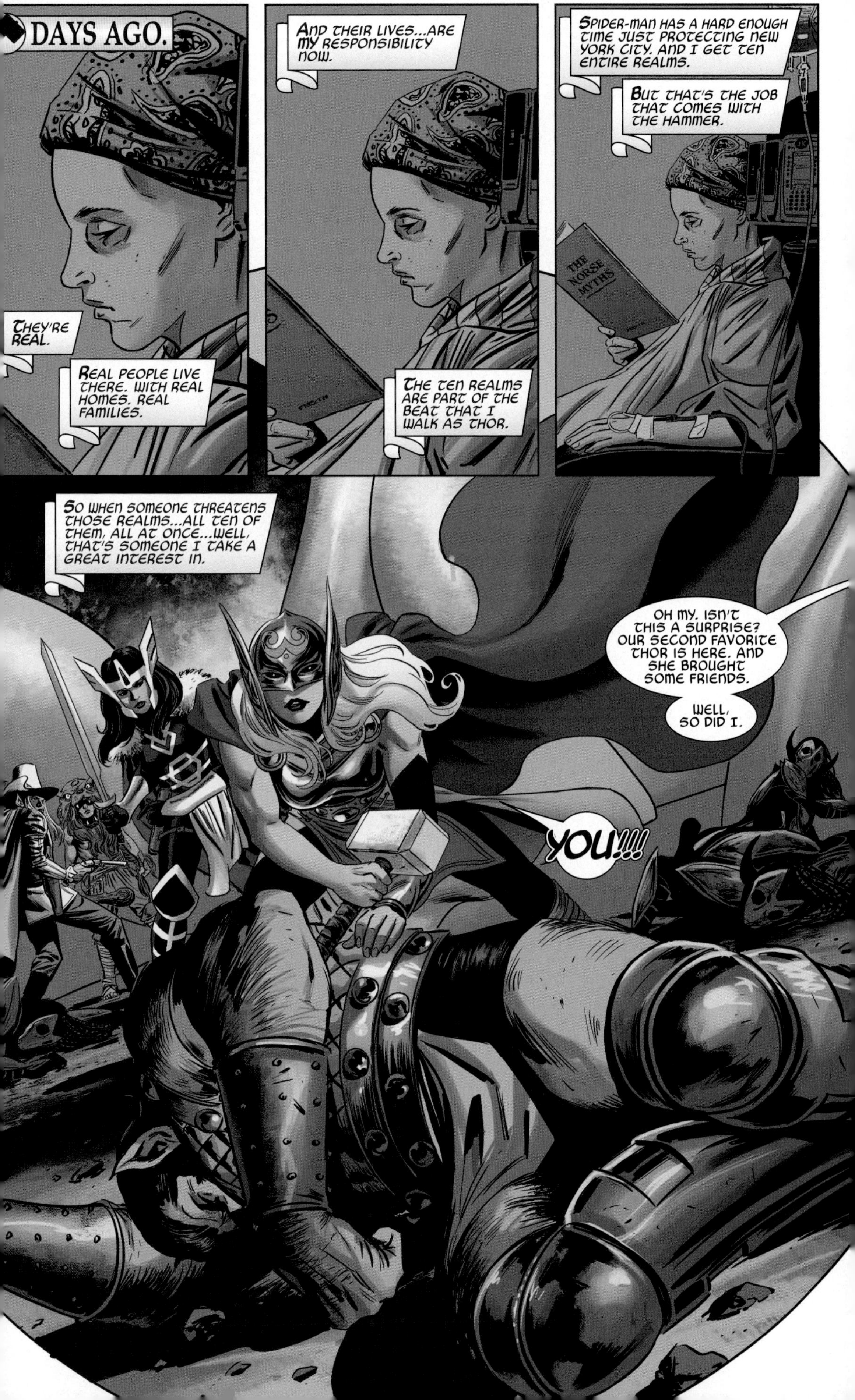
DAYS AGO.
THEY'RE REAL.
REAL PEOPLE LIVE THERE. WITH REAL HOMES. REAL FAMILIES.
AND THEIR LIVES...ARE MY RESPONSIBILITY NOW.
THE TEN REALMS ARE PART OF THE BEAT THAT I WALK AS THOR.
SPIDER-MAN HAS A HARD ENOUGH TIME JUST PROTECTING NEW YORK CITY. AND I GET TEN ENTIRE REALMS.
BUT THAT'S THE JOB THAT COMES WITH THE HAMMER.
THE NORSE MYTHS
SO WHEN SOMEONE THREATENS THOSE REALMS...ALL TEN OF THEM, ALL AT ONCE...WELL, THAT'S SOMEONE I TAKE A GREAT INTEREST IN.
OH MY. ISN'T THIS A SURPRISE? OUR SECOND FAVORITE THOR IS HERE. AND SHE BROUGHT SOME FRIENDS.
WELL, SO DID I.
YOU!!!!

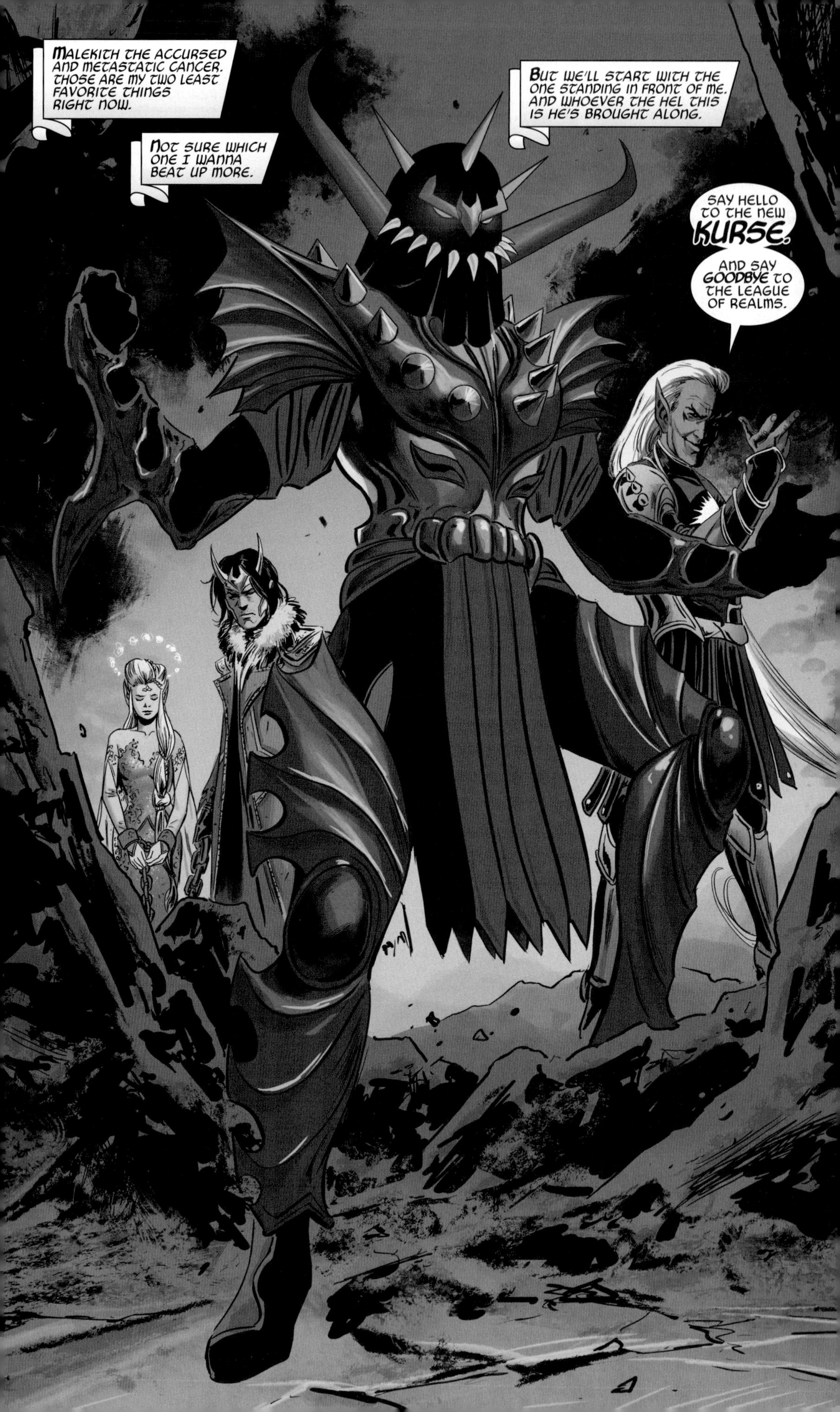
MALEKITH THE ACCURSED AND METASTATIC CANCER. THOSE ARE MY TWO LEAST FAVORITE THINGS RIGHT NOW.
NOT SURE WHICH ONE I WANNA BEAT UP MORE.
BUT WE'LL START WITH THE ONE STANDING IN FRONT OF ME. AND WHOEVER THE HEL THIS IS HE'S BROUGHT ALONG.
SAY HELLO TO THE NEW KURSE.
AND SAY GOODBYE TO THE LEAGUE OF REALMS.

14

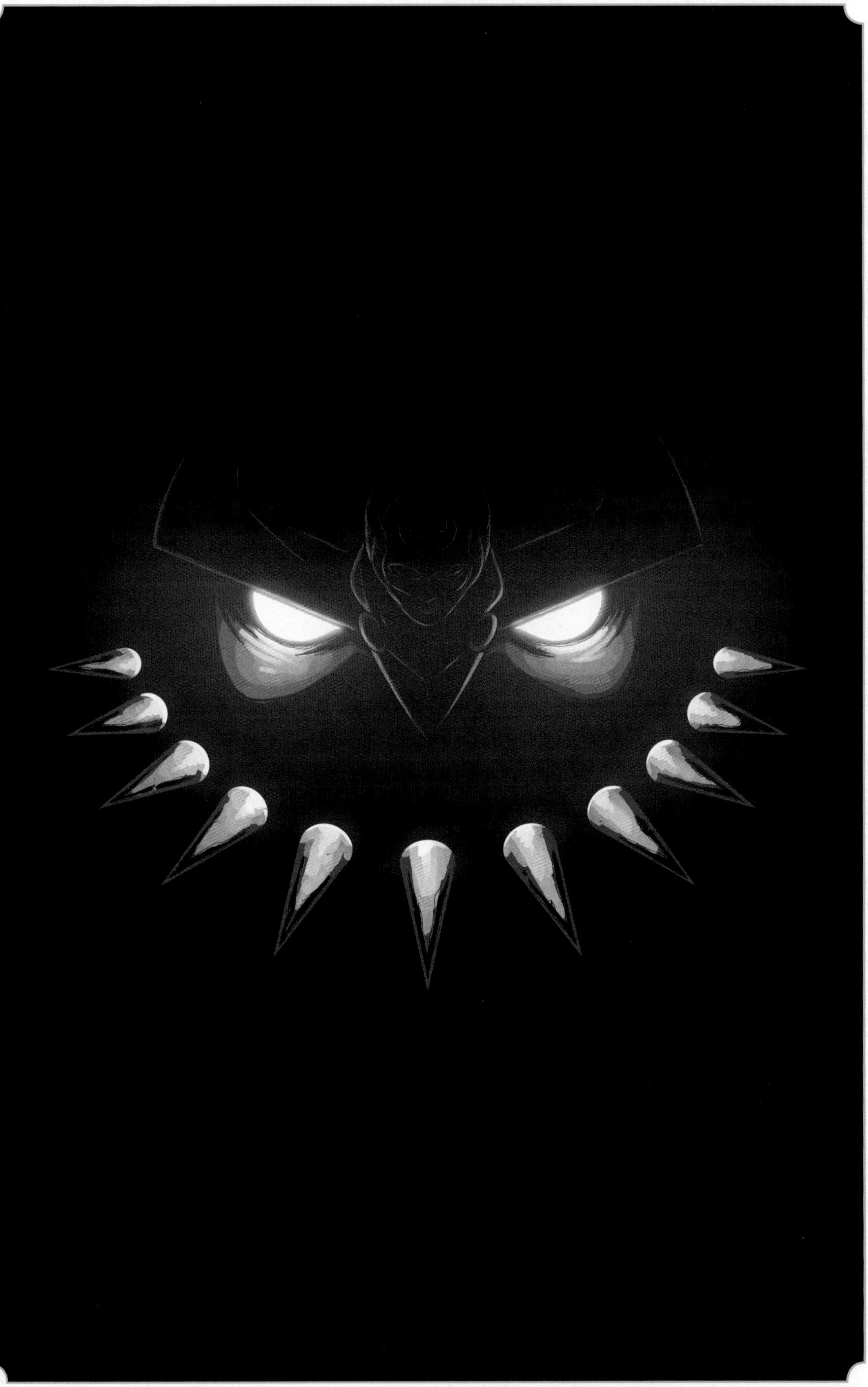

LJOSALFGARD'S BURNING

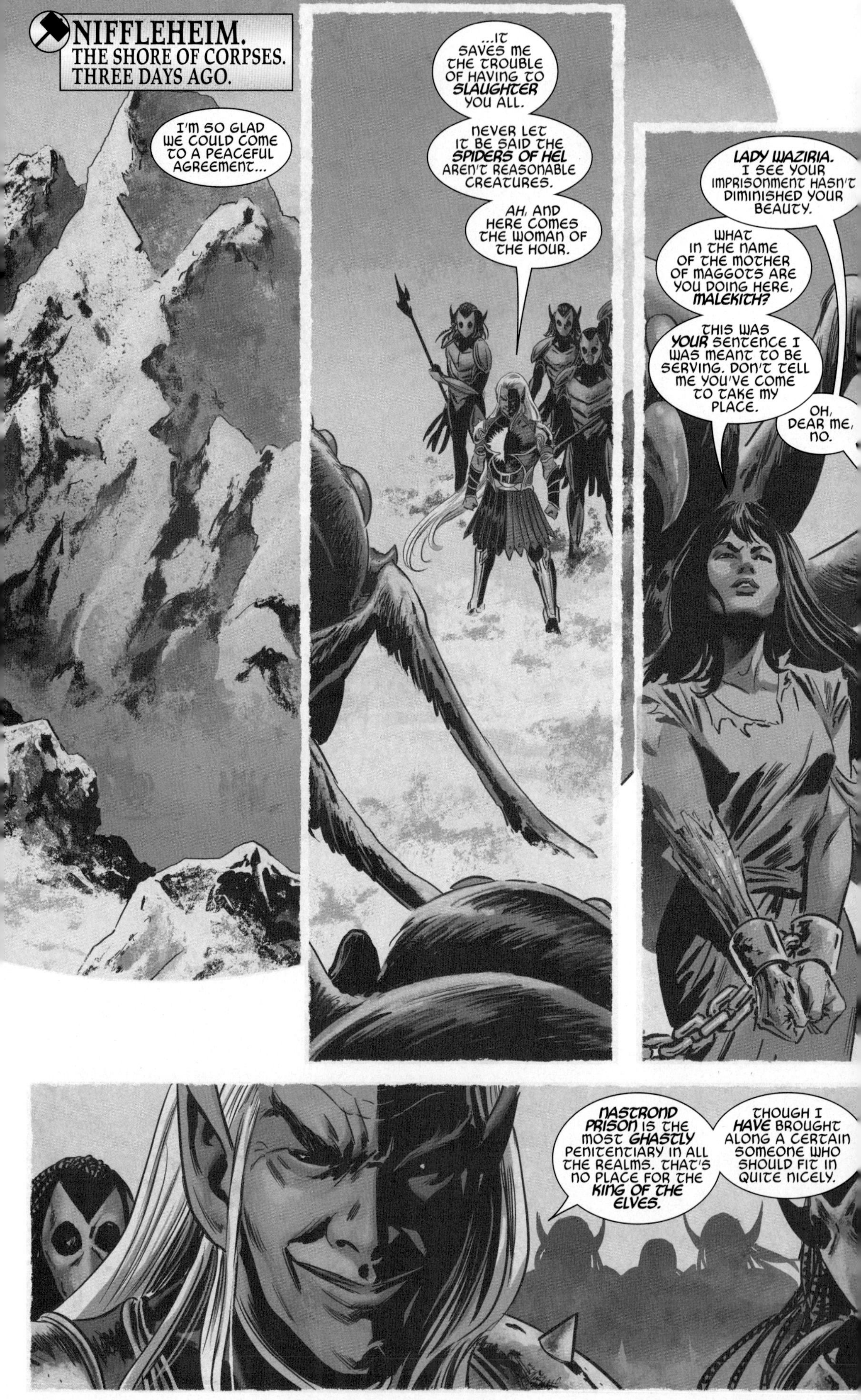
NIFFLEHEIM.
THE SHORE OF CORPSES.
THREE DAYS AGO.
I'M SO GLAD WE COULD COME TO A PEACEFUL AGREEMENT...
...IT SAVES ME THE TROUBLE OF HAVING TO SLAUGHTER YOU ALL.
NEVER LET IT BE SAID THE SPIDERS OF HEL AREN'T REASONABLE CREATURES.
AH, AND HERE COMES THE WOMAN OF THE HOUR.
LADY WAZIRIA. I SEE YOUR IMPRISONMENT HASN'T DIMINISHED YOUR BEAUTY.
WHAT IN THE NAME OF THE MOTHER OF MAGGOTS ARE YOU DOING HERE, MALEKITH?
THIS WAS YOUR SENTENCE I WAS MEANT TO BE SERVING. DON'T TELL ME YOU'VE COME TO TAKE MY PLACE.
OH, DEAR ME, NO.
NASTROND PRISON IS THE MOST GHASTLY PENITENTIARY IN ALL THE REALMS. THAT'S NO PLACE FOR THE KING OF THE ELVES.
THOUGH I HAVE BROUGHT ALONG A CERTAIN SOMEONE WHO SHOULD FIT IN QUITE NICELY.

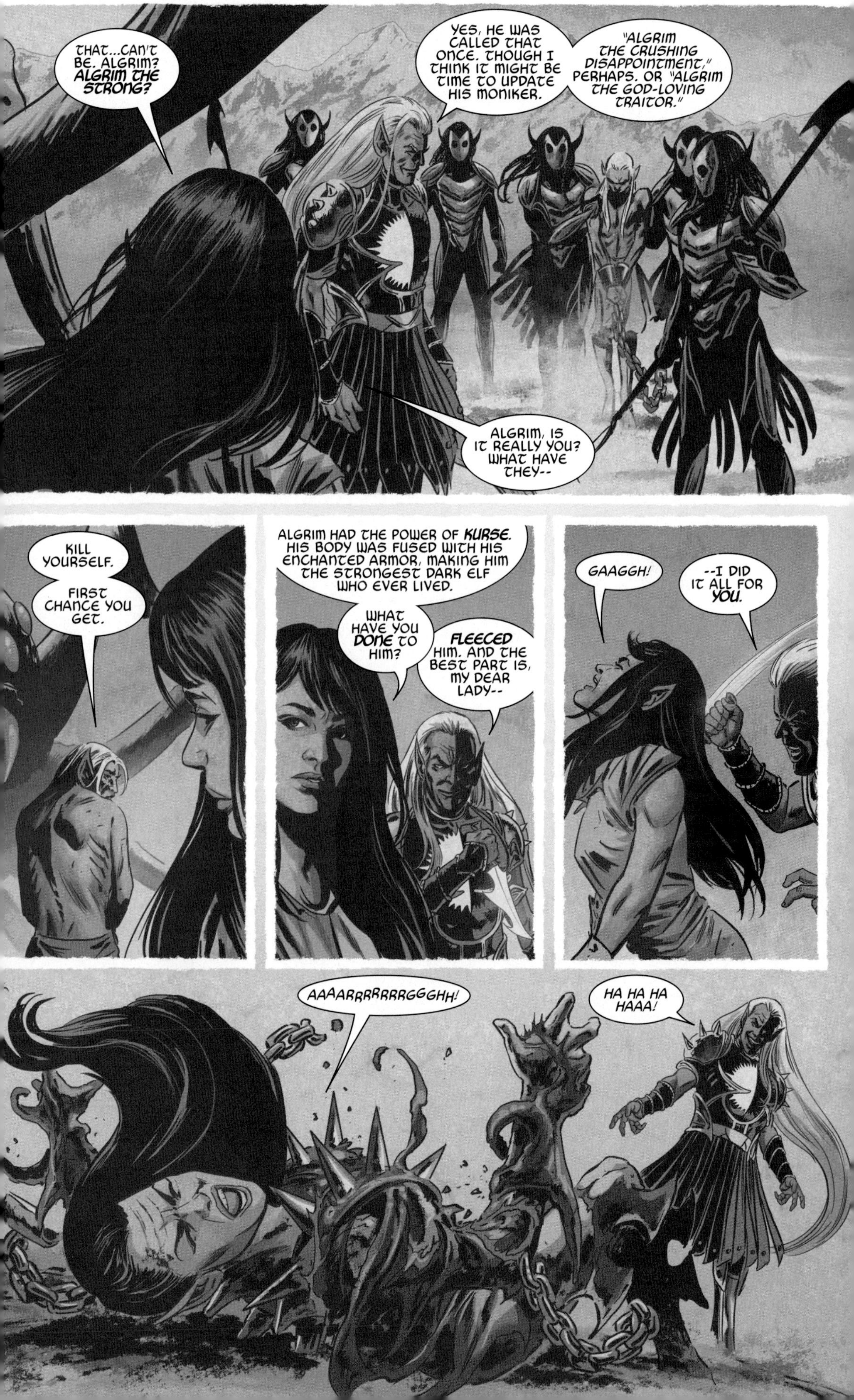
THAT...CAN'T BE. ALGRIM? ALGRIM THE STRONG?
YES, HE WAS CALLED THAT ONCE. THOUGH I THINK IT MIGHT BE TIME TO UPDATE HIS MONIKER.
"ALGRIM THE CRUSHING DISAPPOINTMENT," PERHAPS. OR "ALGRIM THE GOD-LOVING TRAITOR."
ALGRIM, IS IT REALLY YOU? WHAT HAVE THEY--
KILL YOURSELF.
FIRST CHANCE YOU GET.
ALGRIM HAD THE POWER OF KURSE. HIS BODY WAS FUSED WITH HIS ENCHANTED ARMOR, MAKING HIM THE STRONGEST DARK ELF WHO EVER LIVED.
WHAT HAVE YOU DONE TO HIM?
FLEECED HIM. AND THE BEST PART IS, MY DEAR LADY--
GAAGGH!
--I DID IT ALL FOR YOU.
AAAARRRRRRGGGHH!
HA HA HA HAAA!

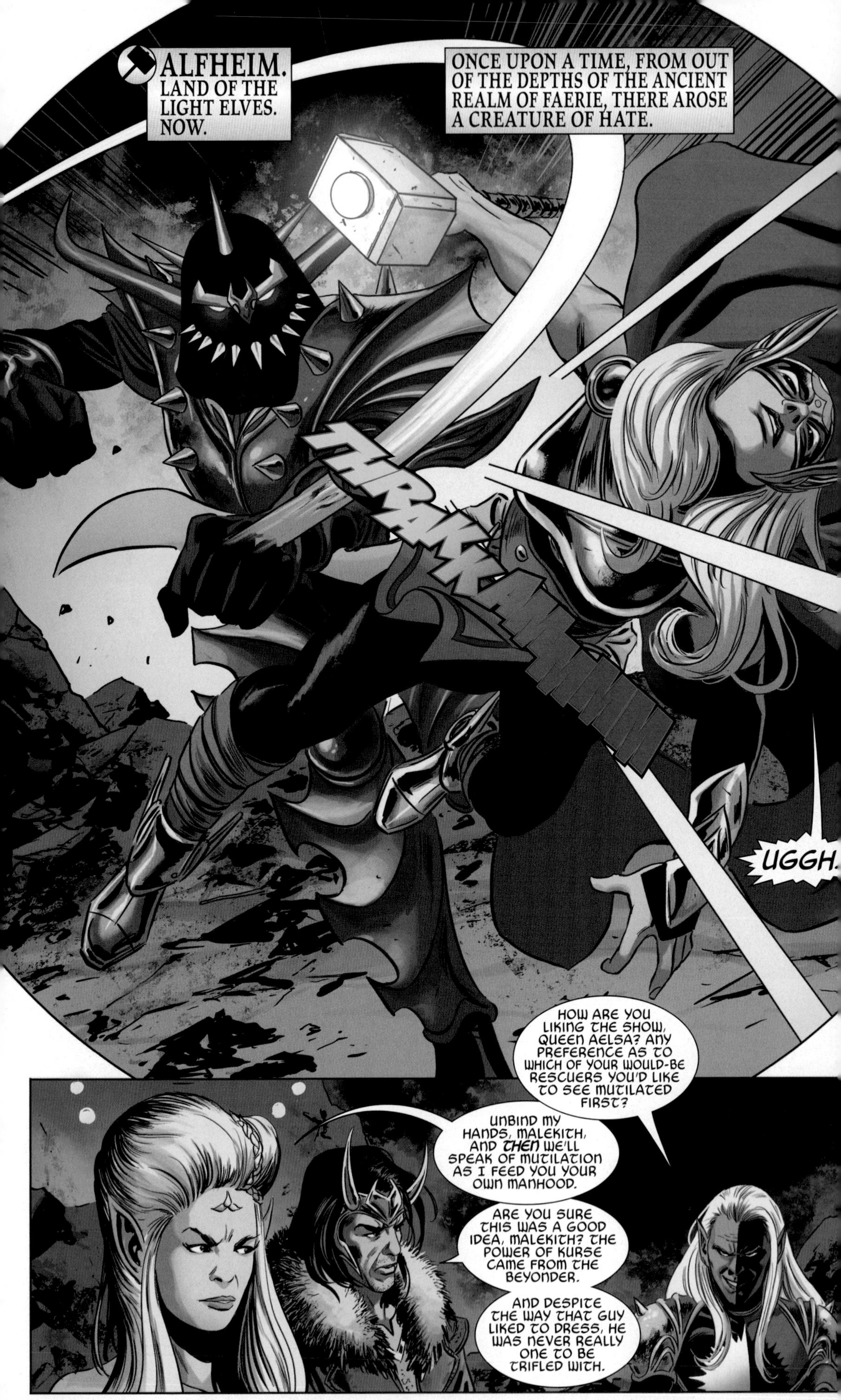
ALFHEIM. LAND OF THE LIGHT ELVES. NOW.
ONCE UPON A TIME, FROM OUT OF THE DEPTHS OF THE ANCIENT REALM OF FAERIE, THERE AROSE A CREATURE OF HATE.
THRAKKAMMM
UGGH.
HOW ARE YOU LIKING THE SHOW, QUEEN AELSA? ANY PREFERENCE AS TO WHICH OF YOUR WOULD-BE RESCUERS YOU'D LIKE TO SEE MUTILATED FIRST?
UNBIND MY HANDS, MALEKITH, AND THEN WE'LL SPEAK OF MUTILATION AS I FEED YOU YOUR OWN MANHOOD.
ARE YOU SURE THIS WAS A GOOD IDEA, MALEKITH? THE POWER OF KURSE CAME FROM THE BEYONDER.
AND DESPITE THE WAY THAT GUY LIKED TO DRESS, HE WAS NEVER REALLY ONE TO BE TRIFLED WITH.

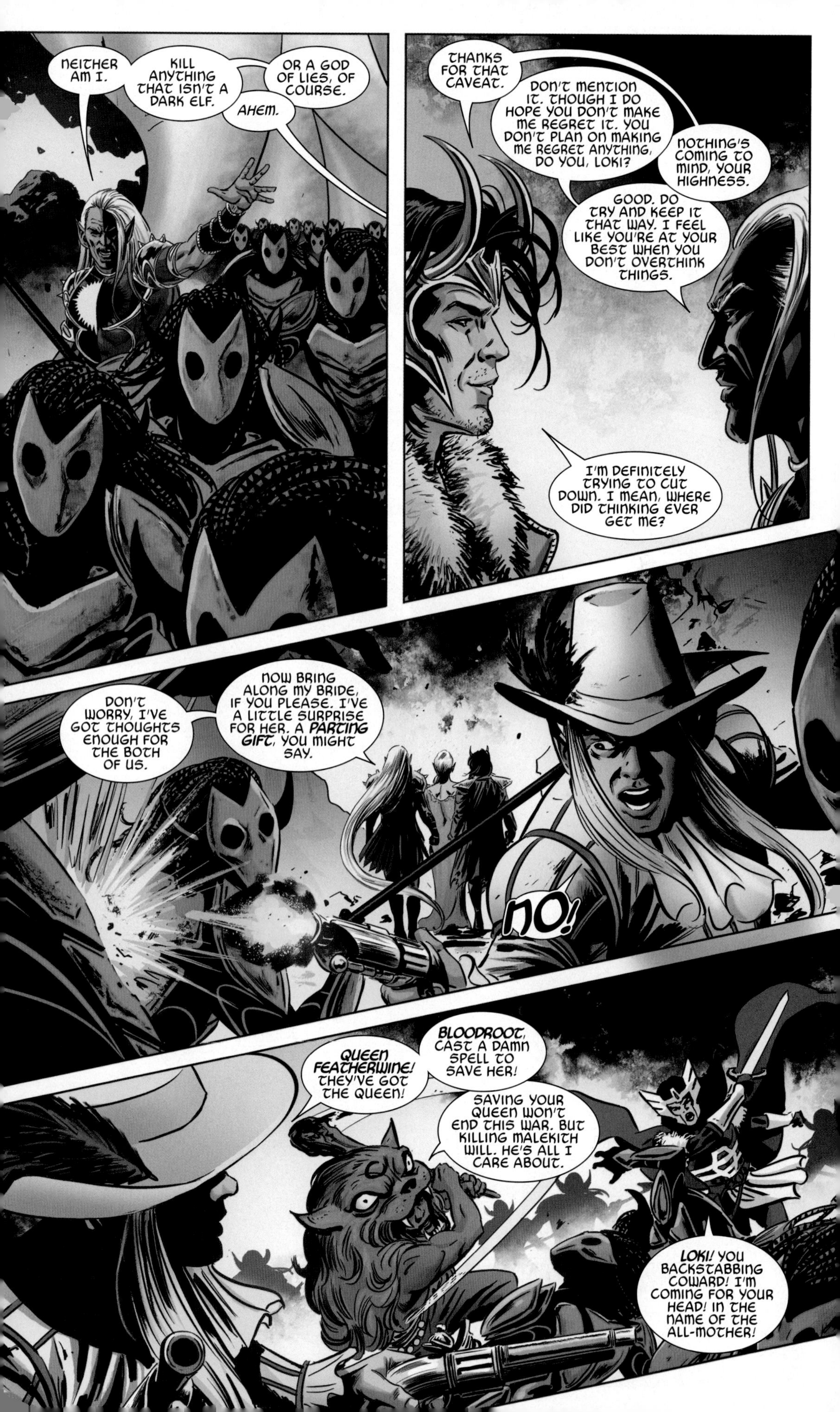
NEITHER AM I.
KILL ANYTHING THAT ISN'T A DARK ELF.
OR A GOD OF LIES, OF COURSE.
AHEM.
THANKS FOR THAT CAVEAT.
DON'T MENTION IT. THOUGH I DO HOPE YOU DON'T MAKE ME REGRET IT. YOU DON'T PLAN ON MAKING ME REGRET ANYTHING, DO YOU, LOKI?
NOTHING'S COMING TO MIND, YOUR HIGHNESS.
GOOD. DO TRY AND KEEP IT THAT WAY. I FEEL LIKE YOU'RE AT YOUR BEST WHEN YOU DON'T OVERTHINK THINGS.
I'M DEFINITELY TRYING TO CUT DOWN. I MEAN, WHERE DID THINKING EVER GET ME?
DON'T WORRY, I'VE GOT THOUGHTS ENOUGH FOR THE BOTH OF US.
NOW BRING ALONG MY BRIDE, IF YOU PLEASE. I'VE A LITTLE SURPRISE FOR HER. A PARTING GIFT, YOU MIGHT SAY.
NO!
QUEEN FEATHERWINE! THEY'VE GOT THE QUEEN!
BLOODROOT, CAST A DAMN SPELL TO SAVE HER!
SAVING YOUR QUEEN WON'T END THIS WAR. BUT KILLING MALEKITH WILL. HE'S ALL I CARE ABOUT.
LOKI! YOU BACKSTABBING COWARD! I'M COMING FOR YOUR HEAD! IN THE NAME OF THE ALL-MOTHER!

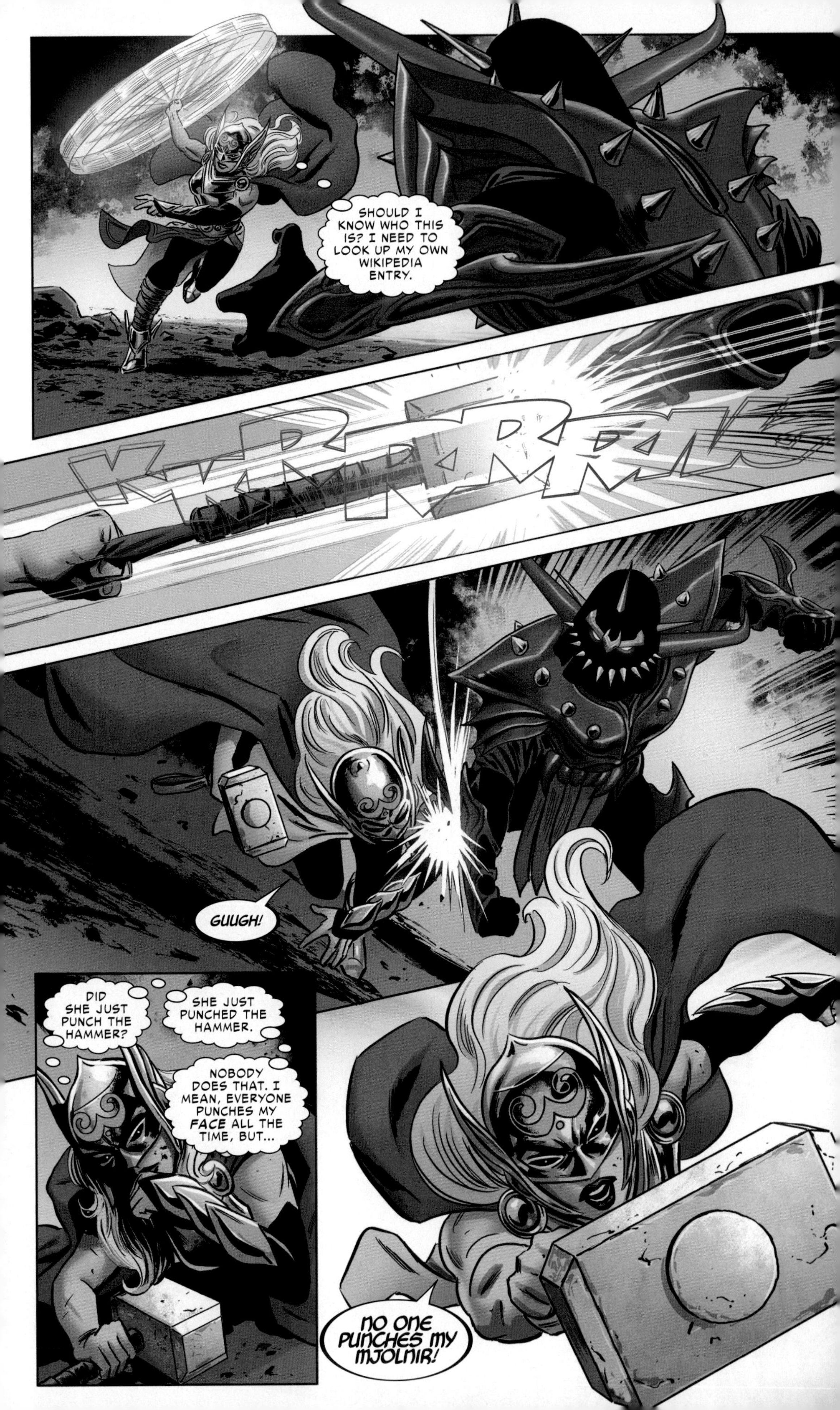
SHOULD I KNOW WHO THIS IS? I NEED TO LOOK UP MY OWN WIKIPEDIA ENTRY.
KRRRRRKRRRASH
GUUGH!
DID SHE JUST PUNCH THE HAMMER?
SHE JUST PUNCHED THE HAMMER.
NOBODY DOES THAT. I MEAN, EVERYONE PUNCHES MY FACE ALL THE TIME, BUT...
NO ONE PUNCHES MY MJOLNIR!

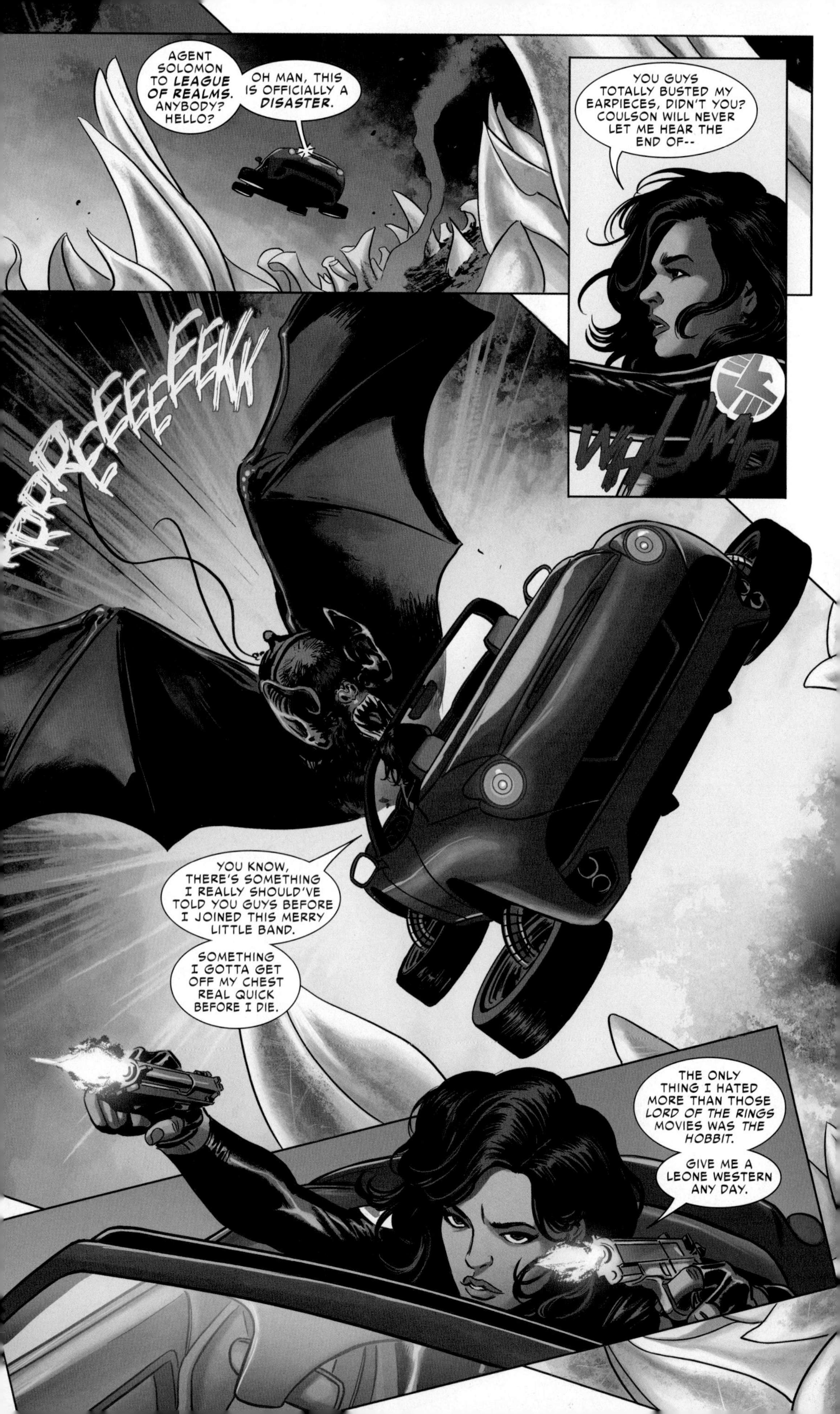
AGENT SOLOMON TO **LEAGUE OF REALMS.** ANYBODY? HELLO?
OH MAN, THIS IS OFFICIALLY A ***DISASTER.***
YOU GUYS TOTALLY BUSTED MY EARPIECES, DIDN'T YOU? COULSON WILL NEVER LET ME HEAR THE END OF--
WHUMP
RRREEEEEEKK
YOU KNOW, THERE'S SOMETHING I REALLY SHOULD'VE TOLD YOU GUYS BEFORE I JOINED THIS MERRY LITTLE BAND.
SOMETHING I GOTTA GET OFF MY CHEST REAL QUICK BEFORE I DIE.
THE ONLY THING I HATED MORE THAN THOSE *LORD OF THE RINGS* MOVIES WAS *THE HOBBIT.*
GIVE ME A LEONE WESTERN ANY DAY.

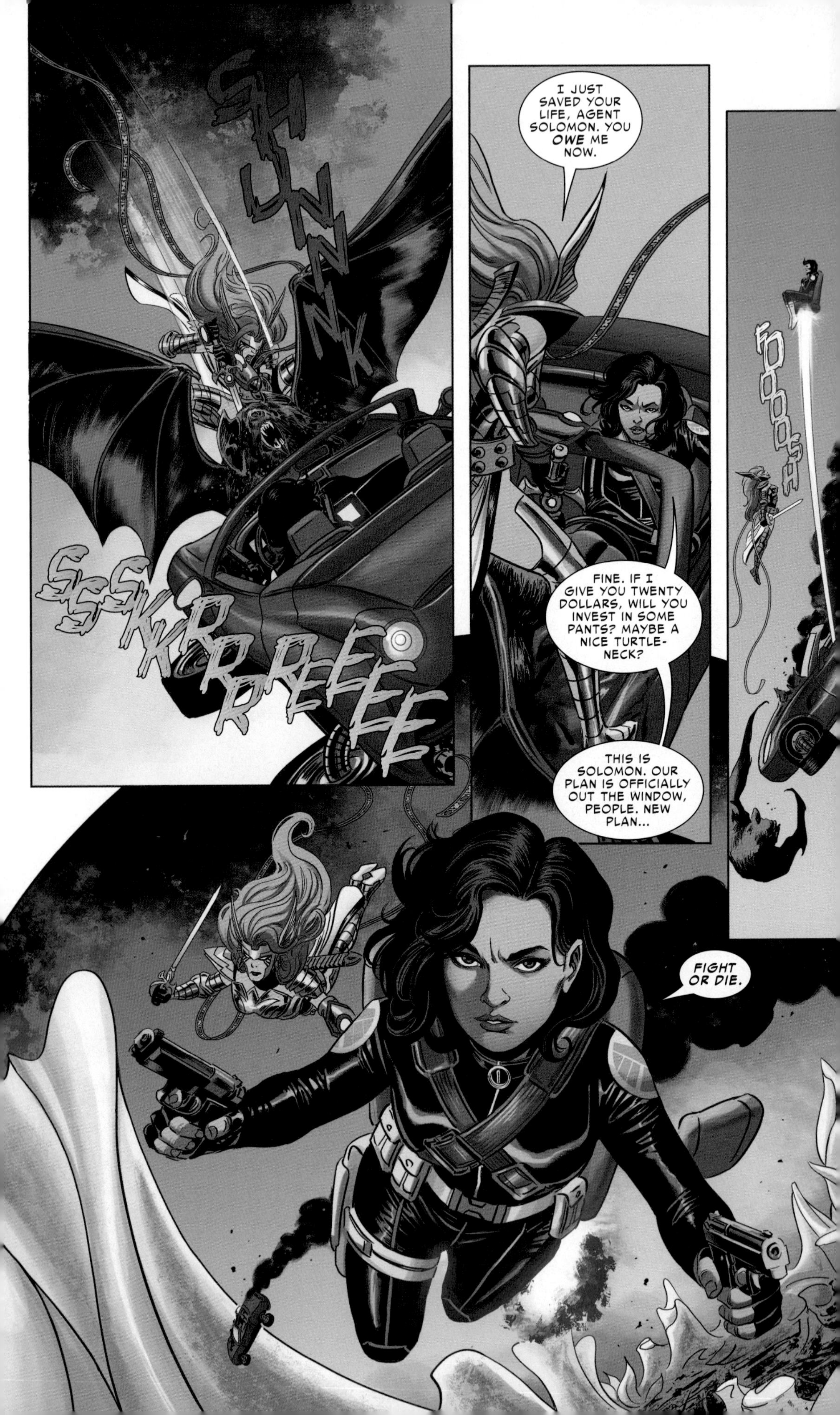
SHUNNNK
SSSKRRRREEEEEE
I JUST SAVED YOUR LIFE, AGENT SOLOMON. YOU OWE ME NOW.
FINE. IF I GIVE YOU TWENTY DOLLARS, WILL YOU INVEST IN SOME PANTS? MAYBE A NICE TURTLE-NECK?
THIS IS SOLOMON. OUR PLAN IS OFFICIALLY OUT THE WINDOW, PEOPLE. NEW PLAN...
FWOOOOSH
FIGHT OR DIE.

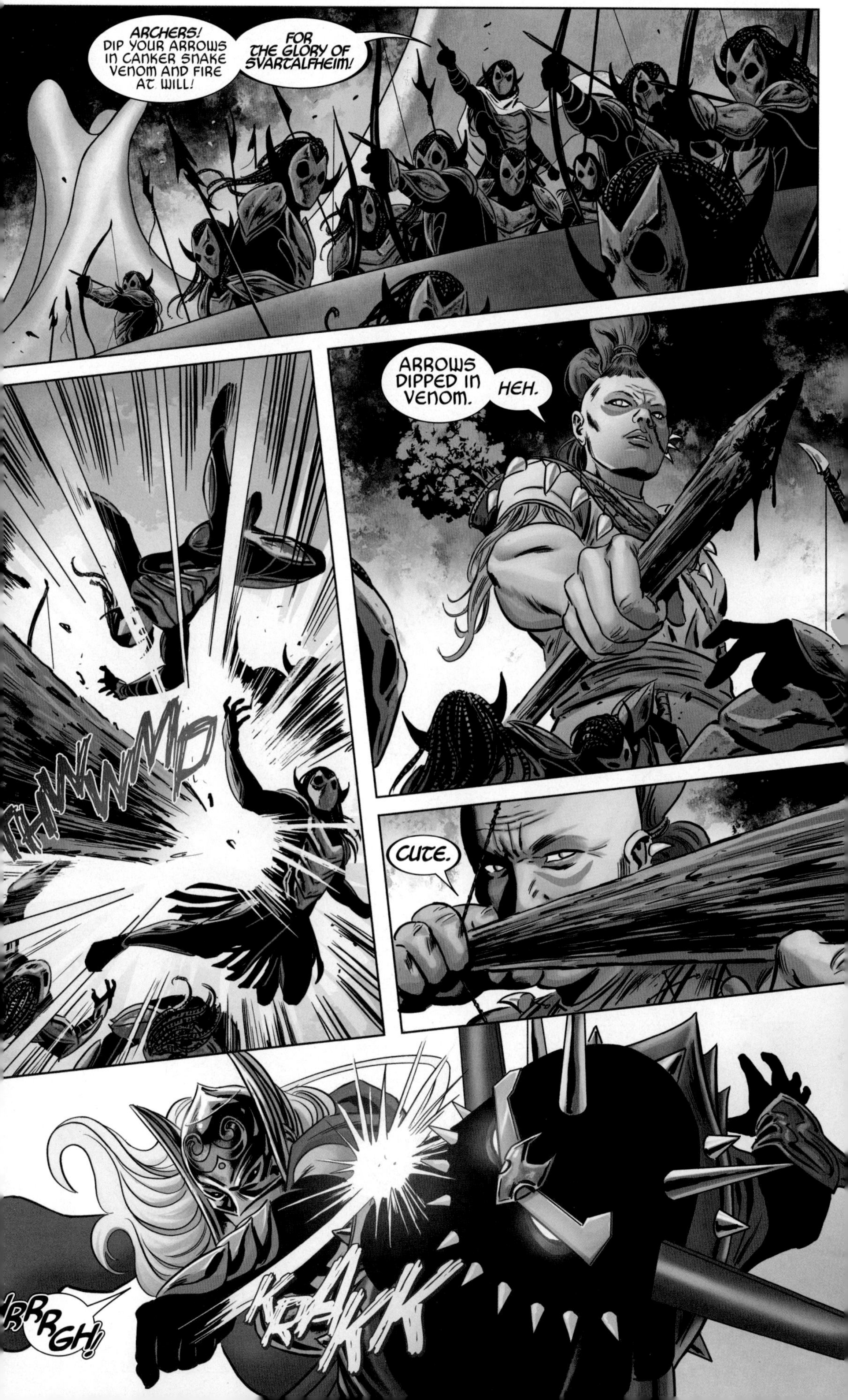
ARCHERS! DIP YOUR ARROWS IN CANKER SNAKE VENOM AND FIRE AT WILL!
FOR THE GLORY OF SVARTALFHEIM!
ARROWS DIPPED IN VENOM.
HEH.
THWWMP
CUTE.
RRRGH!
KRAKK

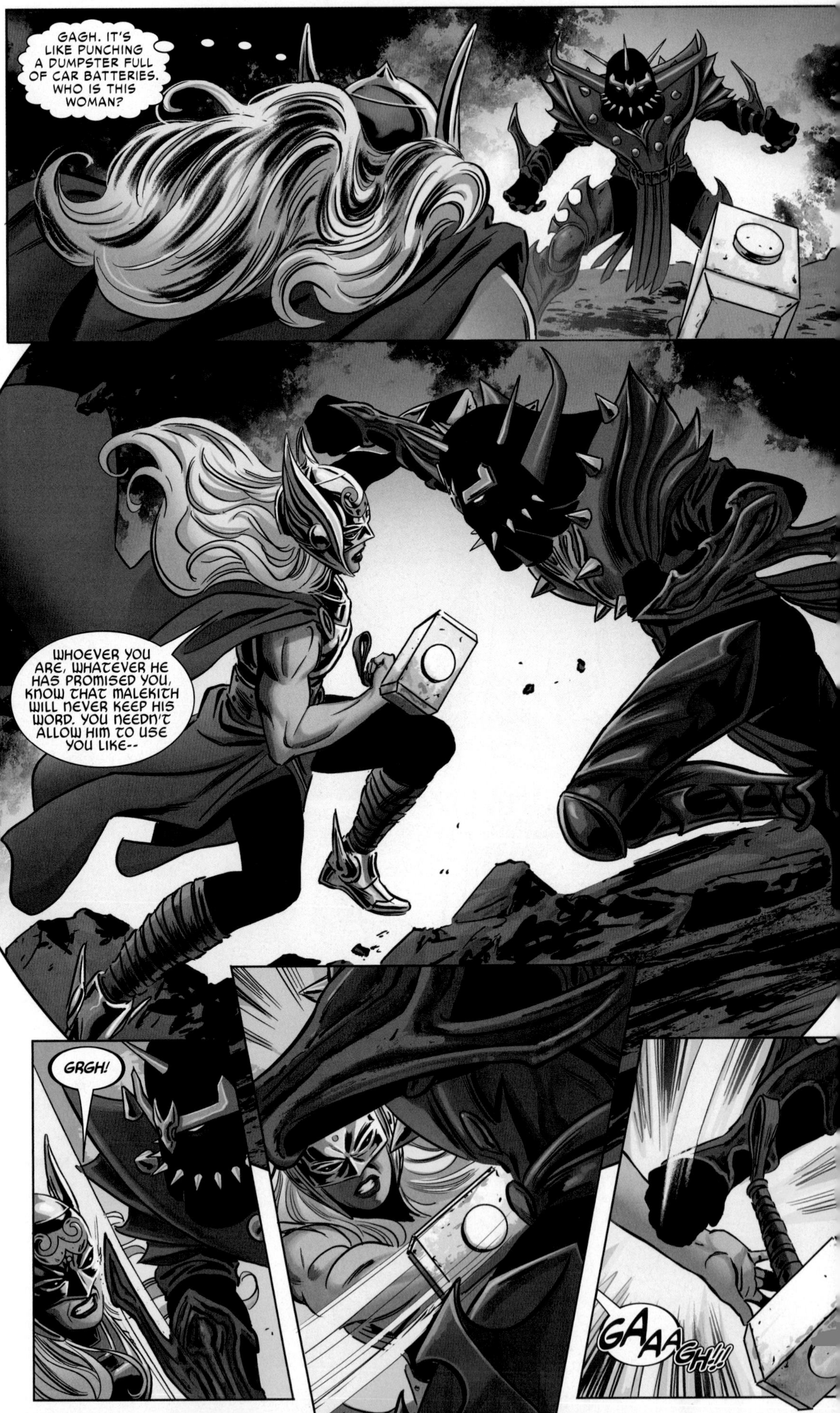
GAGH. IT'S LIKE PUNCHING A DUMPSTER FULL OF CAR BATTERIES. WHO IS THIS WOMAN?
WHOEVER YOU ARE, WHATEVER HE HAS PROMISED YOU, KNOW THAT MALEKITH WILL NEVER KEEP HIS WORD. YOU NEEDN'T ALLOW HIM TO USE YOU LIKE--
GRGH!
GAAAGH!!

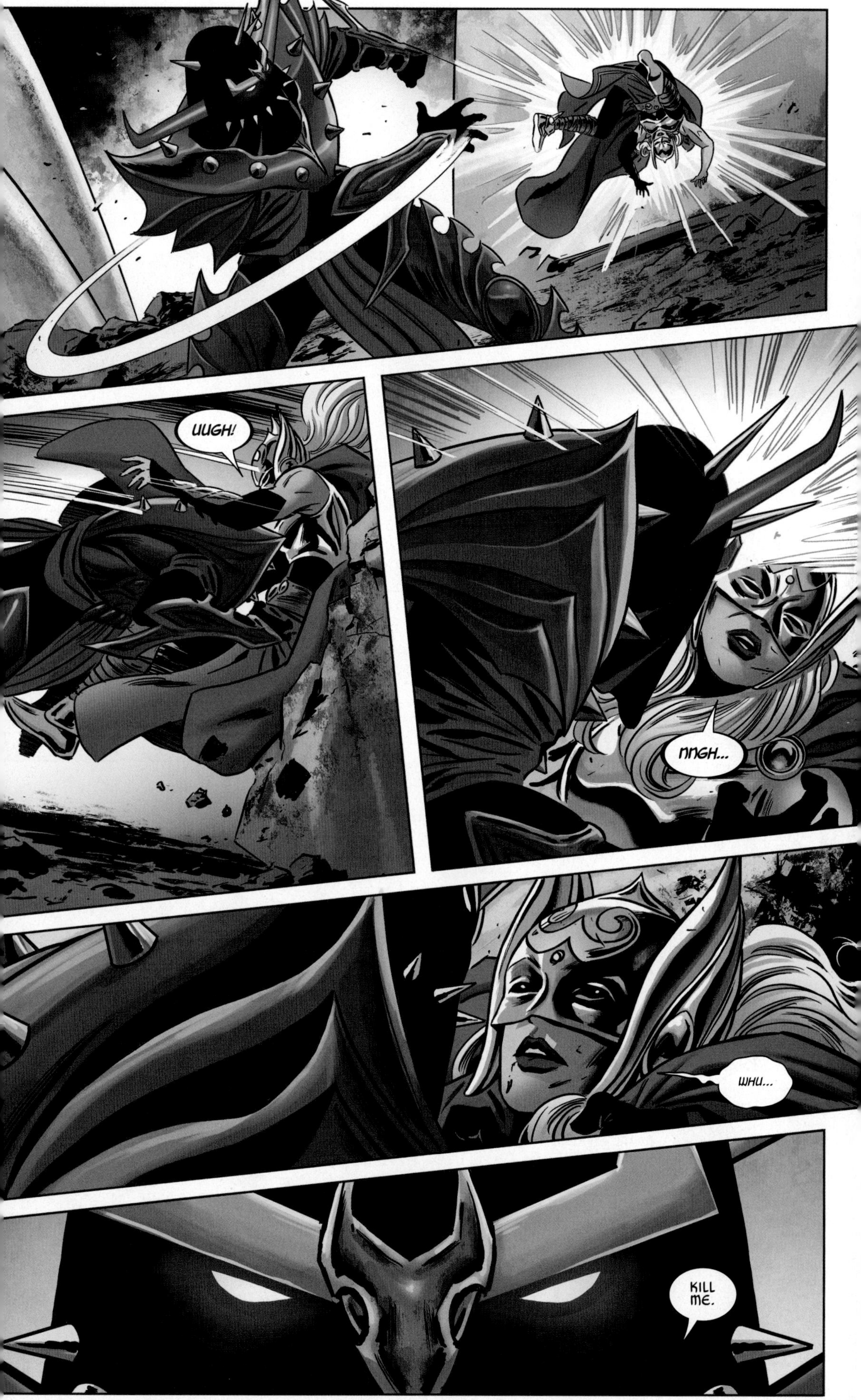
UUGH!
NNGH...
WHU...
KILL ME.

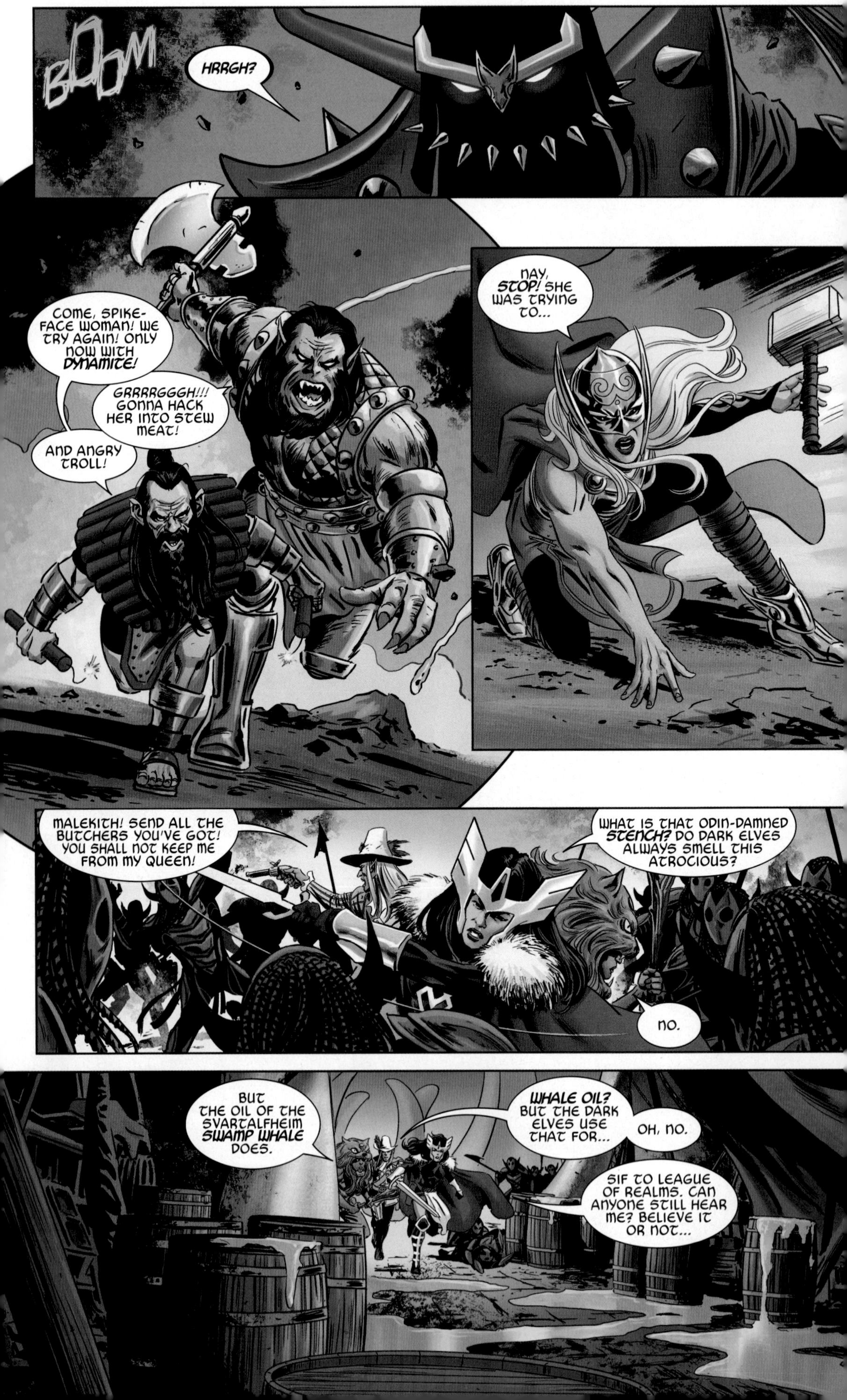

BOOM
HRRGH?
COME, SPIKE-FACE WOMAN! WE TRY AGAIN! ONLY NOW WITH DYNAMITE!
GRRRRGGGH!!! GONNA HACK HER INTO STEW MEAT!
AND ANGRY TROLL!
NAY, STOP! SHE WAS TRYING TO...
MALEKITH! SEND ALL THE BUTCHERS YOU'VE GOT! YOU SHALL NOT KEEP ME FROM MY QUEEN!
WHAT IS THAT ODIN-DAMNED STENCH? DO DARK ELVES ALWAYS SMELL THIS ATROCIOUS?
NO.
BUT THE OIL OF THE SVARTALFHEIM SWAMP WHALE DOES.
WHALE OIL? BUT THE DARK ELVES USE THAT FOR...
OH, NO.
SIF TO LEAGUE OF REALMS. CAN ANYONE STILL HEAR ME? BELIEVE IT OR NOT...

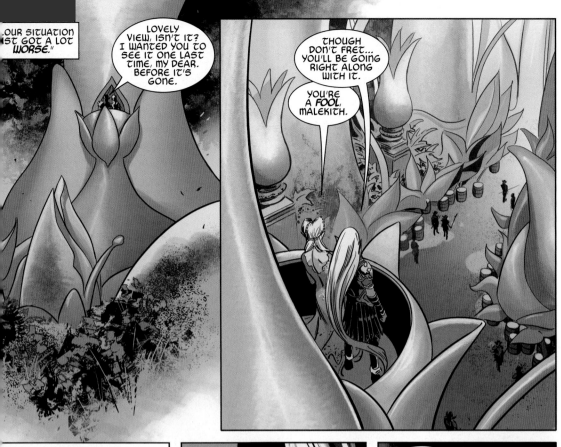

"OUR SITUATION JUST GOT A LOT *WORSE.*"

LOVELY VIEW, ISN'T IT? I WANTED YOU TO SEE IT ONE LAST TIME, MY DEAR. BEFORE IT'S GONE.

THOUGH DON'T FRET... YOU'LL BE GOING RIGHT ALONG WITH IT.

YOU'RE A *FOOL,* MALEKITH.

...UR MAGIC MAY HAVE BEEN STRONG ENOUGH TO *BRAINWASH* ME INTO MARRYING YOU, BUT THE LIGHT ELVES OF ALFHEIM WILL NEVER SUBMIT TO YOUR RULE, NO MATTER WHAT YOU DO TO ME.

YOU'RE RIGHT, DEAR AELSA. BUT WHO EVER SAID I WANTED TO *RULE* YOUR PATHETIC PEOPLE?

YOUR ARMY HAS BEEN SLAUGHTERED, YOUR CITIZENS SCATTERED TO THE WINDS.

AND WHILE WE'VE BEEN OCCUPYING THIS LOVELY LITTLE CAPITAL OF YOURS, MY TROOPS HAVE DRANK YOUR RIVERS DRY, EATEN EVERY LAST MORSEL FROM YOUR LARDERS, AND HUNTED ALL THE BEASTS OF YOUR FIELDS TO ABSOLUTE EXTINCTION.

YOUR REALM HAS SERVED ITS PURPOSE, MY QUEEN.

MY ARMY HAS BEEN FED AND BLOODED. AND NOW IT MARCHES TO CLAIM FAR GREATER PRIZES.

BUT NOT WITHOUT LEAVING YOU A LITTLE SOMETHING TO REMEMBER US BY.

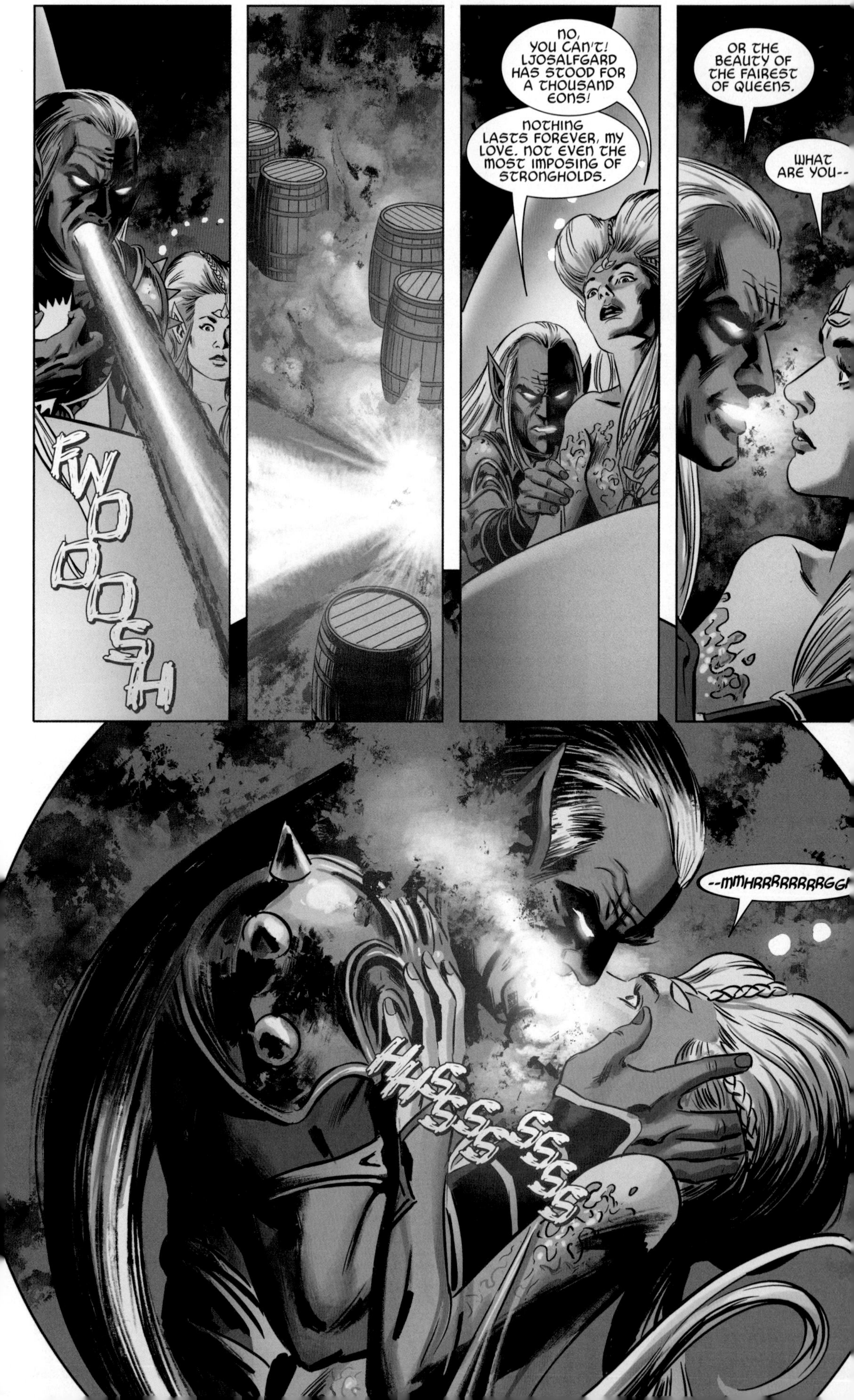
FWOOOOSH
NO, YOU CAN'T! LJOSALFGARD HAS STOOD FOR A THOUSAND EONS!
NOTHING LASTS FOREVER, MY LOVE. NOT EVEN THE MOST IMPOSING OF STRONGHOLDS.
OR THE BEAUTY OF THE FAIREST OF QUEENS.
WHAT ARE YOU--
--MMHRRRRRRRRGG!
HHSSSSSSSSSS

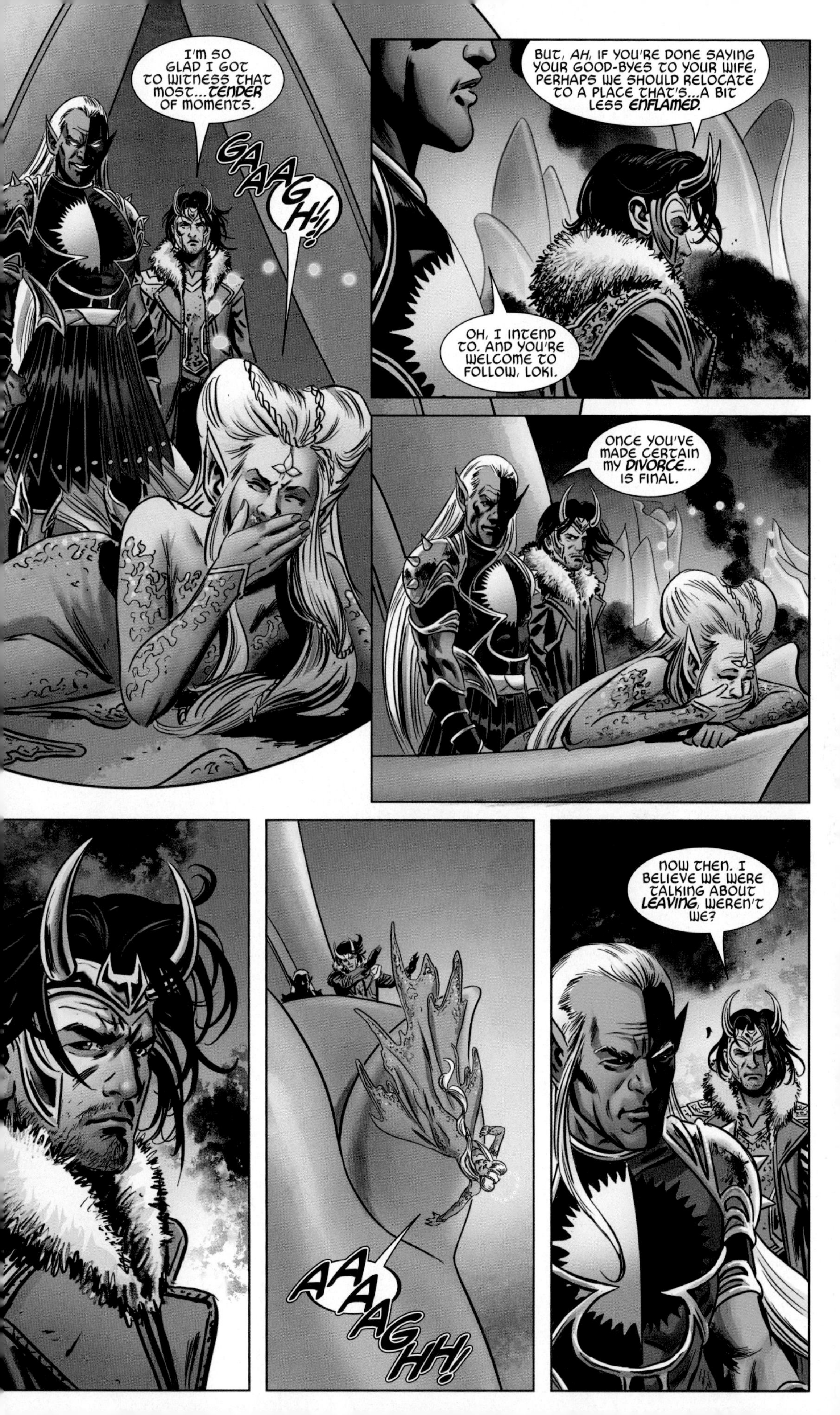
I'M SO GLAD I GOT TO WITNESS THAT MOST...TENDER OF MOMENTS.
GAAAAGH-!!
BUT, AH, IF YOU'RE DONE SAYING YOUR GOOD-BYES TO YOUR WIFE, PERHAPS WE SHOULD RELOCATE TO A PLACE THAT'S...A BIT LESS ENFLAMED.
OH, I INTEND TO. AND YOU'RE WELCOME TO FOLLOW, LOKI.
ONCE YOU'VE MADE CERTAIN MY DIVORCE... IS FINAL.
AAAAAGHH!
NOW THEN. I BELIEVE WE WERE TALKING ABOUT LEAVING, WEREN'T WE?

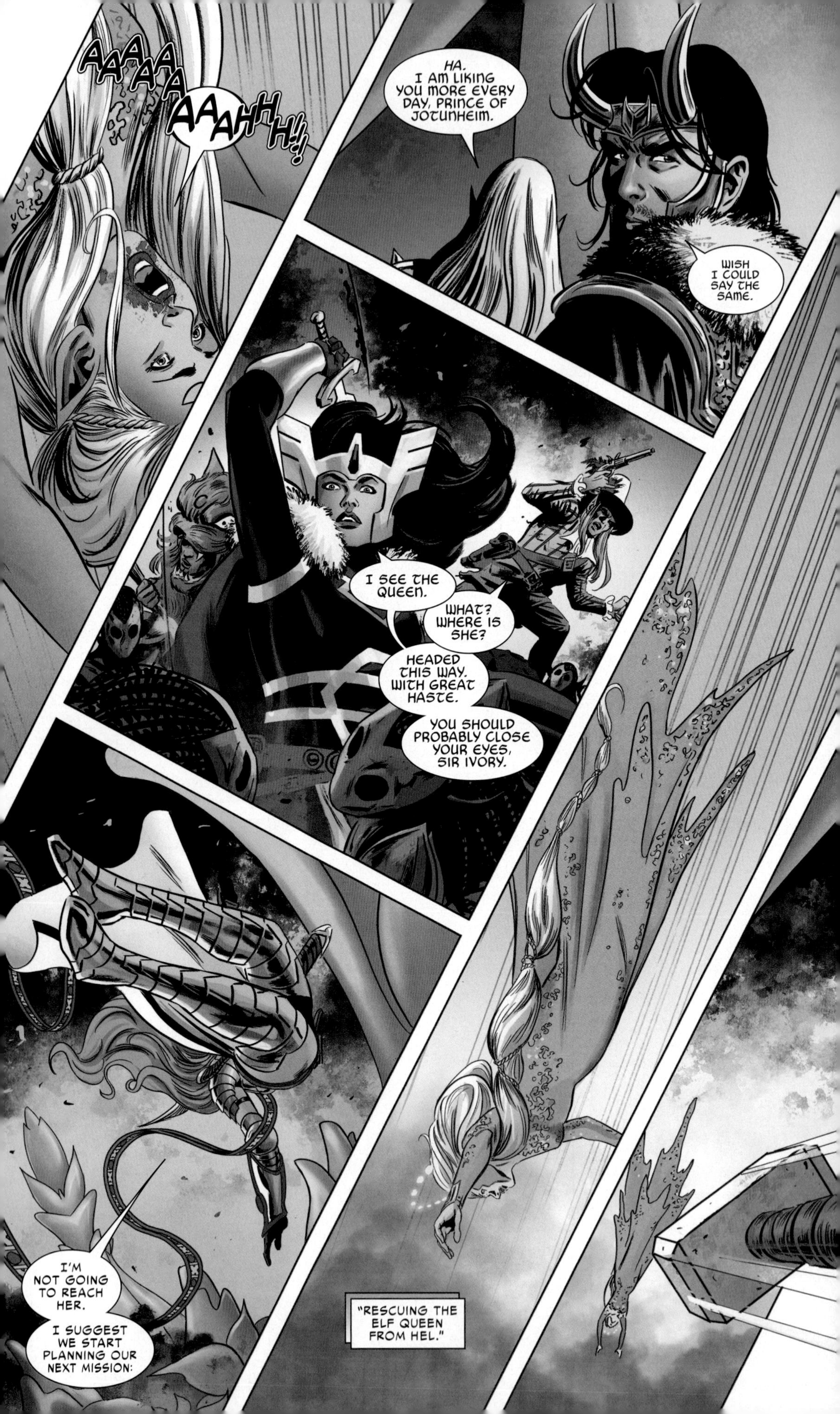
AAAAAAAAAHHH!!!
HA. I AM LIKING YOU MORE EVERY DAY, PRINCE OF JOTUNHEIM.
WISH I COULD SAY THE SAME.
I SEE THE QUEEN.
WHAT? WHERE IS SHE?
HEADED THIS WAY. WITH GREAT HASTE.
YOU SHOULD PROBABLY CLOSE YOUR EYES, SIR IVORY.
I'M NOT GOING TO REACH HER.
I SUGGEST WE START PLANNING OUR NEXT MISSION:
"RESCUING THE ELF QUEEN FROM HEL."

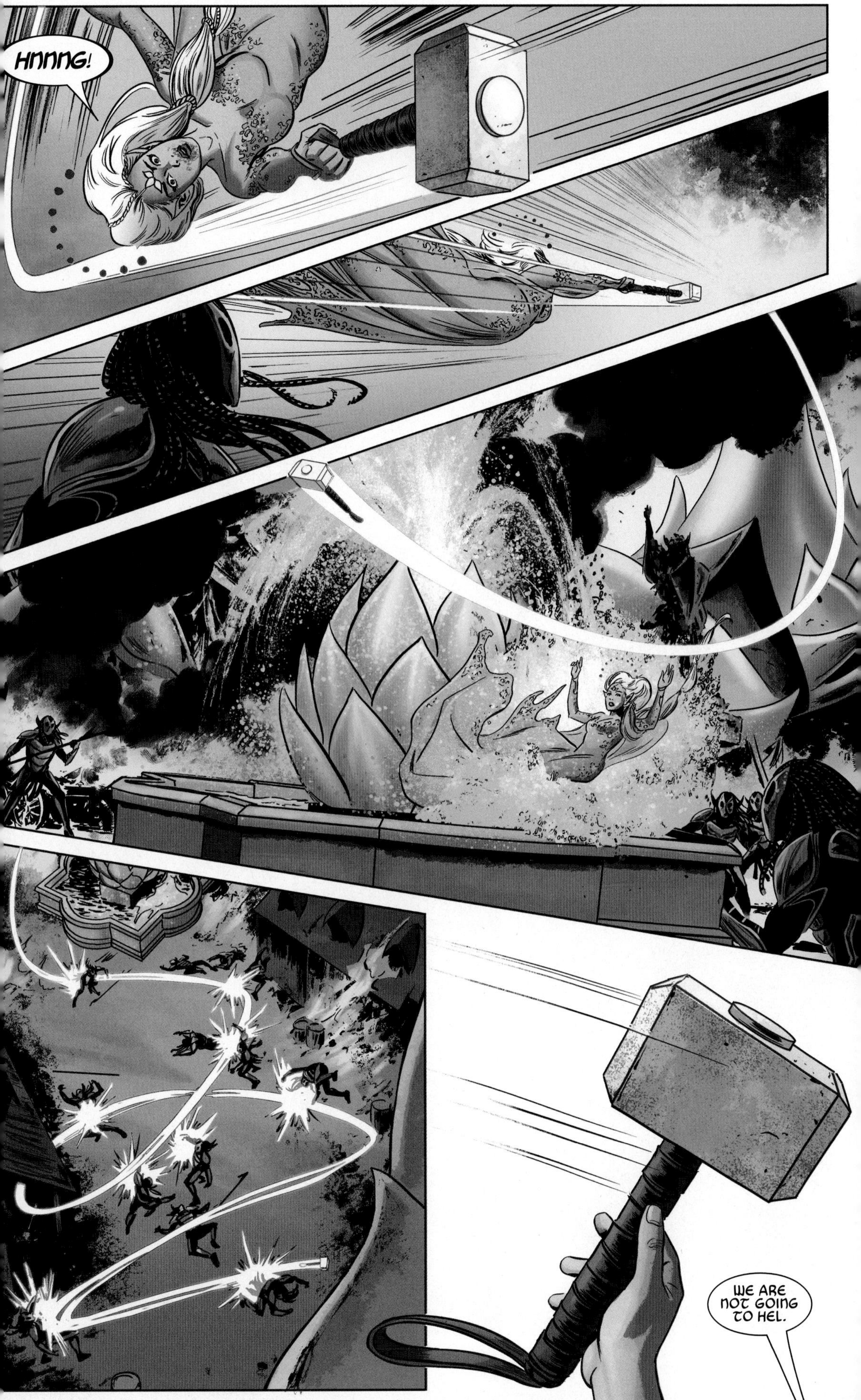
HNNNG!
WE ARE NOT GOING TO HEL.

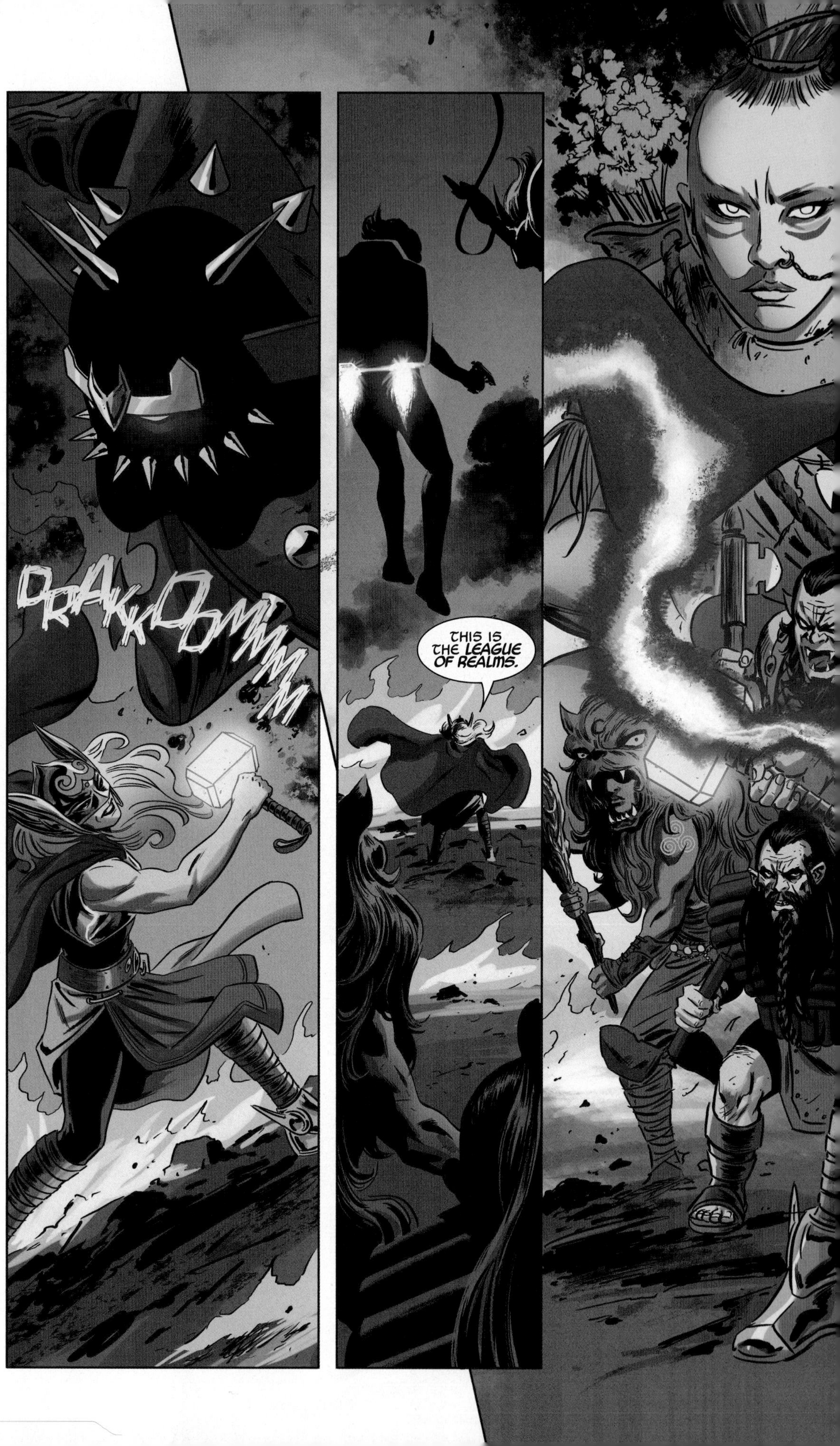
DRAKOOMMMM
THIS IS THE LEAGUE OF REALMS.

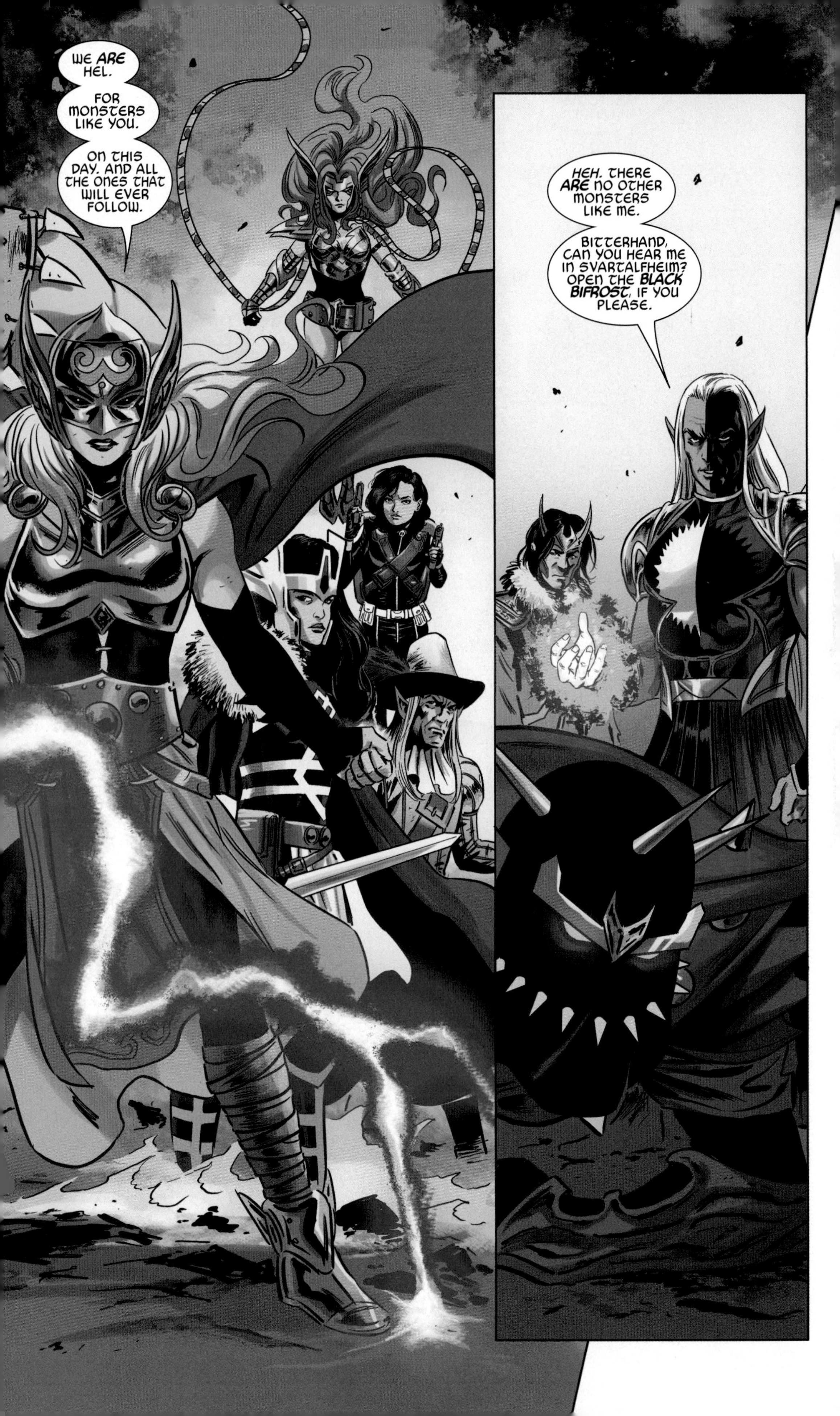
WE ARE HEL.
FOR MONSTERS LIKE YOU.
ON THIS DAY. AND ALL THE ONES THAT WILL EVER FOLLOW.
HEH. THERE ARE NO OTHER MONSTERS LIKE ME.
BITTERHAND, CAN YOU HEAR ME IN SVARTALFHEIM? OPEN THE BLACK BIFROST, IF YOU PLEASE.

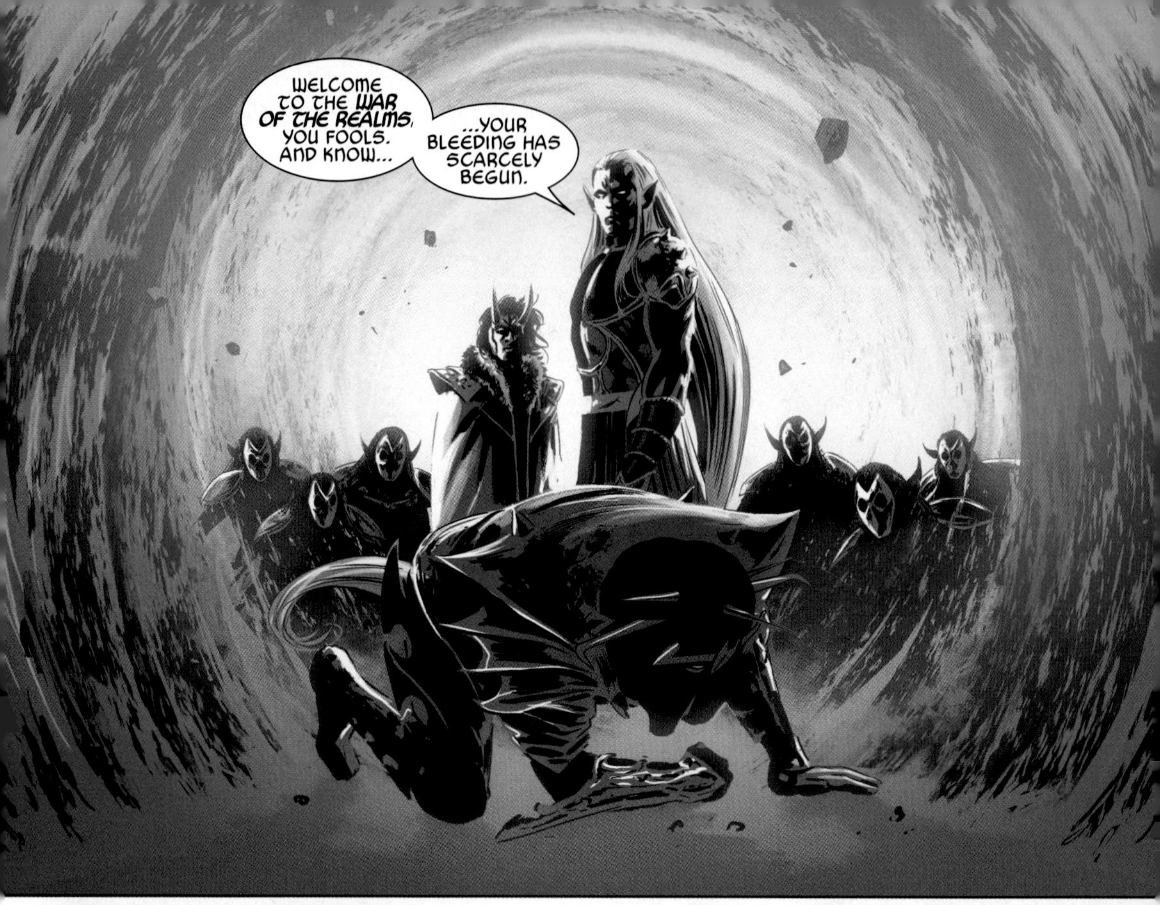
WELCOME TO THE WAR OF THE REALMS, YOU FOOLS. AND KNOW...
...YOUR BLEEDING HAS SCARCELY BEGUN.

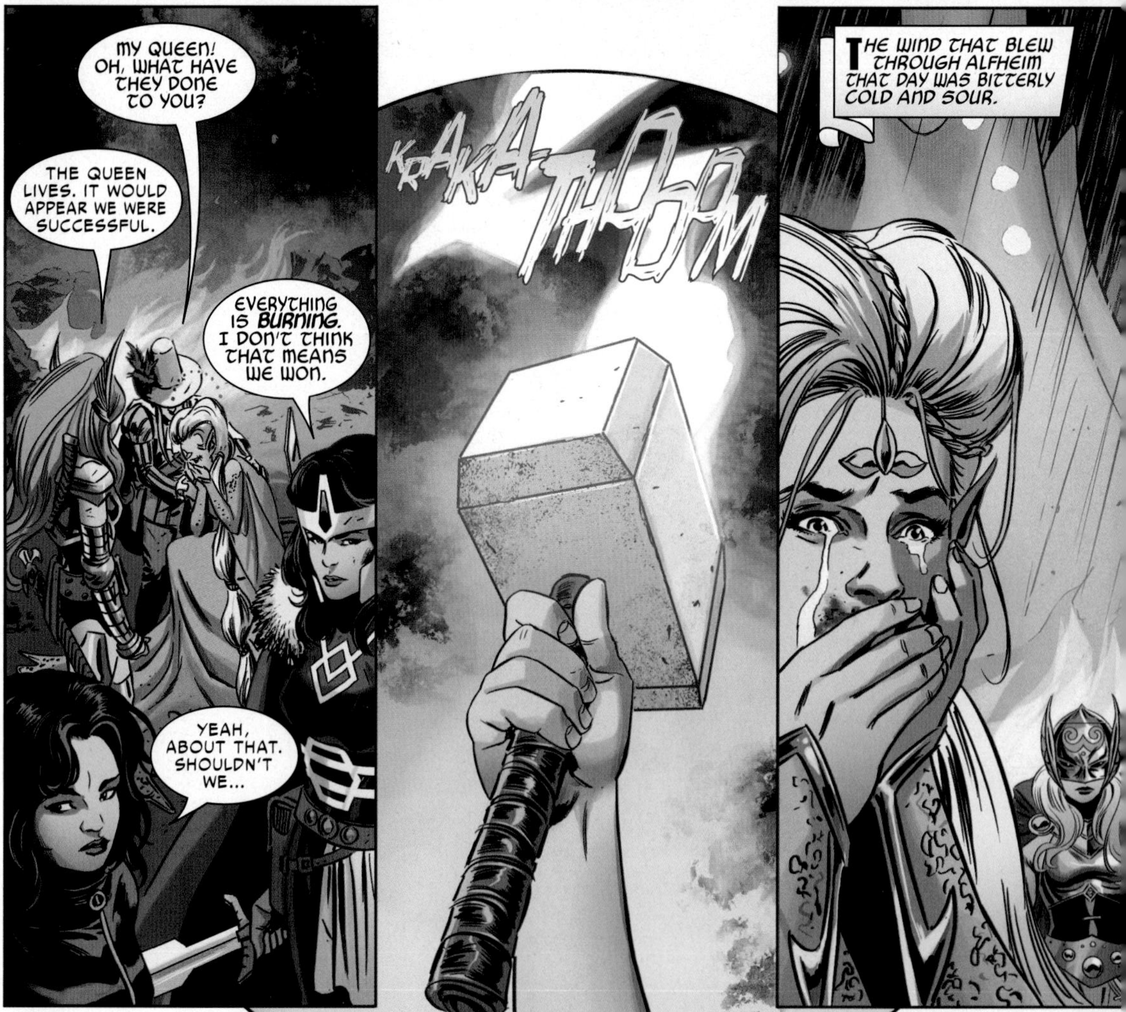
MY QUEEN! OH, WHAT HAVE THEY DONE TO YOU?
THE QUEEN LIVES. IT WOULD APPEAR WE WERE SUCCESSFUL.
EVERYTHING IS BURNING. I DON'T THINK THAT MEANS WE WON.
YEAH, ABOUT THAT. SHOULDN'T WE...
KRAKA-THOOM
THE WIND THAT BLEW THROUGH ALFHEIM THAT DAY WAS BITTERLY COLD AND SOUR.

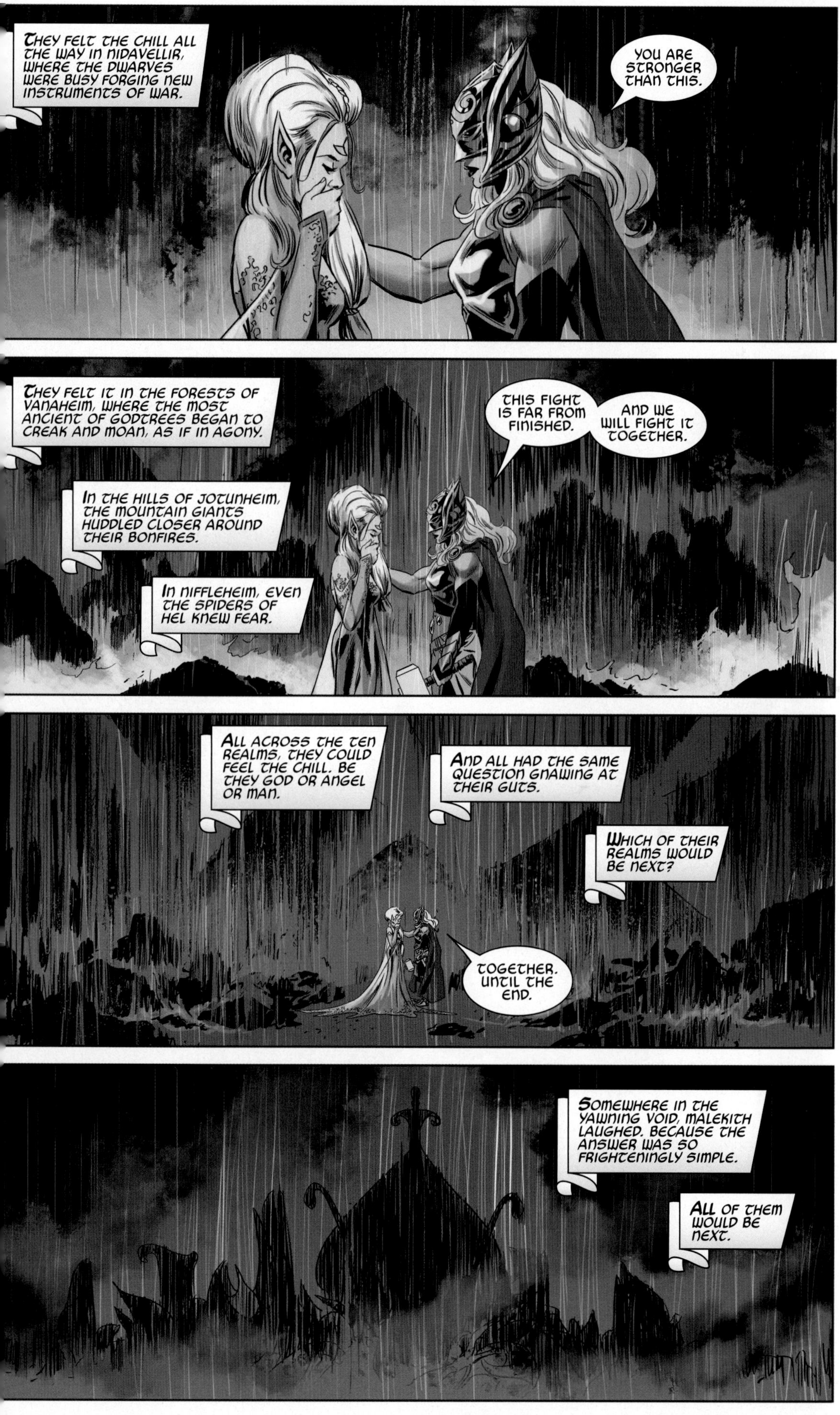
THEY FELT THE CHILL ALL THE WAY IN NIDAVELLIR, WHERE THE DWARVES WERE BUSY FORGING NEW INSTRUMENTS OF WAR.
YOU ARE STRONGER THAN THIS.
THEY FELT IT IN THE FORESTS OF VANAHEIM, WHERE THE MOST ANCIENT OF GODTREES BEGAN TO CREAK AND MOAN, AS IF IN AGONY.
THIS FIGHT IS FAR FROM FINISHED.
AND WE WILL FIGHT IT TOGETHER.
IN THE HILLS OF JOTUNHEIM, THE MOUNTAIN GIANTS HUDDLED CLOSER AROUND THEIR BONFIRES.
IN NIFFLEHEIM, EVEN THE SPIDERS OF HEL KNEW FEAR.
ALL ACROSS THE TEN REALMS, THEY COULD FEEL THE CHILL. BE THEY GOD OR ANGEL OR MAN.
AND ALL HAD THE SAME QUESTION GNAWING AT THEIR GUTS.
WHICH OF THEIR REALMS WOULD BE NEXT?
TOGETHER. UNTIL THE END.
SOMEWHERE IN THE YAWNING VOID, MALEKITH LAUGHED. BECAUSE THE ANSWER WAS SO FRIGHTENINGLY SIMPLE.
ALL OF THEM WOULD BE NEXT.

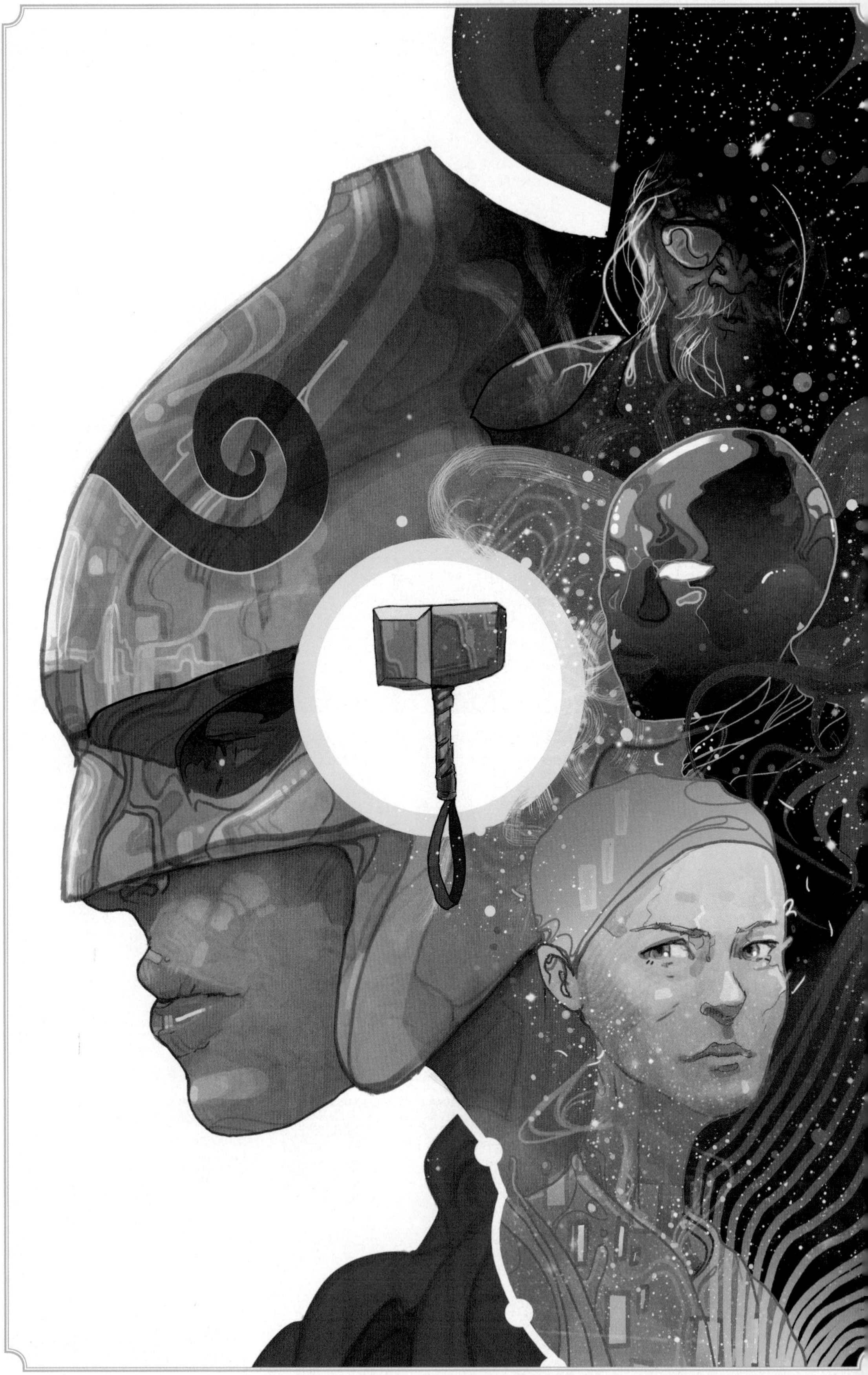

MIGHTY THOR # 15 STORY THUS FAR VARIANT
BY **CHRISTIAN WARD**

15

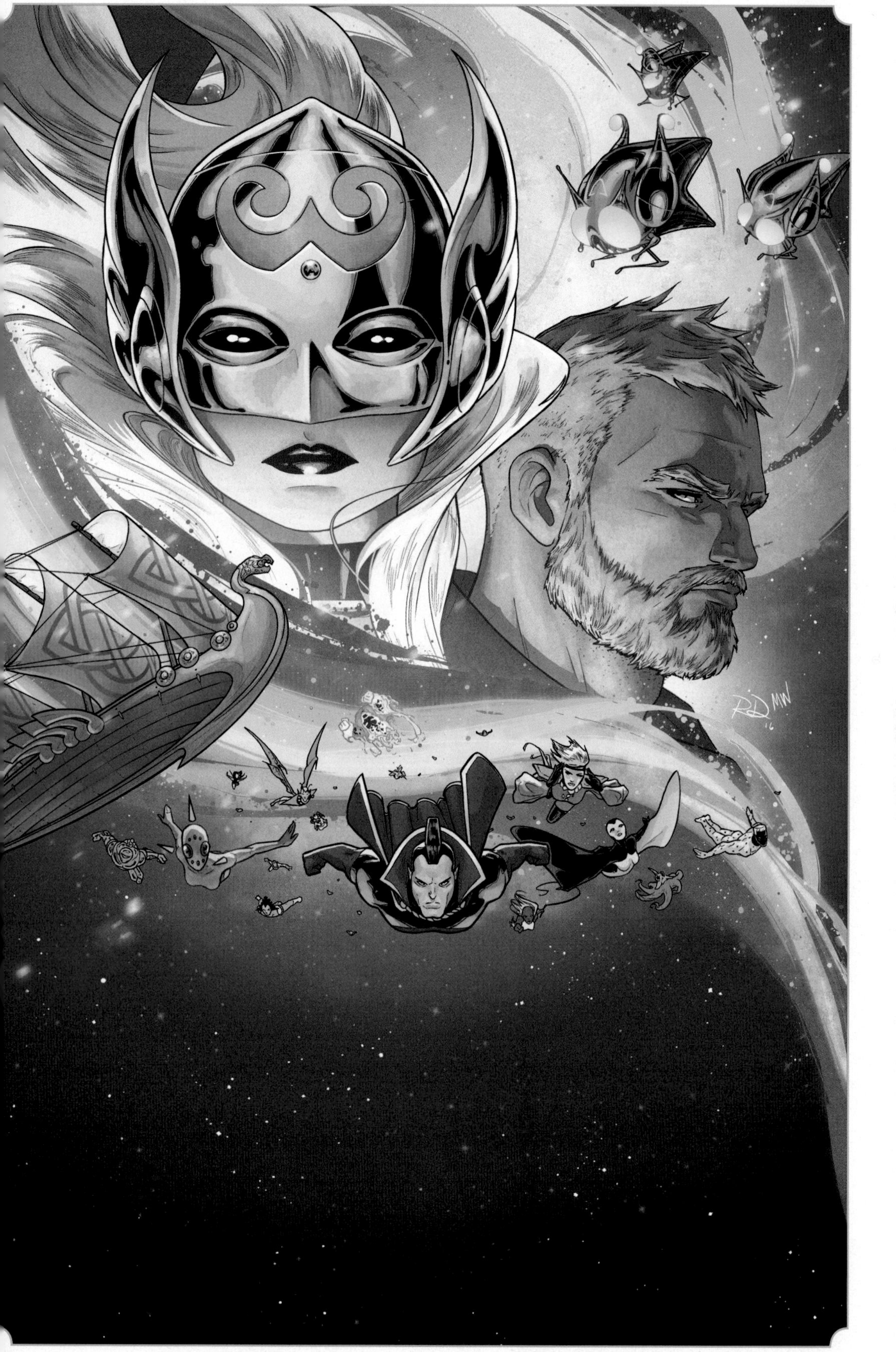
RD MW '16

THE ASGARD/SHI'AR WAR, PART ONE:

DAY WHICH WILL LIVE IN IMMORTAL INFAMY

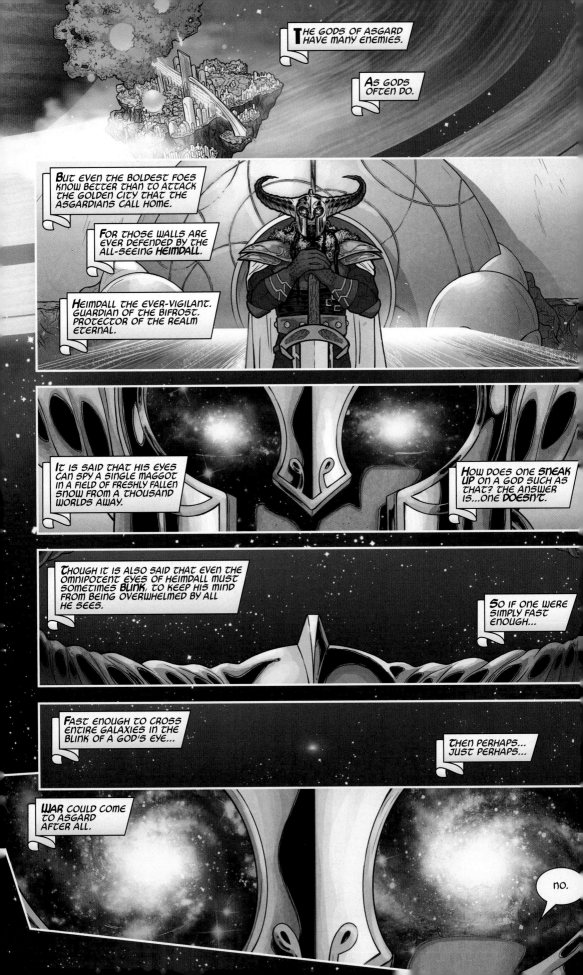

THE GODS OF ASGARD HAVE MANY ENEMIES.

AS GODS OFTEN DO.

BUT EVEN THE BOLDEST FOES KNOW BETTER THAN TO ATTACK THE GOLDEN CITY THAT THE ASGARDIANS CALL HOME.

FOR THOSE WALLS ARE EVER DEFENDED BY THE ALL-SEEING HEIMDALL.

HEIMDALL THE EVER-VIGILANT. GUARDIAN OF THE BIFROST. PROTECTOR OF THE REALM ETERNAL.

IT IS SAID THAT HIS EYES CAN SPY A SINGLE MAGGOT IN A FIELD OF FRESHLY FALLEN SNOW FROM A THOUSAND WORLDS AWAY.

HOW DOES ONE SNEAK UP ON A GOD SUCH AS THAT? THE ANSWER IS...ONE DOESN'T.

THOUGH IT IS ALSO SAID THAT EVEN THE OMNIPOTENT EYES OF HEIMDALL MUST SOMETIMES BLINK, TO KEEP HIS MIND FROM BEING OVERWHELMED BY ALL HE SEES.

SO IF ONE WERE SIMPLY FAST ENOUGH...

FAST ENOUGH TO CROSS ENTIRE GALAXIES IN THE BLINK OF A GOD'S EYE...

THEN PERHAPS... JUST PERHAPS...

WAR COULD COME TO ASGARD AFTER ALL.

no.

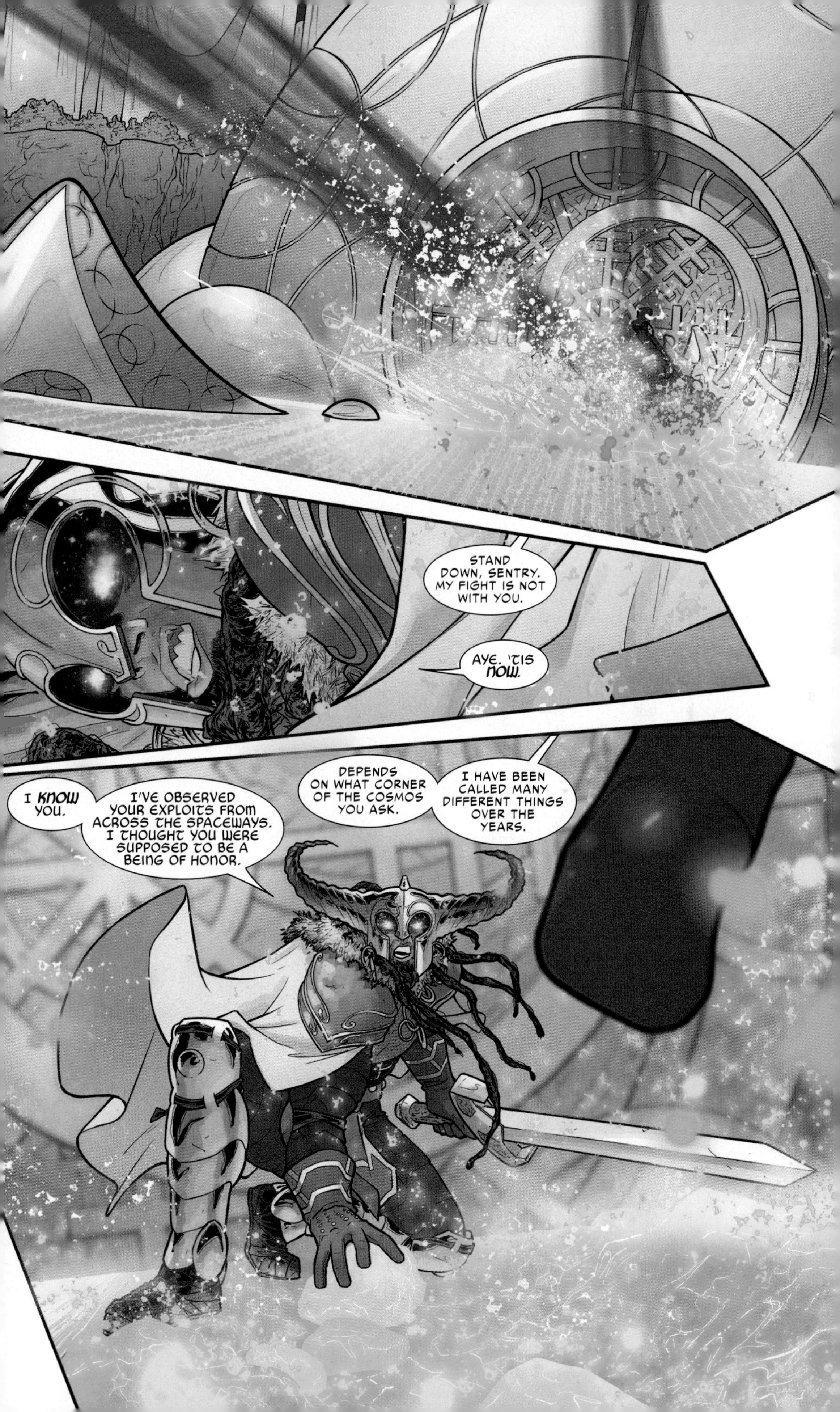
STAND DOWN, SENTRY. MY FIGHT IS NOT WITH YOU.
AYE. 'TIS NOW.
I KNOW YOU.
I'VE OBSERVED YOUR EXPLOITS FROM ACROSS THE SPACEWAYS. I THOUGHT YOU WERE SUPPOSED TO BE A BEING OF HONOR.
DEPENDS ON WHAT CORNER OF THE COSMOS YOU ASK.
I HAVE BEEN CALLED MANY DIFFERENT THINGS OVER THE YEARS.

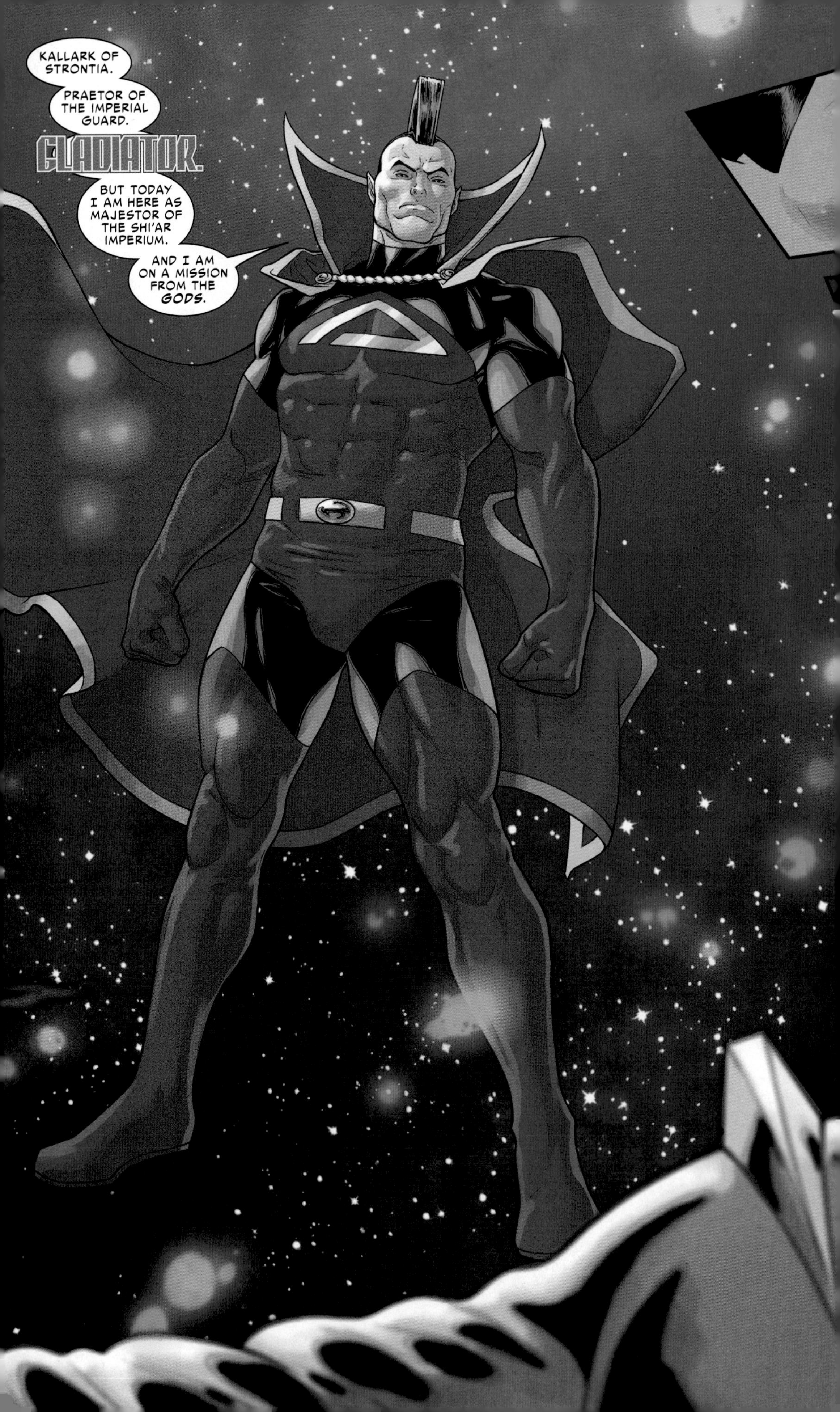
KALLARK OF STRONTIA.
PRAETOR OF THE IMPERIAL GUARD.
GLADIATOR.
BUT TODAY I AM HERE AS MAJESTOR OF THE SHI'AR IMPERIUM.
AND I AM ON A MISSION FROM THE GODS.

THEN YOU'VE COME TO THE RIGHT PLACE. WE'VE PLENTY OF THOSE AROUND.
I ONLY NEED ONE.
THE REST OF YOU CAN BURN FOR ALL I CARE.
AND YOU CAN EAT RAINBOW BRIDGE!
BUT I PROMISE YOU, GLADIATOR, ON THE EYES OF MY NINE MOTHERS...
...YOU SHALL NOT CROSS IT!

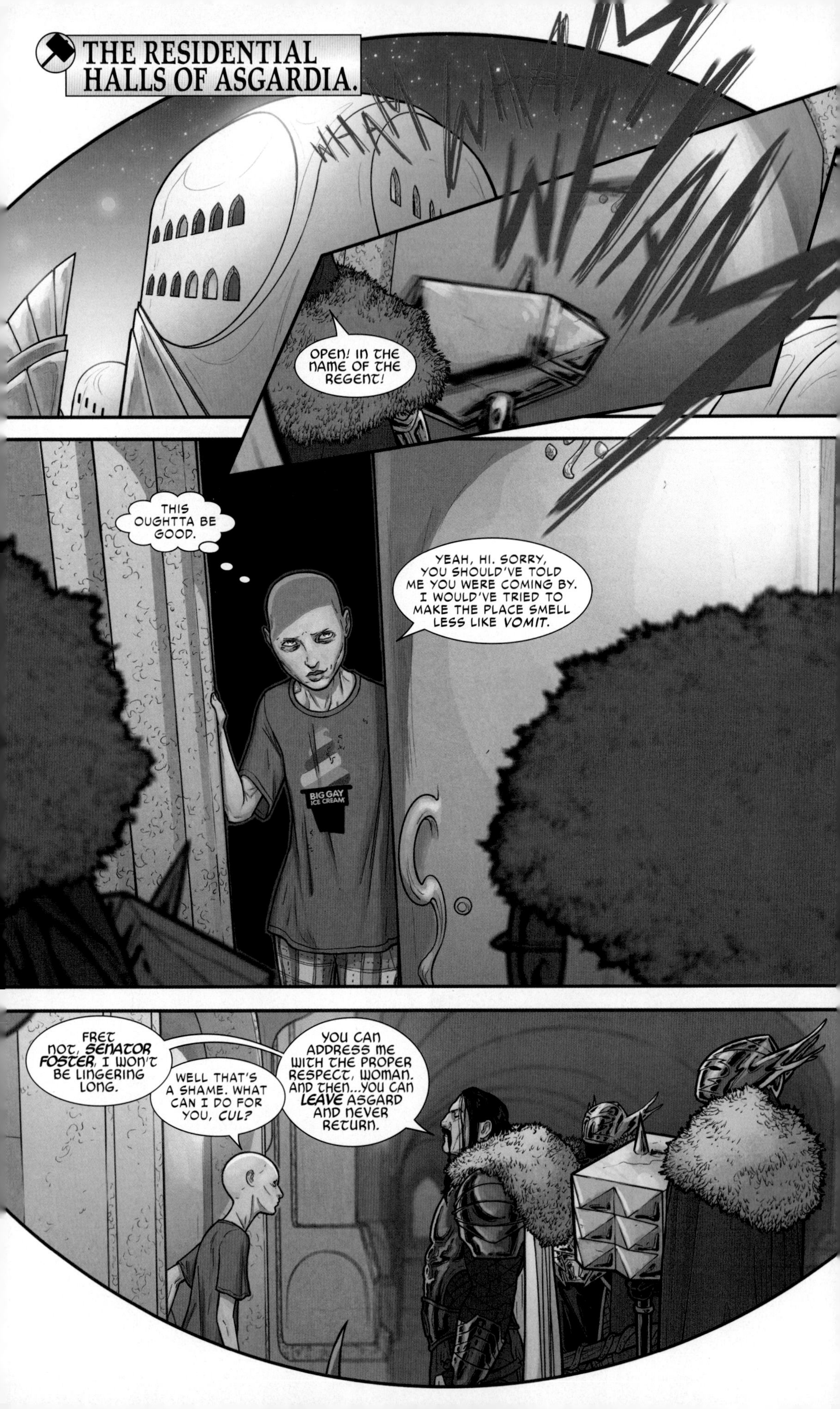
THE RESIDENTIAL HALLS OF ASGARDIA.
WHAM WHAM WHAM WHAM
OPEN! IN THE NAME OF THE REGENT!
THIS OUGHTTA BE GOOD.
YEAH, HI. SORRY, YOU SHOULD'VE TOLD ME YOU WERE COMING BY. I WOULD'VE TRIED TO MAKE THE PLACE SMELL LESS LIKE VOMIT.
BIG GAY ICE CREAM
FRET NOT, SENATOR FOSTER, I WON'T BE LINGERING LONG.
WELL THAT'S A SHAME. WHAT CAN I DO FOR YOU, CUL?
YOU CAN ADDRESS ME WITH THE PROPER RESPECT, WOMAN. AND THEN...YOU CAN LEAVE ASGARD AND NEVER RETURN.

AFRAID I CAN'T DO THAT. I REPRESENT *MIDGARD* IN THE *CONGRESS OF WORLDS.*

LIKE IT OR NOT, CULLY, I'M AS MUCH A PART OF THE COURT OF ASGARDIA AS YOU ARE.

YES, BUT EXACTLY HOW ARE YOU SUPPOSED TO EFFECTIVELY REPRESENT YOUR BELOVED LITTLE MUDBALL...

...WHEN YOU ARE HOLED UP INSIDE YOUR QUARTERS FOR DAYS ON END, *VOMITING* LIKE A DRUNKEN DWARF?

IT'S BEEN A ROUGH WEEK. BUT YOU'LL FORGIVE ME IF I DON'T FEEL LIKE TALKING CHEMOTHERAPY WITH THE GOD OF FEAR. NOW IF YOU'LL EXCUSE--

NINE DAYS.

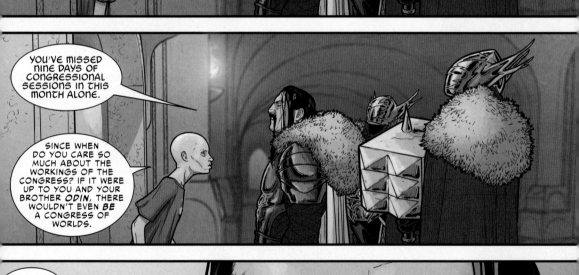

YOU'VE MISSED NINE DAYS OF CONGRESSIONAL SESSIONS IN THIS MONTH ALONE.

SINCE WHEN DO YOU CARE SO MUCH ABOUT THE WORKINGS OF THE CONGRESS? IF IT WERE UP TO YOU AND YOUR BROTHER *ODIN,* THERE WOULDN'T EVEN *BE* A CONGRESS OF WORLDS.

YOU ARE RIGHT.

IF IT WERE UP TO CUL BORSON, MIDGARD WOULD STILL BE BURNING IN A BONFIRE OF FEAR.

AND ALL THE OTHER REALMS WOULD BE GROVELING IN THEIR OWN BLOOD BEFORE THE FEARSOME, UNRELENTING MAJESTY OF ASGARD.

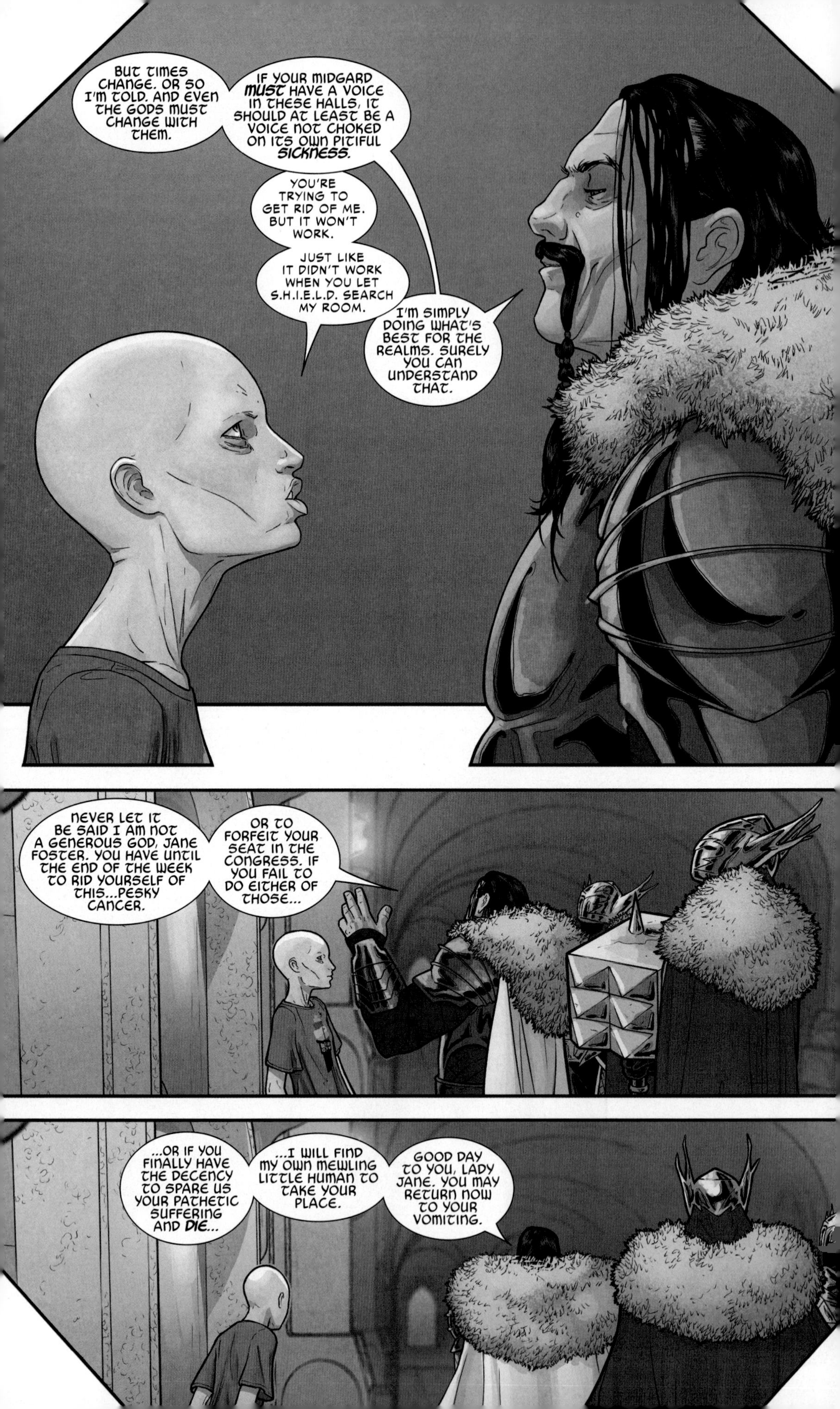
BUT TIMES CHANGE. OR SO I'M TOLD. AND EVEN THE GODS MUST CHANGE WITH THEM.
IF YOUR MIDGARD MUST HAVE A VOICE IN THESE HALLS, IT SHOULD AT LEAST BE A VOICE NOT CHOKED ON ITS OWN PITIFUL SICKNESS.
YOU'RE TRYING TO GET RID OF ME. BUT IT WON'T WORK.
JUST LIKE IT DIDN'T WORK WHEN YOU LET S.H.I.E.L.D. SEARCH MY ROOM.
I'M SIMPLY DOING WHAT'S BEST FOR THE REALMS. SURELY YOU CAN UNDERSTAND THAT.
NEVER LET IT BE SAID I AM NOT A GENEROUS GOD, JANE FOSTER. YOU HAVE UNTIL THE END OF THE WEEK TO RID YOURSELF OF THIS...PESKY CANCER.
OR TO FORFEIT YOUR SEAT IN THE CONGRESS. IF YOU FAIL TO DO EITHER OF THOSE...
...OR IF YOU FINALLY HAVE THE DECENCY TO SPARE US YOUR PATHETIC SUFFERING AND DIE...
...I WILL FIND MY OWN MEWLING LITTLE HUMAN TO TAKE YOUR PLACE.
GOOD DAY TO YOU, LADY JANE. YOU MAY RETURN NOW TO YOUR VOMITING.

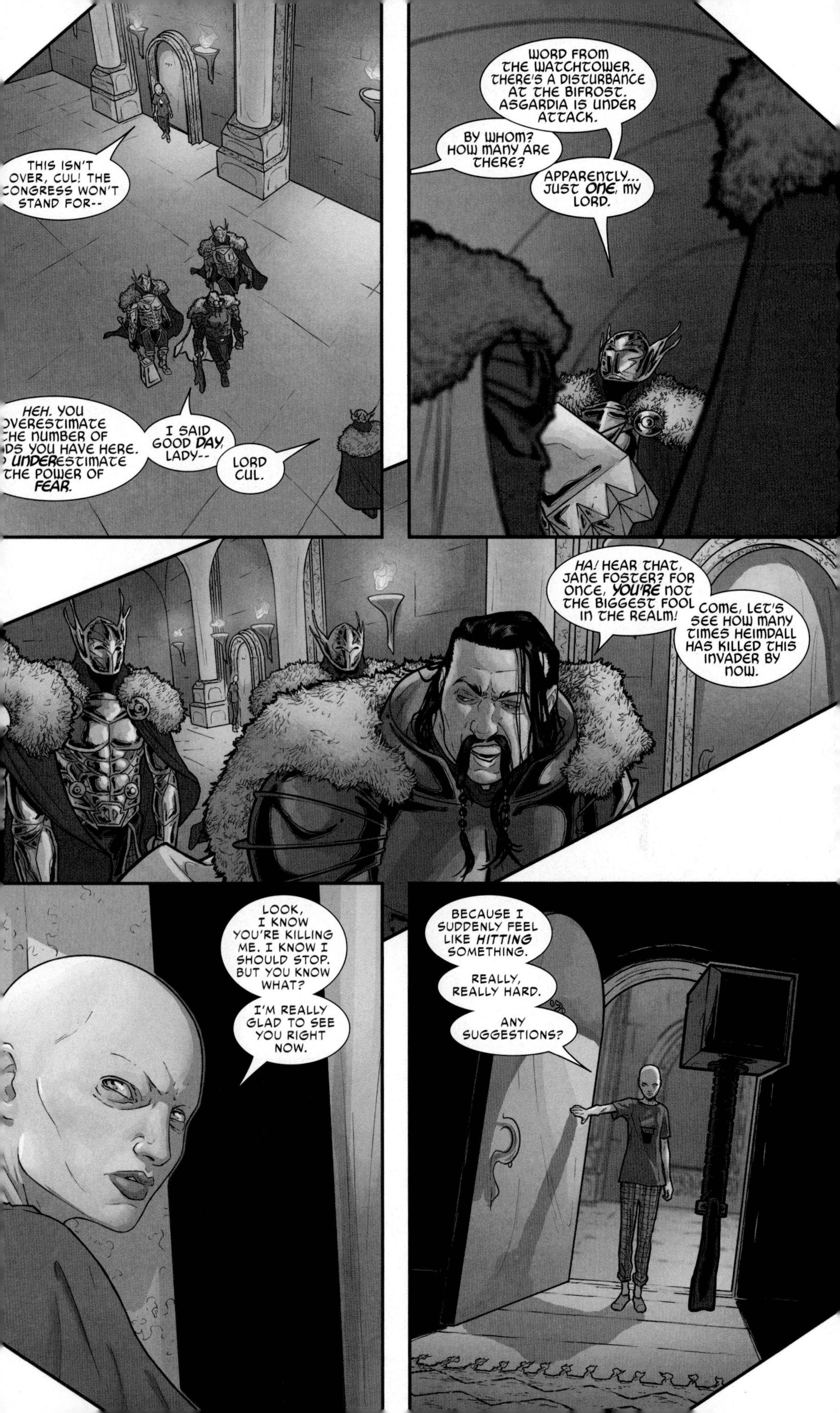
THIS ISN'T OVER, CUL! THE CONGRESS WON'T STAND FOR--
HEH. YOU OVERESTIMATE THE NUMBER OF ODS YOU HAVE HERE. D UNDERESTIMATE THE POWER OF FEAR.
I SAID GOOD DAY, LADY--
LORD CUL.
WORD FROM THE WATCHTOWER. THERE'S A DISTURBANCE AT THE BIFROST. ASGARDIA IS UNDER ATTACK.
BY WHOM? HOW MANY ARE THERE?
APPARENTLY... JUST ONE, MY LORD.
HA! HEAR THAT, JANE FOSTER? FOR ONCE, YOU'RE NOT THE BIGGEST FOOL IN THE REALM!
COME, LET'S SEE HOW MANY TIMES HEIMDALL HAS KILLED THIS INVADER BY NOW.
LOOK, I KNOW YOU'RE KILLING ME. I KNOW I SHOULD STOP. BUT YOU KNOW WHAT?
I'M REALLY GLAD TO SEE YOU RIGHT NOW.
BECAUSE I SUDDENLY FEEL LIKE HITTING SOMETHING.
REALLY, REALLY HARD.
ANY SUGGESTIONS?

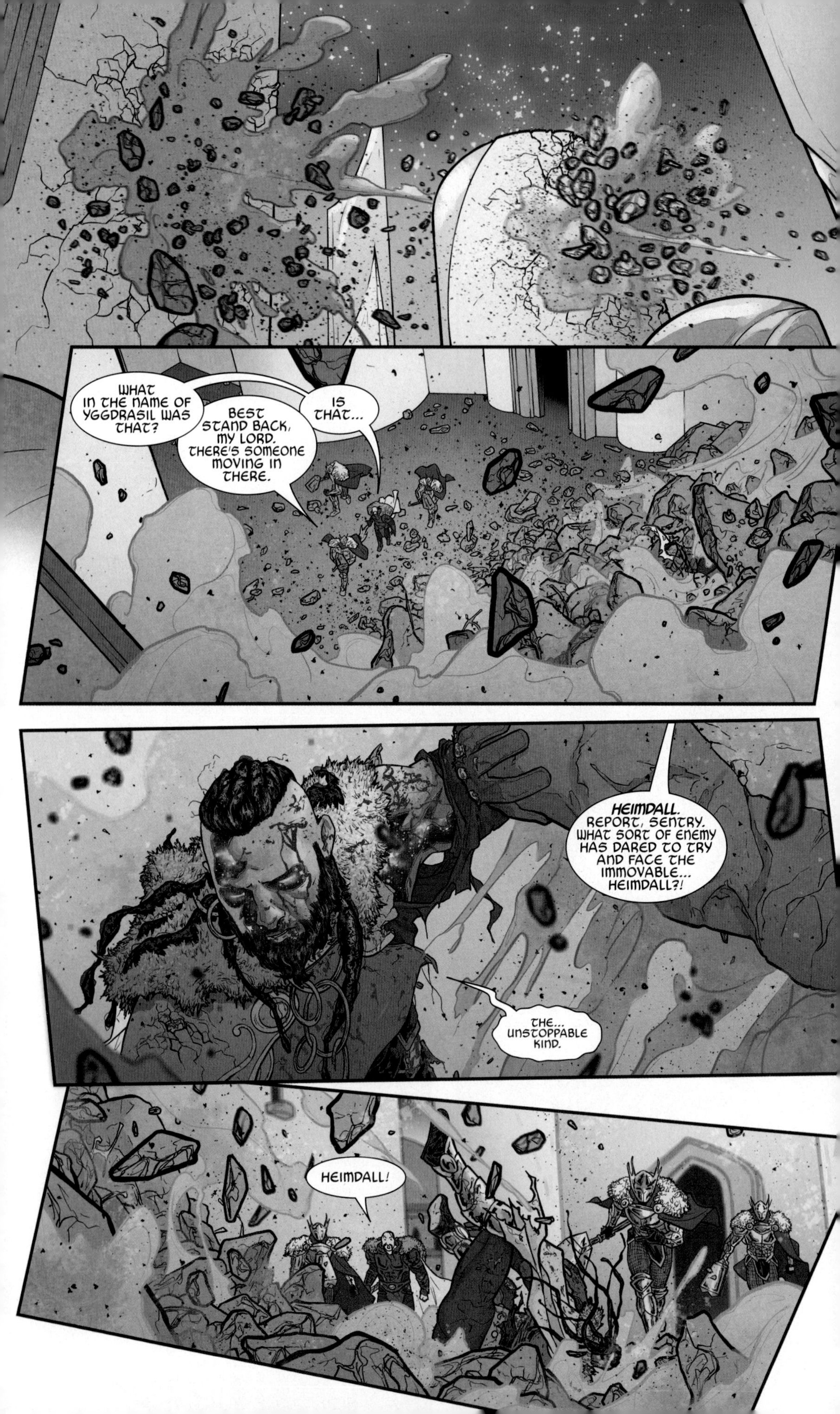
WHAT IN THE NAME OF YGGDRASIL WAS THAT?
BEST STAND BACK, MY LORD. THERE'S SOMEONE MOVING IN THERE.
IS THAT...
HEIMDALL. REPORT, SENTRY. WHAT SORT OF ENEMY HAS DARED TO TRY AND FACE THE IMMOVABLE... HEIMDALL?!
THE... UNSTOPPABLE KIND.
HEIMDALL!

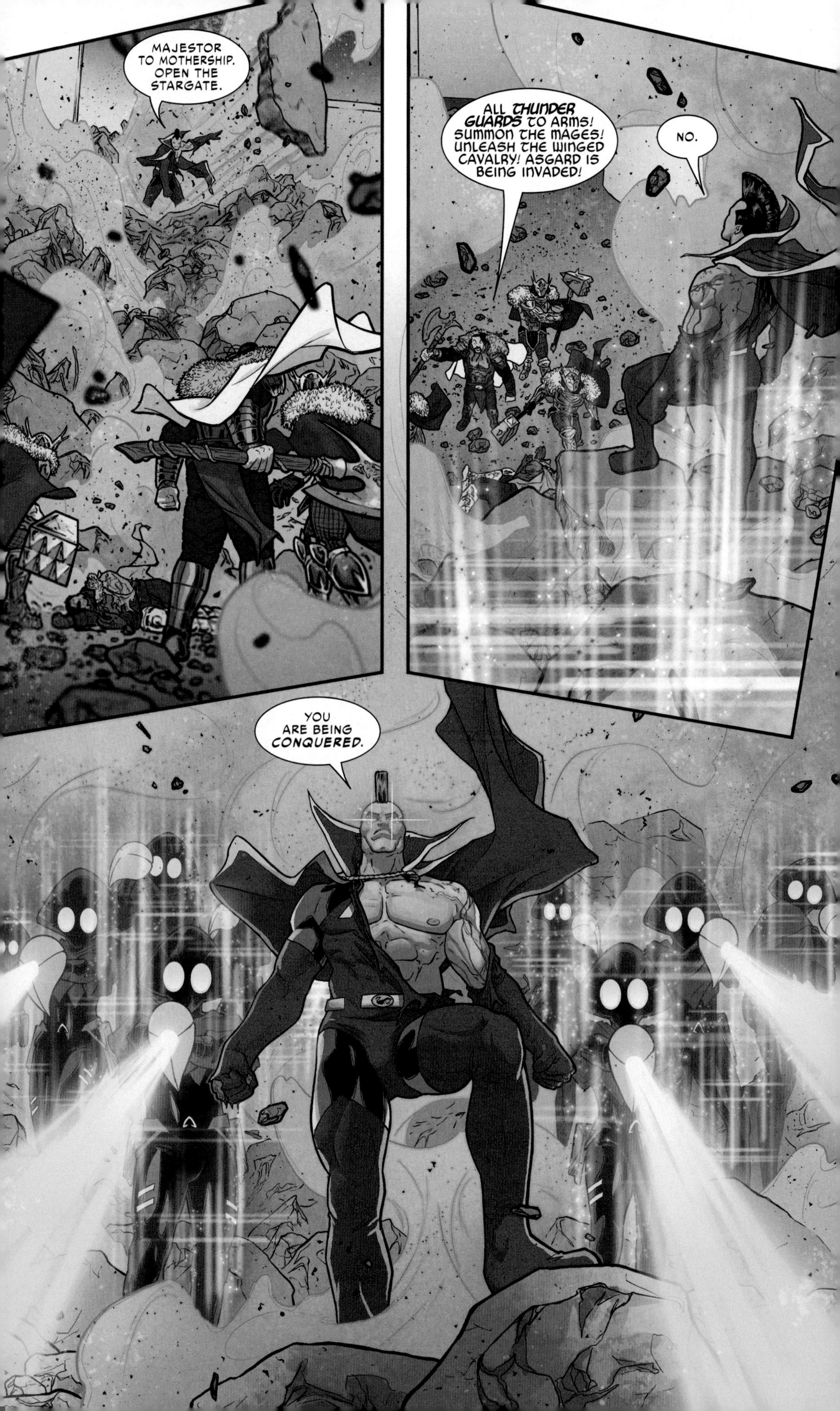
MAJESTOR TO MOTHERSHIP. OPEN THE STARGATE.
ALL THUNDER GUARDS TO ARMS! SUMMON THE MAGES! UNLEASH THE WINGED CAVALRY! ASGARD IS BEING INVADED!
NO.
YOU ARE BEING CONQUERED.

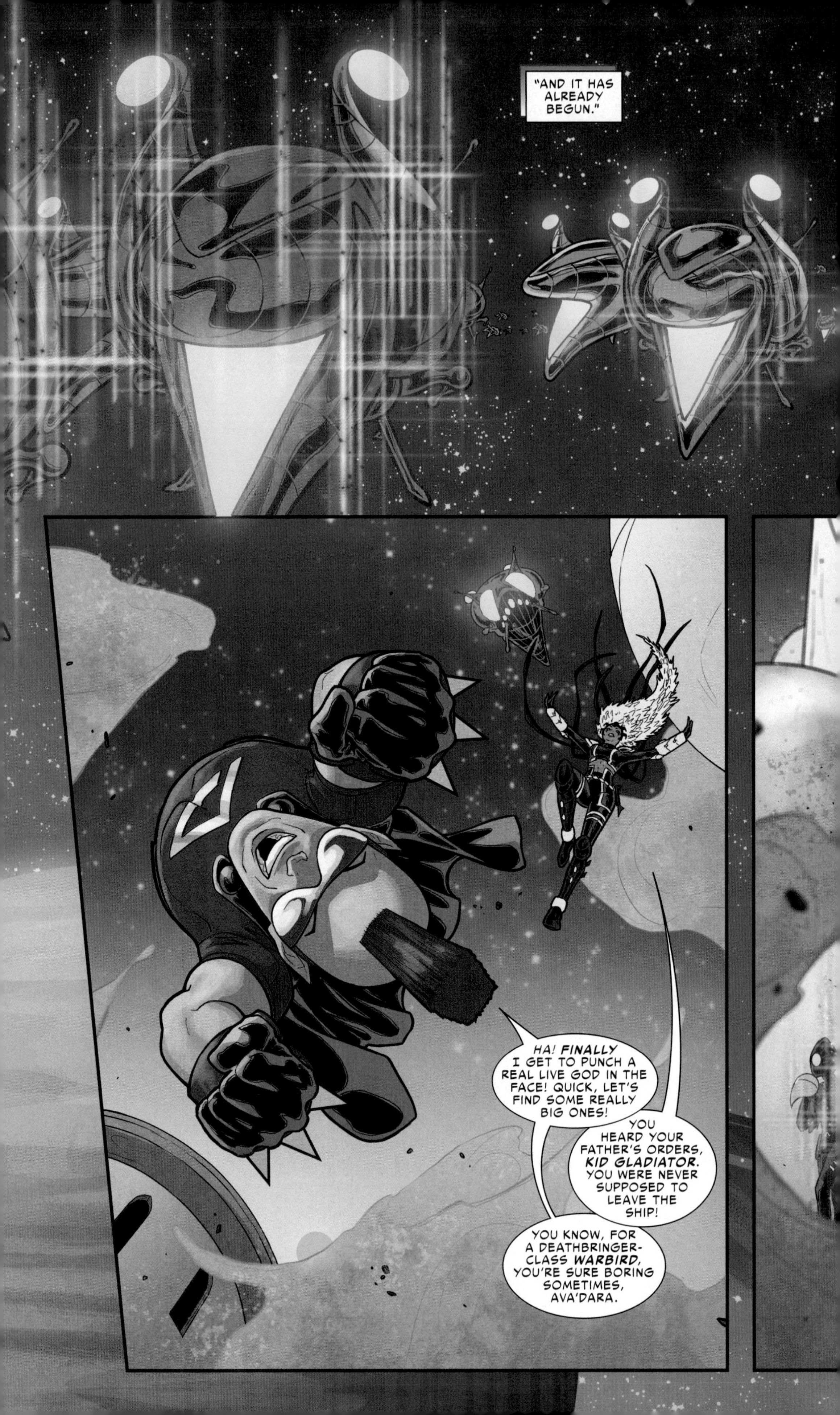
"AND IT HAS ALREADY BEGUN."
HA! FINALLY I GET TO PUNCH A REAL LIVE GOD IN THE FACE! QUICK, LET'S FIND SOME REALLY BIG ONES!
YOU HEARD YOUR FATHER'S ORDERS, KID GLADIATOR. YOU WERE NEVER SUPPOSED TO LEAVE THE SHIP!
YOU KNOW, FOR A DEATHBRINGER-CLASS WARBIRD, YOU'RE SURE BORING SOMETIMES, AVA'DARA.

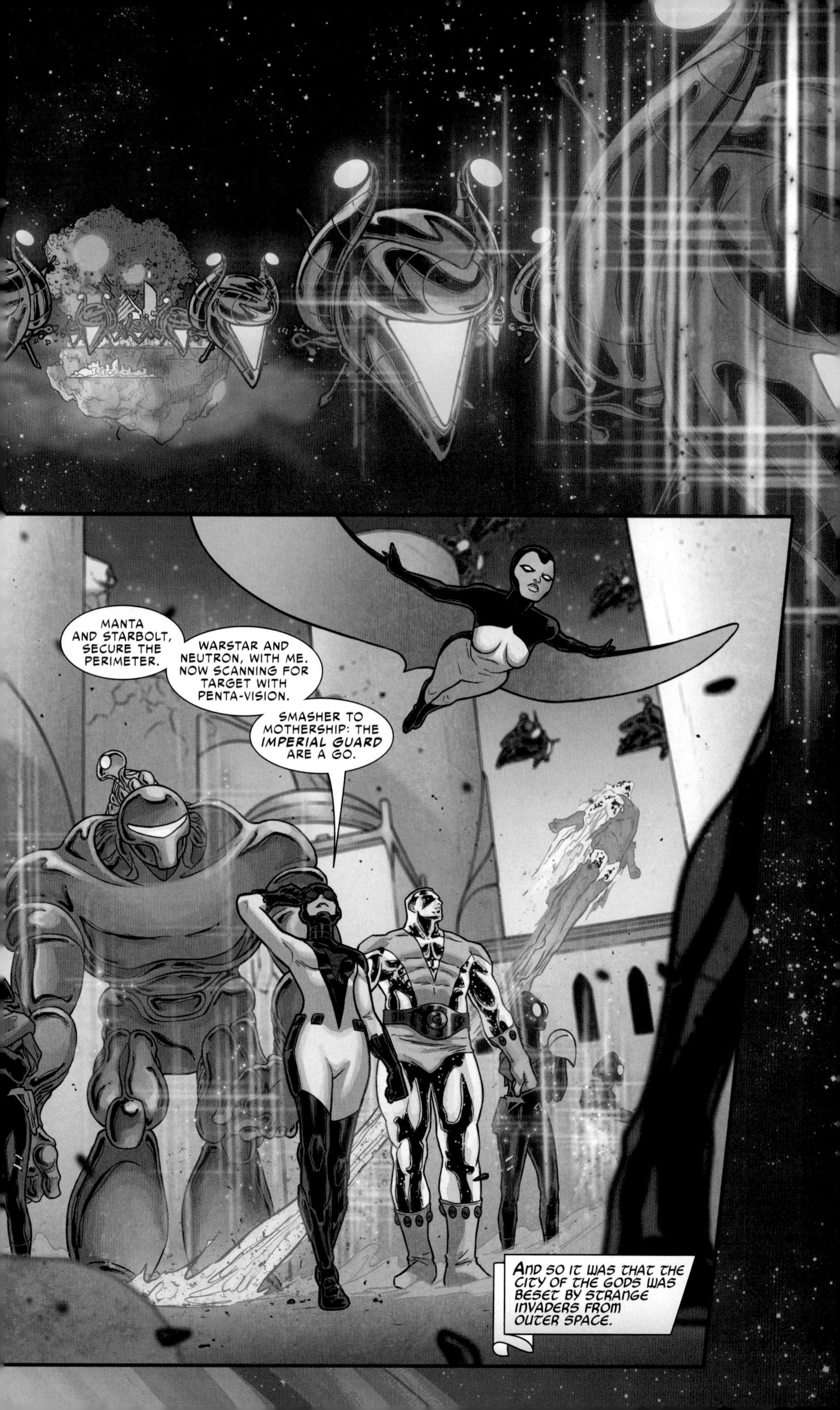
MANTA AND STARBOLT, SECURE THE PERIMETER.
WARSTAR AND NEUTRON, WITH ME. NOW SCANNING FOR TARGET WITH PENTA-VISION.
SMASHER TO MOTHERSHIP: THE *IMPERIAL GUARD* ARE A GO.
AND SO IT WAS THAT THE CITY OF THE GODS WAS BESET BY STRANGE INVADERS FROM OUTER SPACE.

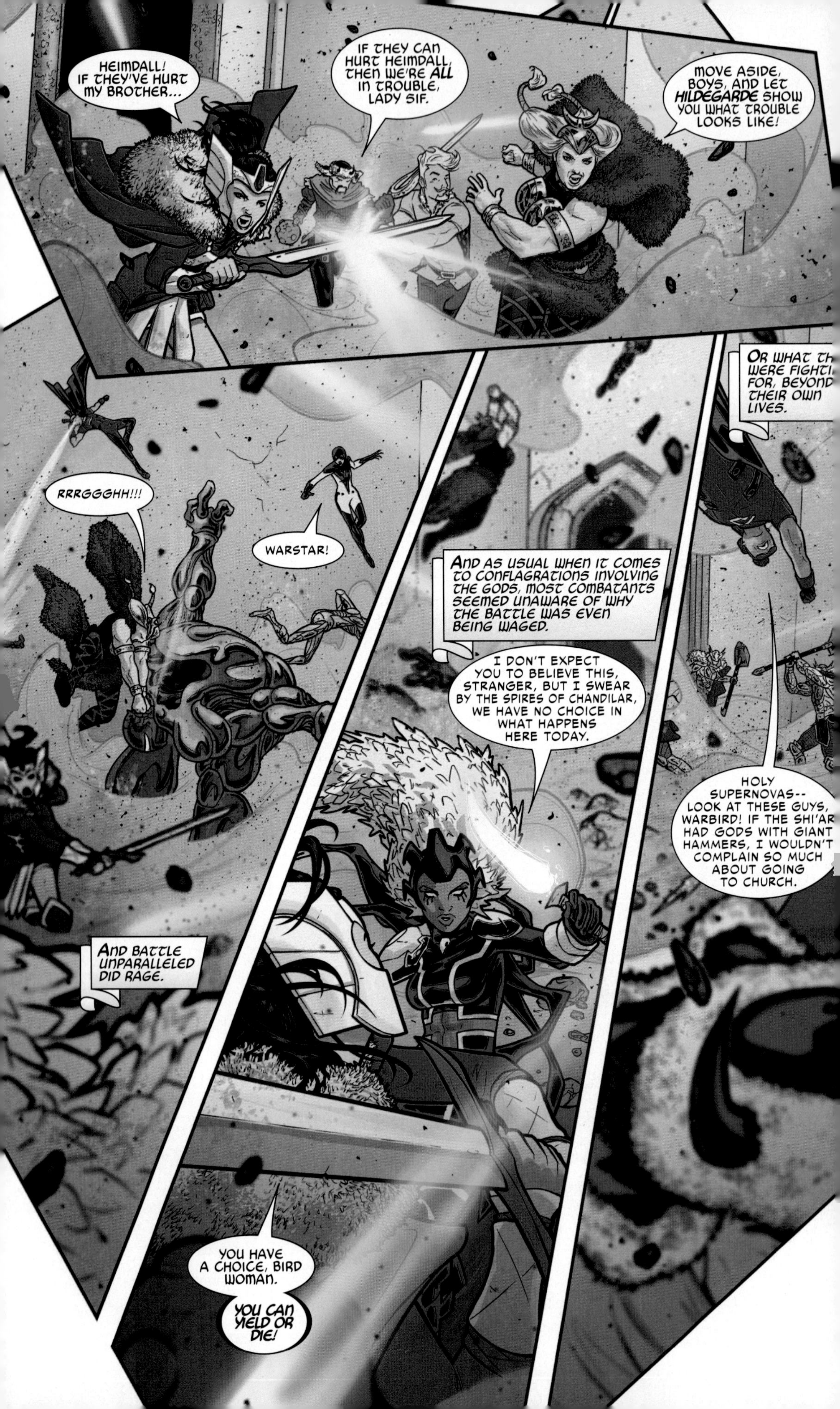
HEIMDALL! IF THEY'VE HURT MY BROTHER...
IF THEY CAN HURT HEIMDALL, THEN WE'RE ALL IN TROUBLE, LADY SIF.
MOVE ASIDE, BOYS, AND LET HILDEGARDE SHOW YOU WHAT TROUBLE LOOKS LIKE!
RRRGGGHH!!!
WARSTAR!
AND BATTLE UNPARALLELED DID RAGE.
AND AS USUAL WHEN IT COMES TO CONFLAGRATIONS INVOLVING THE GODS, MOST COMBATANTS SEEMED UNAWARE OF WHY THE BATTLE WAS EVEN BEING WAGED.
I DON'T EXPECT YOU TO BELIEVE THIS, STRANGER, BUT I SWEAR BY THE SPIRES OF CHANDILAR, WE HAVE NO CHOICE IN WHAT HAPPENS HERE TODAY.
YOU HAVE A CHOICE, BIRD WOMAN.
YOU CAN YIELD OR DIE!
OR WHAT TH WERE FIGHTI FOR, BEYOND THEIR OWN LIVES.
HOLY SUPERNOVAS-- LOOK AT THESE GUYS, WARBIRD! IF THE SHI'AR HAD GODS WITH GIANT HAMMERS, I WOULDN'T COMPLAIN SO MUCH ABOUT GOING TO CHURCH.

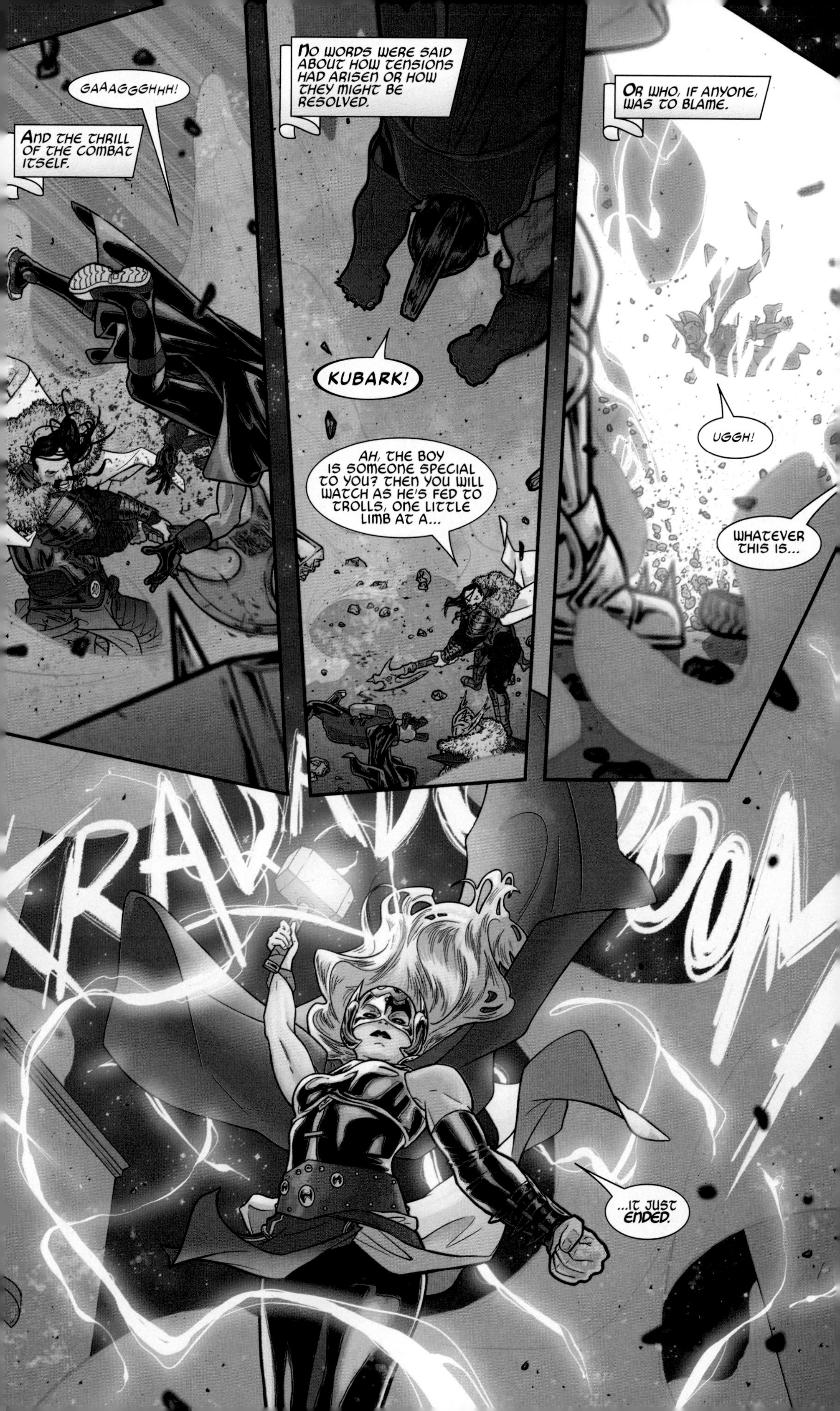

GAAAGGGHHH!
AND THE THRILL OF THE COMBAT ITSELF.
NO WORDS WERE SAID ABOUT HOW TENSIONS HAD ARISEN OR HOW THEY MIGHT BE RESOLVED.
KUBARK!
AH, THE BOY IS SOMEONE SPECIAL TO YOU? THEN YOU WILL WATCH AS HE'S FED TO TROLLS, ONE LITTLE LIMB AT A...
OR WHO, IF ANYONE, WAS TO BLAME.
UGGH!
WHATEVER THIS IS...
...IT JUST ENDED.

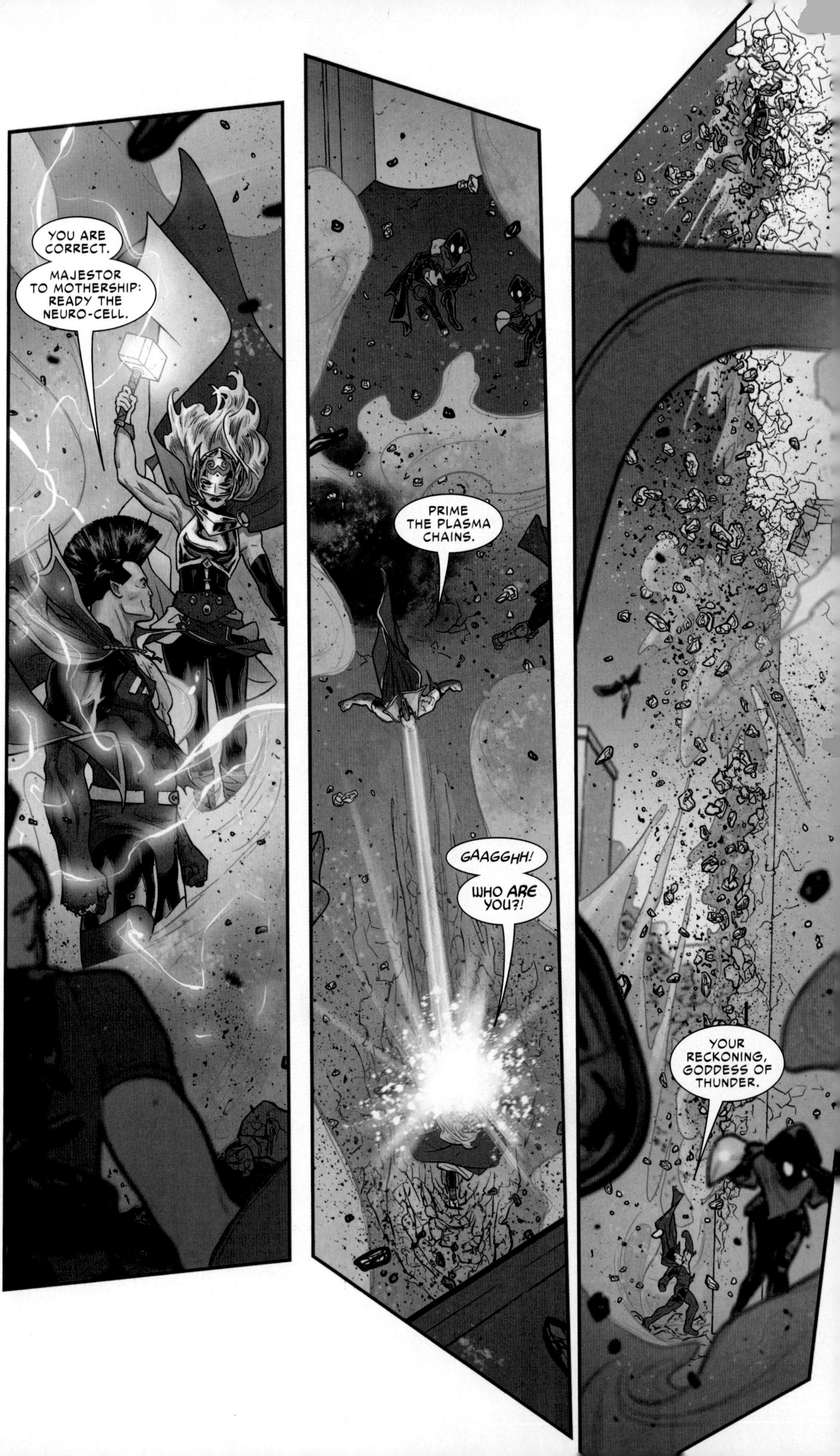
YOU ARE CORRECT.
MAJESTOR TO MOTHERSHIP: READY THE NEURO-CELL.
PRIME THE PLASMA CHAINS.
GAAGGHH!
WHO ARE YOU?!
YOUR RECKONING, GODDESS OF THUNDER.

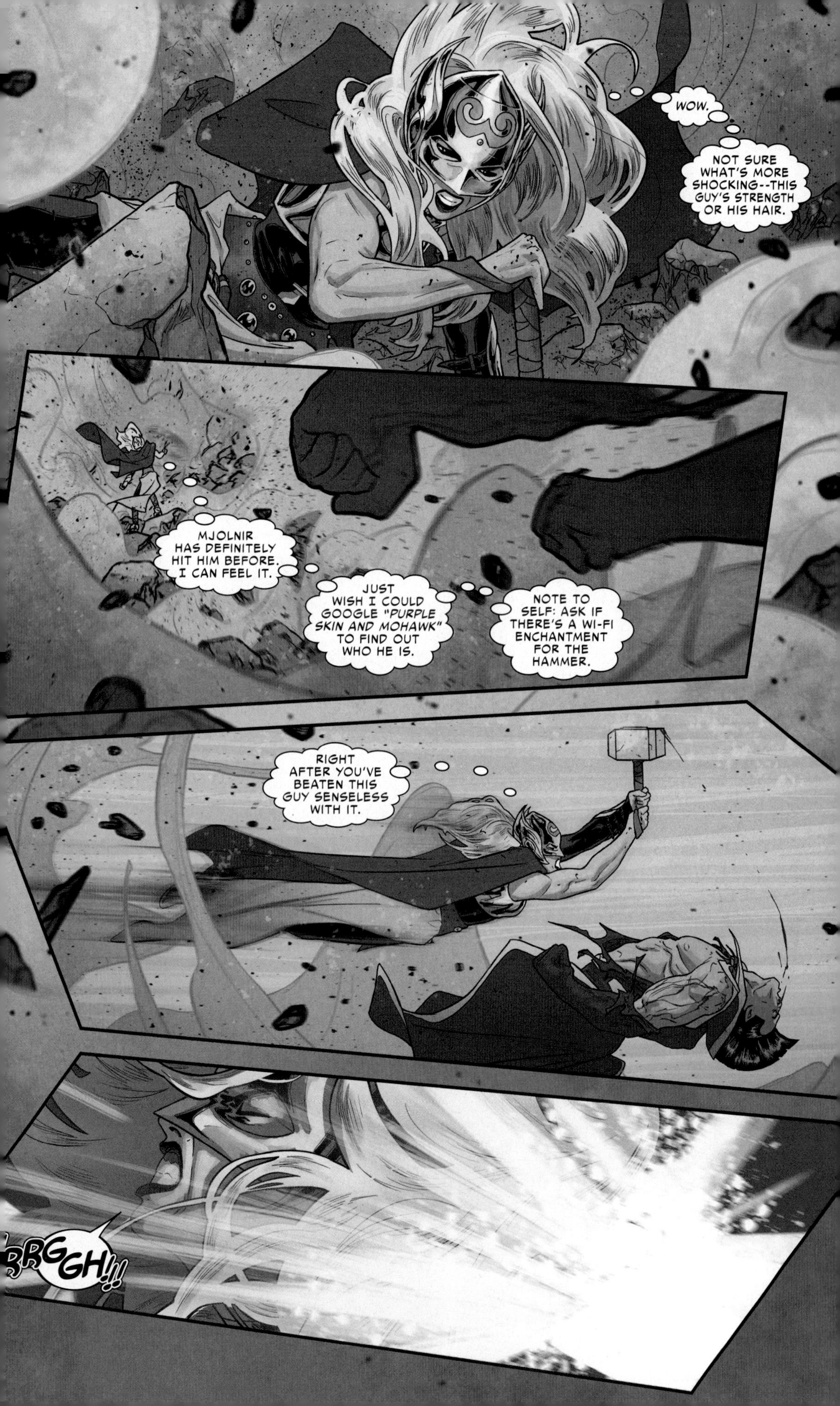
WOW.
NOT SURE WHAT'S MORE SHOCKING--THIS GUY'S STRENGTH OR HIS HAIR.
MJOLNIR HAS DEFINITELY HIT HIM BEFORE. I CAN FEEL IT.
JUST WISH I COULD GOOGLE "PURPLE SKIN AND MOHAWK" TO FIND OUT WHO HE IS.
NOTE TO SELF: ASK IF THERE'S A WI-FI ENCHANTMENT FOR THE HAMMER.
RIGHT AFTER YOU'VE BEATEN THIS GUY SENSELESS WITH IT.
RRGGH!!!

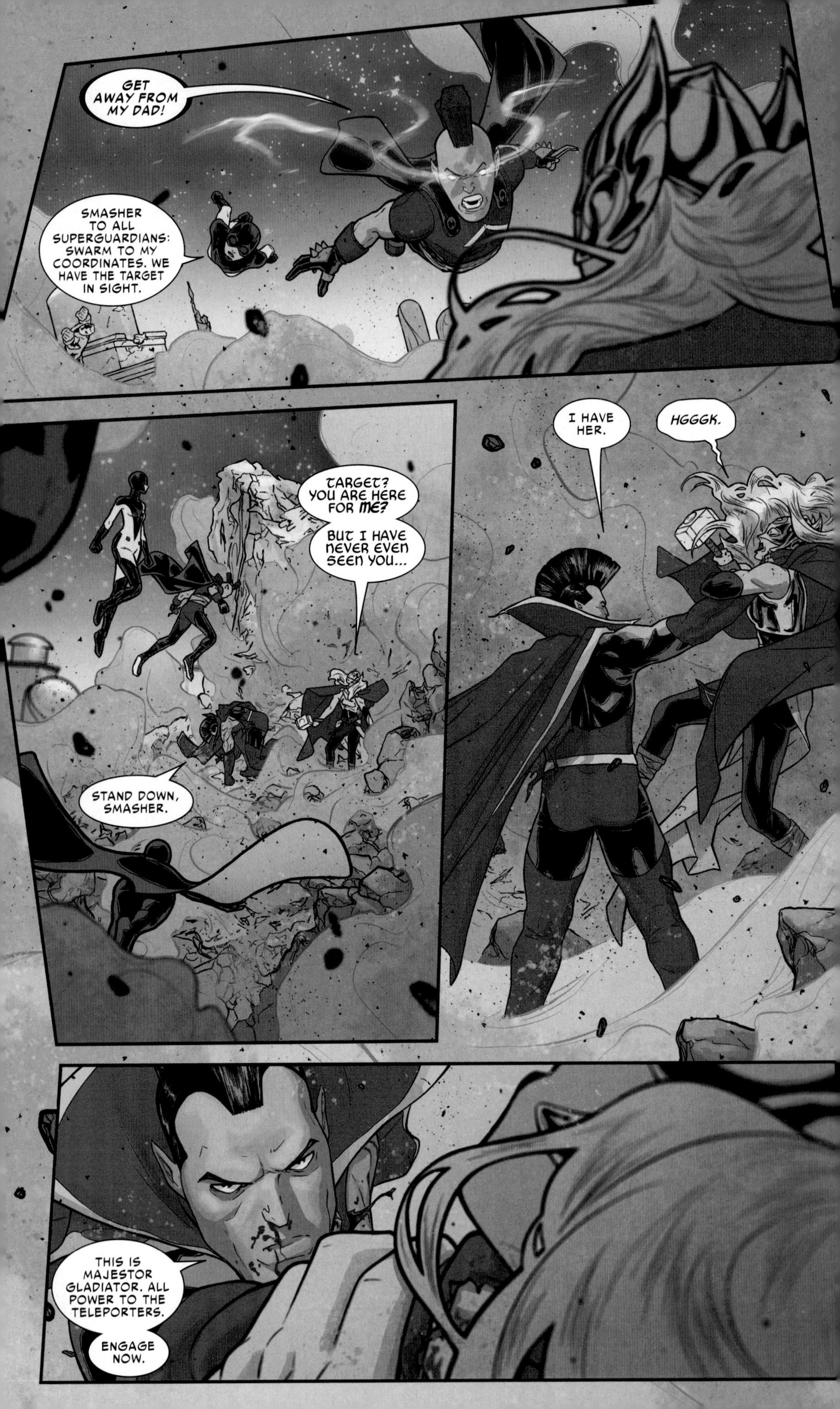
GET AWAY FROM MY DAD!
SMASHER TO ALL SUPERGUARDIANS: SWARM TO MY COORDINATES. WE HAVE THE TARGET IN SIGHT.
TARGET? YOU ARE HERE FOR ME?
BUT I HAVE NEVER EVEN SEEN YOU...
STAND DOWN, SMASHER.
I HAVE HER.
HGGGK.
THIS IS MAJESTOR GLADIATOR. ALL POWER TO THE TELEPORTERS.
ENGAGE NOW.

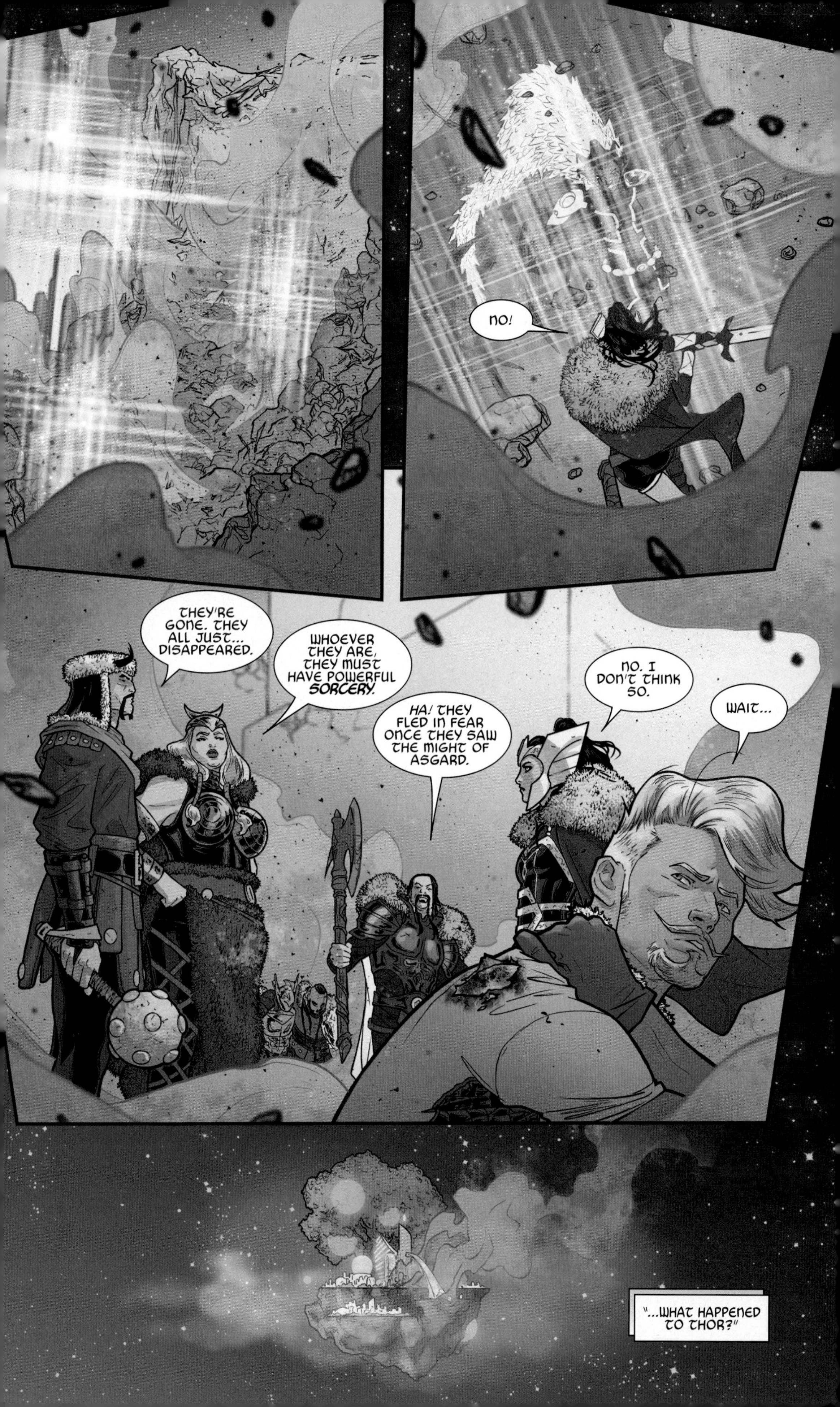
NO!
THEY'RE GONE. THEY ALL JUST... DISAPPEARED.
WHOEVER THEY ARE, THEY MUST HAVE POWERFUL SORCERY.
HA! THEY FLED IN FEAR ONCE THEY SAW THE MIGHT OF ASGARD.
NO. I DON'T THINK SO.
WAIT...
"...WHAT HAPPENED TO THOR?"

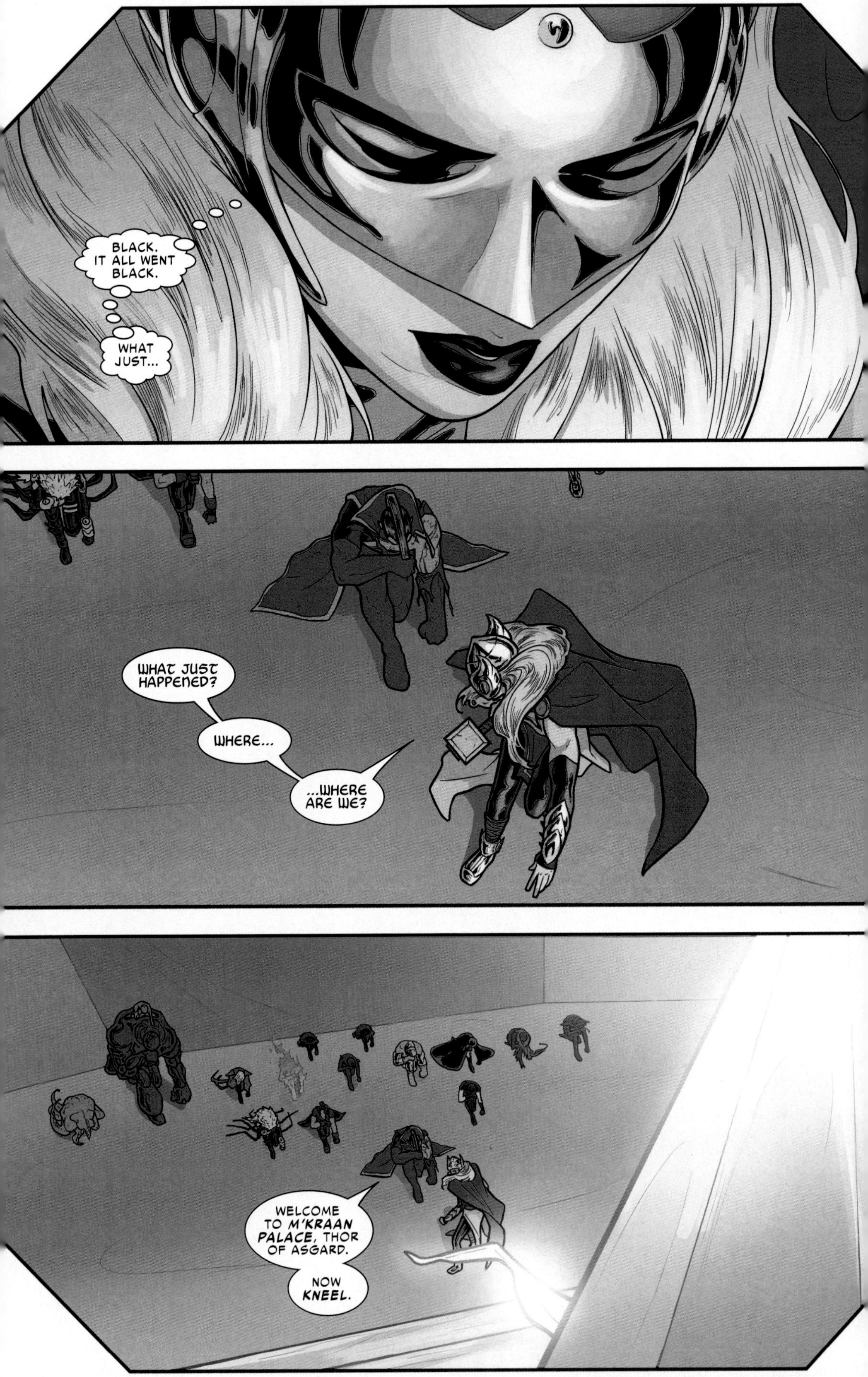
BLACK. IT ALL WENT BLACK.
WHAT JUST...
WHAT JUST HAPPENED?
WHERE...
...WHERE ARE WE?
WELCOME TO M'KRAAN PALACE, THOR OF ASGARD.
NOW KNEEL.

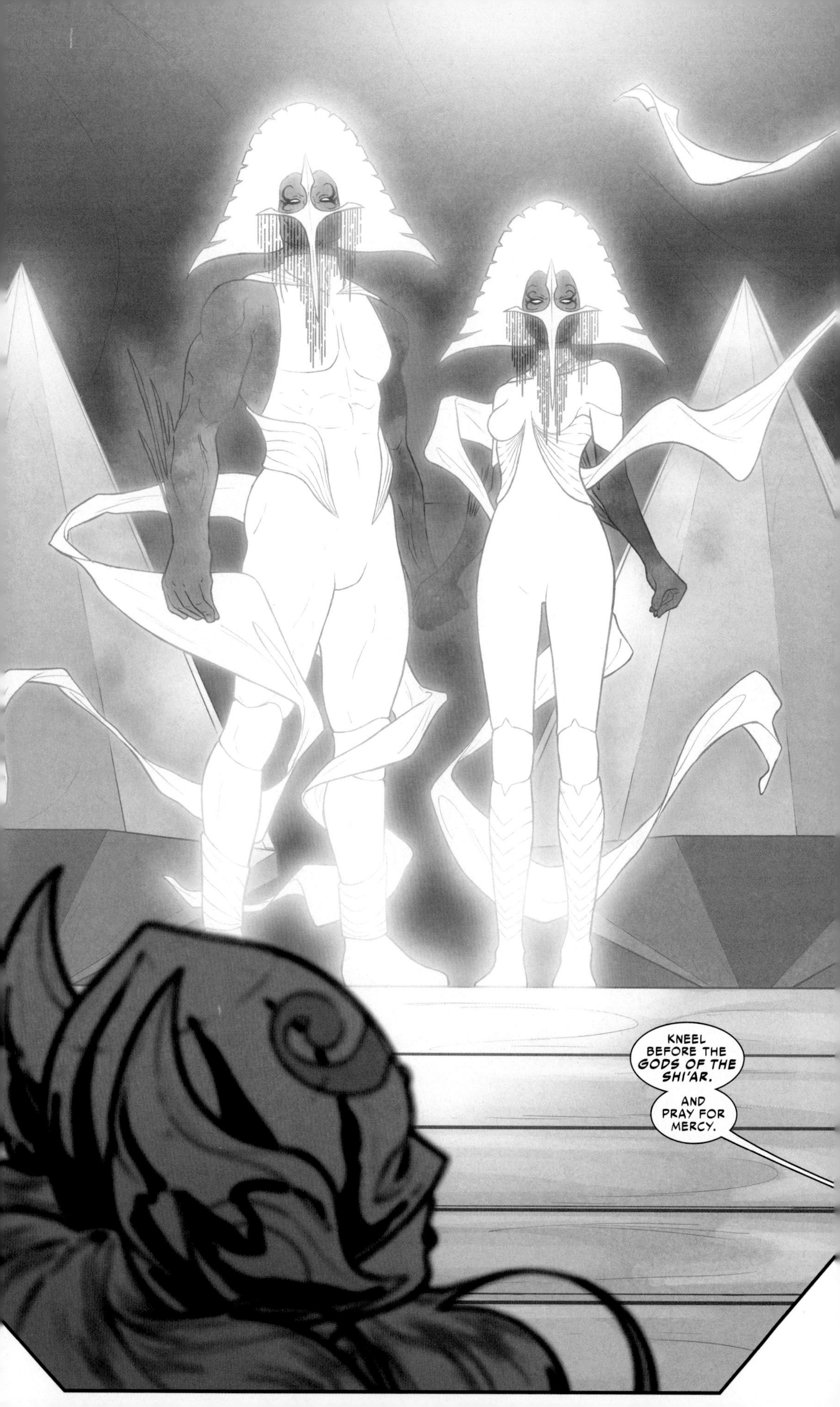
KNEEL BEFORE THE GODS OF THE SHI'AR.
AND PRAY FOR MERCY.

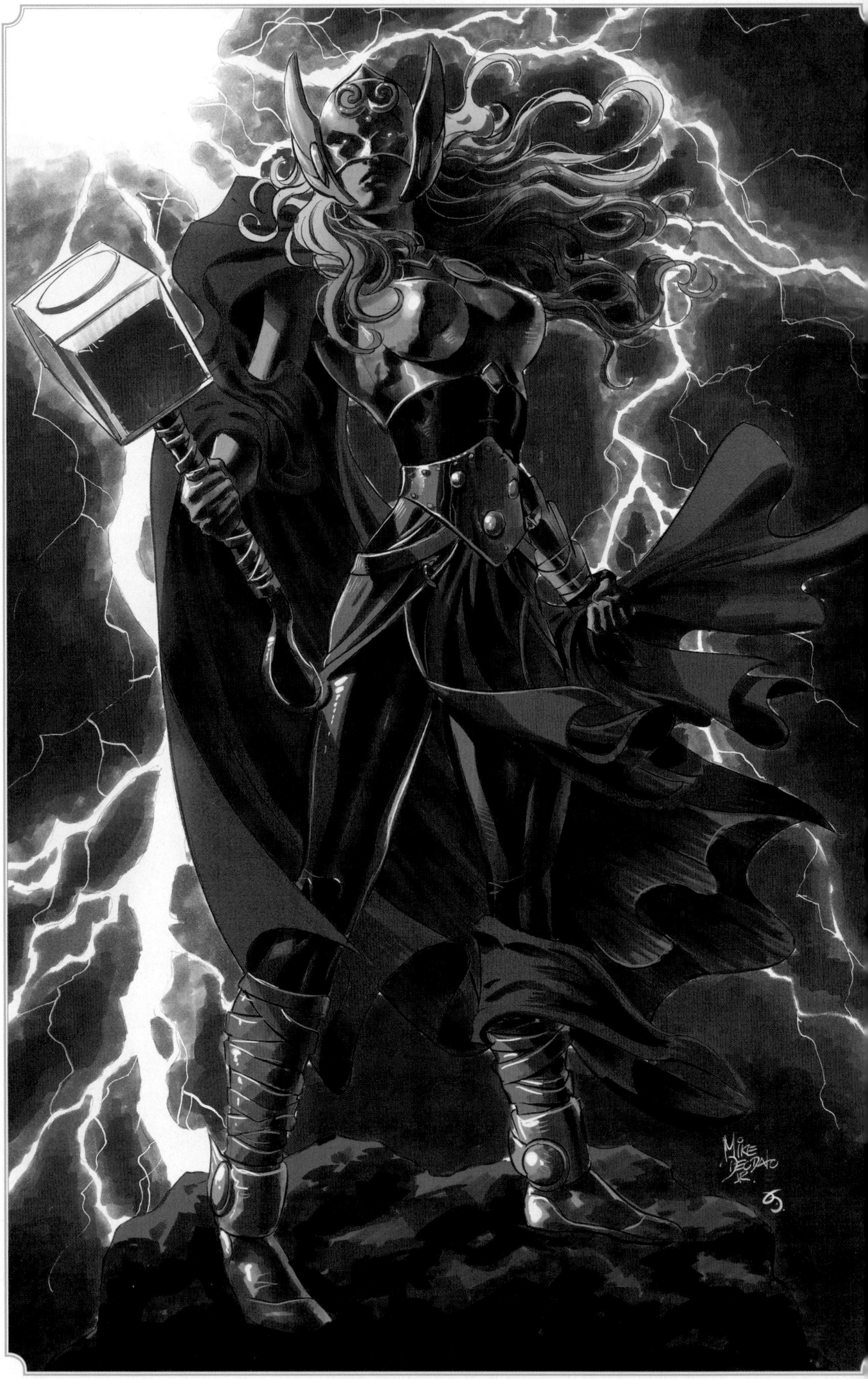

MIGHTY THOR # 15 VARIANT
BY **MIKE DEODATO JR.** & **FRANK MARTIN**

16

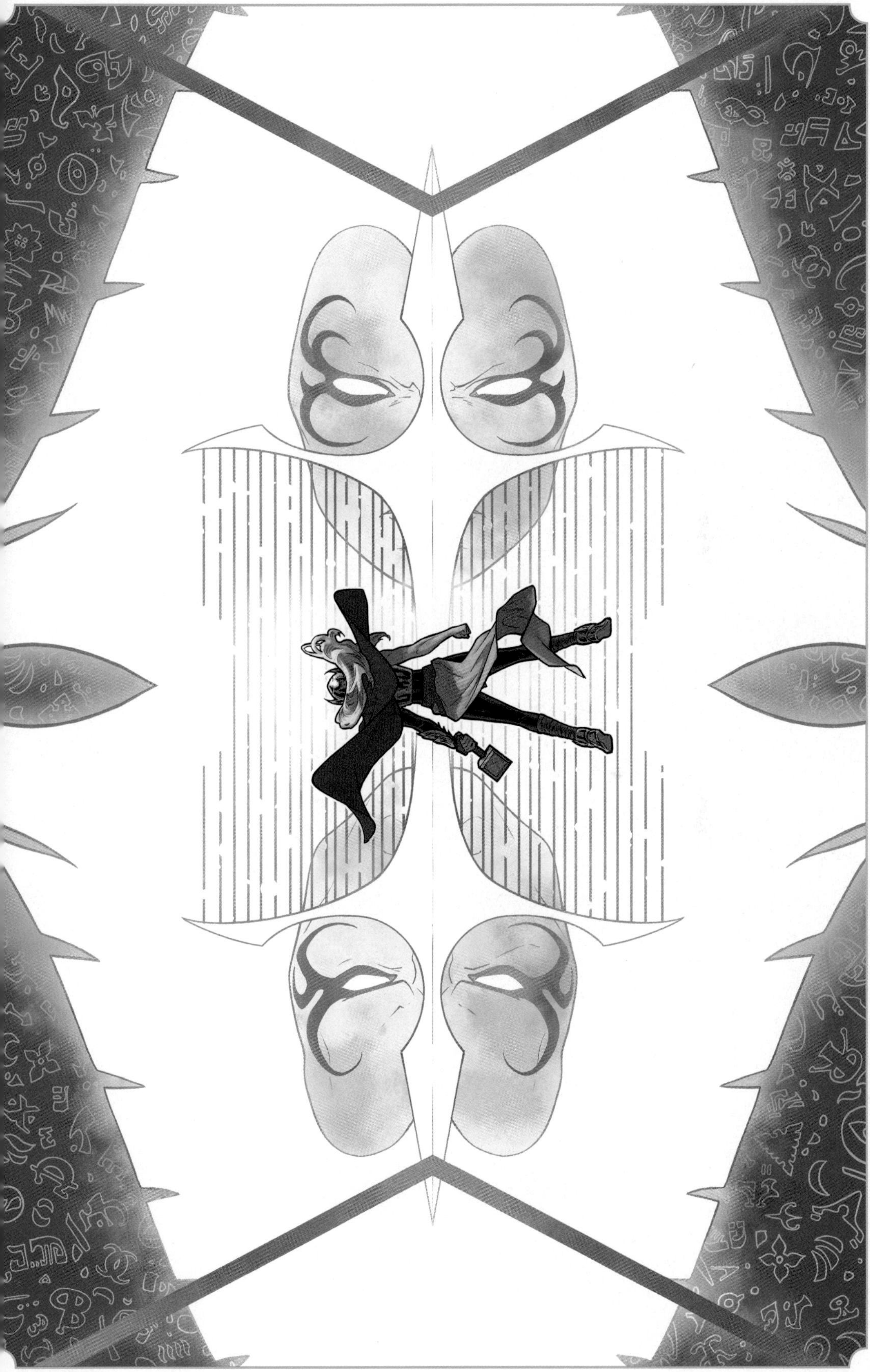

THE ASGARD/SHI'AR WAR, PART TWO:

THE CHALLENGE OF THE GODS

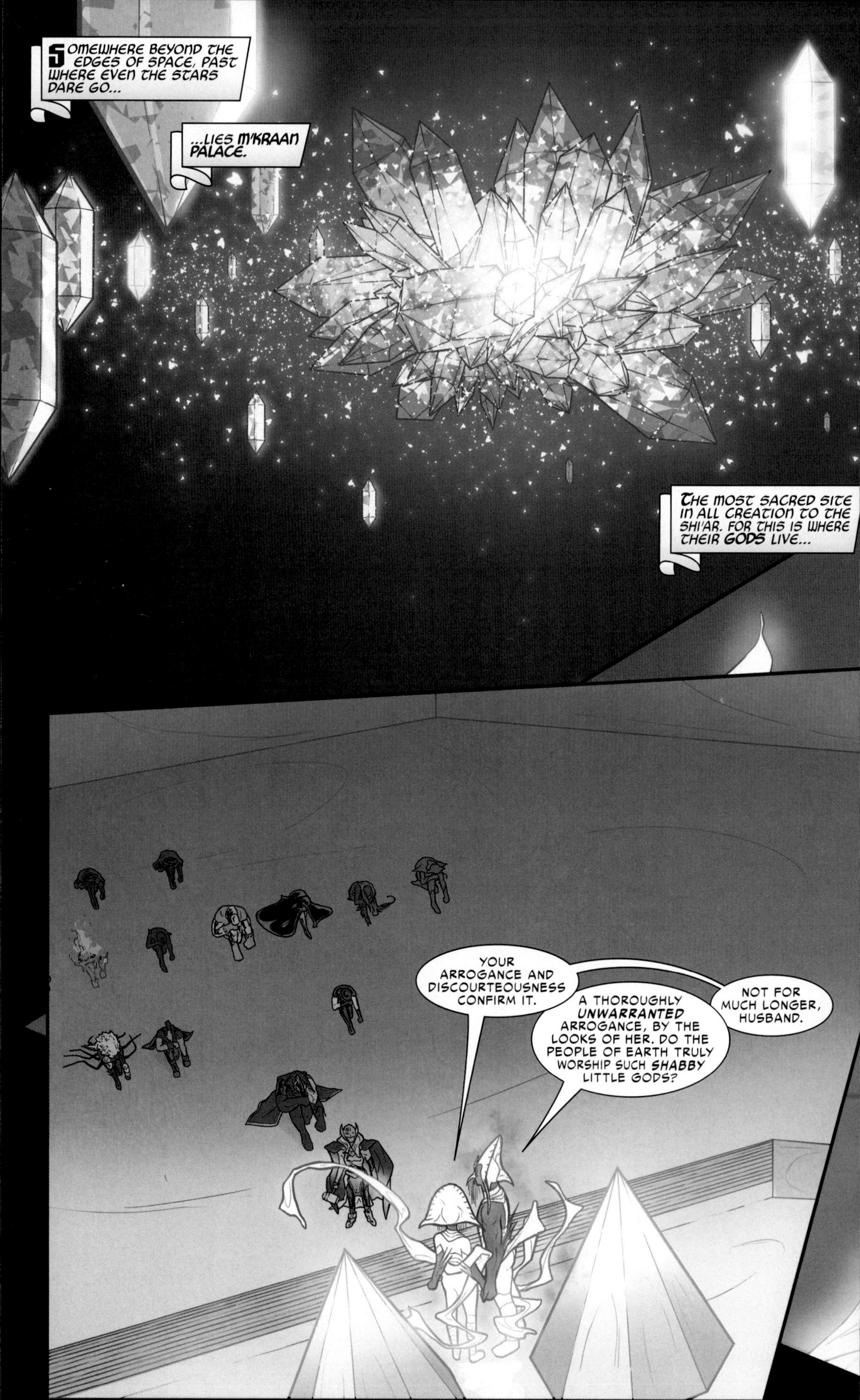
SOMEWHERE BEYOND THE EDGES OF SPACE, PAST WHERE EVEN THE STARS DARE GO...
...LIES M'KRAAN PALACE.
THE MOST SACRED SITE IN ALL CREATION TO THE SHI'AR. FOR THIS IS WHERE THEIR GODS LIVE...
YOUR ARROGANCE AND DISCOURTEOUSNESS CONFIRM IT.
A THOROUGHLY UNWARRANTED ARROGANCE, BY THE LOOKS OF HER. DO THE PEOPLE OF EARTH TRULY WORSHIP SUCH SHABBY LITTLE GODS?
NOT FOR MUCH LONGER, HUSBAND.

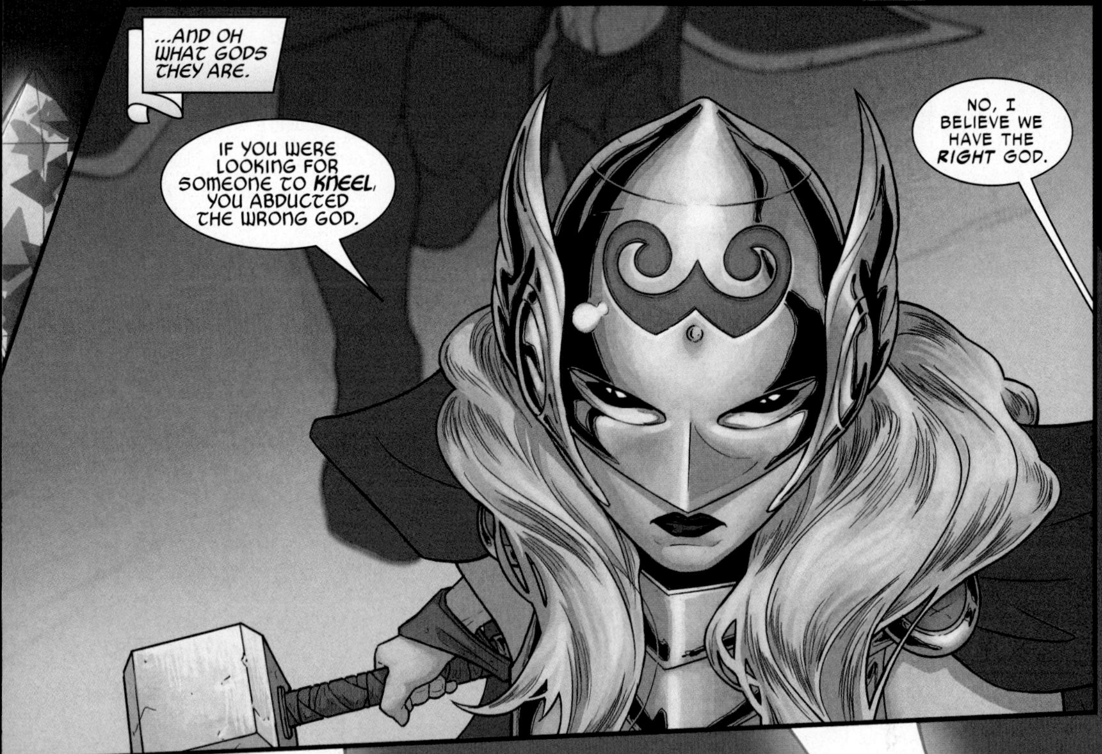
...AND OH WHAT GODS THEY ARE.
IF YOU WERE LOOKING FOR SOMEONE TO KNEEL, YOU ABDUCTED THE WRONG GOD.
NO, I BELIEVE WE HAVE THE RIGHT GOD.

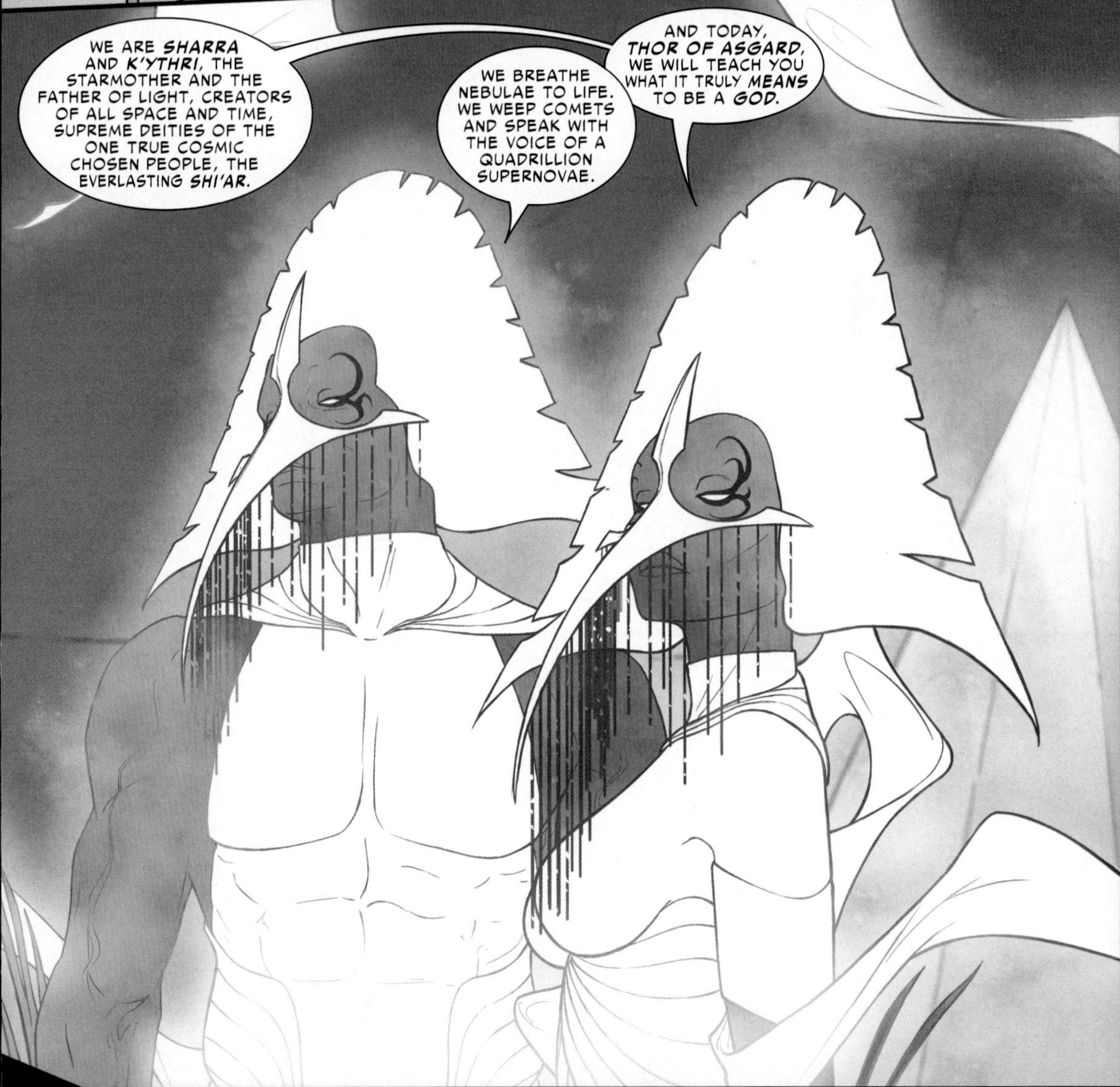
WE ARE SHARRA AND K'YTHRI, THE STARMOTHER AND THE FATHER OF LIGHT, CREATORS OF ALL SPACE AND TIME, SUPREME DEITIES OF THE ONE TRUE COSMIC CHOSEN PEOPLE, THE EVERLASTING SHI'AR.
WE BREATHE NEBULAE TO LIFE. WE WEEP COMETS AND SPEAK WITH THE VOICE OF A QUADRILLION SUPERNOVAE.
AND TODAY, THOR OF ASGARD, WE WILL TEACH YOU WHAT IT TRULY MEANS TO BE A GOD.

...YOU WISH TO *TEACH* ME WHAT IT MEANS TO BE A...

THREE DAYS AGO, WHILE YOU WERE FIDDLING WITH YOUR COMETS, I WAS HOLDING A MORTAL WOMAN IN MY ARMS AS THE *CANCER* THAT HAD RAVAGED HER BRAIN SLOWLY CONSUMED WHAT WAS LEFT OF HER LIFE.

ALL I COULD DO WAS LISTEN AS SHE *PRAYED.* SHE PRAYED TO ALL THE GODS.

AND THERE ARE SO VERY MANY OF THEM SPREAD ACROSS THIS COSMOS, ARE THERE NOT? AND OH, HOW EACH LOVES TO BOAST OF THEIR OWN MAJESTY AND ALMIGHTINESS.

YET WHERE IS THAT WOMAN NOW? TELL ME, IN WHAT *HEAVEN* DOES SHE RESIDE?

NONE OF THEM. BECAUSE NO GOD BOTHERED TO LISTEN OR CARE.

IF *THAT* IS WHAT YOU THINK IT MEANS TO BE A GOD, THEN YOU AND ALL YOUR TEACHINGS ARE WELCOME TO DO AS THAT POOR WOMAN DID.

AND *VANISH* FROM THESE REALMS FOREVER.

WHAT IN THE NAME OF THE IMPERIUM IS SHE GOING ON ABOUT? SOME EXPIRED MORTAL? IS SHE FEEBLE-MINDED, DO YOU THINK?

IT WOULD APPEAR SO. PERHAPS W SHOULD SPE MORE SLOWL

THE ONLY THING I WISH TO LEARN FROM YOU IS *WHY.* WHY A I HERE? I HAVE DONE NOTHING TO THESE SHI'AR.

YET.

YOU ARE HERE BECAUSE WE WISH IT.

BECAUSE WE DEMAND IT.

YOU ARE HERE TO ANSWER OUR CHALLENGE.

A CHALLENGE OF THE--

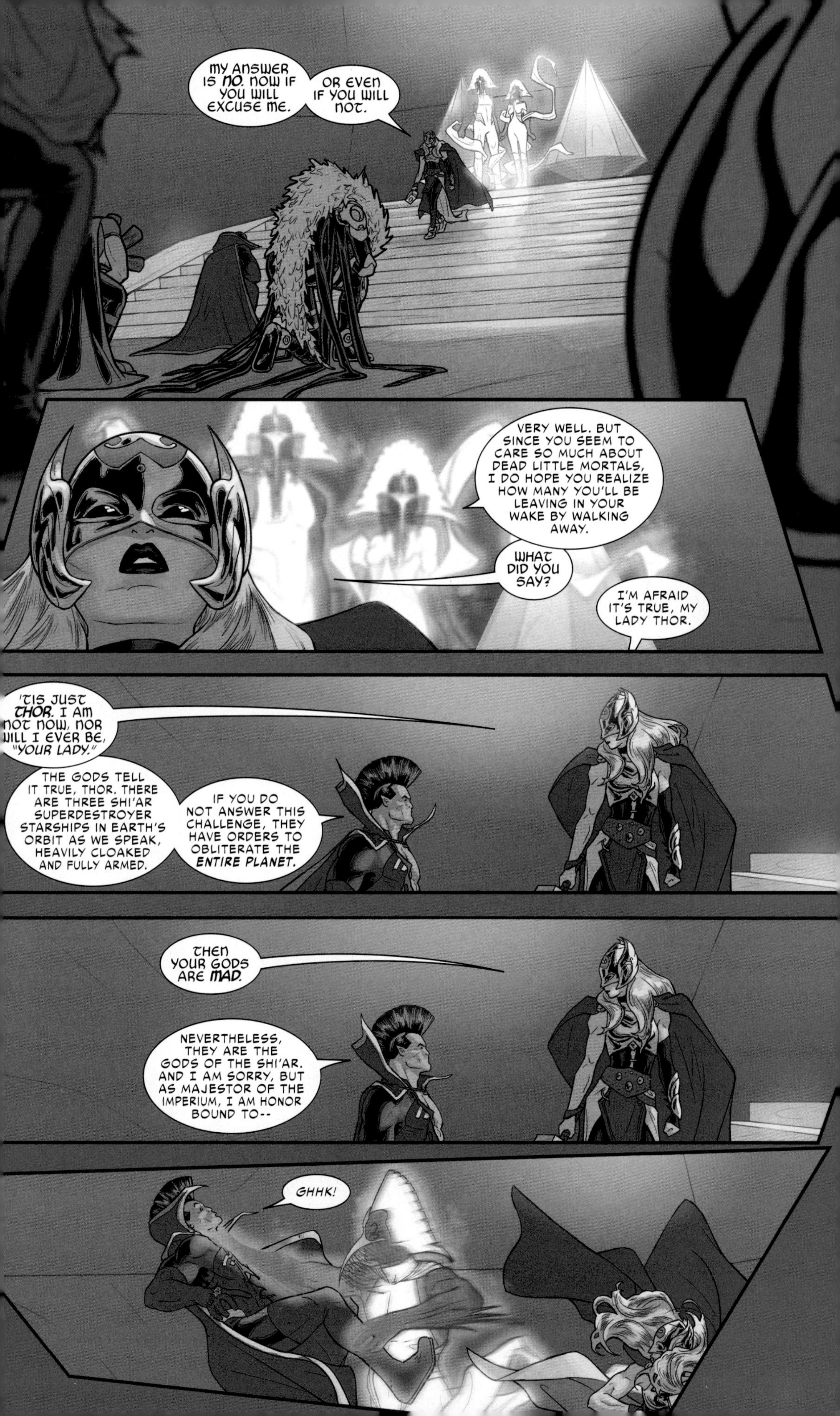
MY ANSWER IS NO. NOW IF YOU WILL EXCUSE ME.
OR EVEN IF YOU WILL NOT.
VERY WELL. BUT SINCE YOU SEEM TO CARE SO MUCH ABOUT DEAD LITTLE MORTALS, I DO HOPE YOU REALIZE HOW MANY YOU'LL BE LEAVING IN YOUR WAKE BY WALKING AWAY.
WHAT DID YOU SAY?
I'M AFRAID IT'S TRUE, MY LADY THOR.
'TIS JUST THOR. I AM NOT NOW, NOR WILL I EVER BE, "YOUR LADY."
THE GODS TELL IT TRUE, THOR. THERE ARE THREE SHI'AR SUPERDESTROYER STARSHIPS IN EARTH'S ORBIT AS WE SPEAK, HEAVILY CLOAKED AND FULLY ARMED.
IF YOU DO NOT ANSWER THIS CHALLENGE, THEY HAVE ORDERS TO OBLITERATE THE ENTIRE PLANET.
THEN YOUR GODS ARE MAD.
NEVERTHELESS, THEY ARE THE GODS OF THE SHI'AR. AND I AM SORRY, BUT AS MAJESTOR OF THE IMPERIUM, I AM HONOR BOUND TO--
GHHK!

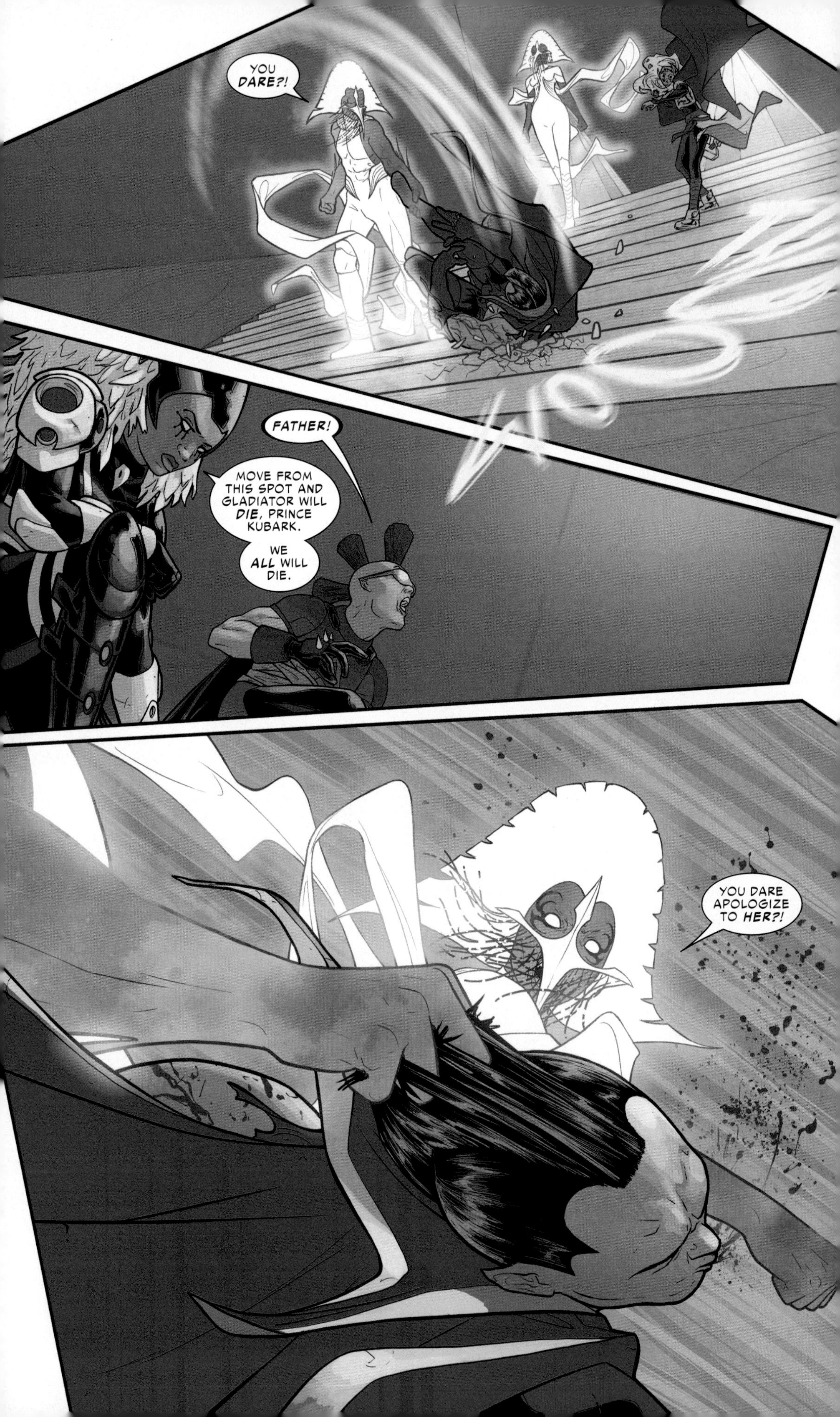

YOU DARE?!
FATHER!
MOVE FROM THIS SPOT AND GLADIATOR WILL DIE, PRINCE KUBARK.
WE ALL WILL DIE.
YOU DARE APOLOGIZE TO HER?!

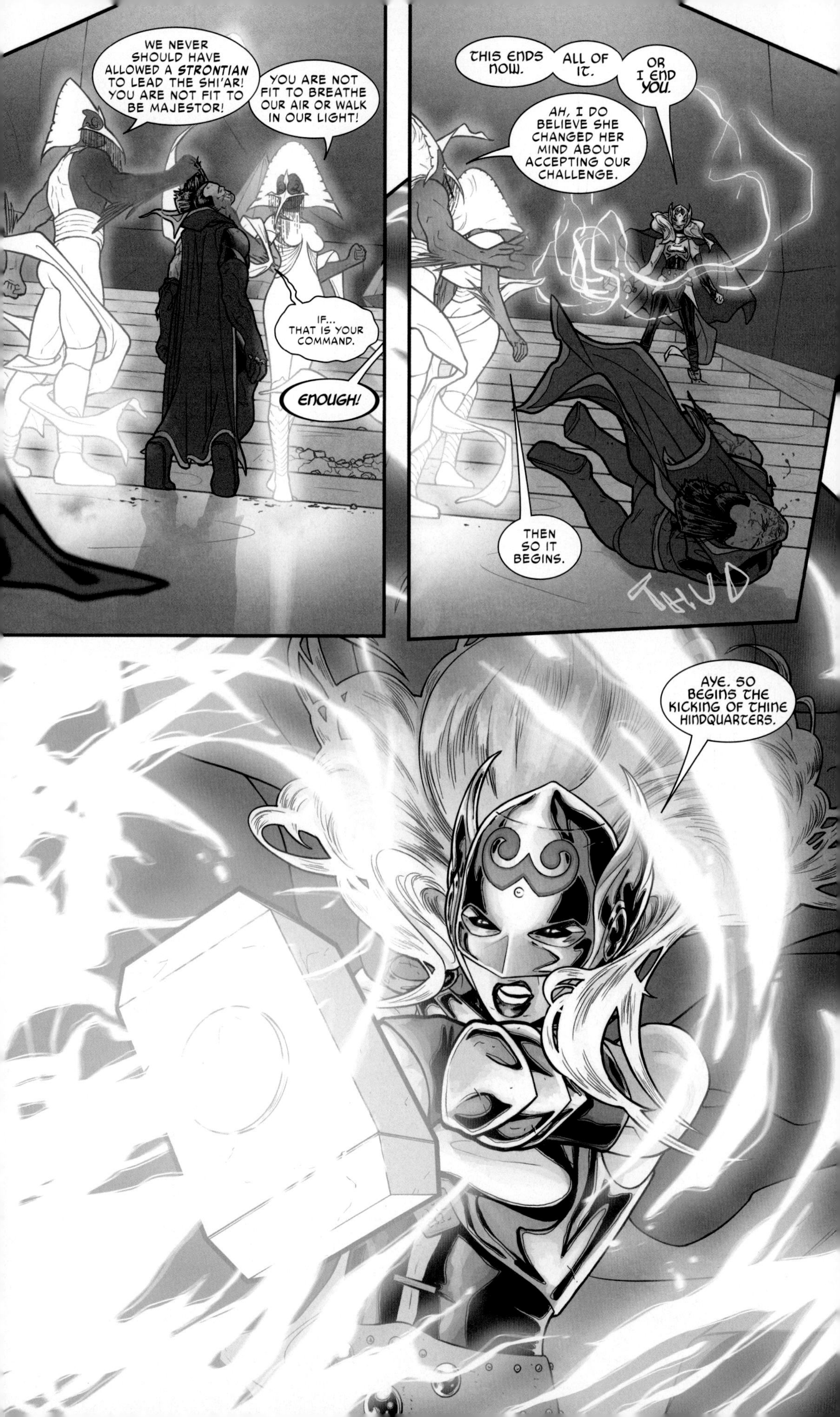
WE NEVER SHOULD HAVE ALLOWED A STRONTIAN TO LEAD THE SHI'AR! YOU ARE NOT FIT TO BE MAJESTOR!
YOU ARE NOT FIT TO BREATHE OUR AIR OR WALK IN OUR LIGHT!
IF... THAT IS YOUR COMMAND.
ENOUGH!
THIS ENDS NOW.
ALL OF IT.
OR I END YOU.
AH, I DO BELIEVE SHE CHANGED HER MIND ABOUT ACCEPTING OUR CHALLENGE.
THEN SO IT BEGINS.
THUD
AYE. SO BEGINS THE KICKING OF THINE HINDQUARTERS.

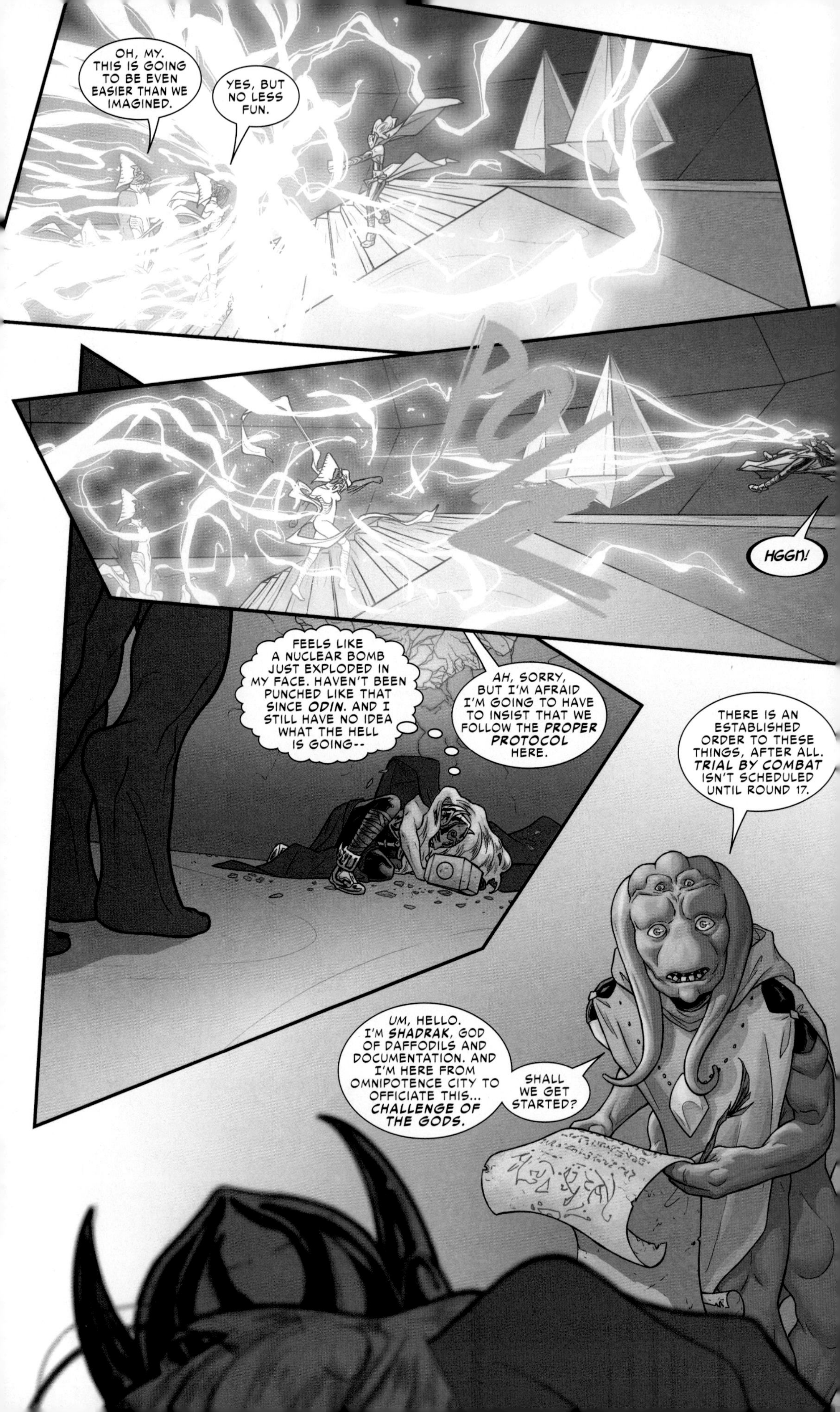

OH, MY. THIS IS GOING TO BE EVEN EASIER THAN WE IMAGINED.
YES, BUT NO LESS FUN.
HGGN!
FEELS LIKE A NUCLEAR BOMB JUST EXPLODED IN MY FACE. HAVEN'T BEEN PUNCHED LIKE THAT SINCE ODIN. AND I STILL HAVE NO IDEA WHAT THE HELL IS GOING--
AH, SORRY, BUT I'M AFRAID I'M GOING TO HAVE TO INSIST THAT WE FOLLOW THE PROPER PROTOCOL HERE.
THERE IS AN ESTABLISHED ORDER TO THESE THINGS, AFTER ALL. TRIAL BY COMBAT ISN'T SCHEDULED UNTIL ROUND 17.
UM, HELLO. I'M SHADRAK, GOD OF DAFFODILS AND DOCUMENTATION. AND I'M HERE FROM OMNIPOTENCE CITY TO OFFICIATE THIS... CHALLENGE OF THE GODS.
SHALL WE GET STARTED?

AND THEN THERE WAS THE TIME I DONNED THE ARMOR OF THE DESTROYER AND WENT OFF, SWORD IN HAND, TO BATTLE THE CELESTIALS!

THE CONGRESS OF WORLDS.

÷SIGH÷

OR WAIT, WAS IT *ODIN* WHO DID THAT?

NO, NO, IT WAS DEFINITELY ME. I REMEMBER IT LIKE IT WAS YESTERDAY!

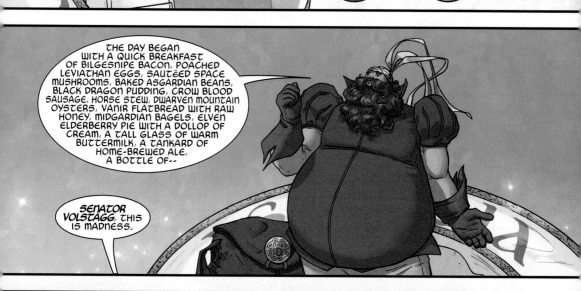

THE DAY BEGAN WITH A QUICK BREAKFAST OF BILGESNIPE BACON, POACHED LEVIATHAN EGGS, SAUTÉED SPACE MUSHROOMS, BAKED ASGARDIAN BEANS, BLACK DRAGON PUDDING, CROW BLOOD SAUSAGE, HORSE STEW, DWARVEN MOUNTAIN OYSTERS, VANIR FLATBREAD WITH RAW HONEY, MIDGARDIAN BAGELS, ELVEN ELDERBERRY PIE WITH A DOLLOP OF CREAM, A TALL GLASS OF WARM BUTTERMILK, A TANKARD OF HOME-BREWED ALE, A BOTTLE OF--

SENATOR VOLSTAGG, THIS IS MADNESS.

THE DELEGATION FROM *NIFFLEHEIM* DEMANDS THAT THE ASGARDIAN YIELD THE FLOOR.

SORRY, ARE EVEN THE ESTEEMED *GHOST SENATORS* GROWING HUNGRY?

ALL THIS *CONGRESS OF WORLDS* MUST DO IS VOTE TO APPROVE ASGARDIAN ACTION AGAINST THE SHI'AR, AND WE ALL MAY THEN BREAK FOR LUNCH. MY TREAT.

THE SHI'AR-- FAH!

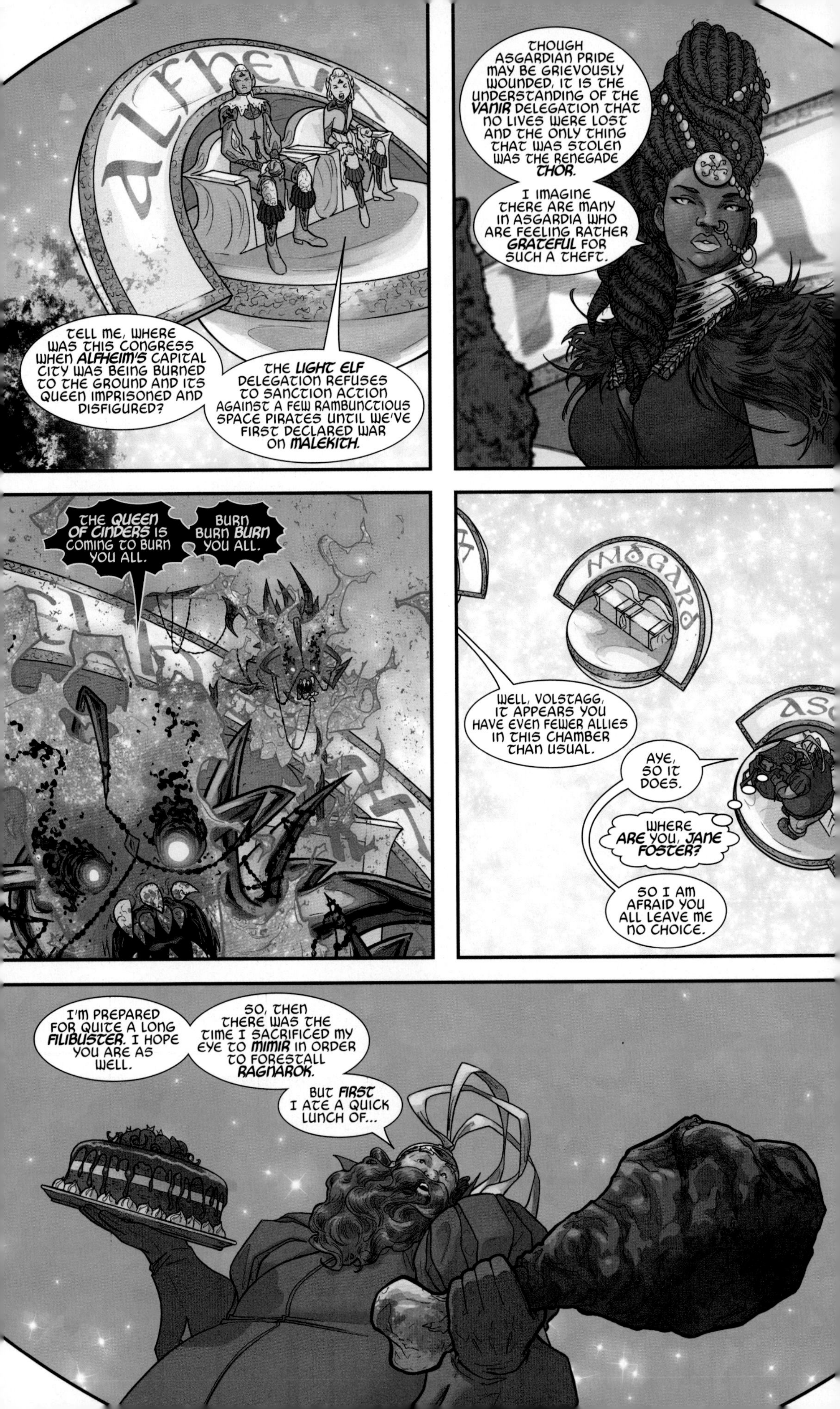

ALFHEIM
TELL ME, WHERE WAS THIS CONGRESS WHEN ALFHEIM'S CAPITAL CITY WAS BEING BURNED TO THE GROUND AND ITS QUEEN IMPRISONED AND DISFIGURED?
THE LIGHT ELF DELEGATION REFUSES TO SANCTION ACTION AGAINST A FEW RAMBUNCTIOUS SPACE PIRATES UNTIL WE'VE FIRST DECLARED WAR ON MALEKITH.
THOUGH ASGARDIAN PRIDE MAY BE GRIEVOUSLY WOUNDED, IT IS THE UNDERSTANDING OF THE VANIR DELEGATION THAT NO LIVES WERE LOST AND THE ONLY THING THAT WAS STOLEN WAS THE RENEGADE THOR.
I IMAGINE THERE ARE MANY IN ASGARDIA WHO ARE FEELING RATHER GRATEFUL FOR SUCH A THEFT.
THE QUEEN OF CINDERS IS COMING TO BURN YOU ALL.
BURN BURN BURN YOU ALL.
MIDGARD
WELL, VOLSTAGG, IT APPEARS YOU HAVE EVEN FEWER ALLIES IN THIS CHAMBER THAN USUAL.
AYE, SO IT DOES.
WHERE ARE YOU, JANE FOSTER?
SO I AM AFRAID YOU ALL LEAVE ME NO CHOICE.
I'M PREPARED FOR QUITE A LONG FILIBUSTER. I HOPE YOU ARE AS WELL.
SO, THEN THERE WAS THE TIME I SACRIFICED MY EYE TO MIMIR IN ORDER TO FORESTALL RAGNAROK.
BUT FIRST I ATE A QUICK LUNCH OF...

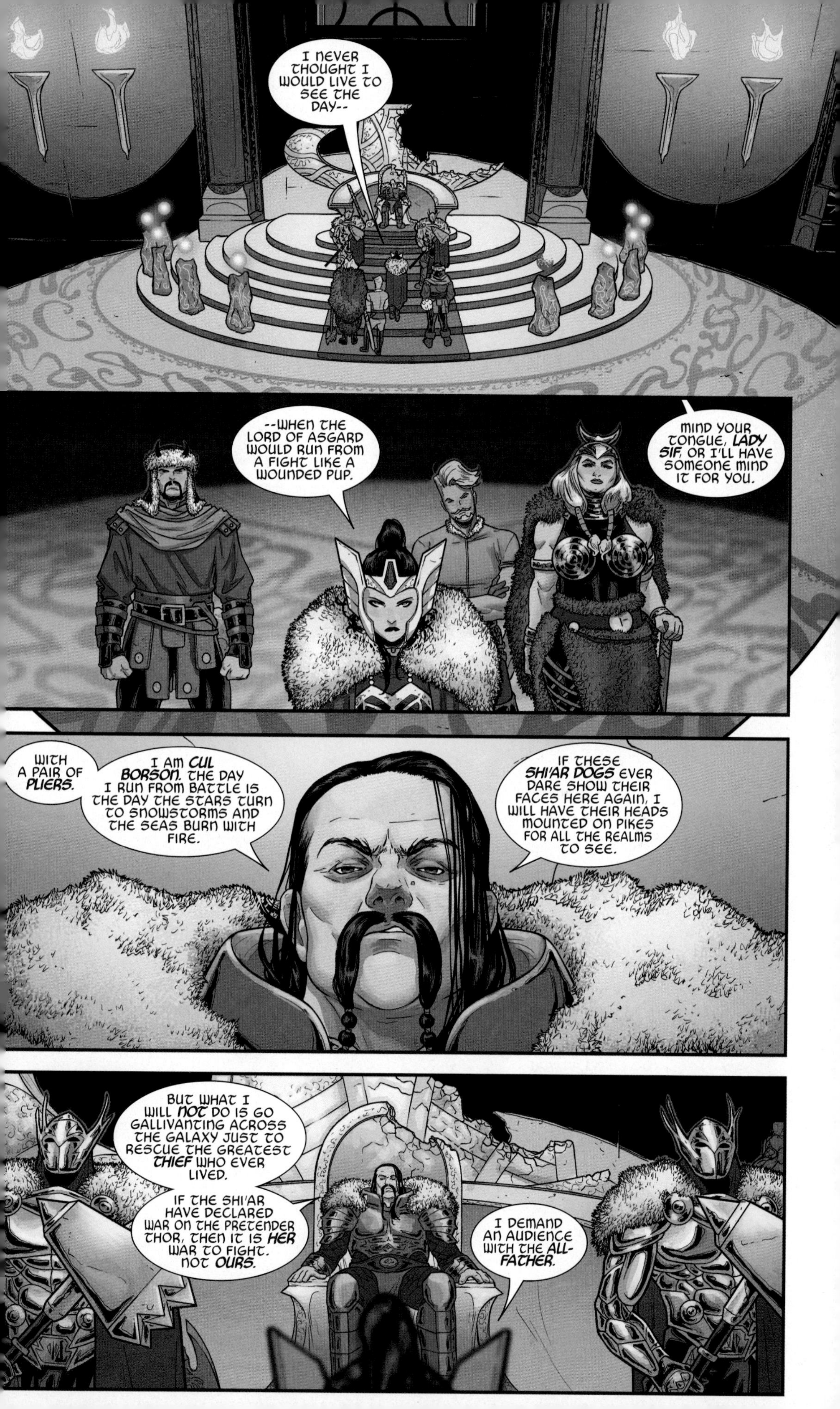

I NEVER THOUGHT I WOULD LIVE TO SEE THE DAY--
--WHEN THE LORD OF ASGARD WOULD RUN FROM A FIGHT LIKE A WOUNDED PUP.
MIND YOUR TONGUE, LADY SIF, OR I'LL HAVE SOMEONE MIND IT FOR YOU.
WITH A PAIR OF PLIERS.
I AM CUL BORSON. THE DAY I RUN FROM BATTLE IS THE DAY THE STARS TURN TO SNOWSTORMS AND THE SEAS BURN WITH FIRE.
IF THESE SHI'AR DOGS EVER DARE SHOW THEIR FACES HERE AGAIN, I WILL HAVE THEIR HEADS MOUNTED ON PIKES FOR ALL THE REALMS TO SEE.
BUT WHAT I WILL NOT DO IS GO GALLIVANTING ACROSS THE GALAXY JUST TO RESCUE THE GREATEST THIEF WHO EVER LIVED.
IF THE SHI'AR HAVE DECLARED WAR ON THE PRETENDER THOR, THEN IT IS HER WAR TO FIGHT. NOT OURS.
I DEMAND AN AUDIENCE WITH THE ALL-FATHER.

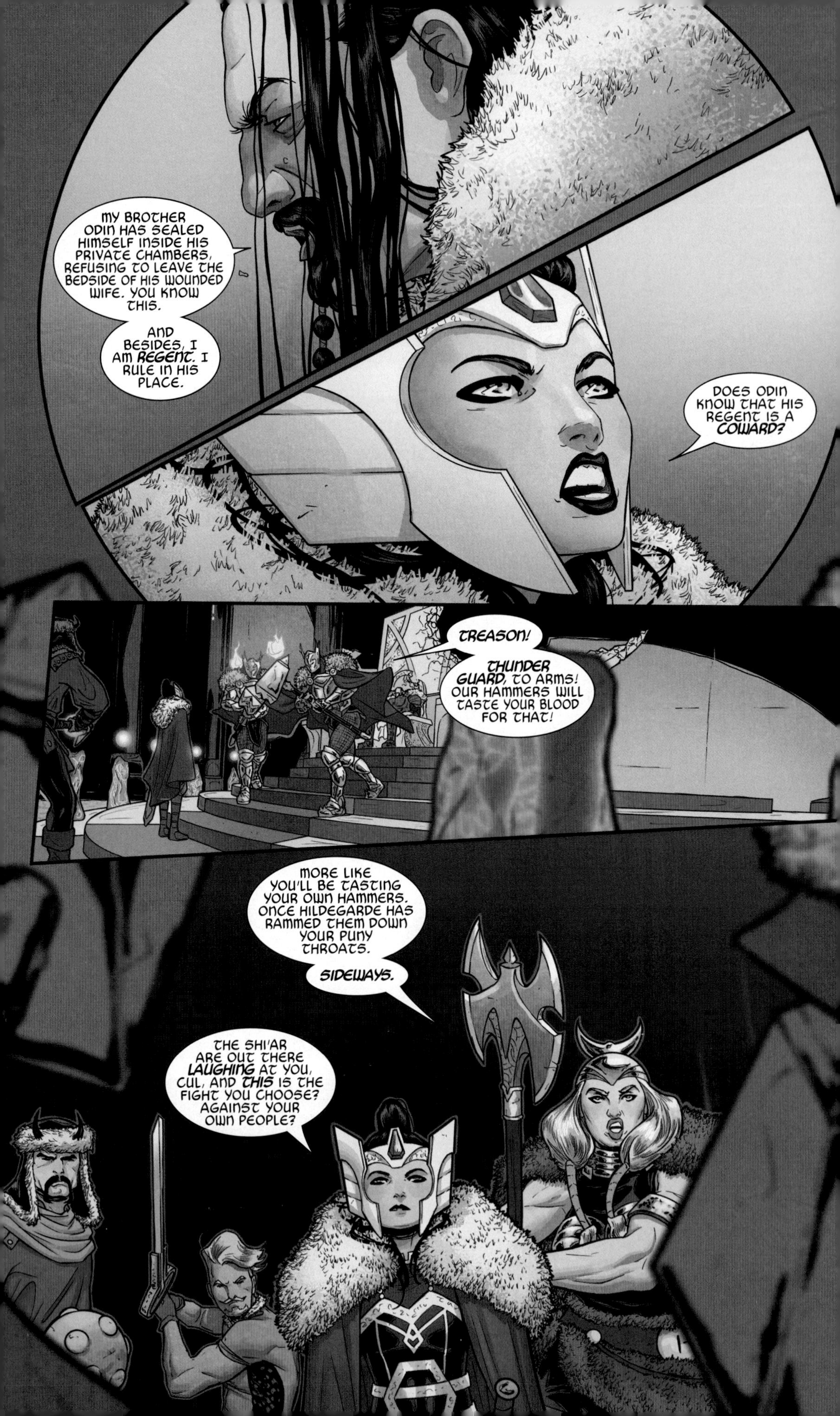
MY BROTHER ODIN HAS SEALED HIMSELF INSIDE HIS PRIVATE CHAMBERS, REFUSING TO LEAVE THE BEDSIDE OF HIS WOUNDED WIFE. YOU KNOW THIS.
AND BESIDES, I AM REGENT. I RULE IN HIS PLACE.
DOES ODIN KNOW THAT HIS REGENT IS A COWARD?
TREASON!
THUNDER GUARD, TO ARMS! OUR HAMMERS WILL TASTE YOUR BLOOD FOR THAT!
MORE LIKE YOU'LL BE TASTING YOUR OWN HAMMERS. ONCE HILDEGARDE HAS RAMMED THEM DOWN YOUR PUNY THROATS.
SIDEWAYS.
THE SHI'AR ARE OUT THERE LAUGHING AT YOU, CUL, AND THIS IS THE FIGHT YOU CHOOSE? AGAINST YOUR OWN PEOPLE?

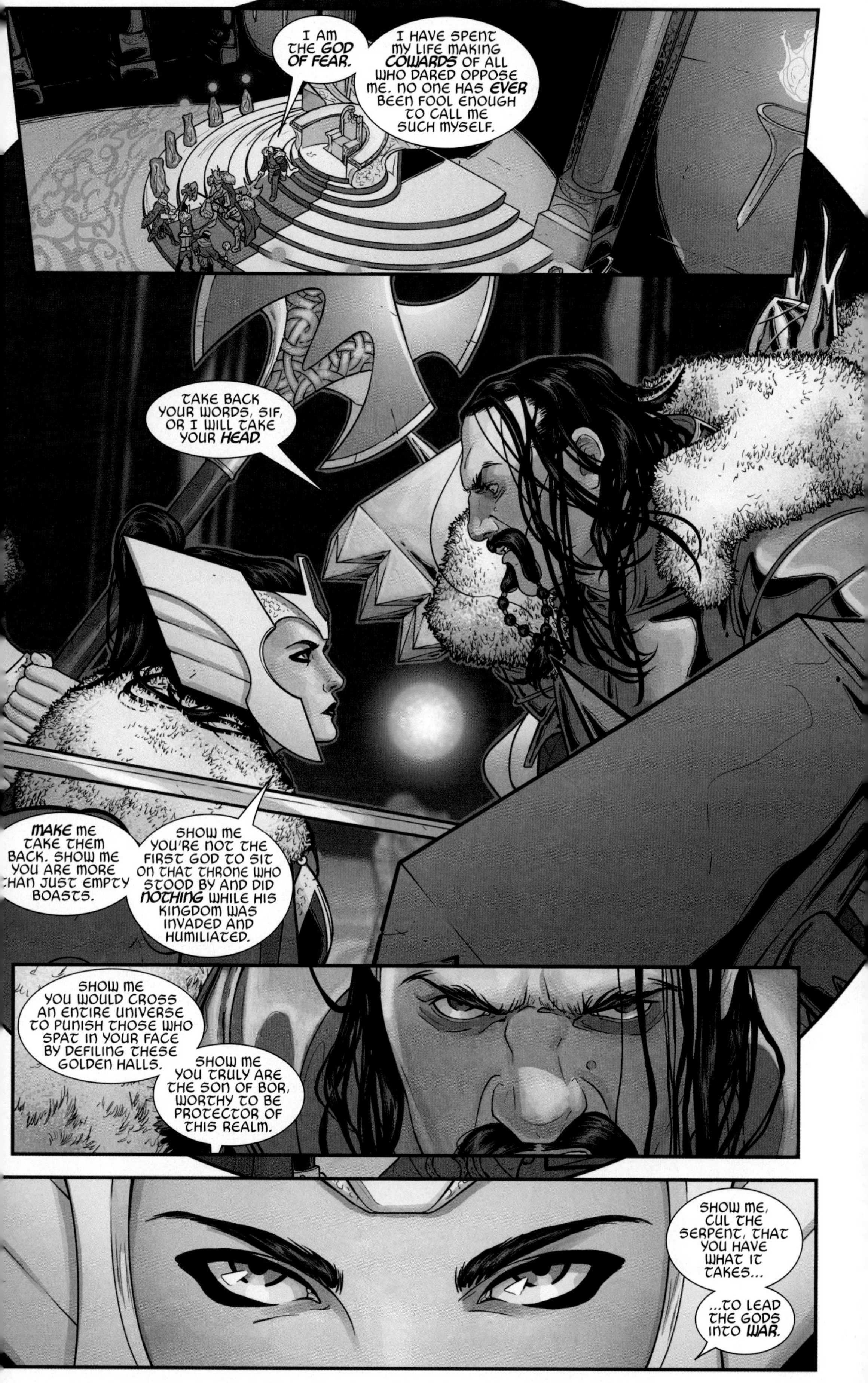

I AM THE GOD OF FEAR.
I HAVE SPENT MY LIFE MAKING COWARDS OF ALL WHO DARED OPPOSE ME. NO ONE HAS EVER BEEN FOOL ENOUGH TO CALL ME SUCH MYSELF.
TAKE BACK YOUR WORDS, SIF, OR I WILL TAKE YOUR HEAD.
MAKE ME TAKE THEM BACK. SHOW ME YOU ARE MORE THAN JUST EMPTY BOASTS.
SHOW ME YOU'RE NOT THE FIRST GOD TO SIT ON THAT THRONE WHO STOOD BY AND DID NOTHING WHILE HIS KINGDOM WAS INVADED AND HUMILIATED.
SHOW ME YOU WOULD CROSS AN ENTIRE UNIVERSE TO PUNISH THOSE WHO SPAT IN YOUR FACE BY DEFILING THESE GOLDEN HALLS.
SHOW ME YOU TRULY ARE THE SON OF BOR, WORTHY TO BE PROTECTOR OF THIS REALM.
SHOW ME, CUL THE SERPENT, THAT YOU HAVE WHAT IT TAKES...
...TO LEAD THE GODS INTO WAR.

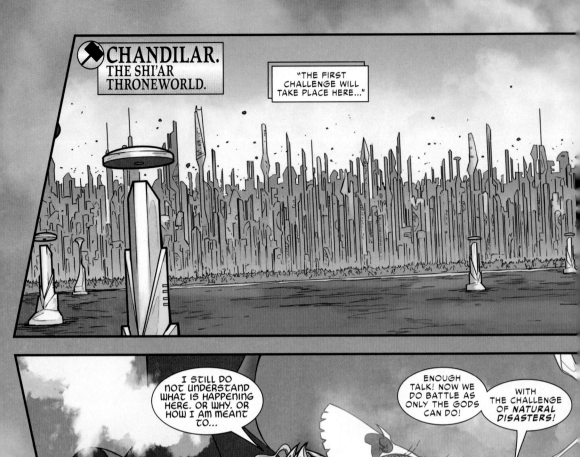

CHANDILAR. THE SHI'AR THRONEWORLD.

"THE FIRST CHALLENGE WILL TAKE PLACE HERE..."

I STILL DO NOT UNDERSTAND WHAT IS HAPPENING HERE. OR WHY. OR HOW I AM MEANT TO...

ENOUGH TALK! NOW WE DO BATTLE AS ONLY THE GODS CAN DO!

WITH THE CHALLENGE OF *NATURAL DISASTERS!*

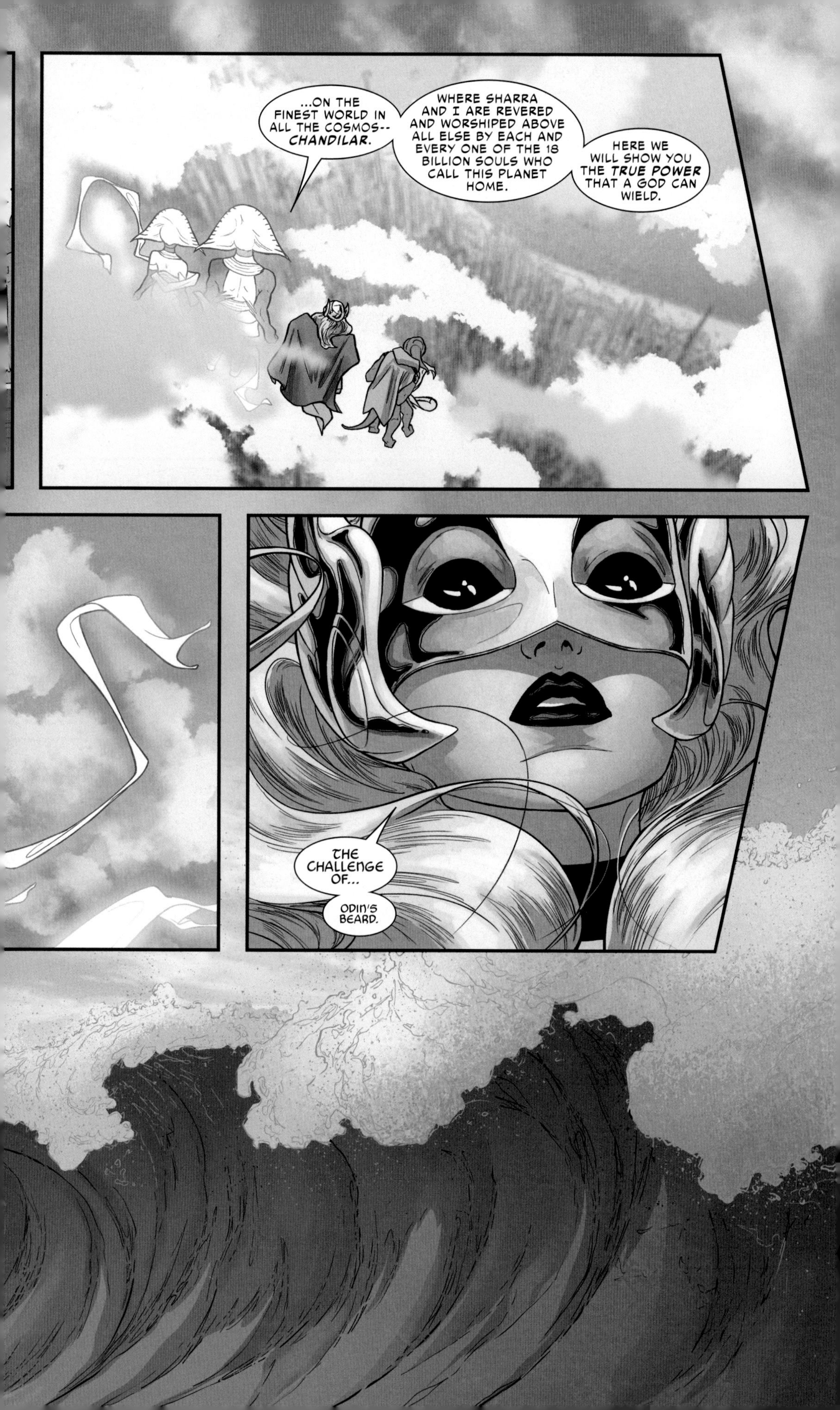
...ON THE FINEST WORLD IN ALL THE COSMOS-- *CHANDILAR*.
WHERE SHARRA AND I ARE REVERED AND WORSHIPED ABOVE ALL ELSE BY EACH AND EVERY ONE OF THE 18 BILLION SOULS WHO CALL THIS PLANET HOME.
HERE WE WILL SHOW YOU THE ***TRUE POWER*** THAT A GOD CAN WIELD.
THE CHALLENGE OF...
ODIN'S BEARD.

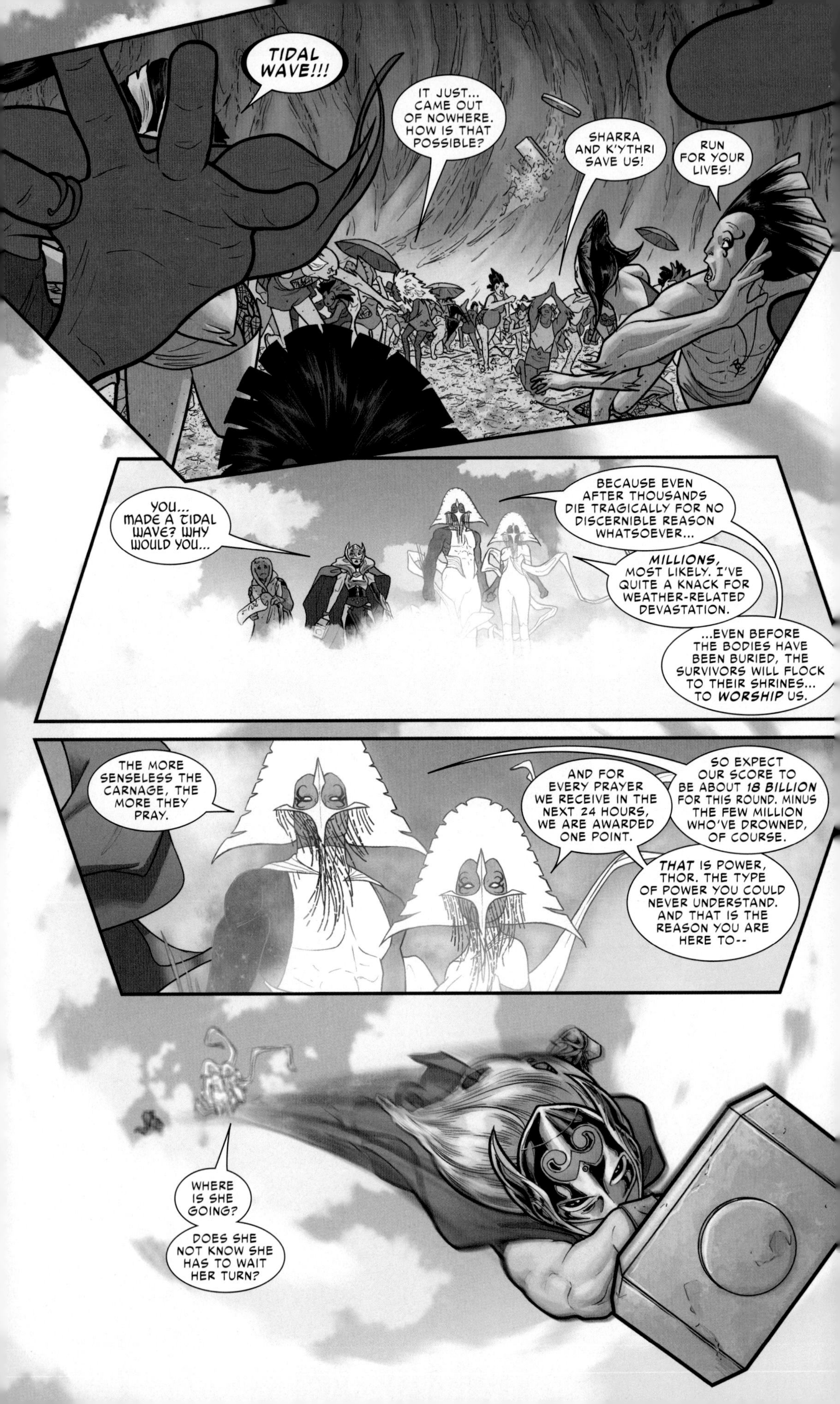
TIDAL WAVE!!!
IT JUST... CAME OUT OF NOWHERE. HOW IS THAT POSSIBLE?
SHARRA AND K'YTHRI SAVE US!
RUN FOR YOUR LIVES!
YOU... MADE A TIDAL WAVE? WHY WOULD YOU...
BECAUSE EVEN AFTER THOUSANDS DIE TRAGICALLY FOR NO DISCERNIBLE REASON WHATSOEVER...
MILLIONS, MOST LIKELY. I'VE QUITE A KNACK FOR WEATHER-RELATED DEVASTATION.
...EVEN BEFORE THE BODIES HAVE BEEN BURIED, THE SURVIVORS WILL FLOCK TO THEIR SHRINES... TO WORSHIP US.
THE MORE SENSELESS THE CARNAGE, THE MORE THEY PRAY.
AND FOR EVERY PRAYER WE RECEIVE IN THE NEXT 24 HOURS, WE ARE AWARDED ONE POINT.
SO EXPECT OUR SCORE TO BE ABOUT 18 BILLION FOR THIS ROUND. MINUS THE FEW MILLION WHO'VE DROWNED, OF COURSE.
THAT IS POWER, THOR. THE TYPE OF POWER YOU COULD NEVER UNDERSTAND. AND THAT IS THE REASON YOU ARE HERE TO--
WHERE IS SHE GOING?
DOES SHE NOT KNOW SHE HAS TO WAIT HER TURN?

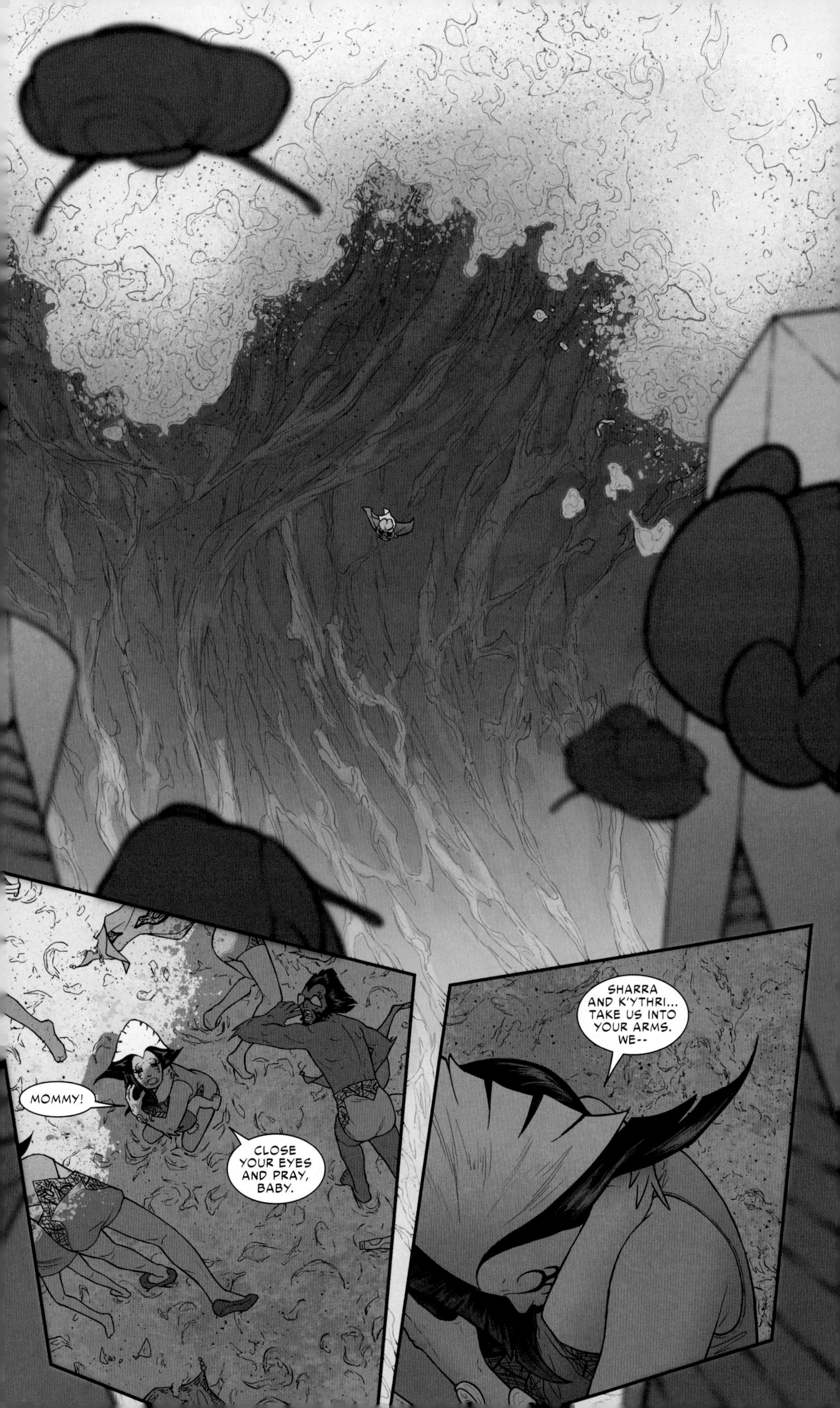
MOMMY!
CLOSE YOUR EYES AND PRAY, BABY.
SHARRA AND K'YTHRI... TAKE US INTO YOUR ARMS. WE--

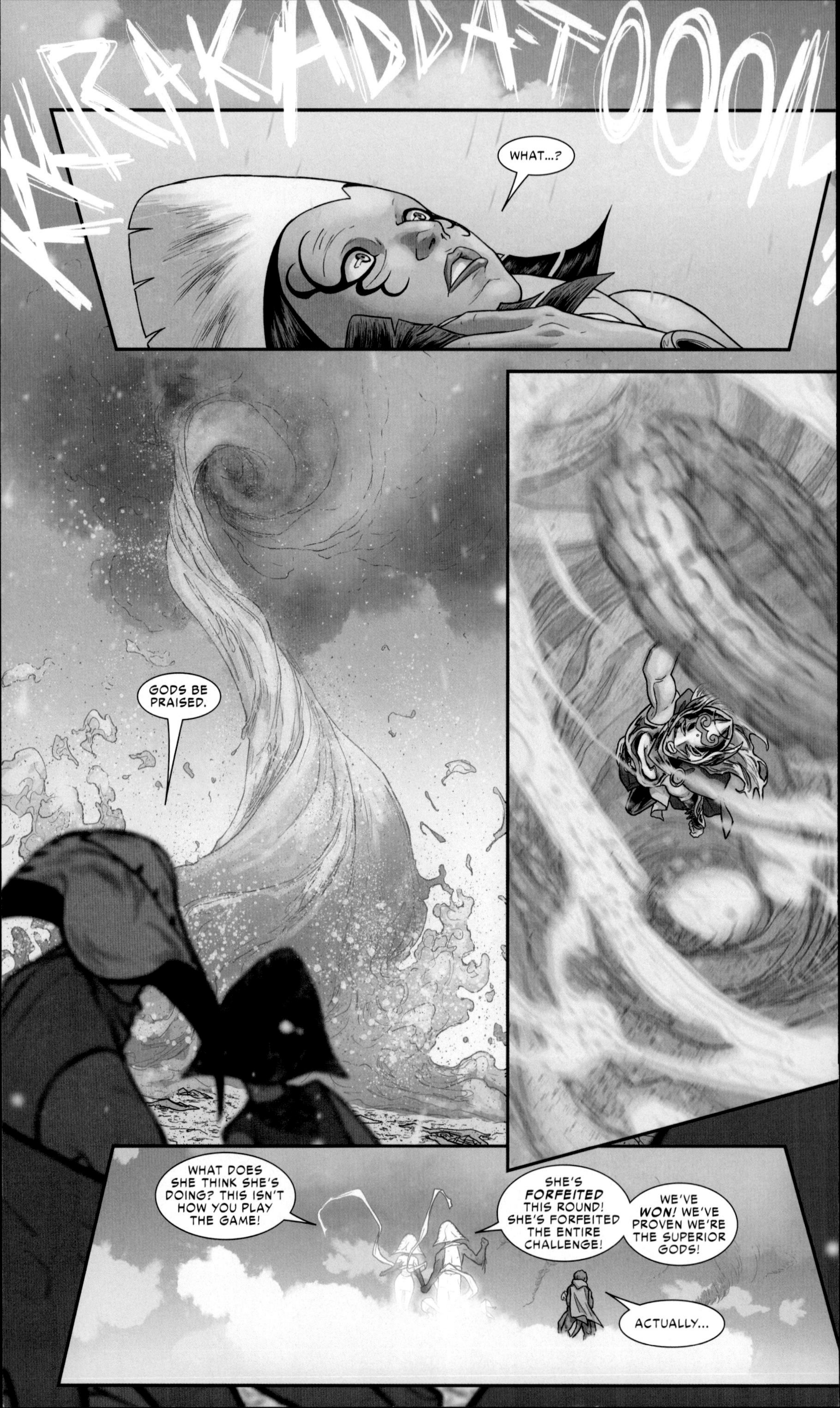
KRAKADDA-TOOOM
WHAT...?
GODS BE PRAISED.
WHAT DOES SHE THINK SHE'S DOING? THIS ISN'T HOW YOU PLAY THE GAME!
SHE'S FORFEITED THIS ROUND! SHE'S FORFEITED THE ENTIRE CHALLENGE!
WE'VE WON! WE'VE PROVEN WE'RE THE SUPERIOR GODS!
ACTUALLY...

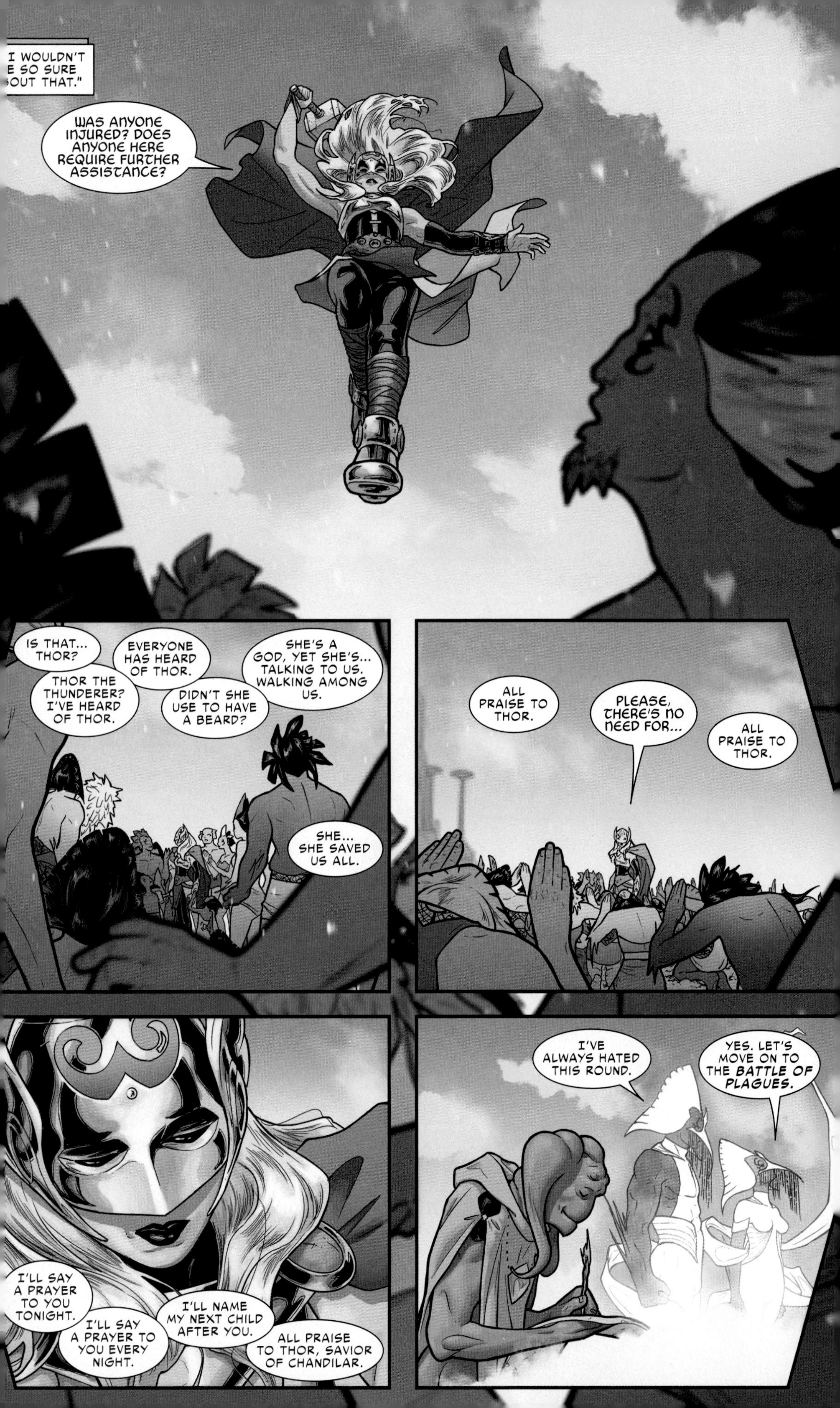

I WOULDN'T
E SO SURE
OUT THAT."
WAS ANYONE INJURED? DOES ANYONE HERE REQUIRE FURTHER ASSISTANCE?
IS THAT... THOR?
EVERYONE HAS HEARD OF THOR.
SHE'S A GOD, YET SHE'S... TALKING TO US. WALKING AMONG US.
THOR THE THUNDERER? I'VE HEARD OF THOR.
DIDN'T SHE USE TO HAVE A BEARD?
SHE... SHE SAVED US ALL.
ALL PRAISE TO THOR.
PLEASE, THERE'S NO NEED FOR...
ALL PRAISE TO THOR.
I'LL SAY A PRAYER TO YOU TONIGHT.
I'LL SAY A PRAYER TO YOU EVERY NIGHT.
I'LL NAME MY NEXT CHILD AFTER YOU.
ALL PRAISE TO THOR, SAVIOR OF CHANDILAR.
I'VE ALWAYS HATED THIS ROUND.
YES. LET'S MOVE ON TO THE *BATTLE OF PLAGUES*.

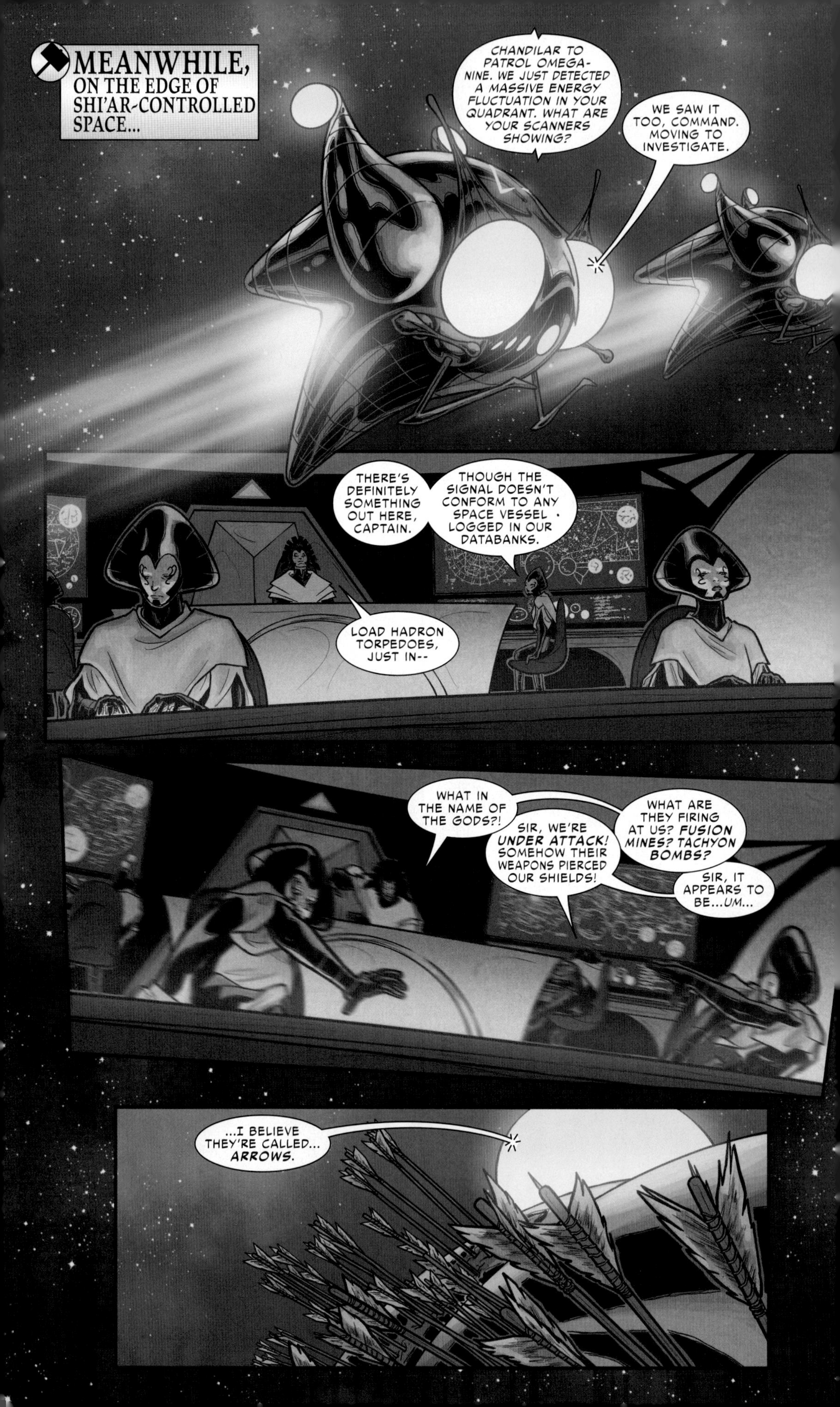
MEANWHILE, ON THE EDGE OF SHI'AR-CONTROLLED SPACE...
CHANDILAR TO PATROL OMEGA-NINE. WE JUST DETECTED A MASSIVE ENERGY FLUCTUATION IN YOUR QUADRANT. WHAT ARE YOUR SCANNERS SHOWING?
WE SAW IT TOO, COMMAND. MOVING TO INVESTIGATE.
THERE'S DEFINITELY SOMETHING OUT HERE, CAPTAIN.
THOUGH THE SIGNAL DOESN'T CONFORM TO ANY SPACE VESSEL LOGGED IN OUR DATABANKS.
LOAD HADRON TORPEDOES, JUST IN--
WHAT IN THE NAME OF THE GODS?!
SIR, WE'RE UNDER ATTACK! SOMEHOW THEIR WEAPONS PIERCED OUR SHIELDS!
WHAT ARE THEY FIRING AT US? FUSION MINES? TACHYON BOMBS?
SIR, IT APPEARS TO BE...UM...
...I BELIEVE THEY'RE CALLED... ARROWS.

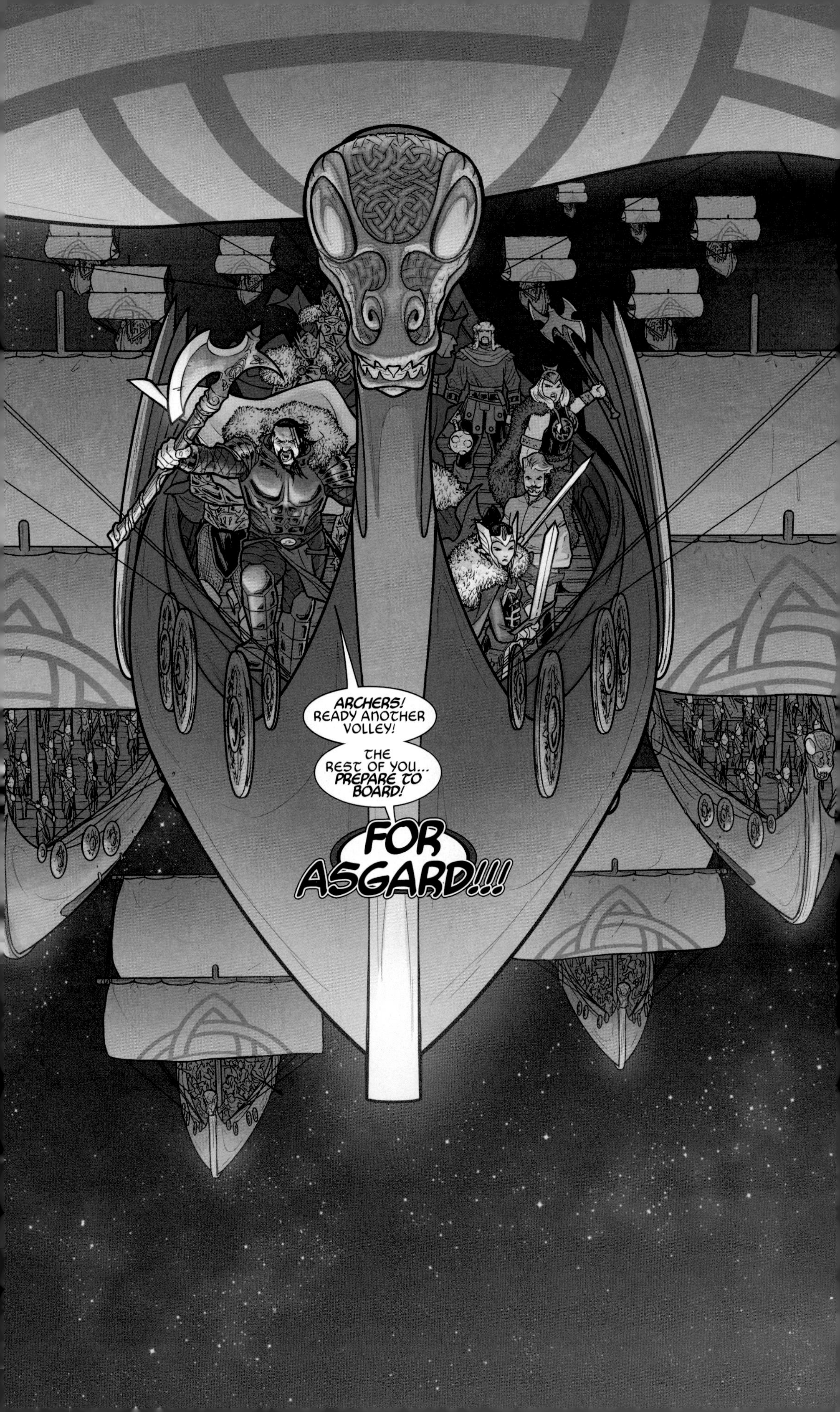
ARCHERS! READY ANOTHER VOLLEY!
THE REST OF YOU... PREPARE TO BOARD!
FOR ASGARD!!!

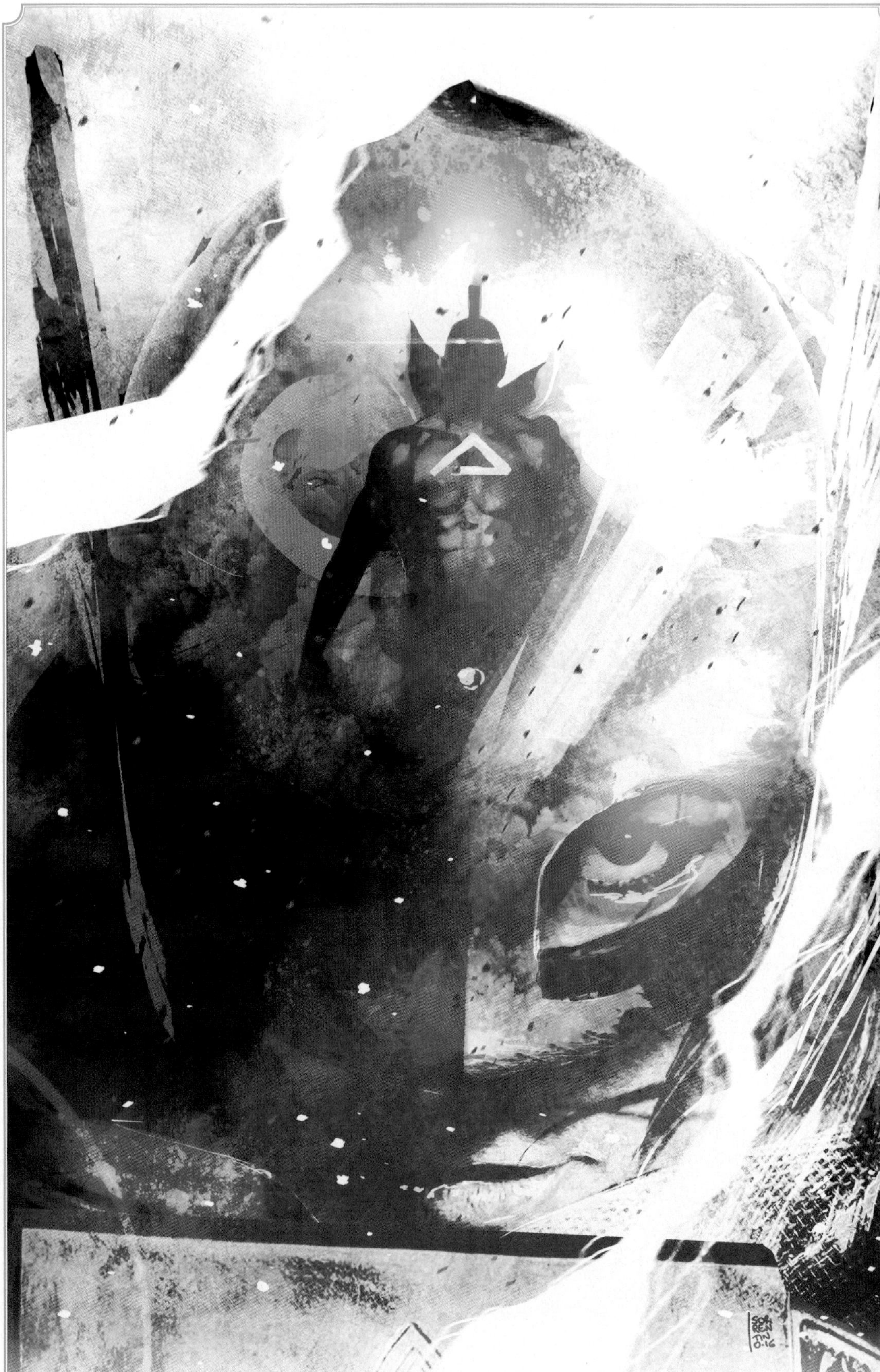

MIGHTY THOR # 15 VARIANT
BY **ANDREA SORRENTINO**

17

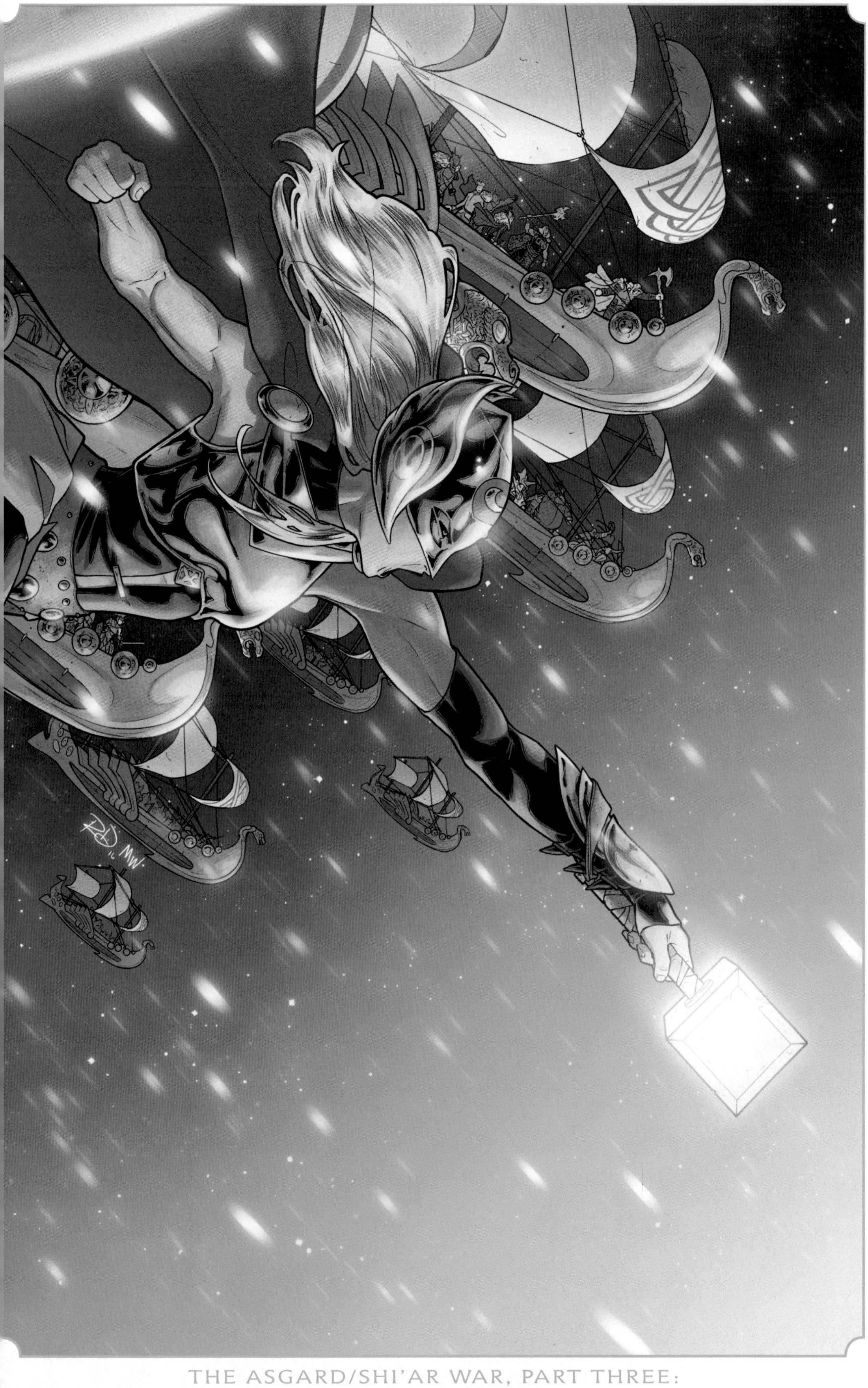

THE ASGARD/SHI'AR WAR, PART THREE:

WHEN THE STARS THREW DOWN THEIR SPEARS

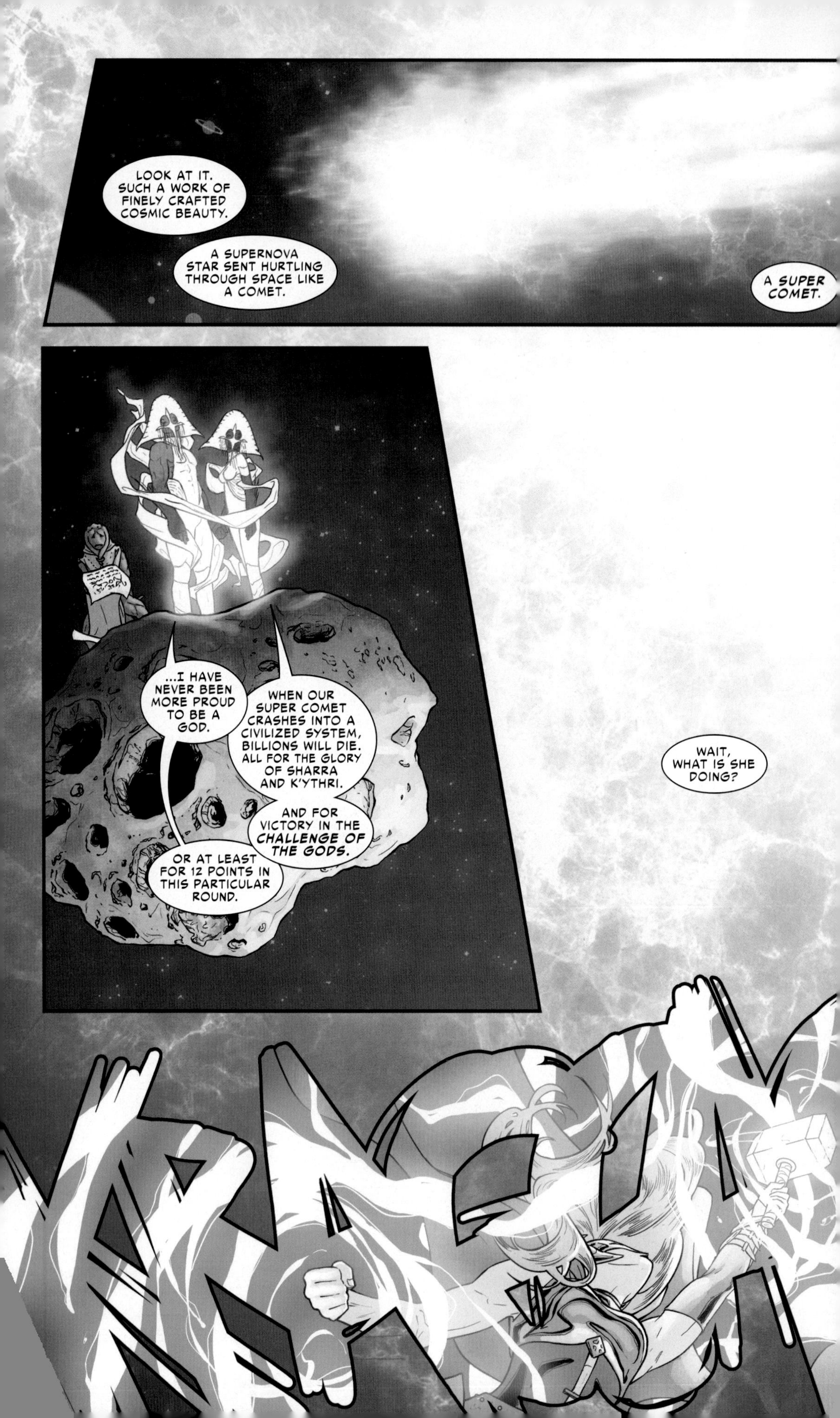
LOOK AT IT. SUCH A WORK OF FINELY CRAFTED COSMIC BEAUTY.
A SUPERNOVA STAR SENT HURTLING THROUGH SPACE LIKE A COMET.
A *SUPER COMET*.
...I HAVE NEVER BEEN MORE PROUD TO BE A GOD.
WHEN OUR SUPER COMET CRASHES INTO A CIVILIZED SYSTEM, BILLIONS WILL DIE. ALL FOR THE GLORY OF SHARRA AND K'YTHRI.
AND FOR VICTORY IN THE *CHALLENGE OF THE GODS*.
OR AT LEAST FOR 12 POINTS IN THIS PARTICULAR ROUND.
WAIT, WHAT IS SHE DOING?

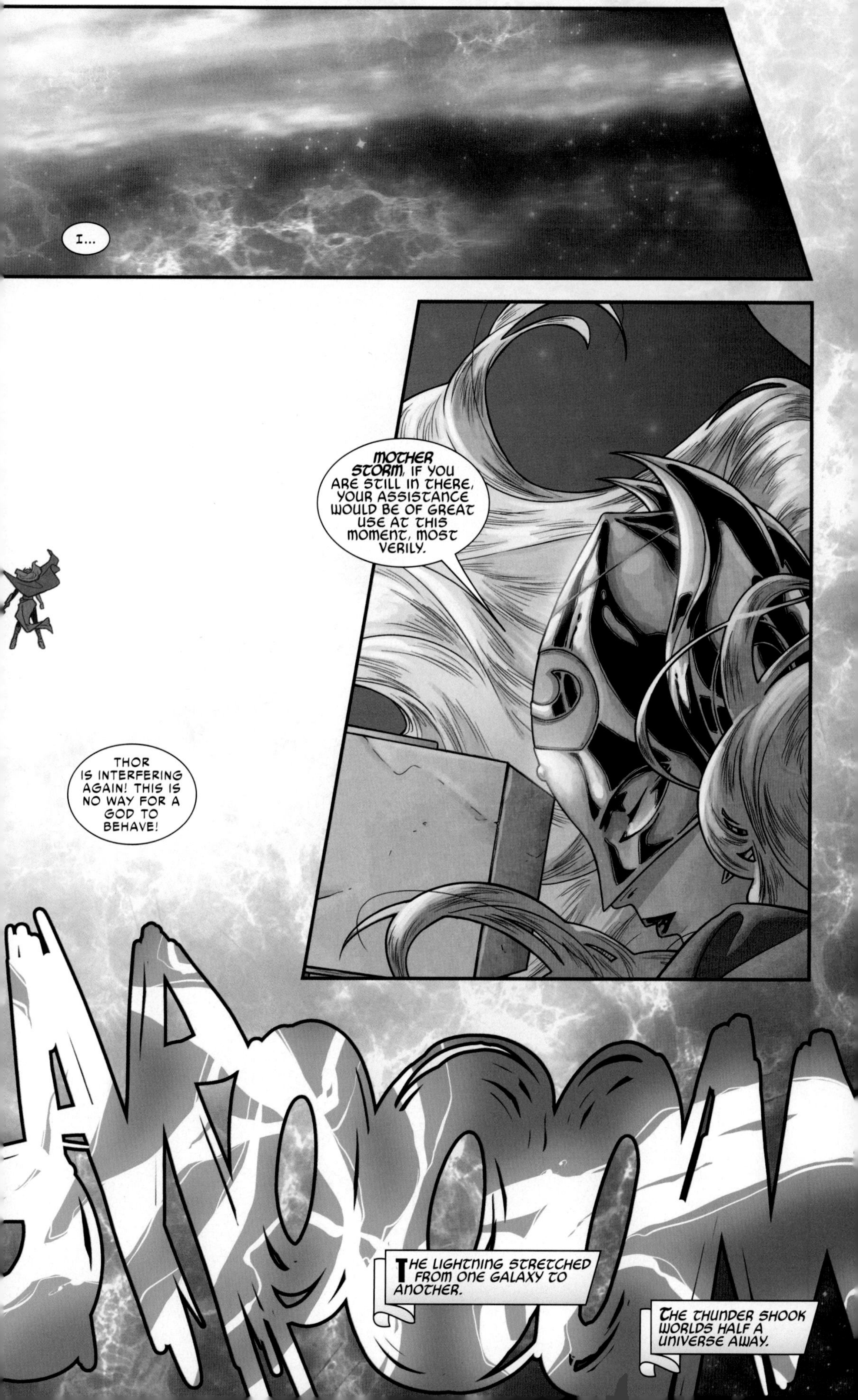
I...
MOTHER STORM, IF YOU ARE STILL IN THERE, YOUR ASSISTANCE WOULD BE OF GREAT USE AT THIS MOMENT, MOST VERILY.
THOR IS INTERFERING AGAIN! THIS IS NO WAY FOR A GOD TO BEHAVE!
THE LIGHTNING STRETCHED FROM ONE GALAXY TO ANOTHER.
THE THUNDER SHOOK WORLDS HALF A UNIVERSE AWAY.

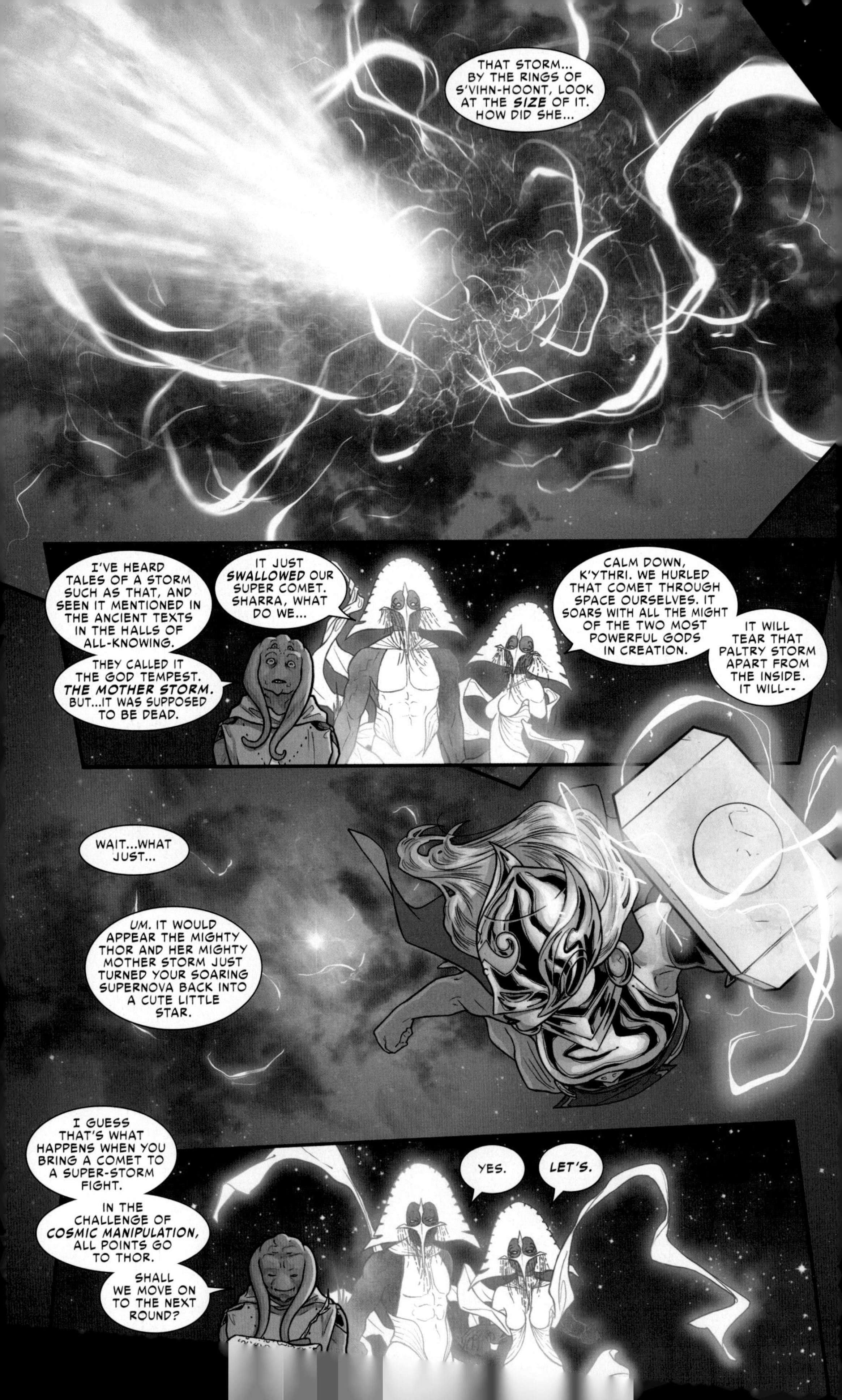
THAT STORM... BY THE RINGS OF S'VIHN-HOONT, LOOK AT THE *SIZE* OF IT. HOW DID SHE...
I'VE HEARD TALES OF A STORM SUCH AS THAT, AND SEEN IT MENTIONED IN THE ANCIENT TEXTS IN THE HALLS OF ALL-KNOWING.
THEY CALLED IT THE GOD TEMPEST. ***THE MOTHER STORM.*** BUT...IT WAS SUPPOSED TO BE DEAD.
IT JUST ***SWALLOWED*** OUR SUPER COMET. SHARRA, WHAT DO WE...
CALM DOWN, K'YTHRI. WE HURLED THAT COMET THROUGH SPACE OURSELVES. IT SOARS WITH ALL THE MIGHT OF THE TWO MOST POWERFUL GODS IN CREATION.
IT WILL TEAR THAT PALTRY STORM APART FROM THE INSIDE. IT WILL--
WAIT...WHAT JUST...
UM. IT WOULD APPEAR THE MIGHTY THOR AND HER MIGHTY MOTHER STORM JUST TURNED YOUR SOARING SUPERNOVA BACK INTO A CUTE LITTLE STAR.
I GUESS THAT'S WHAT HAPPENS WHEN YOU BRING A COMET TO A SUPER-STORM FIGHT.
IN THE CHALLENGE OF ***COSMIC MANIPULATION,*** ALL POINTS GO TO THOR.
SHALL WE MOVE ON TO THE NEXT ROUND?
YES.
LET'S.

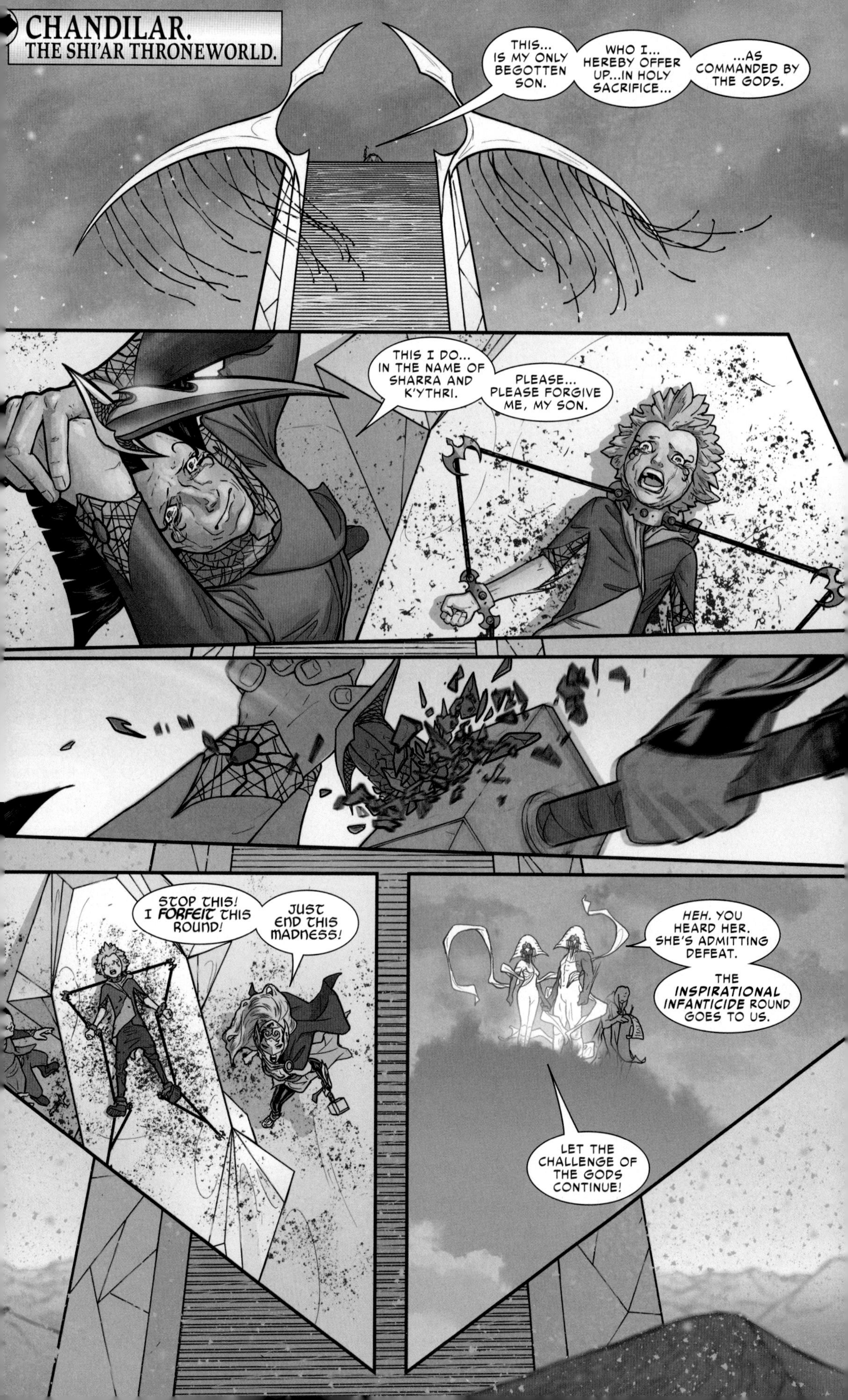
CHANDILAR.
THE SHI'AR THRONEWORLD.
THIS... IS MY ONLY BEGOTTEN SON.
WHO I... HEREBY OFFER UP...IN HOLY SACRIFICE...
...AS COMMANDED BY THE GODS.
THIS I DO... IN THE NAME OF SHARRA AND K'YTHRI.
PLEASE... PLEASE FORGIVE ME, MY SON.
STOP THIS! I FORFEIT THIS ROUND!
JUST END THIS MADNESS!
HEH. YOU HEARD HER. SHE'S ADMITTING DEFEAT.
THE INSPIRATIONAL INFANTICIDE ROUND GOES TO US.
LET THE CHALLENGE OF THE GODS CONTINUE!

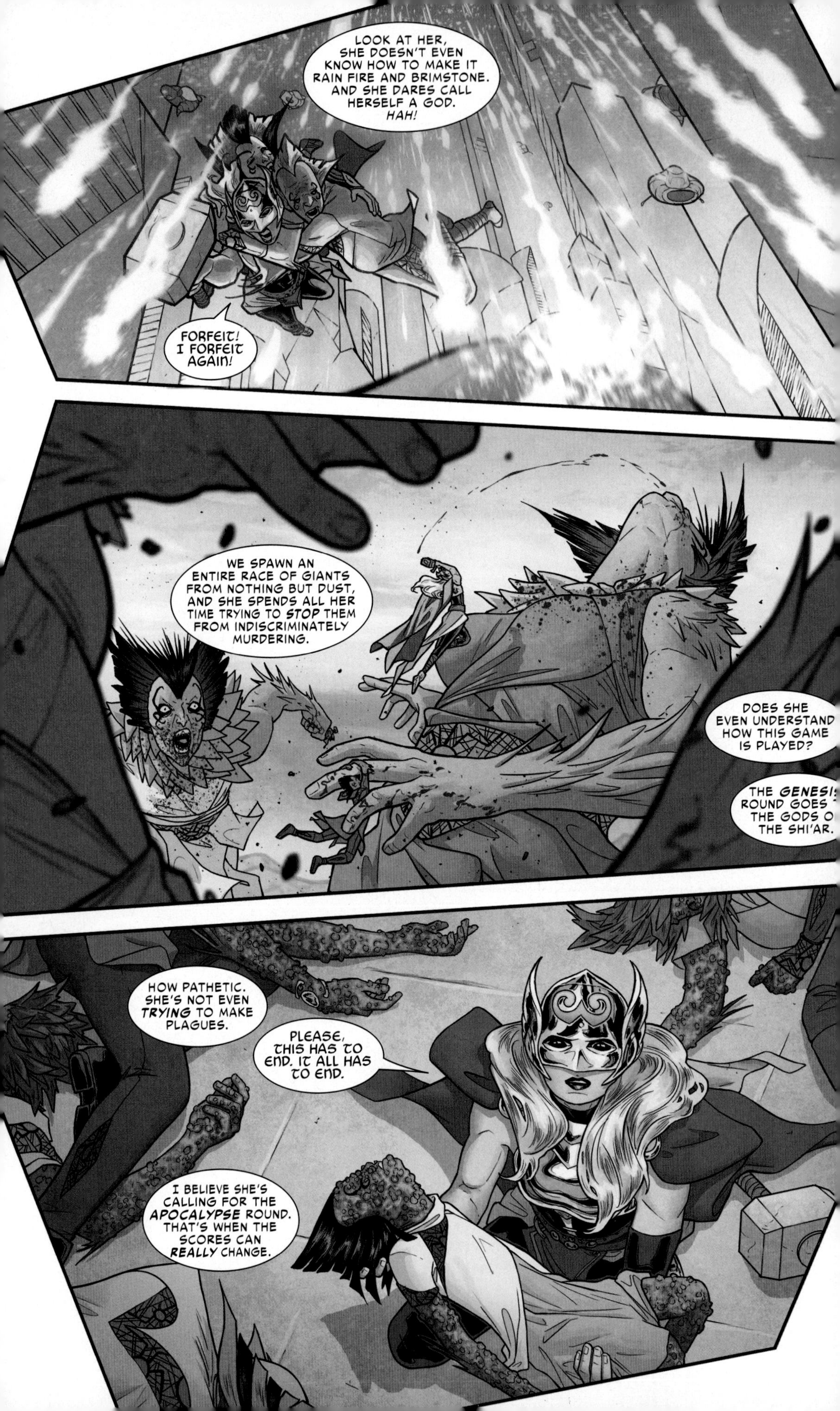
LOOK AT HER, SHE DOESN'T EVEN KNOW HOW TO MAKE IT RAIN FIRE AND BRIMSTONE. AND SHE DARES CALL HERSELF A GOD. HAH!
FORFEIT! I FORFEIT AGAIN!
WE SPAWN AN ENTIRE RACE OF GIANTS FROM NOTHING BUT DUST, AND SHE SPENDS ALL HER TIME TRYING TO STOP THEM FROM INDISCRIMINATELY MURDERING.
DOES SHE EVEN UNDERSTAND HOW THIS GAME IS PLAYED?
THE GENESI ROUND GOES THE GODS O THE SHI'AR.
HOW PATHETIC. SHE'S NOT EVEN TRYING TO MAKE PLAGUES.
PLEASE, THIS HAS TO END. IT ALL HAS TO END.
I BELIEVE SHE'S CALLING FOR THE APOCALYPSE ROUND. THAT'S WHEN THE SCORES CAN REALLY CHANGE.

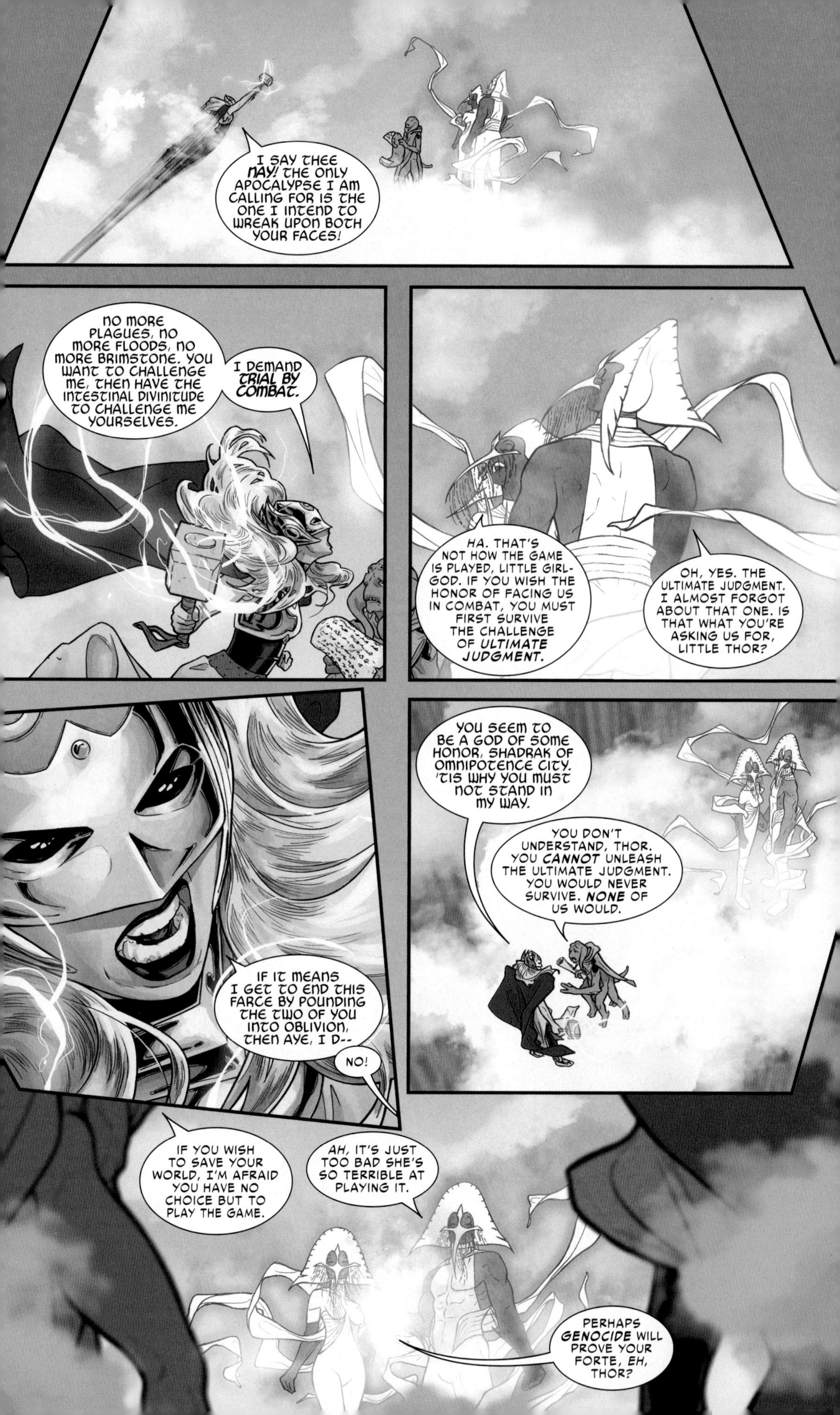
I SAY THEE NAY! THE ONLY APOCALYPSE I AM CALLING FOR IS THE ONE I INTEND TO WREAK UPON BOTH YOUR FACES!
NO MORE PLAGUES, NO MORE FLOODS, NO MORE BRIMSTONE. YOU WANT TO CHALLENGE ME, THEN HAVE THE INTESTINAL DIVINITUDE TO CHALLENGE ME YOURSELVES.
I DEMAND TRIAL BY COMBAT.
HA. THAT'S NOT HOW THE GAME IS PLAYED, LITTLE GIRL-GOD. IF YOU WISH THE HONOR OF FACING US IN COMBAT, YOU MUST FIRST SURVIVE THE CHALLENGE OF ULTIMATE JUDGMENT.
OH, YES. THE ULTIMATE JUDGMENT. I ALMOST FORGOT ABOUT THAT ONE. IS THAT WHAT YOU'RE ASKING US FOR, LITTLE THOR?
IF IT MEANS I GET TO END THIS FARCE BY POUNDING THE TWO OF YOU INTO OBLIVION, THEN AYE, I D--
NO!
YOU SEEM TO BE A GOD OF SOME HONOR, SHADRAK OF OMNIPOTENCE CITY. 'TIS WHY YOU MUST NOT STAND IN MY WAY.
YOU DON'T UNDERSTAND, THOR. YOU CANNOT UNLEASH THE ULTIMATE JUDGMENT. YOU WOULD NEVER SURVIVE. NONE OF US WOULD.
IF YOU WISH TO SAVE YOUR WORLD, I'M AFRAID YOU HAVE NO CHOICE BUT TO PLAY THE GAME.
AH, IT'S JUST TOO BAD SHE'S SO TERRIBLE AT PLAYING IT.
PERHAPS GENOCIDE WILL PROVE YOUR FORTE, EH, THOR?

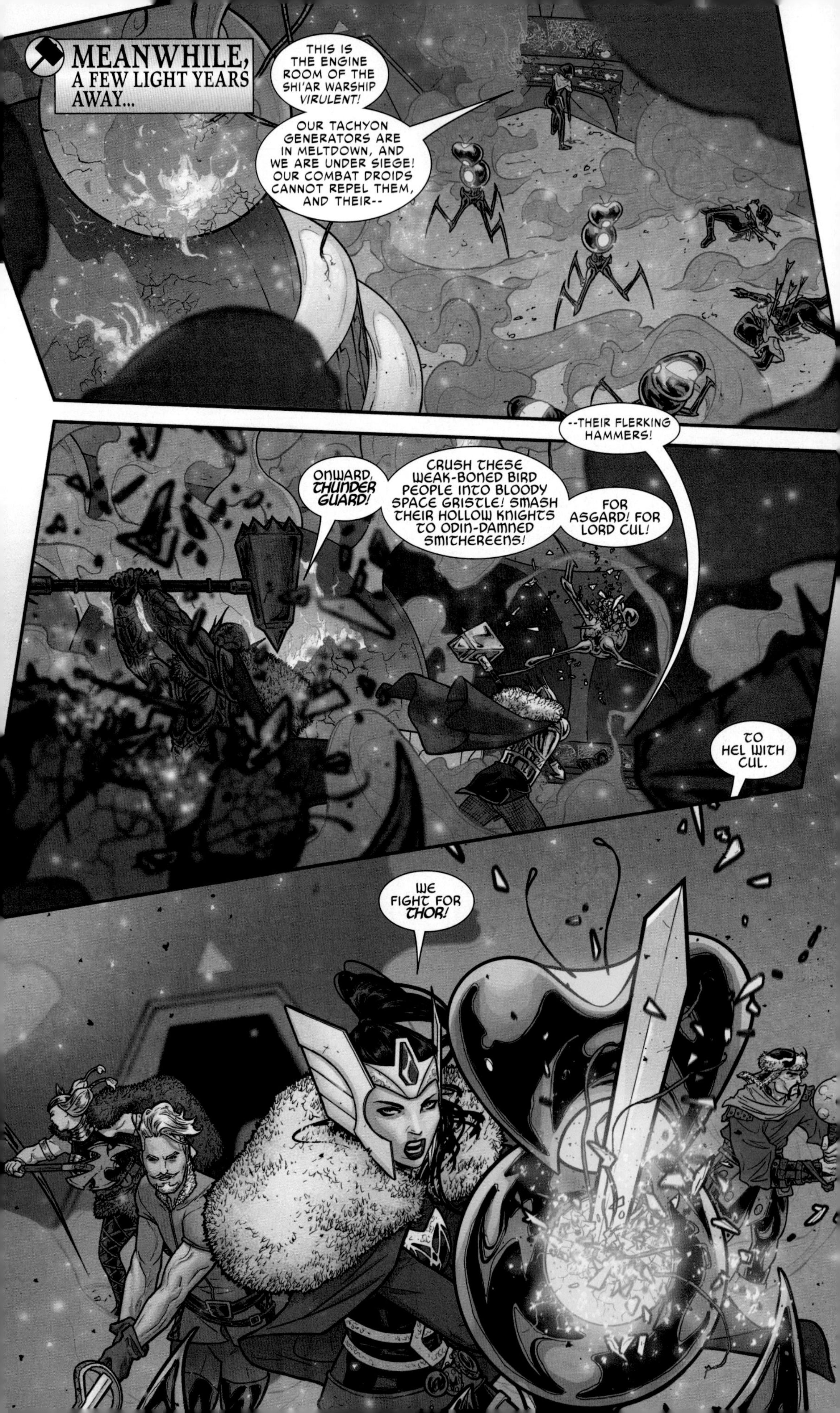
MEANWHILE, A FEW LIGHT YEARS AWAY...
THIS IS THE ENGINE ROOM OF THE SHI'AR WARSHIP *VIRULENT!*
OUR TACHYON GENERATORS ARE IN MELTDOWN, AND WE ARE UNDER SIEGE! OUR COMBAT DROIDS CANNOT REPEL THEM, AND THEIR--
--THEIR FLERKING HAMMERS!
ONWARD, *THUNDER GUARD!*
CRUSH THESE WEAK-BONED BIRD PEOPLE INTO BLOODY SPACE GRISTLE! SMASH THEIR HOLLOW KNIGHTS TO ODIN-DAMNED SMITHEREENS!
FOR ASGARD! FOR LORD CUL!
TO HEL WITH CUL.
WE FIGHT FOR *THOR!*

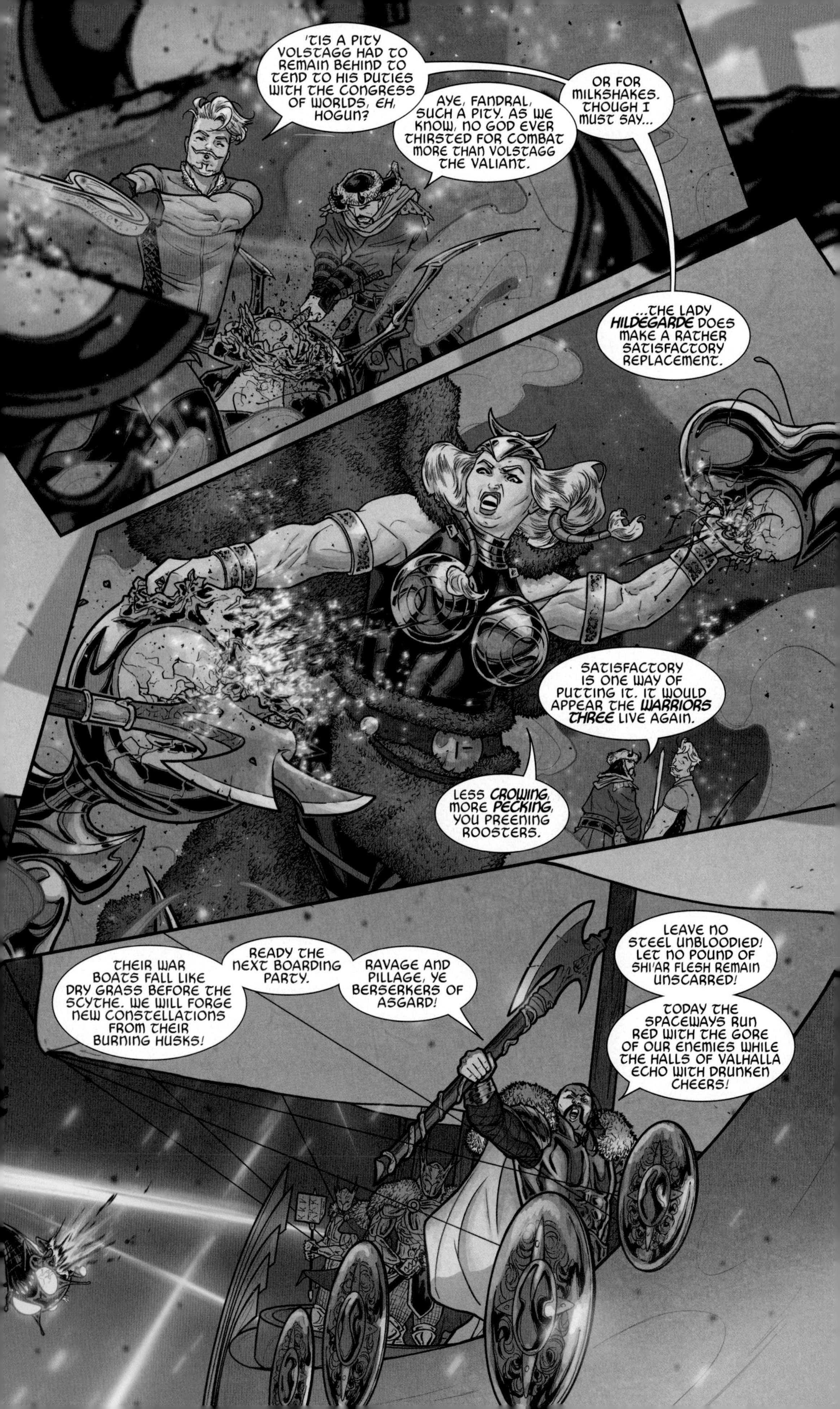

'TIS A PITY VOLSTAGG HAD TO REMAIN BEHIND TO TEND TO HIS DUTIES WITH THE CONGRESS OF WORLDS, EH, HOGUN?
AYE, FANDRAL, SUCH A PITY. AS WE KNOW, NO GOD EVER THIRSTED FOR COMBAT MORE THAN VOLSTAGG THE VALIANT.
OR FOR MILKSHAKES. THOUGH I MUST SAY...
...THE LADY HILDEGARDE DOES MAKE A RATHER SATISFACTORY REPLACEMENT.
SATISFACTORY IS ONE WAY OF PUTTING IT. IT WOULD APPEAR THE WARRIORS THREE LIVE AGAIN.
LESS CROWING, MORE PECKING, YOU PREENING ROOSTERS.
THEIR WAR BOATS FALL LIKE DRY GRASS BEFORE THE SCYTHE. WE WILL FORGE NEW CONSTELLATIONS FROM THEIR BURNING HUSKS!
READY THE NEXT BOARDING PARTY.
RAVAGE AND PILLAGE, YE BERSERKERS OF ASGARD!
LEAVE NO STEEL UNBLOODIED! LET NO POUND OF SHI'AR FLESH REMAIN UNSCARRED!
TODAY THE SPACEWAYS RUN RED WITH THE GORE OF OUR ENEMIES WHILE THE HALLS OF VALHALLA ECHO WITH DRUNKEN CHEERS!

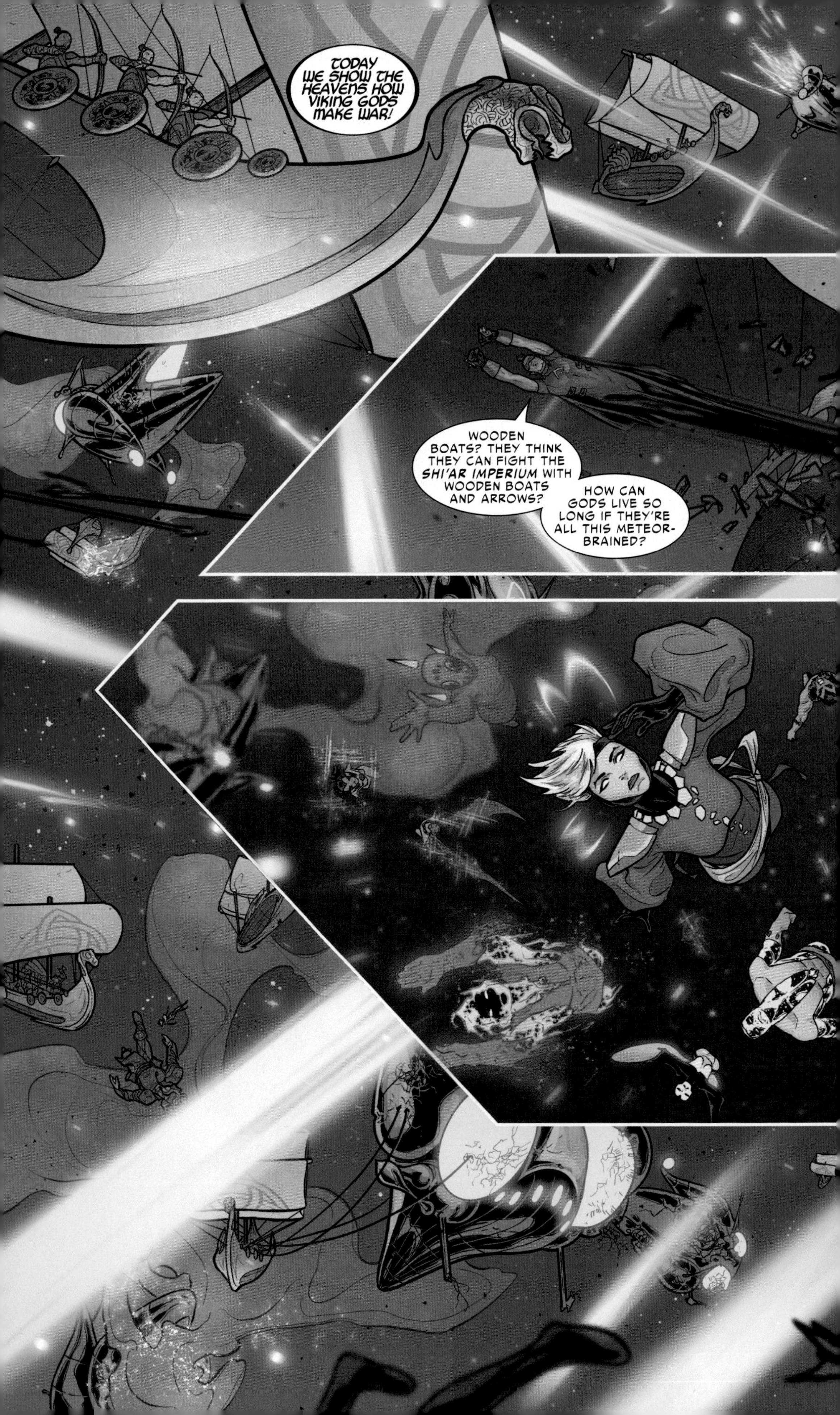
TODAY WE SHOW THE HEAVENS HOW VIKING GODS MAKE WAR!
WOODEN BOATS? THEY THINK THEY CAN FIGHT THE SHI'AR IMPERIUM WITH WOODEN BOATS AND ARROWS?
HOW CAN GODS LIVE SO LONG IF THEY'RE ALL THIS METEOR-BRAINED?

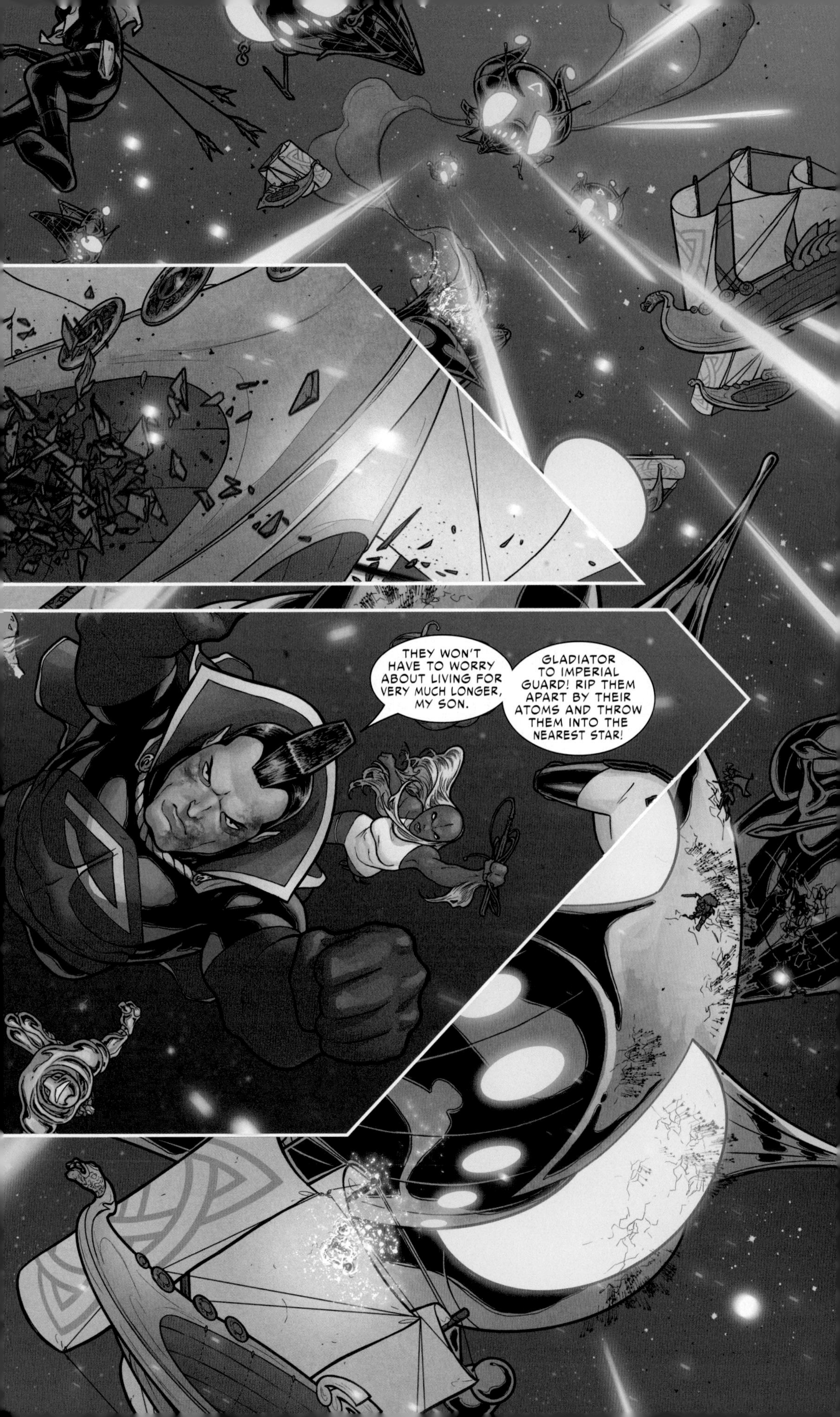
THEY WON'T HAVE TO WORRY ABOUT LIVING FOR VERY MUCH LONGER, MY SON.
GLADIATOR TO IMPERIAL GUARD! RIP THEM APART BY THEIR ATOMS AND THROW THEM INTO THE NEAREST STAR!

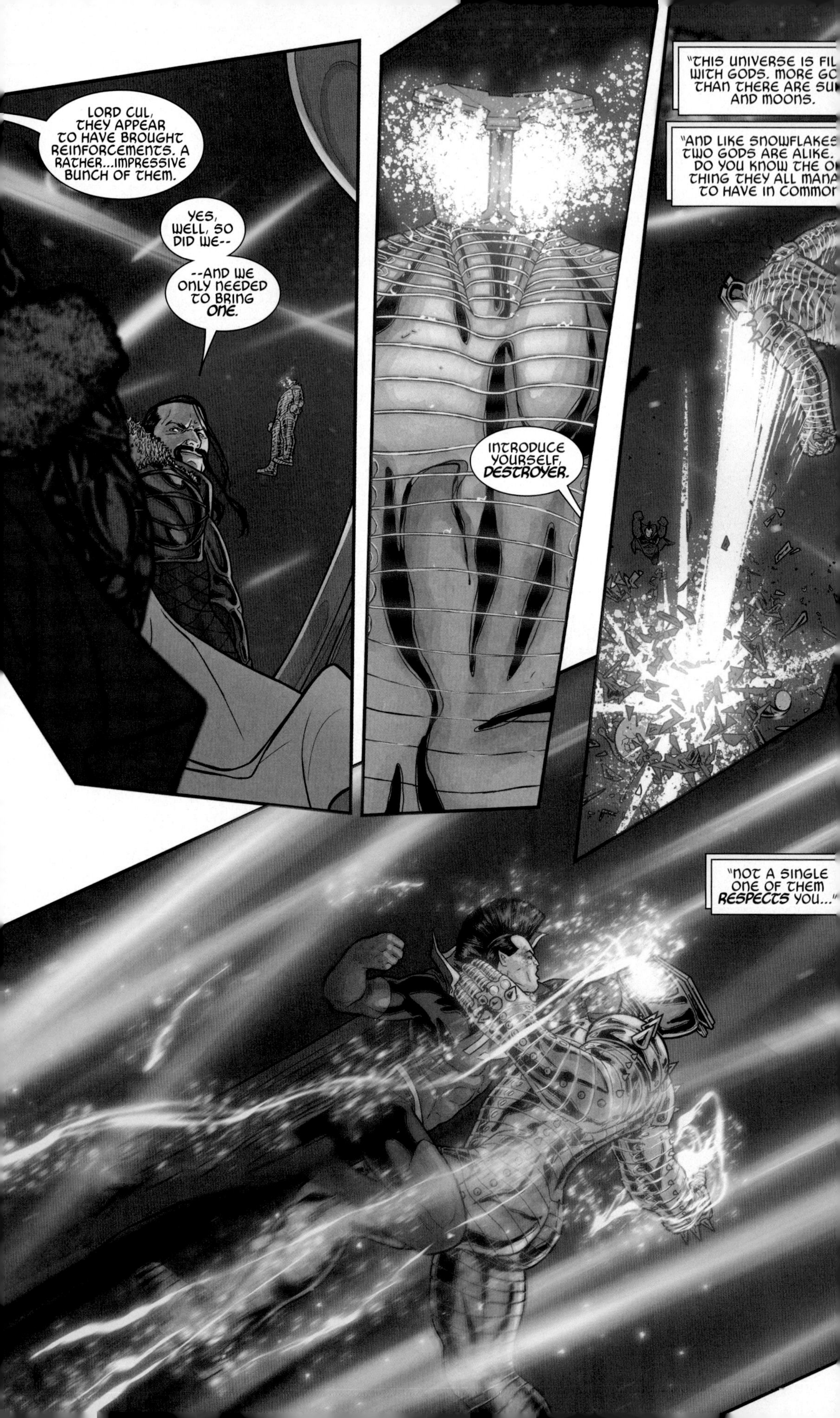
LORD CUL, THEY APPEAR TO HAVE BROUGHT REINFORCEMENTS. A RATHER...IMPRESSIVE BUNCH OF THEM.
YES, WELL, SO DID WE--
--AND WE ONLY NEEDED TO BRING ONE.
INTRODUCE YOURSELF, DESTROYER.
"THIS UNIVERSE IS FIL WITH GODS. MORE GO THAN THERE ARE SU AND MOONS.
"AND LIKE SNOWFLAKES TWO GODS ARE ALIKE. DO YOU KNOW THE O THING THEY ALL MANA TO HAVE IN COMMO
"NOT A SINGLE ONE OF THEM RESPECTS YOU..."

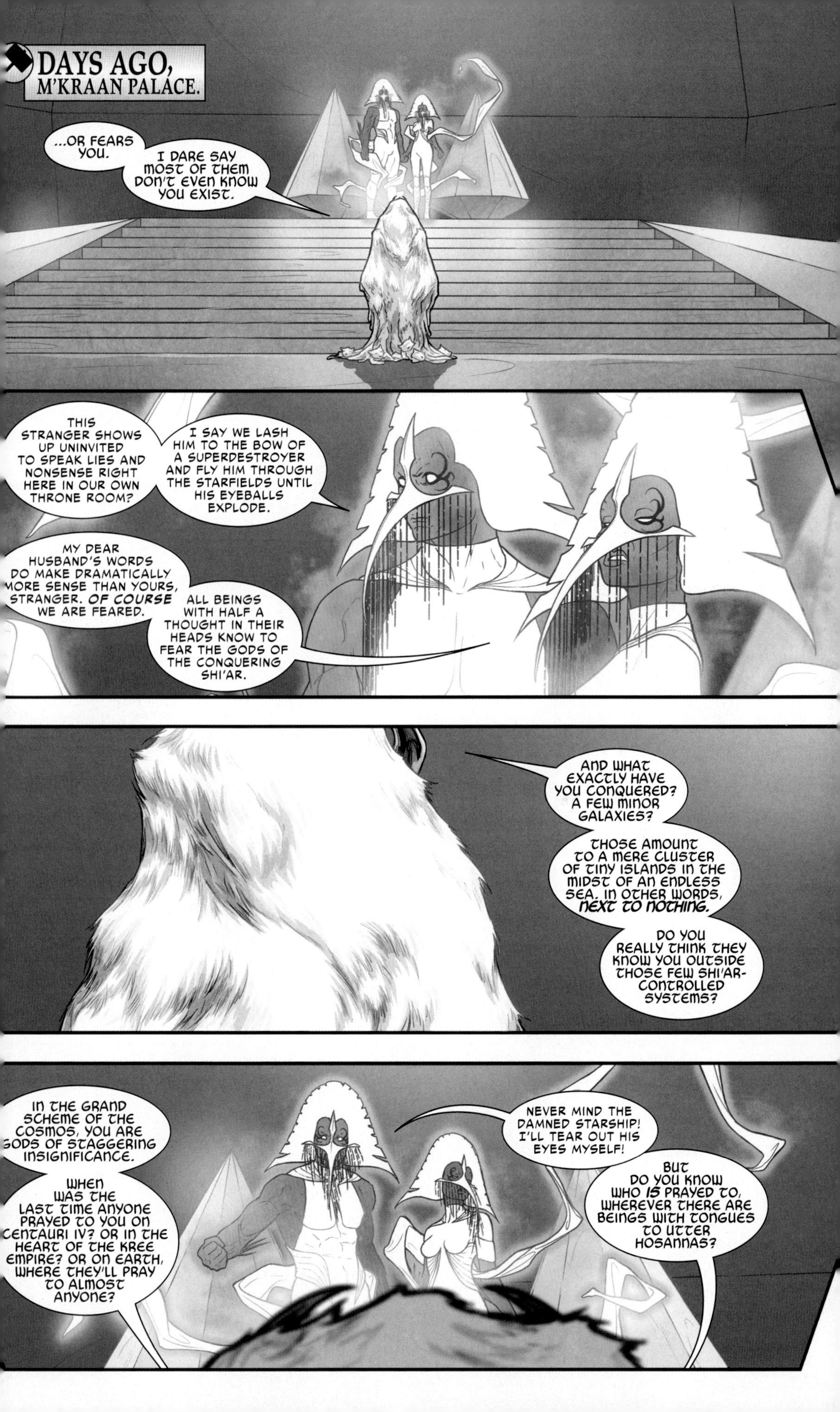
DAYS AGO, M'KRAAN PALACE.
...OR FEARS YOU.
I DARE SAY MOST OF THEM DON'T EVEN KNOW YOU EXIST.
THIS STRANGER SHOWS UP UNINVITED TO SPEAK LIES AND NONSENSE RIGHT HERE IN OUR OWN THRONE ROOM?
I SAY WE LASH HIM TO THE BOW OF A SUPERDESTROYER AND FLY HIM THROUGH THE STARFIELDS UNTIL HIS EYEBALLS EXPLODE.
MY DEAR HUSBAND'S WORDS DO MAKE DRAMATICALLY MORE SENSE THAN YOURS, STRANGER. *OF COURSE* WE ARE FEARED.
ALL BEINGS WITH HALF A THOUGHT IN THEIR HEADS KNOW TO FEAR THE GODS OF THE CONQUERING SHI'AR.
AND WHAT EXACTLY HAVE YOU CONQUERED? A FEW MINOR GALAXIES?
THOSE AMOUNT TO A MERE CLUSTER OF TINY ISLANDS IN THE MIDST OF AN ENDLESS SEA. IN OTHER WORDS, *NEXT TO NOTHING.*
DO YOU REALLY THINK THEY KNOW YOU OUTSIDE THOSE FEW SHI'AR-CONTROLLED SYSTEMS?
IN THE GRAND SCHEME OF THE COSMOS, YOU ARE GODS OF STAGGERING INSIGNIFICANCE.
WHEN WAS THE LAST TIME ANYONE PRAYED TO YOU ON CENTAURI IV? OR IN THE HEART OF THE KREE EMPIRE? OR ON EARTH, WHERE THEY'LL PRAY TO ALMOST ANYONE?
NEVER MIND THE DAMNED STARSHIP! I'LL TEAR OUT HIS EYES MYSELF!
BUT DO YOU KNOW WHO *IS* PRAYED TO, WHEREVER THERE ARE BEINGS WITH TONGUES TO UTTER HOSANNAS?

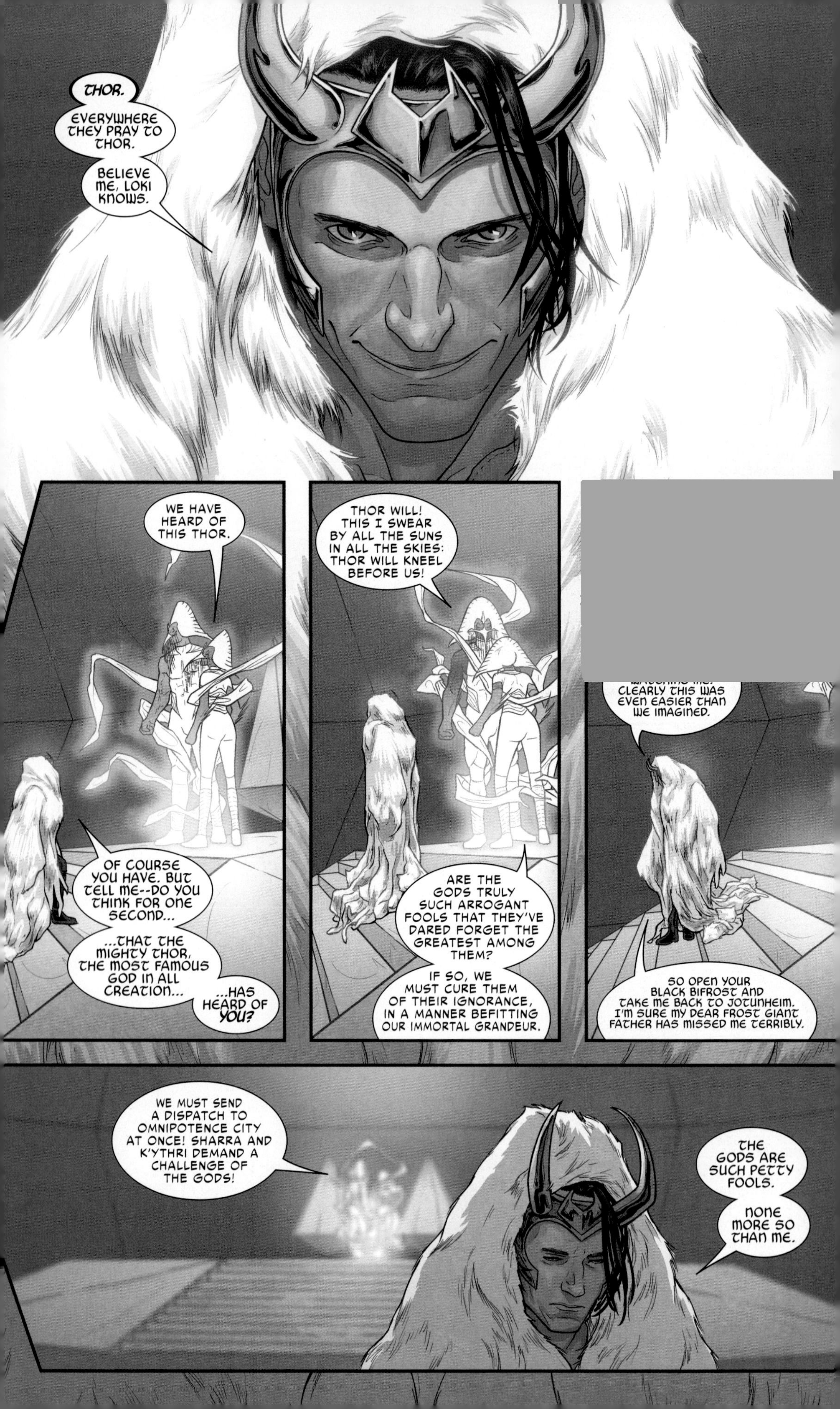
THOR.
EVERYWHERE THEY PRAY TO THOR.
BELIEVE ME, LOKI KNOWS.
WE HAVE HEARD OF THIS THOR.
OF COURSE YOU HAVE. BUT TELL ME--DO YOU THINK FOR ONE SECOND...
...THAT THE MIGHTY THOR, THE MOST FAMOUS GOD IN ALL CREATION...
...HAS HEARD OF YOU?
THOR WILL! THIS I SWEAR BY ALL THE SUNS IN ALL THE SKIES: THOR WILL KNEEL BEFORE US!
ARE THE GODS TRULY SUCH ARROGANT FOOLS THAT THEY'VE DARED FORGET THE GREATEST AMONG THEM?
IF SO, WE MUST CURE THEM OF THEIR IGNORANCE, IN A MANNER BEFITTING OUR IMMORTAL GRANDEUR.
CLEARLY THIS WAS EVEN EASIER THAN WE IMAGINED.
SO OPEN YOUR BLACK BIFROST AND TAKE ME BACK TO JOTUNHEIM. I'M SURE MY DEAR FROST GIANT FATHER HAS MISSED ME TERRIBLY.
WE MUST SEND A DISPATCH TO OMNIPOTENCE CITY AT ONCE! SHARRA AND K'YTHRI DEMAND A CHALLENGE OF THE GODS!
THE GODS ARE SUCH PETTY FOOLS.
NONE MORE SO THAN ME.

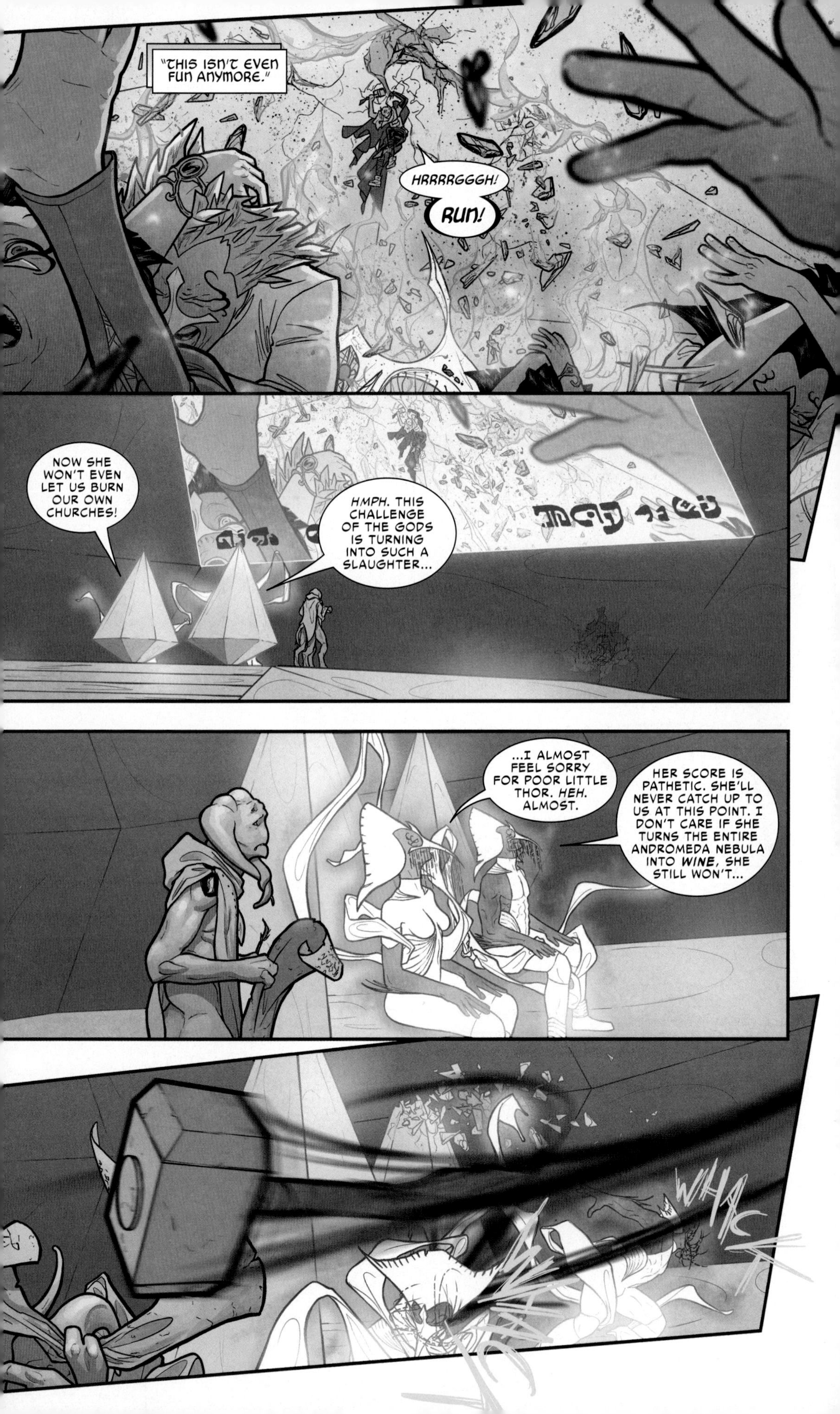
"THIS ISN'T EVEN FUN ANYMORE."
HRRRRGGGH!
RUN!
NOW SHE WON'T EVEN LET US BURN OUR OWN CHURCHES!
HMPH. THIS CHALLENGE OF THE GODS IS TURNING INTO SUCH A SLAUGHTER...
...I ALMOST FEEL SORRY FOR POOR LITTLE THOR. HEH. ALMOST.
HER SCORE IS PATHETIC. SHE'LL NEVER CATCH UP TO US AT THIS POINT. I DON'T CARE IF SHE TURNS THE ENTIRE ANDROMEDA NEBULA INTO WINE, SHE STILL WON'T...
WHACK

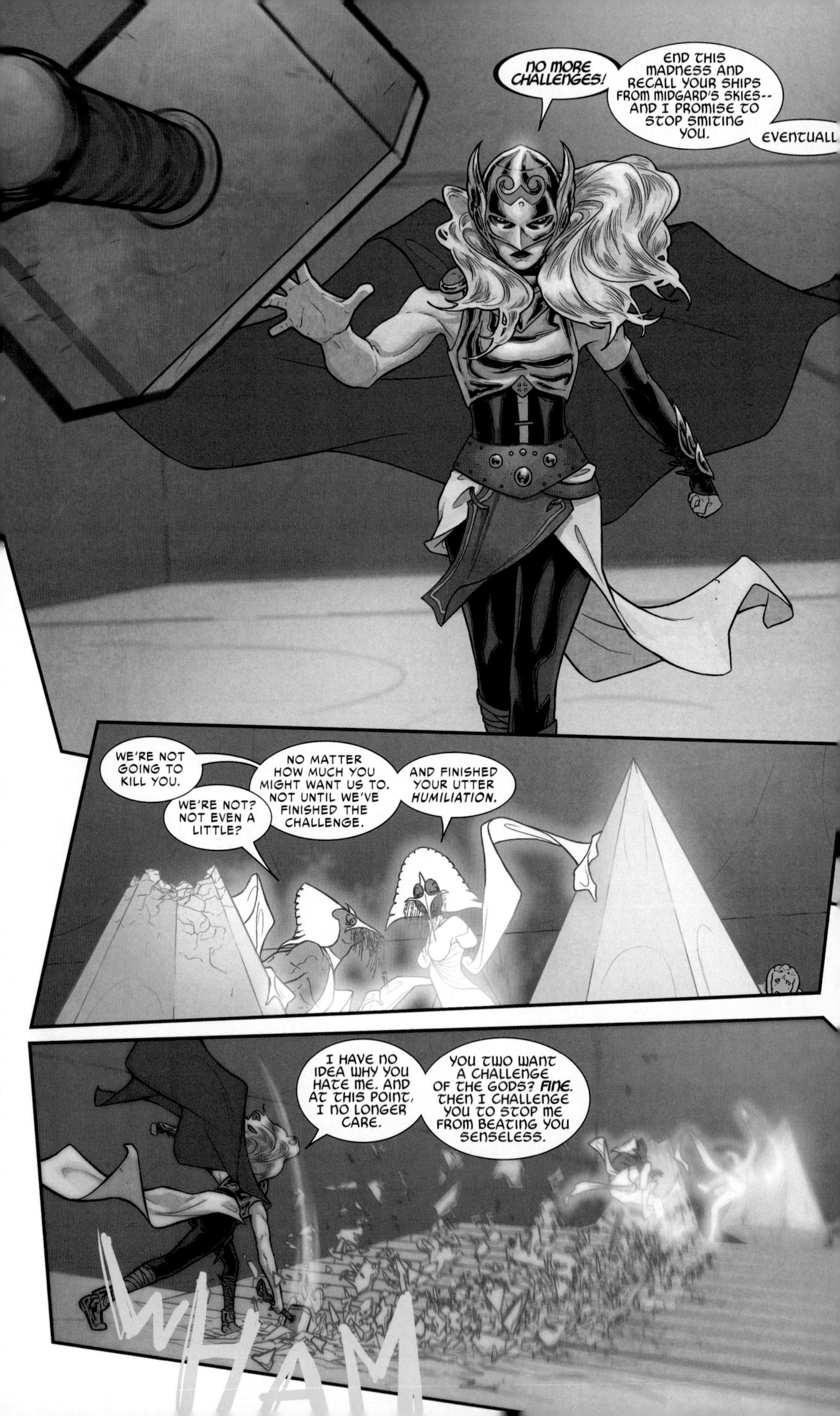

NO MORE CHALLENGES!
END THIS MADNESS AND RECALL YOUR SHIPS FROM MIDGARD'S SKIES-- AND I PROMISE TO STOP SMITING YOU.
EVENTUALL
WE'RE NOT GOING TO KILL YOU.
WE'RE NOT? NOT EVEN A LITTLE?
NO MATTER HOW MUCH YOU MIGHT WANT US TO. NOT UNTIL WE'VE FINISHED THE CHALLENGE.
AND FINISHED YOUR UTTER HUMILIATION.
I HAVE NO IDEA WHY YOU HATE ME. AND AT THIS POINT, I NO LONGER CARE.
YOU TWO WANT A CHALLENGE OF THE GODS? FINE. THEN I CHALLENGE YOU TO STOP ME FROM BEATING YOU SENSELESS.
WHAM

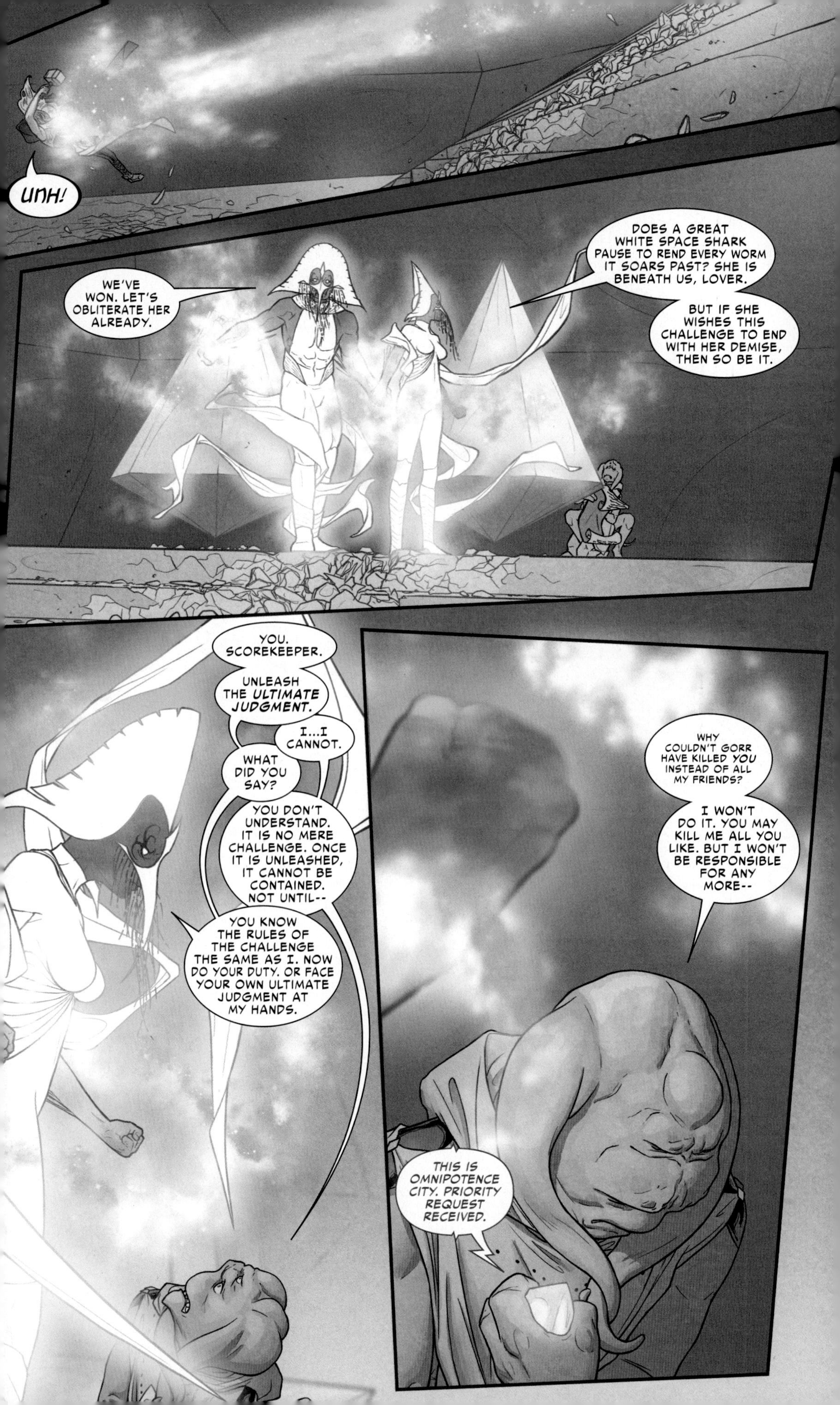
UNH!
WE'VE WON. LET'S OBLITERATE HER ALREADY.
DOES A GREAT WHITE SPACE SHARK PAUSE TO REND EVERY WORM IT SOARS PAST? SHE IS BENEATH US, LOVER.
BUT IF SHE WISHES THIS CHALLENGE TO END WITH HER DEMISE, THEN SO BE IT.
YOU. SCOREKEEPER.
UNLEASH THE *ULTIMATE JUDGMENT.*
I...I CANNOT.
WHAT DID YOU SAY?
YOU DON'T UNDERSTAND. IT IS NO MERE CHALLENGE. ONCE IT IS UNLEASHED, IT CANNOT BE CONTAINED. NOT UNTIL--
YOU KNOW THE RULES OF THE CHALLENGE THE SAME AS I. NOW DO YOUR DUTY. OR FACE YOUR OWN ULTIMATE JUDGMENT AT MY HANDS.
WHY COULDN'T GORR HAVE KILLED *YOU* INSTEAD OF ALL MY FRIENDS?
I WON'T DO IT. YOU MAY KILL ME ALL YOU LIKE. BUT I WON'T BE RESPONSIBLE FOR ANY MORE--
THIS IS OMNIPOTENCE CITY. PRIORITY REQUEST RECEIVED.

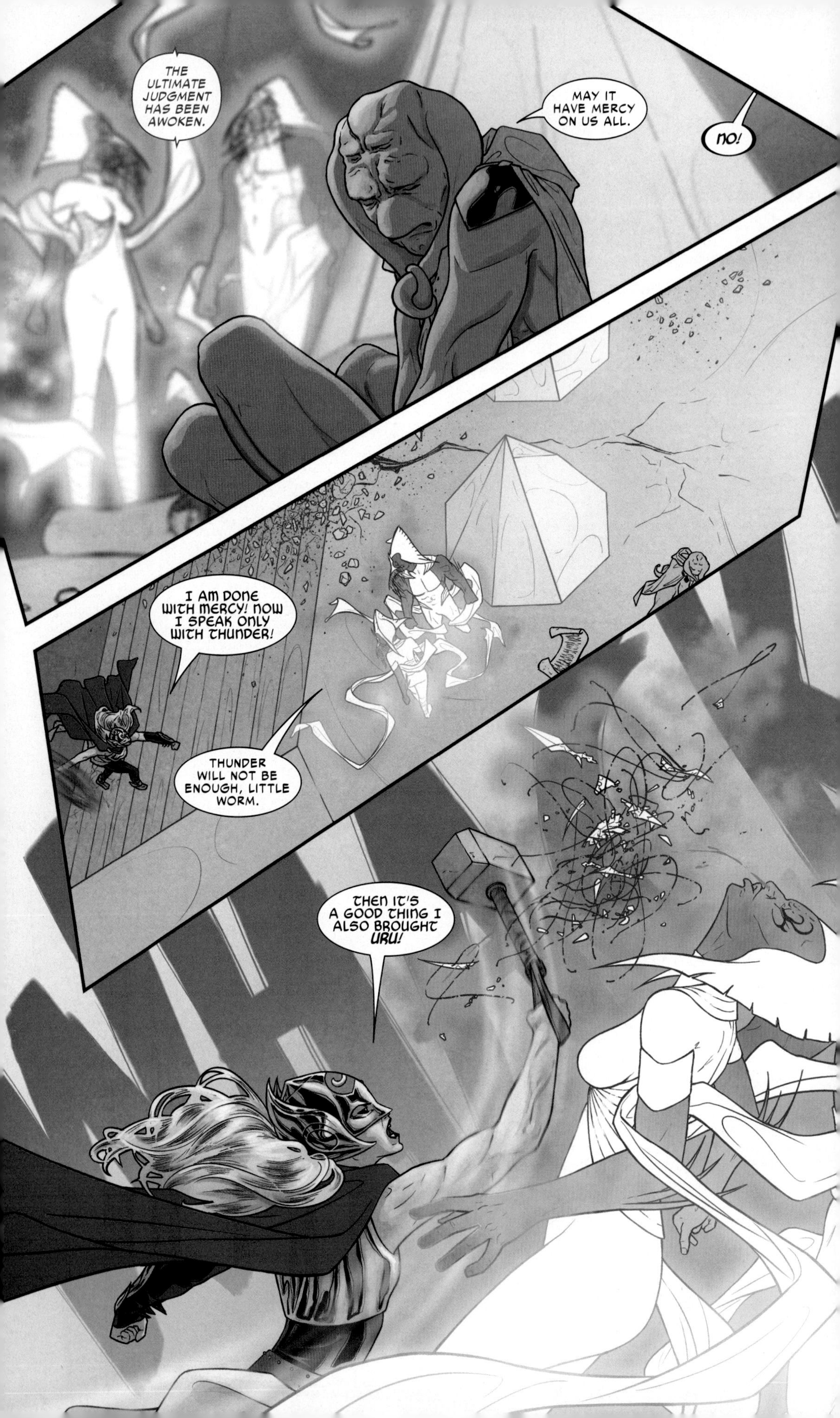
THE ULTIMATE JUDGMENT HAS BEEN AWOKEN.
MAY IT HAVE MERCY ON US ALL.
NO!
I AM DONE WITH MERCY! NOW I SPEAK ONLY WITH THUNDER!
THUNDER WILL NOT BE ENOUGH, LITTLE WORM.
THEN IT'S A GOOD THING I ALSO BROUGHT URU!

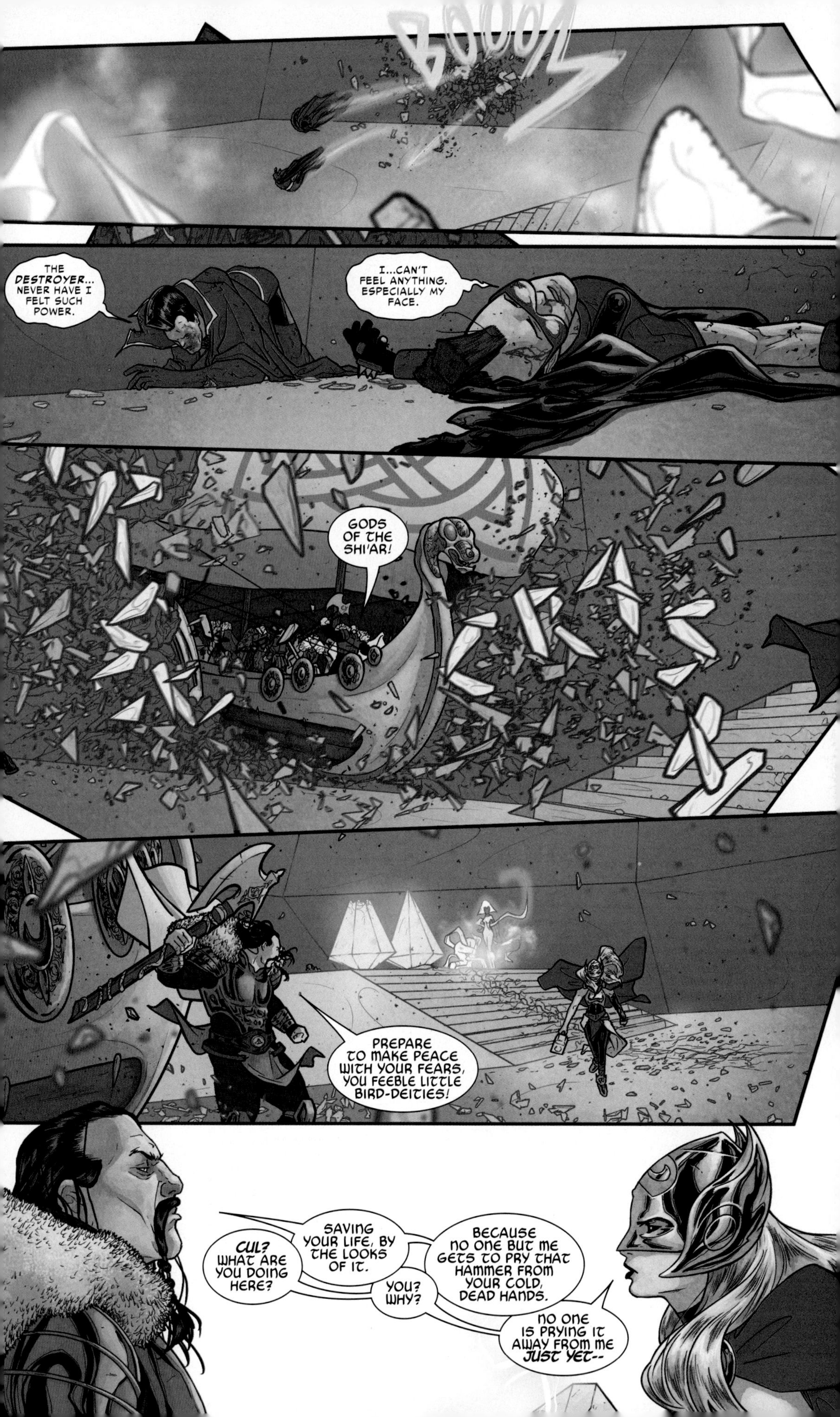
BOOOM
THE DESTROYER... NEVER HAVE I FELT SUCH POWER.
I...CAN'T FEEL ANYTHING. ESPECIALLY MY FACE.
GODS OF THE SHI'AR!
PREPARE TO MAKE PEACE WITH YOUR FEARS, YOU FEEBLE LITTLE BIRD-DEITIES!
CUL? WHAT ARE YOU DOING HERE?
SAVING YOUR LIFE, BY THE LOOKS OF IT.
YOU? WHY?
BECAUSE NO ONE BUT ME GETS TO PRY THAT HAMMER FROM YOUR COLD, DEAD HANDS.
NO ONE IS PRYING IT AWAY FROM ME JUST YET--

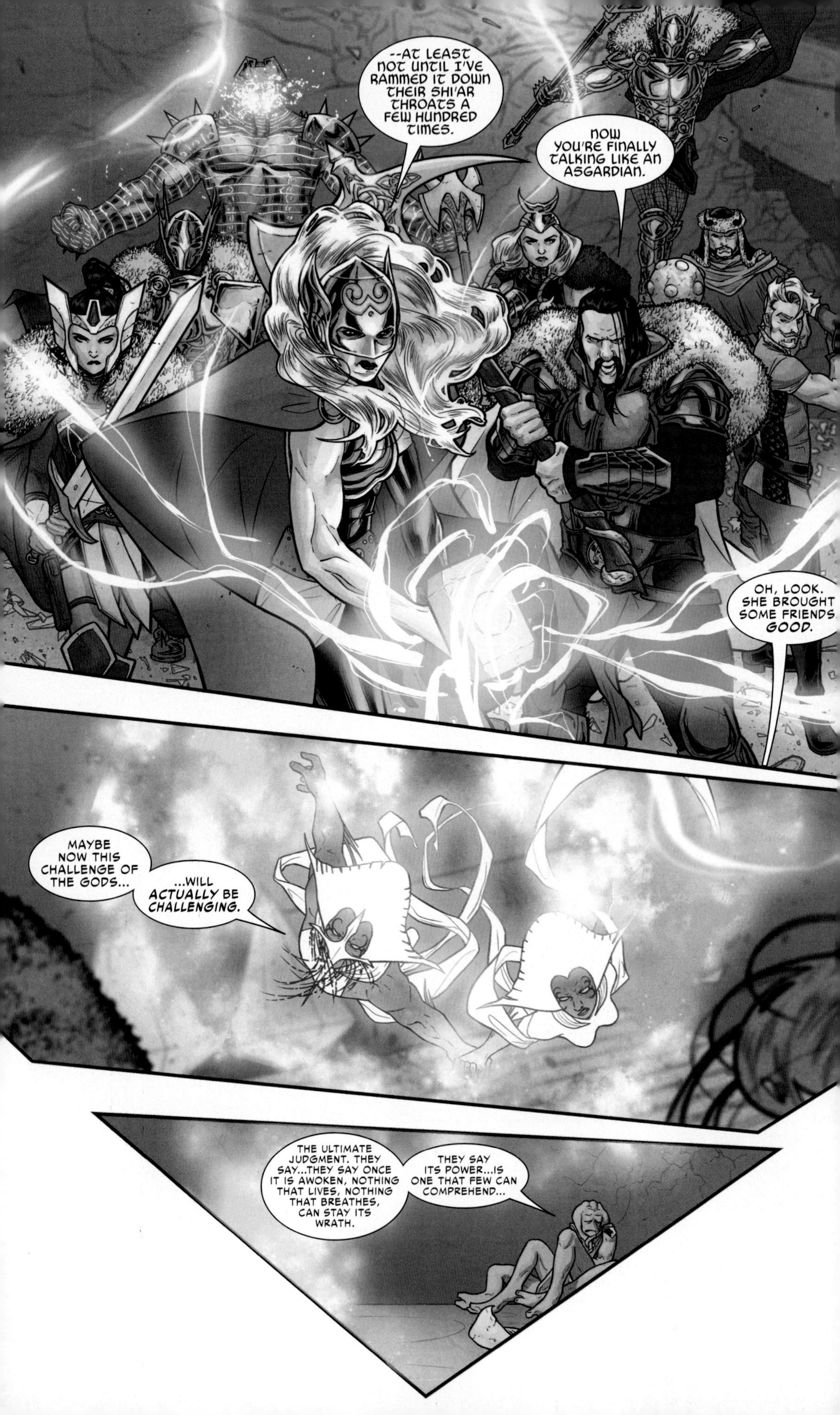
--AT LEAST NOT UNTIL I'VE RAMMED IT DOWN THEIR SHI'AR THROATS A FEW HUNDRED TIMES.
NOW YOU'RE FINALLY TALKING LIKE AN ASGARDIAN.
OH, LOOK. SHE BROUGHT SOME FRIENDS. GOOD.
MAYBE NOW THIS CHALLENGE OF THE GODS...
...WILL ACTUALLY BE CHALLENGING.
THE ULTIMATE JUDGMENT. THEY SAY...THEY SAY ONCE IT IS AWOKEN, NOTHING THAT LIVES, NOTHING THAT BREATHES, CAN STAY ITS WRATH.
THEY SAY ITS POWER...IS ONE THAT FEW CAN COMPREHEND...

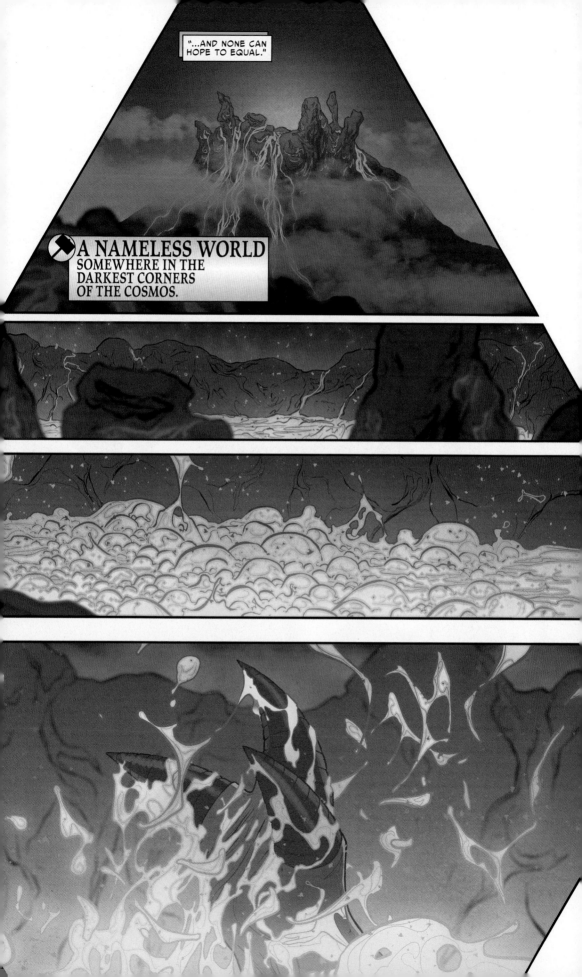

"...AND NONE CAN HOPE TO EQUAL."

A NAMELESS WORLD
SOMEWHERE IN THE DARKEST CORNERS OF THE COSMOS.

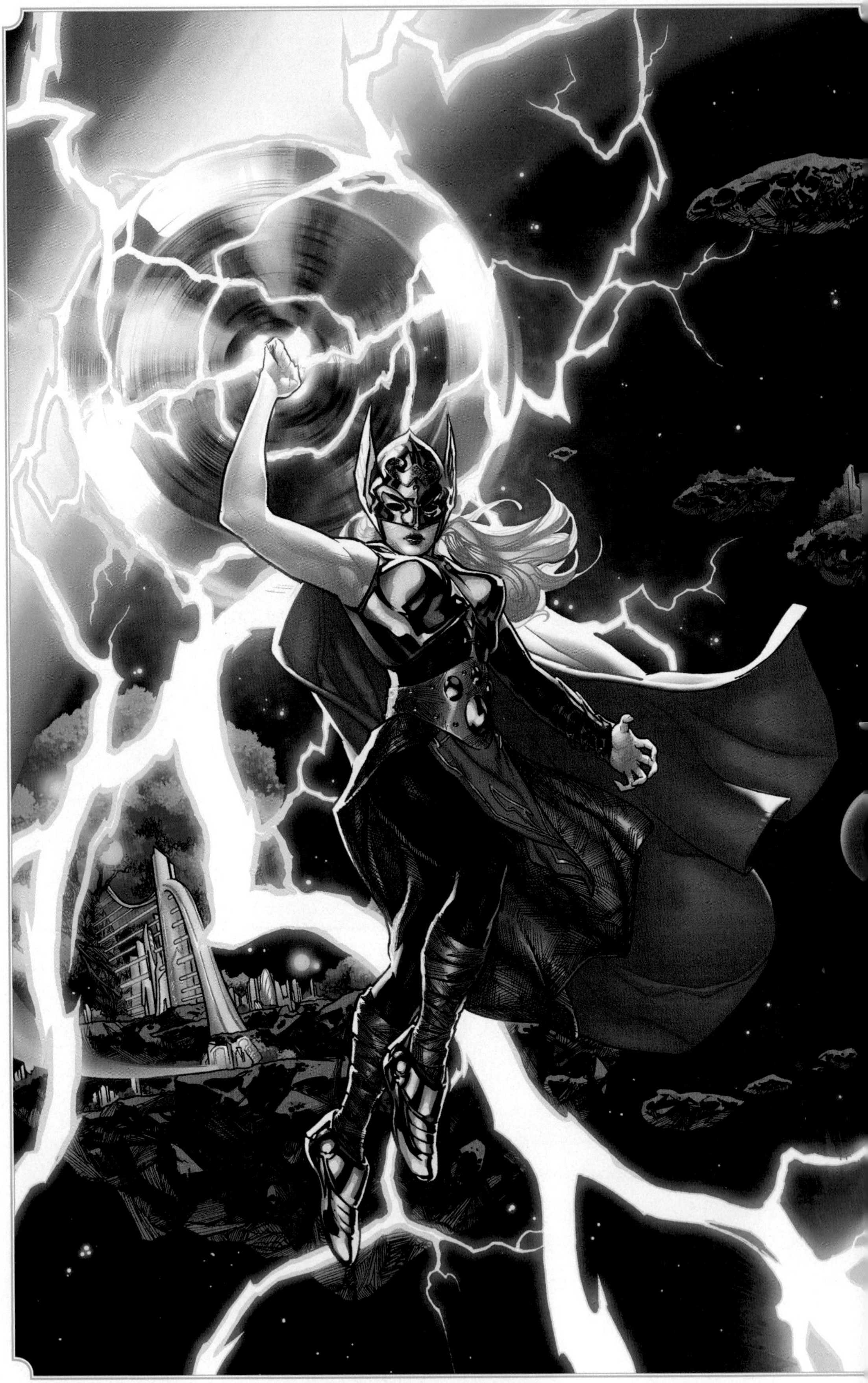

MIGHTY THOR # 15 VARIANT
BY **RYAN SOOK**

18

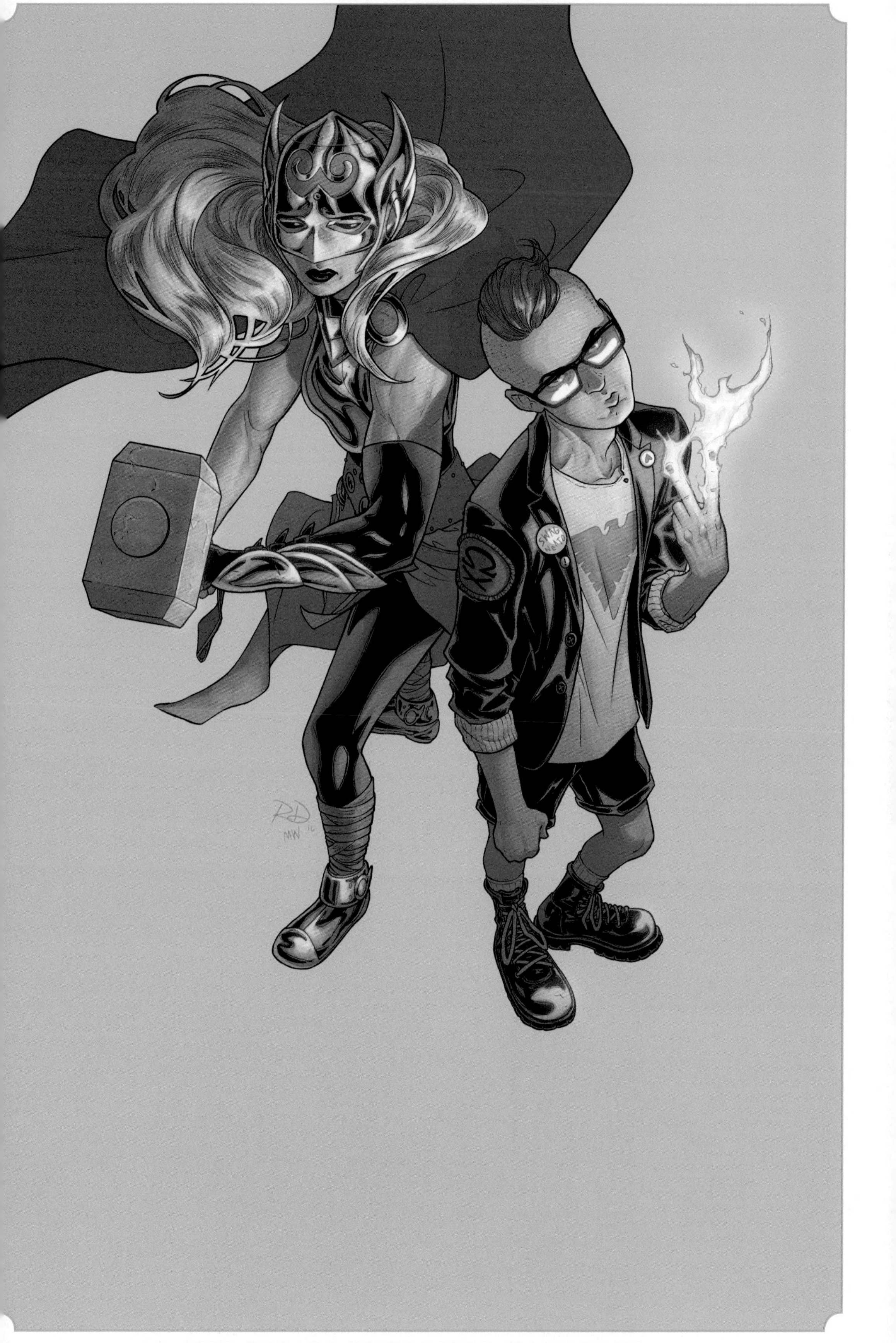

THE ASGARD/SHI'AR WAR, PART FOUR:
THE OMEGA KISS

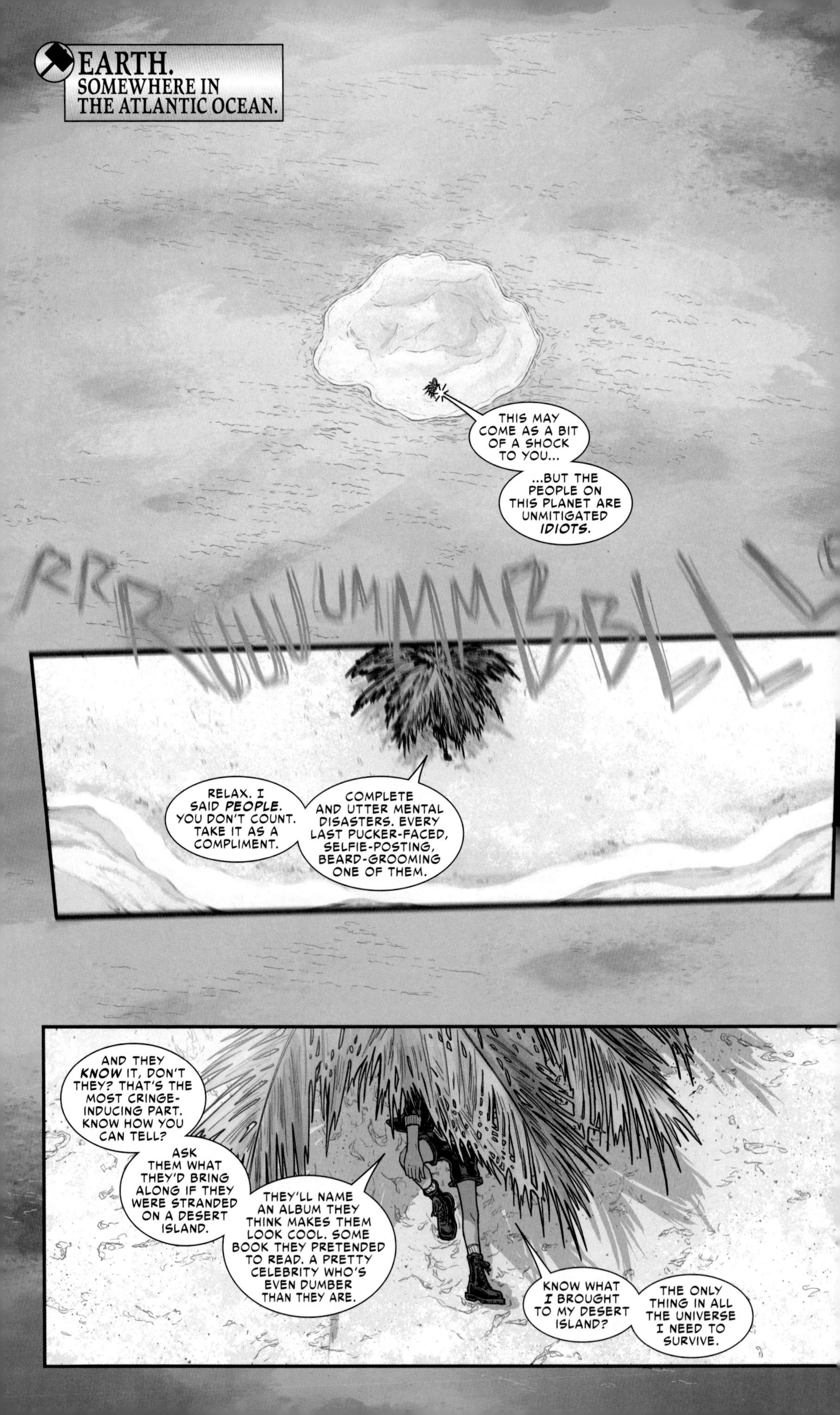
EARTH.
SOMEWHERE IN THE ATLANTIC OCEAN.
THIS MAY COME AS A BIT OF A SHOCK TO YOU...
...BUT THE PEOPLE ON THIS PLANET ARE UNMITIGATED IDIOTS.
RRRUUUMMMBBLLE
COMPLETE AND UTTER MENTAL DISASTERS. EVERY LAST PUCKER-FACED, SELFIE-POSTING, BEARD-GROOMING ONE OF THEM.
RELAX. I SAID PEOPLE. YOU DON'T COUNT. TAKE IT AS A COMPLIMENT.
AND THEY KNOW IT, DON'T THEY? THAT'S THE MOST CRINGE-INDUCING PART. KNOW HOW YOU CAN TELL?
ASK THEM WHAT THEY'D BRING ALONG IF THEY WERE STRANDED ON A DESERT ISLAND.
THEY'LL NAME AN ALBUM THEY THINK MAKES THEM LOOK COOL. SOME BOOK THEY PRETENDED TO READ. A PRETTY CELEBRITY WHO'S EVEN DUMBER THAN THEY ARE.
KNOW WHAT I BROUGHT TO MY DESERT ISLAND?
THE ONLY THING IN ALL THE UNIVERSE I NEED TO SURVIVE.

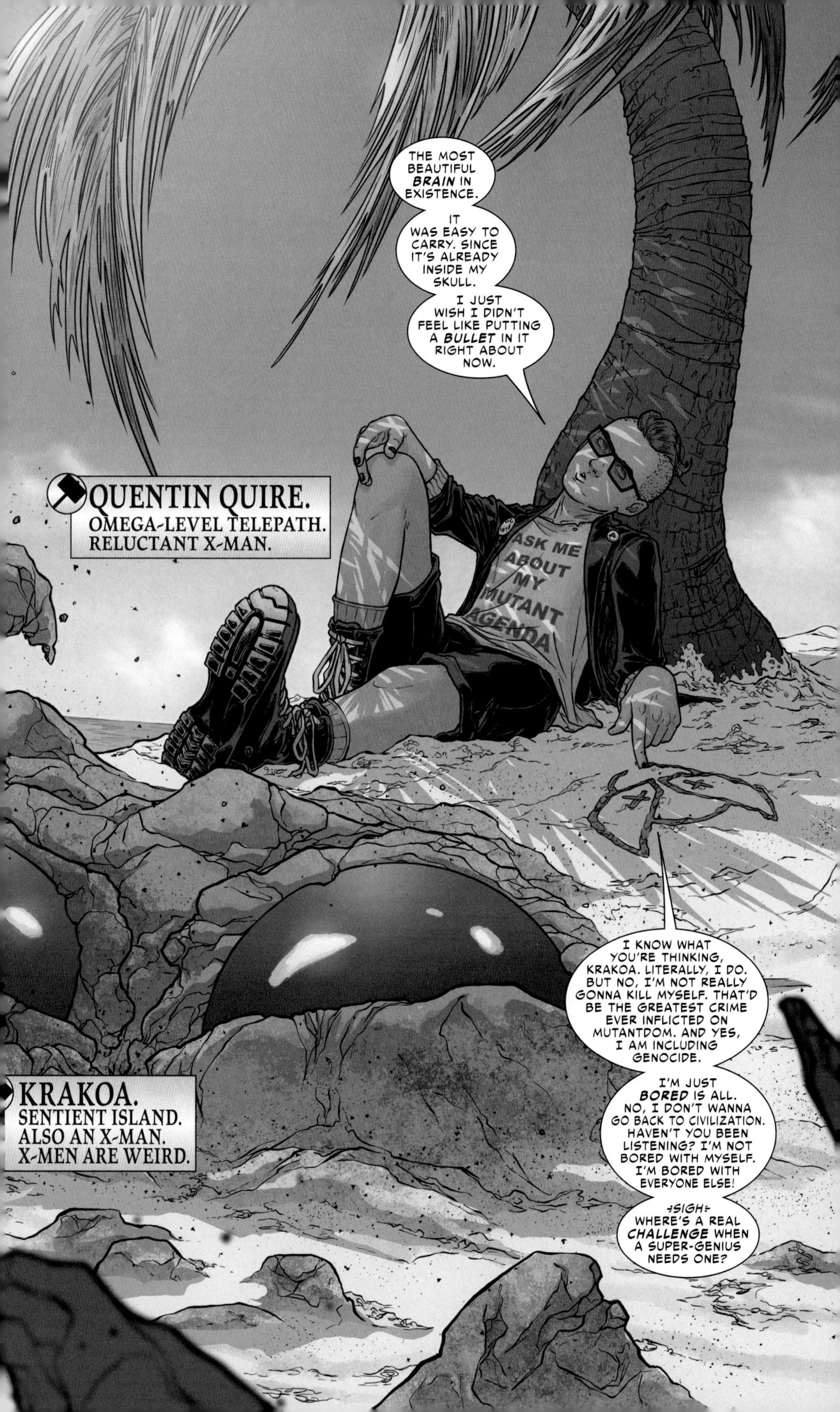
THE MOST BEAUTIFUL BRAIN IN EXISTENCE.
IT WAS EASY TO CARRY. SINCE IT'S ALREADY INSIDE MY SKULL.
I JUST WISH I DIDN'T FEEL LIKE PUTTING A BULLET IN IT RIGHT ABOUT NOW.
QUENTIN QUIRE. OMEGA-LEVEL TELEPATH. RELUCTANT X-MAN.
ASK ME ABOUT MY MUTANT AGENDA
I KNOW WHAT YOU'RE THINKING, KRAKOA. LITERALLY, I DO. BUT NO, I'M NOT REALLY GONNA KILL MYSELF. THAT'D BE THE GREATEST CRIME EVER INFLICTED ON MUTANTDOM. AND YES, I AM INCLUDING GENOCIDE.
I'M JUST BORED IS ALL. NO, I DON'T WANNA GO BACK TO CIVILIZATION. HAVEN'T YOU BEEN LISTENING? I'M NOT BORED WITH MYSELF. I'M BORED WITH EVERYONE ELSE!
KRAKOA. SENTIENT ISLAND. ALSO AN X-MAN. X-MEN ARE WEIRD.
⇒SIGH⇐ WHERE'S A REAL CHALLENGE WHEN A SUPER-GENIUS NEEDS ONE?

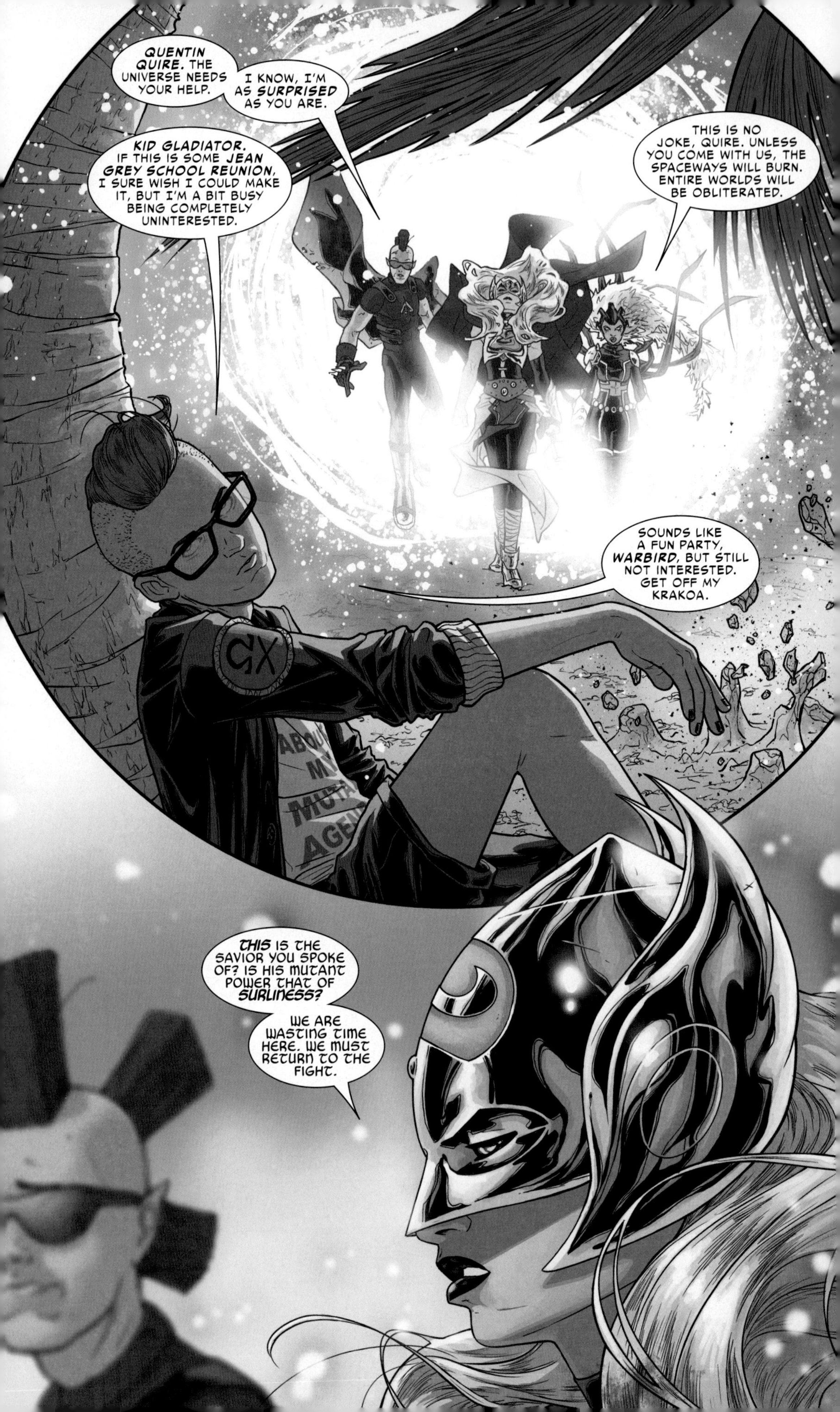
QUENTIN QUIRE. THE UNIVERSE NEEDS YOUR HELP.
I KNOW, I'M AS SURPRISED AS YOU ARE.
KID GLADIATOR. IF THIS IS SOME JEAN GREY SCHOOL REUNION, I SURE WISH I COULD MAKE IT, BUT I'M A BIT BUSY BEING COMPLETELY UNINTERESTED.
THIS IS NO JOKE, QUIRE. UNLESS YOU COME WITH US, THE SPACEWAYS WILL BURN. ENTIRE WORLDS WILL BE OBLITERATED.
SOUNDS LIKE A FUN PARTY, WARBIRD, BUT STILL NOT INTERESTED. GET OFF MY KRAKOA.
THIS IS THE SAVIOR YOU SPOKE OF? IS HIS MUTANT POWER THAT OF SURLINESS?
WE ARE WASTING TIME HERE. WE MUST RETURN TO THE FIGHT.

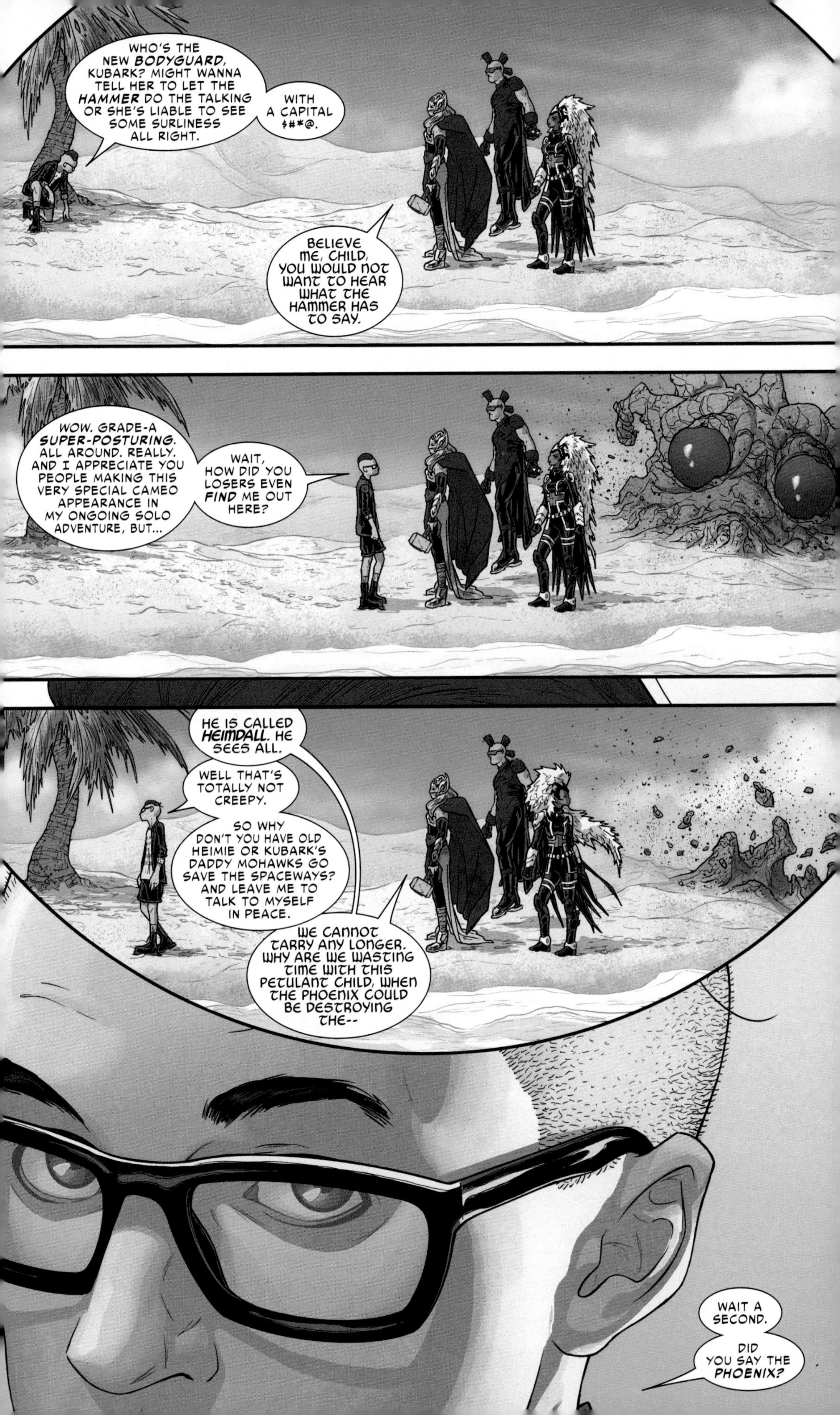
WHO'S THE NEW BODYGUARD, KUBARK? MIGHT WANNA TELL HER TO LET THE HAMMER DO THE TALKING OR SHE'S LIABLE TO SEE SOME SURLINESS ALL RIGHT.
WITH A CAPITAL $#*@.
BELIEVE ME, CHILD, YOU WOULD NOT WANT TO HEAR WHAT THE HAMMER HAS TO SAY.
WOW. GRADE-A SUPER-POSTURING. ALL AROUND. REALLY. AND I APPRECIATE YOU PEOPLE MAKING THIS VERY SPECIAL CAMEO APPEARANCE IN MY ONGOING SOLO ADVENTURE, BUT...
WAIT, HOW DID YOU LOSERS EVEN FIND ME OUT HERE?
HE IS CALLED HEIMDALL. HE SEES ALL.
WELL THAT'S TOTALLY NOT CREEPY.
SO WHY DON'T YOU HAVE OLD HEIMIE OR KUBARK'S DADDY MOHAWKS GO SAVE THE SPACEWAYS? AND LEAVE ME TO TALK TO MYSELF IN PEACE.
WE CANNOT TARRY ANY LONGER. WHY ARE WE WASTING TIME WITH THIS PETULANT CHILD, WHEN THE PHOENIX COULD BE DESTROYING THE--
WAIT A SECOND.
DID YOU SAY THE PHOENIX?

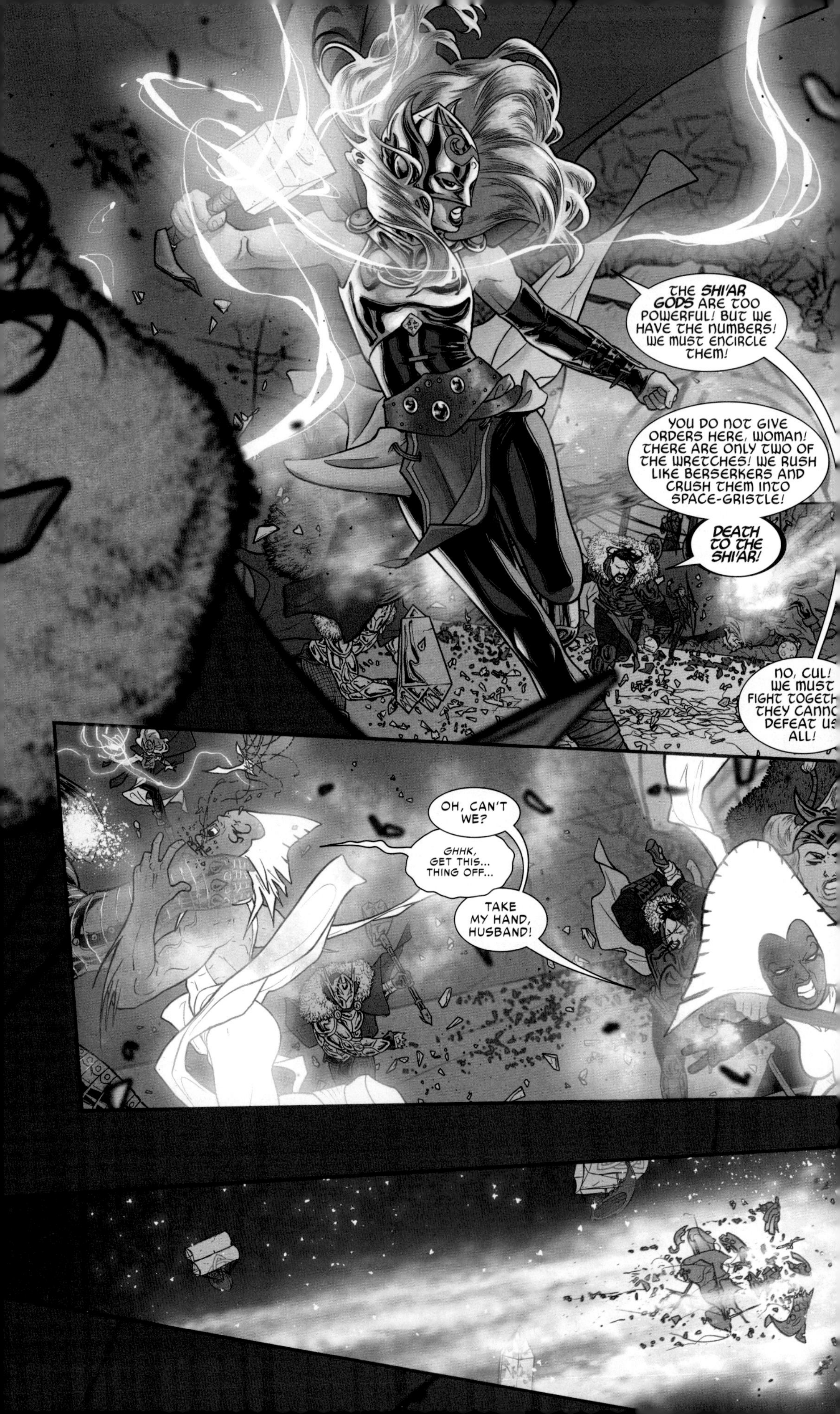
THE SHI'AR GODS ARE TOO POWERFUL! BUT WE HAVE THE NUMBERS! WE MUST ENCIRCLE THEM!
YOU DO NOT GIVE ORDERS HERE, WOMAN! THERE ARE ONLY TWO OF THE WRETCHES! WE RUSH LIKE BERSERKERS AND CRUSH THEM INTO SPACE-GRISTLE!
DEATH TO THE SHI'AR!
NO, CUL! WE MUST FIGHT TOGETH THEY CANNO DEFEAT US ALL!
OH, CAN'T WE?
GHHK, GET THIS... THING OFF...
TAKE MY HAND, HUSBAND!

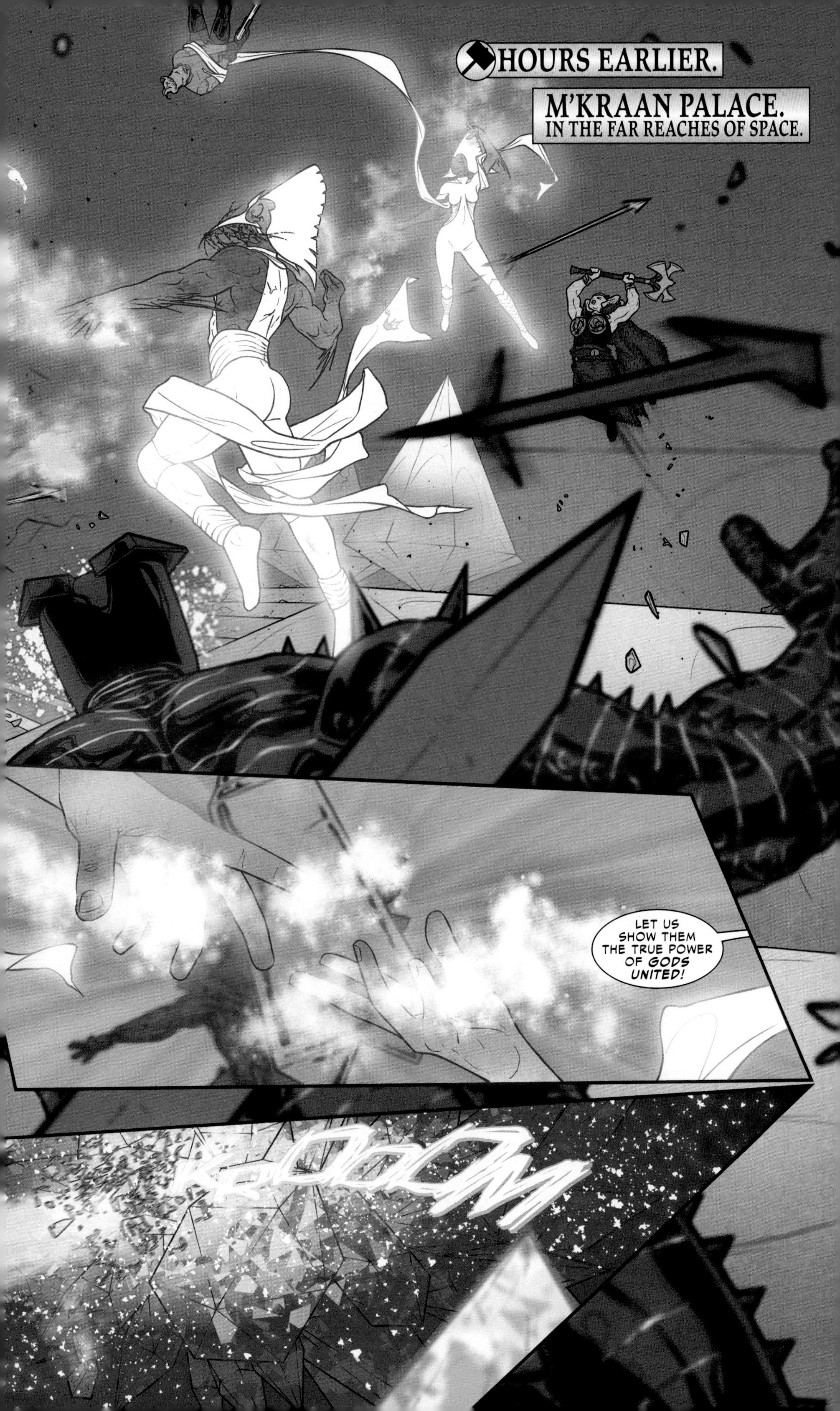
HOURS EARLIER.
M'KRAAN PALACE.
IN THE FAR REACHES OF SPACE.
LET US SHOW THEM THE TRUE POWER OF GODS UNITED!
KRAOOOOM

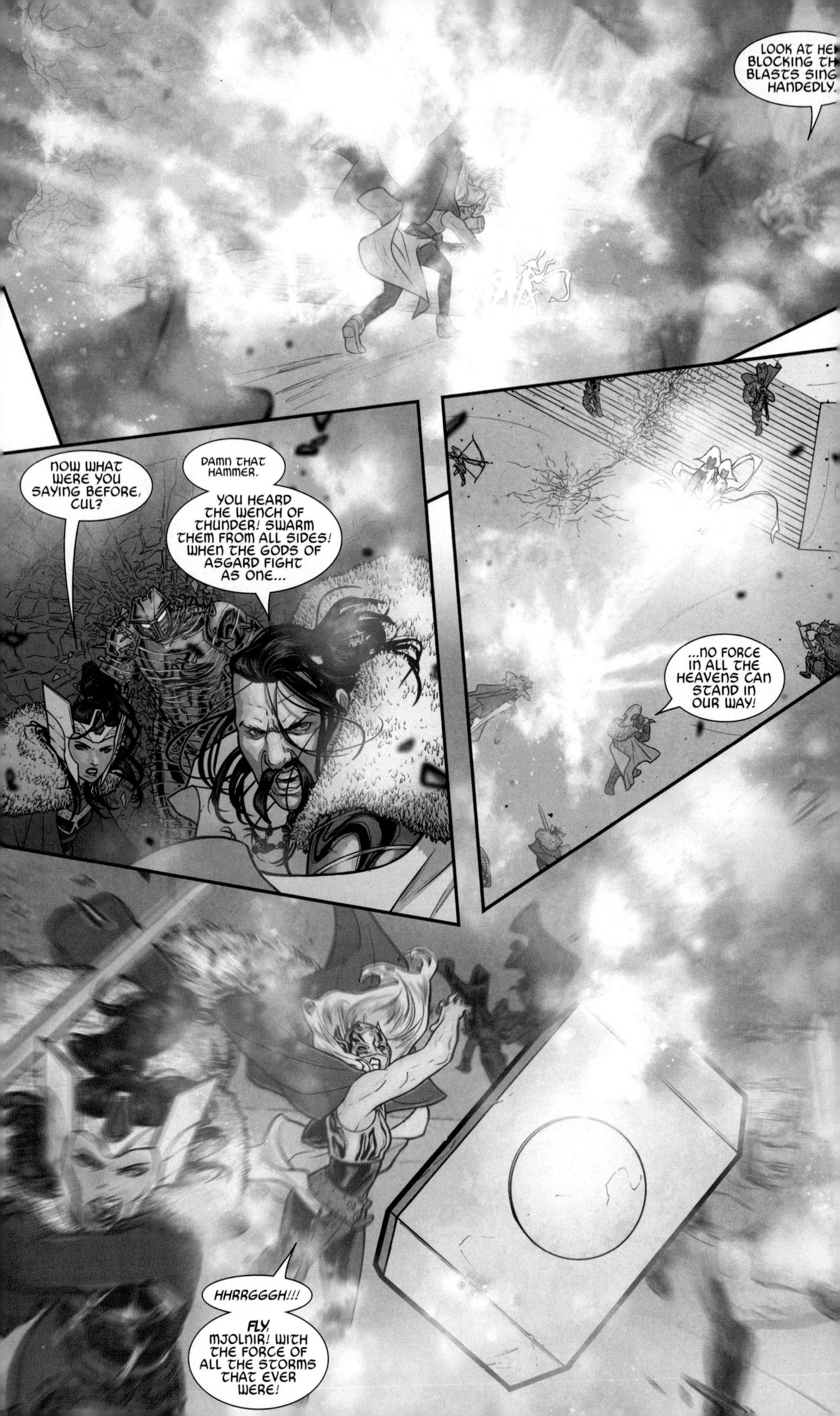
LOOK AT HE BLOCKING TH BLASTS SING HANDEDLY.
NOW WHAT WERE YOU SAYING BEFORE, CUL?
DAMN THAT HAMMER.
YOU HEARD THE WENCH OF THUNDER! SWARM THEM FROM ALL SIDES! WHEN THE GODS OF ASGARD FIGHT AS ONE...
...NO FORCE IN ALL THE HEAVENS CAN STAND IN OUR WAY!
HHRRGGGH!!!
FLY, MJOLNIR! WITH THE FORCE OF ALL THE STORMS THAT EVER WERE!

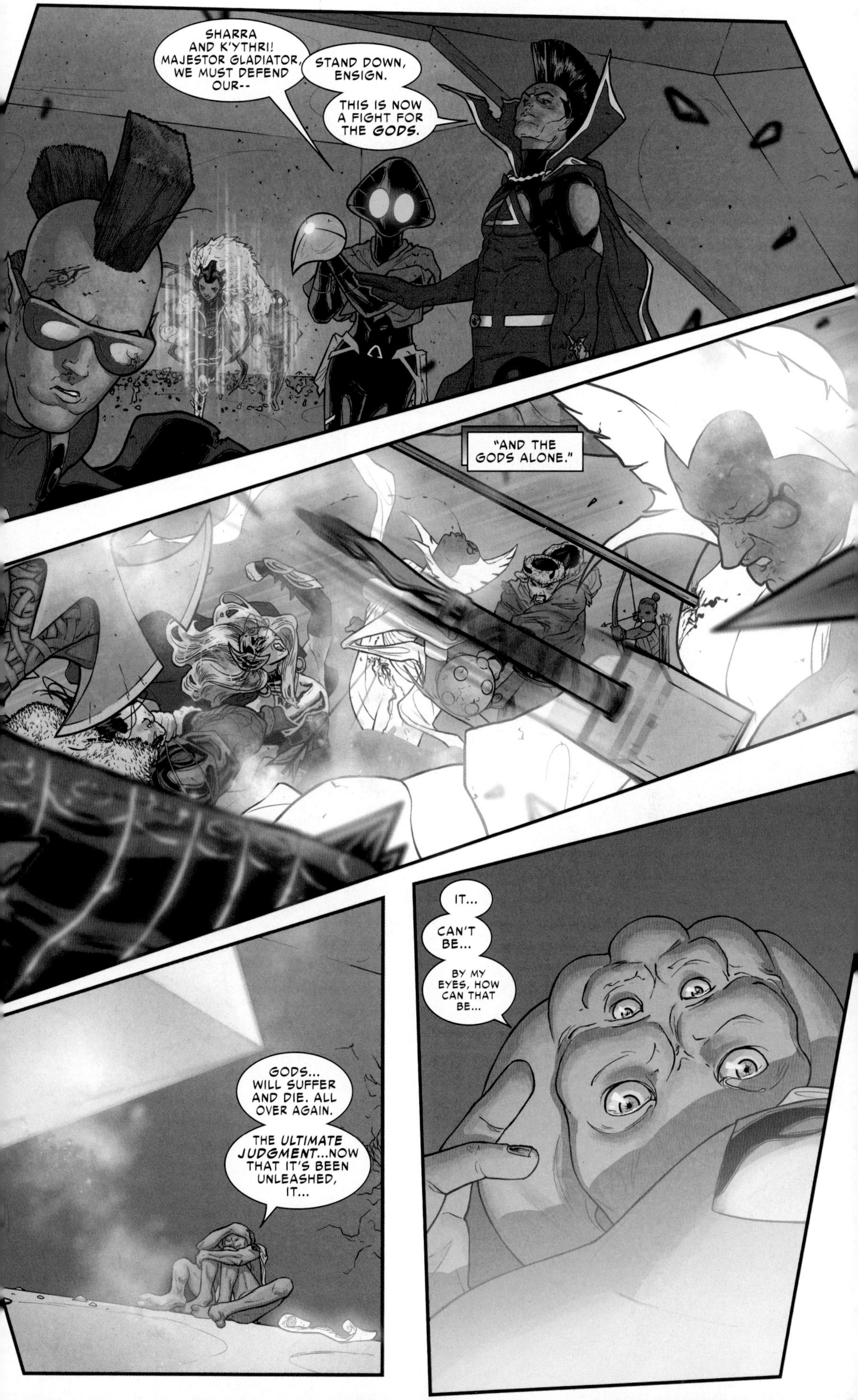
SHARRA AND K'YTHRI! MAJESTOR GLADIATOR, WE MUST DEFEND OUR--
STAND DOWN, ENSIGN.
THIS IS NOW A FIGHT FOR THE *GODS*.
"AND THE GODS ALONE."
IT...
CAN'T BE...
BY MY EYES, HOW CAN THAT BE...
GODS... WILL SUFFER AND DIE. ALL OVER AGAIN.
THE *ULTIMATE JUDGMENT*...NOW THAT IT'S BEEN UNLEASHED, IT...

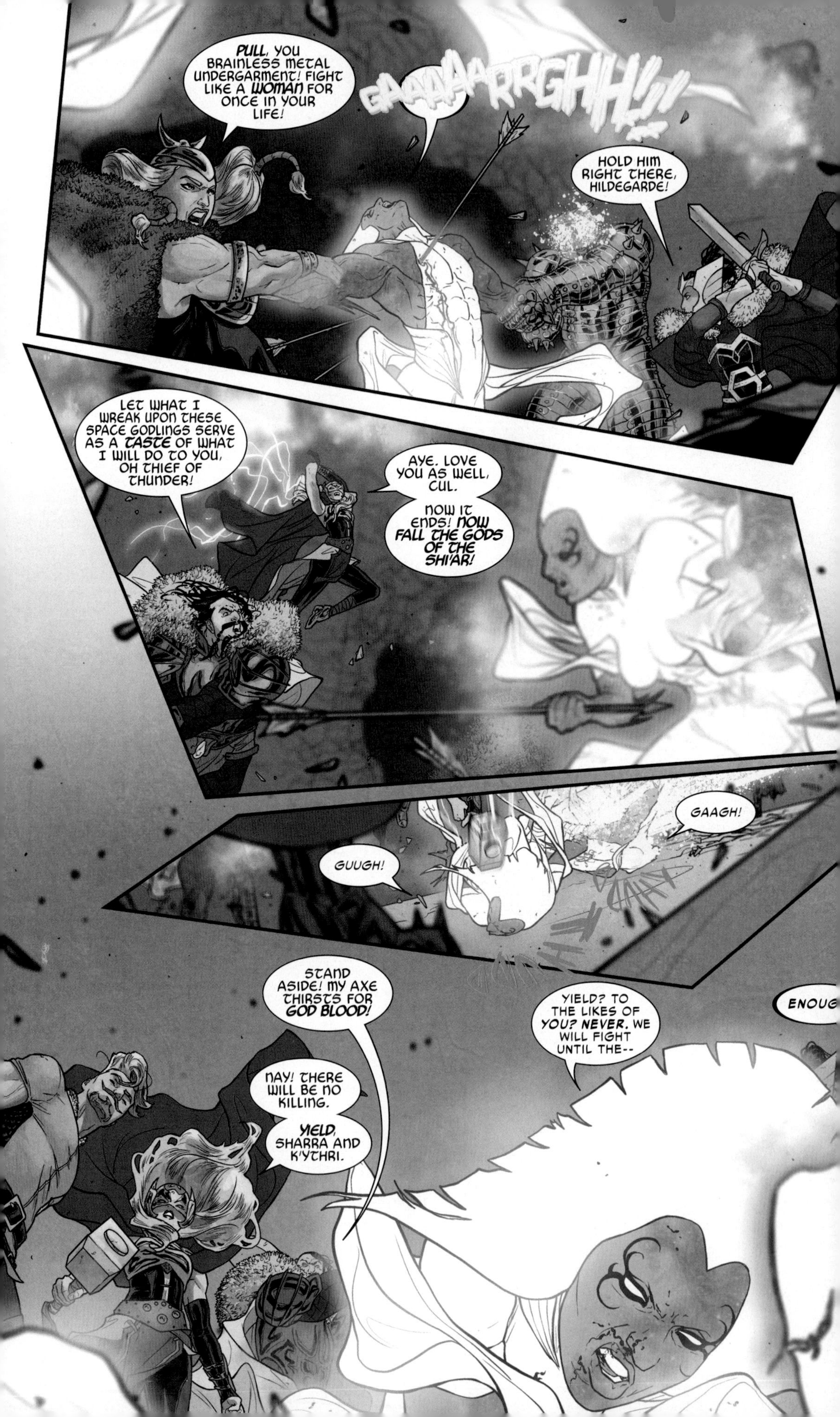
PULL, YOU BRAINLESS METAL UNDERGARMENT! FIGHT LIKE A WOMAN FOR ONCE IN YOUR LIFE!
GAAAAARRGHH!!!
HOLD HIM RIGHT THERE, HILDEGARDE!
LET WHAT I WREAK UPON THESE SPACE GODLINGS SERVE AS A TASTE OF WHAT I WILL DO TO YOU, OH THIEF OF THUNDER!
AYE. LOVE YOU AS WELL, CUL.
NOW IT ENDS! NOW FALL THE GODS OF THE SHI'AR!
GAAGH!
GUUGH!
STAND ASIDE! MY AXE THIRSTS FOR GOD BLOOD!
NAY! THERE WILL BE NO KILLING.
YIELD, SHARRA AND K'YTHRI.
YIELD? TO THE LIKES OF YOU? NEVER. WE WILL FIGHT UNTIL THE--
ENOUG

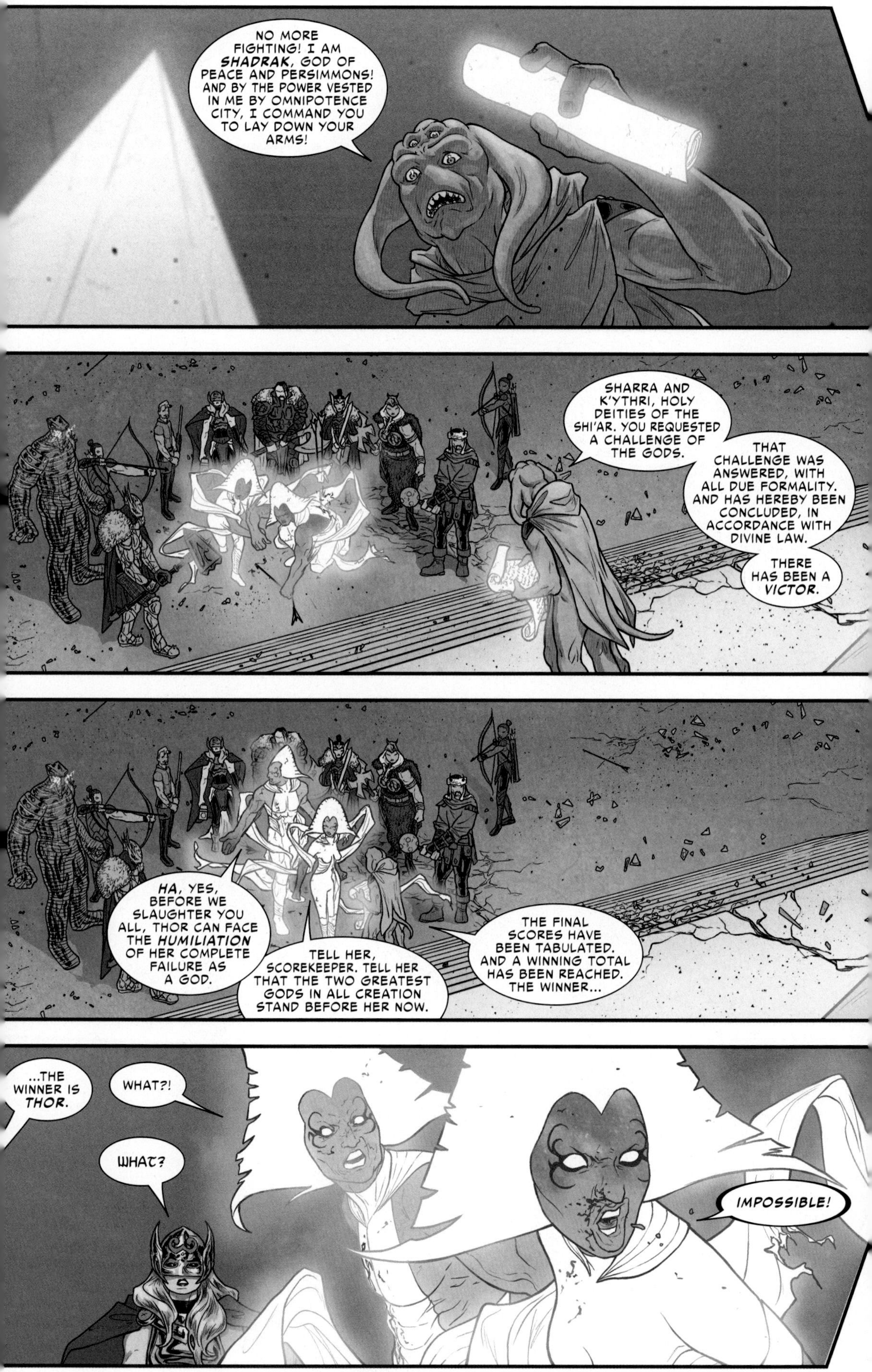
NO MORE FIGHTING! I AM SHADRAK, GOD OF PEACE AND PERSIMMONS! AND BY THE POWER VESTED IN ME BY OMNIPOTENCE CITY, I COMMAND YOU TO LAY DOWN YOUR ARMS!
SHARRA AND K'YTHRI, HOLY DEITIES OF THE SHI'AR. YOU REQUESTED A CHALLENGE OF THE GODS.
THAT CHALLENGE WAS ANSWERED, WITH ALL DUE FORMALITY. AND HAS HEREBY BEEN CONCLUDED, IN ACCORDANCE WITH DIVINE LAW.
THERE HAS BEEN A VICTOR.
HA, YES, BEFORE WE SLAUGHTER YOU ALL, THOR CAN FACE THE HUMILIATION OF HER COMPLETE FAILURE AS A GOD.
TELL HER, SCOREKEEPER. TELL HER THAT THE TWO GREATEST GODS IN ALL CREATION STAND BEFORE HER NOW.
THE FINAL SCORES HAVE BEEN TABULATED. AND A WINNING TOTAL HAS BEEN REACHED. THE WINNER...
...THE WINNER IS THOR.
WHAT?!
WHAT?
IMPOSSIBLE!

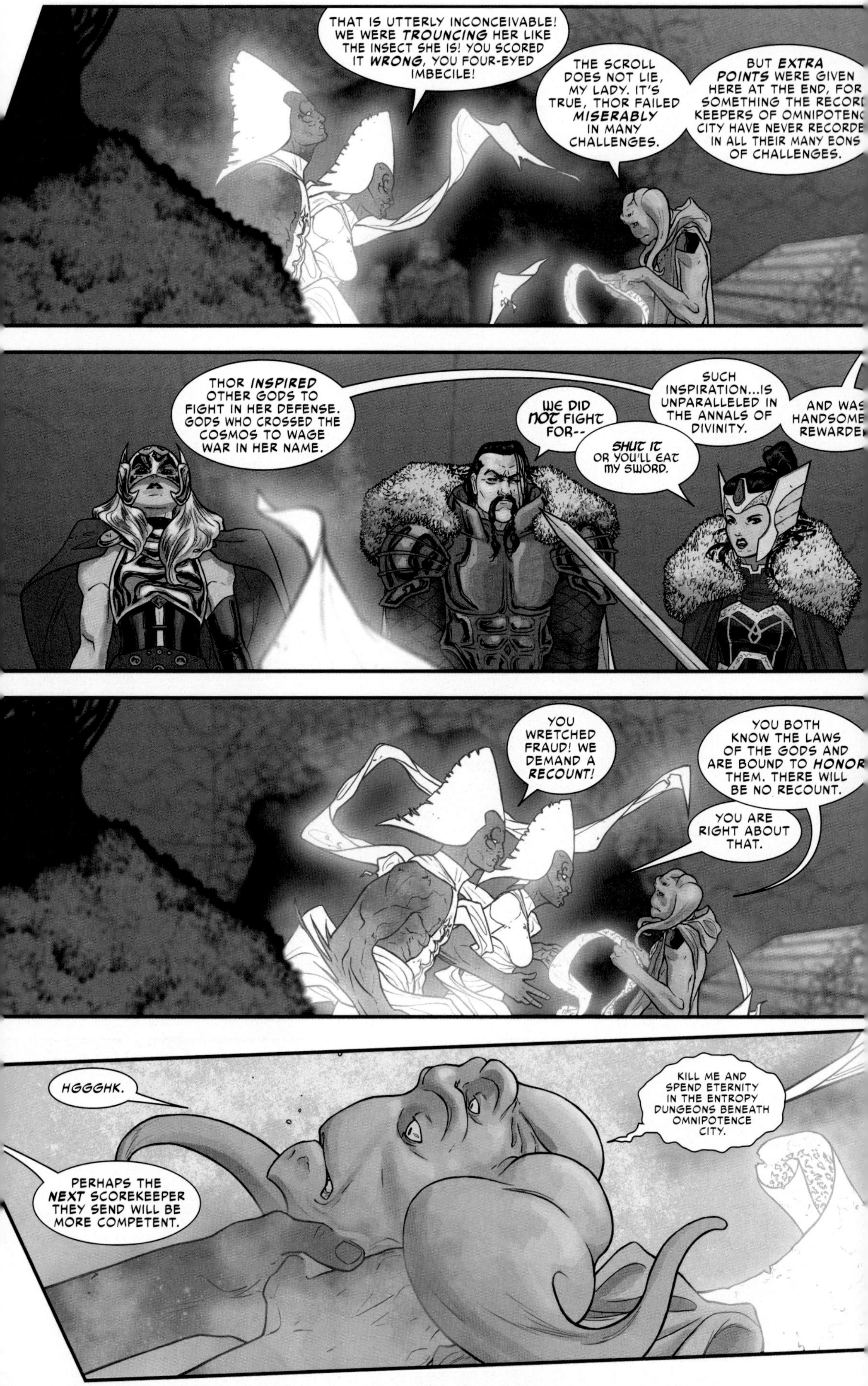
THAT IS UTTERLY INCONCEIVABLE! WE WERE TROUNCING HER LIKE THE INSECT SHE IS! YOU SCORED IT WRONG, YOU FOUR-EYED IMBECILE!
THE SCROLL DOES NOT LIE, MY LADY. IT'S TRUE, THOR FAILED MISERABLY IN MANY CHALLENGES.
BUT EXTRA POINTS WERE GIVEN HERE AT THE END, FOR SOMETHING THE RECORD KEEPERS OF OMNIPOTENC CITY HAVE NEVER RECORDE IN ALL THEIR MANY EONS OF CHALLENGES.
THOR INSPIRED OTHER GODS TO FIGHT IN HER DEFENSE. GODS WHO CROSSED THE COSMOS TO WAGE WAR IN HER NAME.
WE DID NOT FIGHT FOR--
SHUT IT OR YOU'LL EAT MY SWORD.
SUCH INSPIRATION...IS UNPARALLELED IN THE ANNALS OF DIVINITY.
AND WAS HANDSOME REWARDE
YOU WRETCHED FRAUD! WE DEMAND A RECOUNT!
YOU BOTH KNOW THE LAWS OF THE GODS AND ARE BOUND TO HONOR THEM. THERE WILL BE NO RECOUNT.
YOU ARE RIGHT ABOUT THAT.
HGGGHK.
KILL ME AND SPEND ETERNITY IN THE ENTROPY DUNGEONS BENEATH OMNIPOTENCE CITY.
PERHAPS THE NEXT SCOREKEEPER THEY SEND WILL BE MORE COMPETENT.

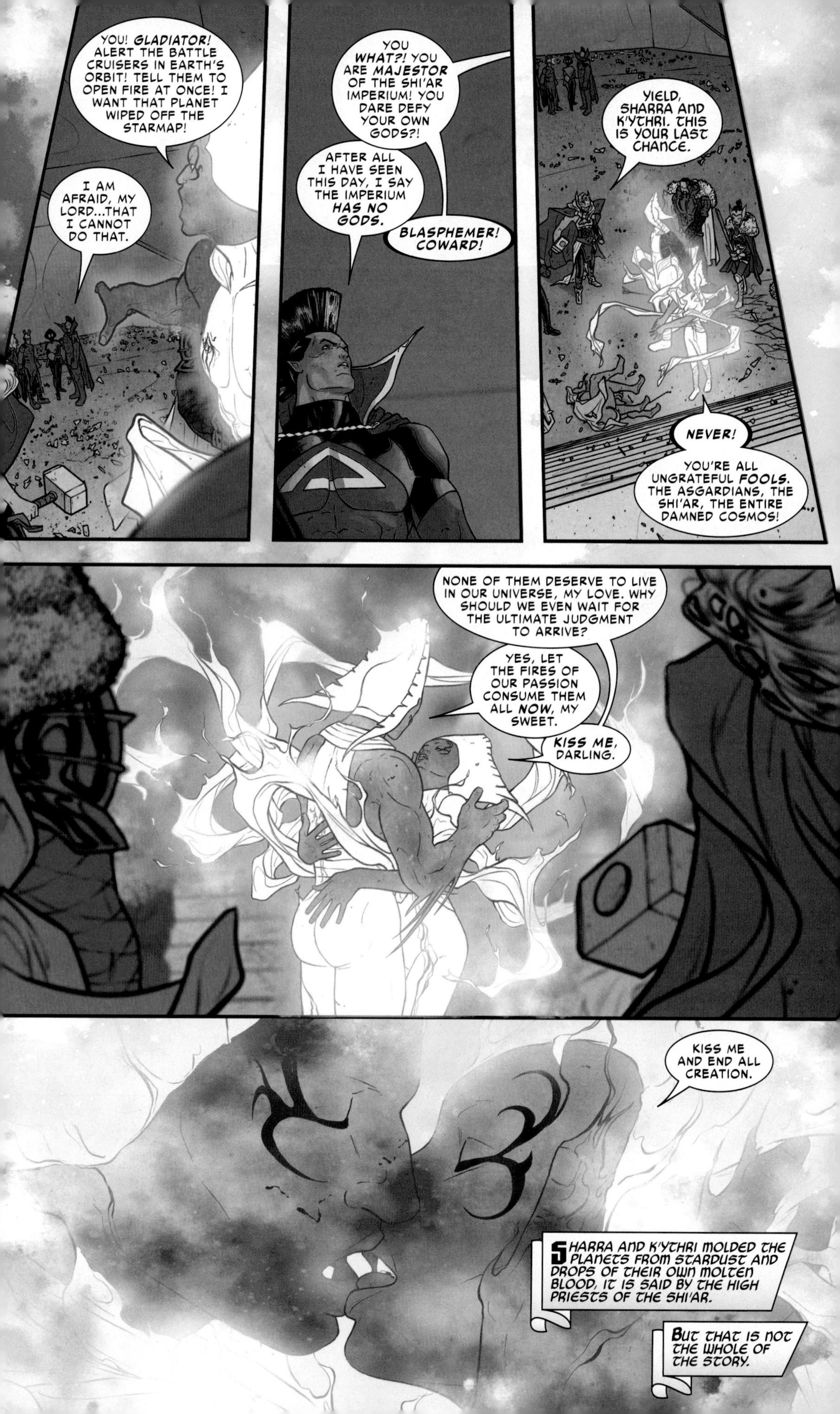
YOU! GLADIATOR! ALERT THE BATTLE CRUISERS IN EARTH'S ORBIT! TELL THEM TO OPEN FIRE AT ONCE! I WANT THAT PLANET WIPED OFF THE STARMAP!
I AM AFRAID, MY LORD...THAT I CANNOT DO THAT.
YOU WHAT?! YOU ARE MAJESTOR OF THE SHI'AR IMPERIUM! YOU DARE DEFY YOUR OWN GODS?!
AFTER ALL I HAVE SEEN THIS DAY, I SAY THE IMPERIUM HAS NO GODS.
BLASPHEMER! COWARD!
YIELD, SHARRA AND K'YTHRI. THIS IS YOUR LAST CHANCE.
NEVER!
YOU'RE ALL UNGRATEFUL FOOLS. THE ASGARDIANS, THE SHI'AR, THE ENTIRE DAMNED COSMOS!
NONE OF THEM DESERVE TO LIVE IN OUR UNIVERSE, MY LOVE. WHY SHOULD WE EVEN WAIT FOR THE ULTIMATE JUDGMENT TO ARRIVE?
YES, LET THE FIRES OF OUR PASSION CONSUME THEM ALL NOW, MY SWEET.
KISS ME, DARLING.
KISS ME AND END ALL CREATION.
SHARRA AND K'YTHRI MOLDED THE PLANETS FROM STARDUST AND DROPS OF THEIR OWN MOLTEN BLOOD, IT IS SAID BY THE HIGH PRIESTS OF THE SHI'AR.
BUT THAT IS NOT THE WHOLE OF THE STORY.

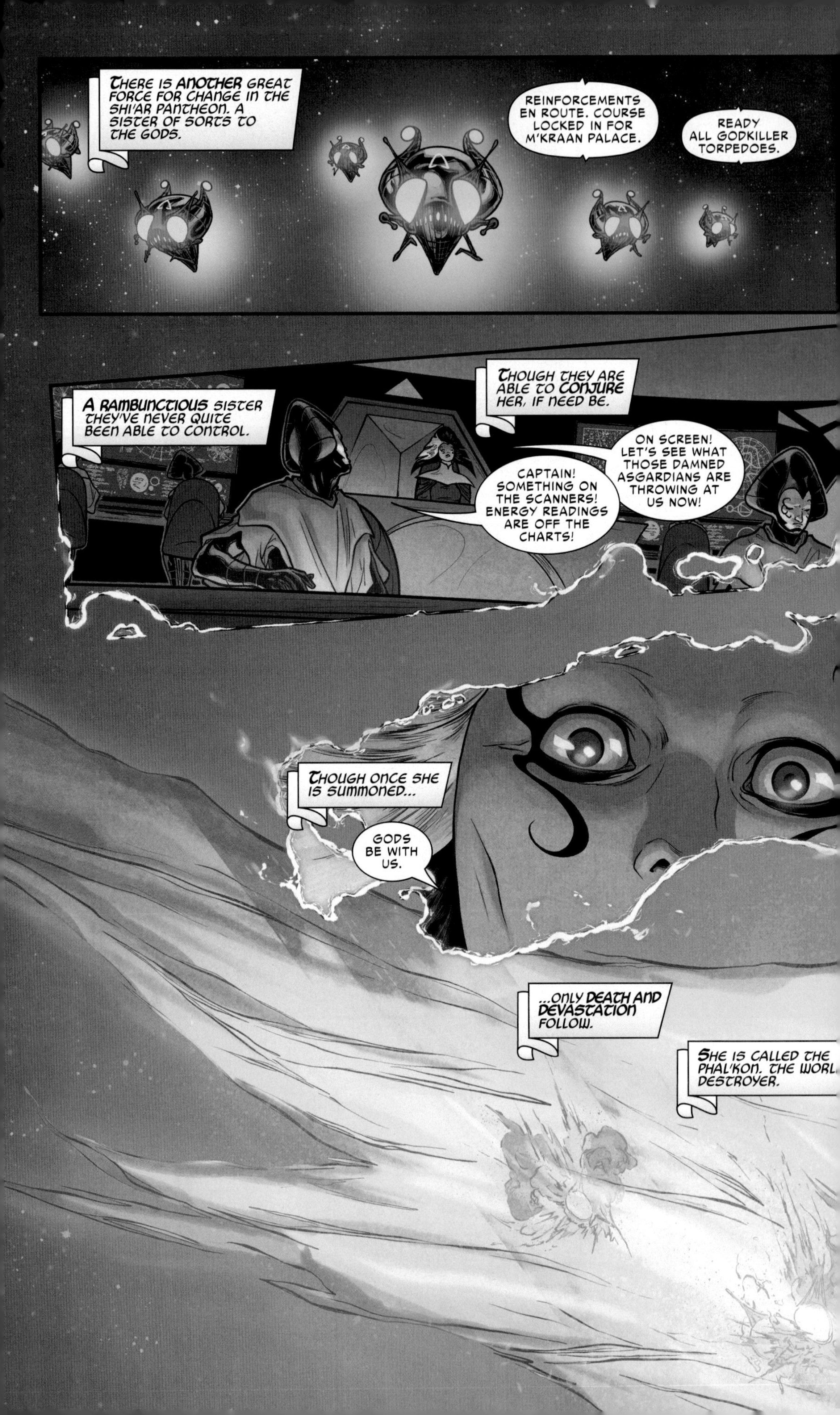
THERE IS ANOTHER GREAT FORCE FOR CHANGE IN THE SHI'AR PANTHEON. A SISTER OF SORTS TO THE GODS.
REINFORCEMENTS EN ROUTE. COURSE LOCKED IN FOR M'KRAAN PALACE.
READY ALL GODKILLER TORPEDOES.
A RAMBUNCTIOUS SISTER THEY'VE NEVER QUITE BEEN ABLE TO CONTROL.
THOUGH THEY ARE ABLE TO CONJURE HER, IF NEED BE.
CAPTAIN! SOMETHING ON THE SCANNERS! ENERGY READINGS ARE OFF THE CHARTS!
ON SCREEN! LET'S SEE WHAT THOSE DAMNED ASGARDIANS ARE THROWING AT US NOW!
THOUGH ONCE SHE IS SUMMONED...
GODS BE WITH US.
...ONLY DEATH AND DEVASTATION FOLLOW.
SHE IS CALLED THE PHAL'KON. THE WORL DESTROYER.

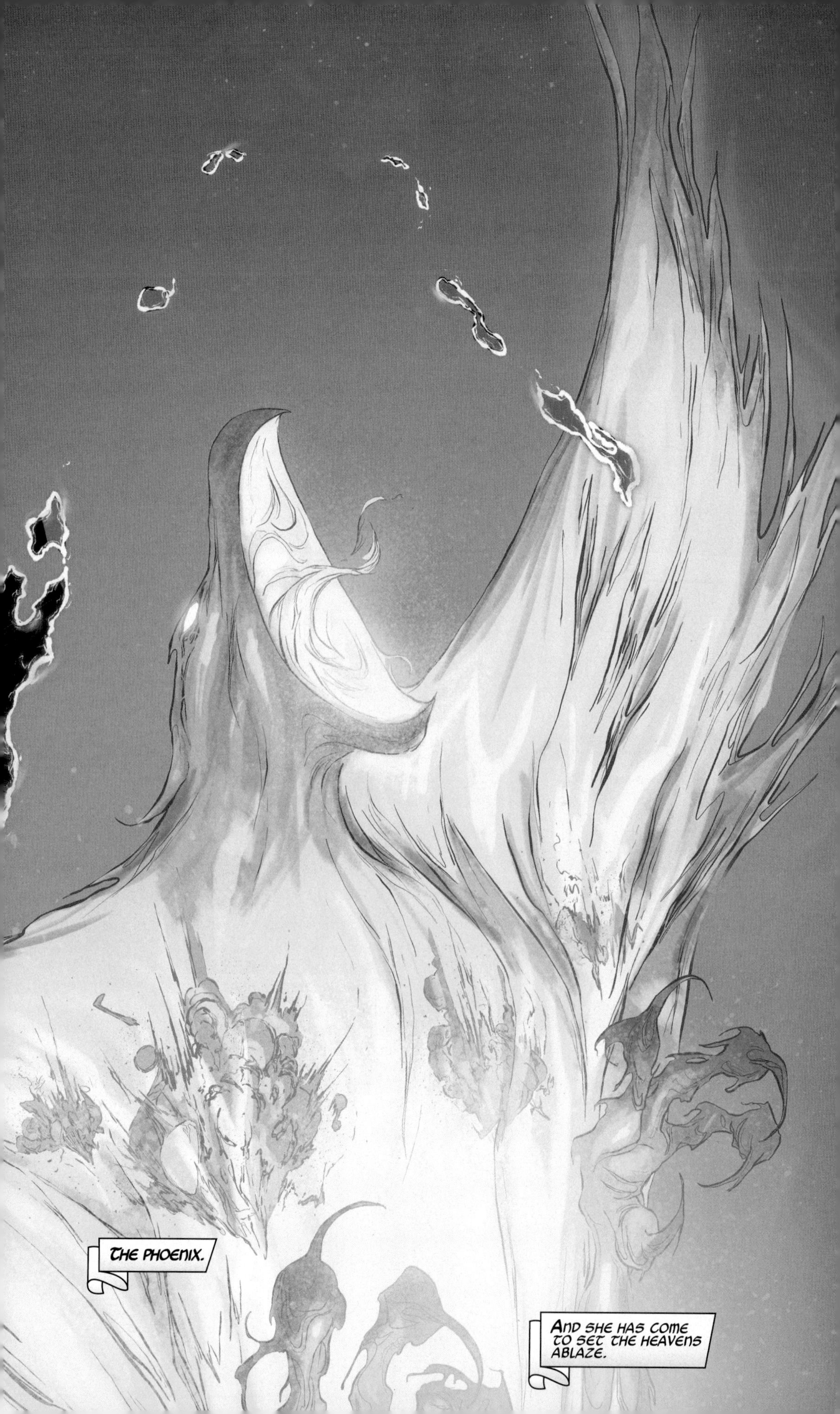
THE PHOENIX.
AND SHE HAS COME TO SET THE HEAVENS ABLAZE.

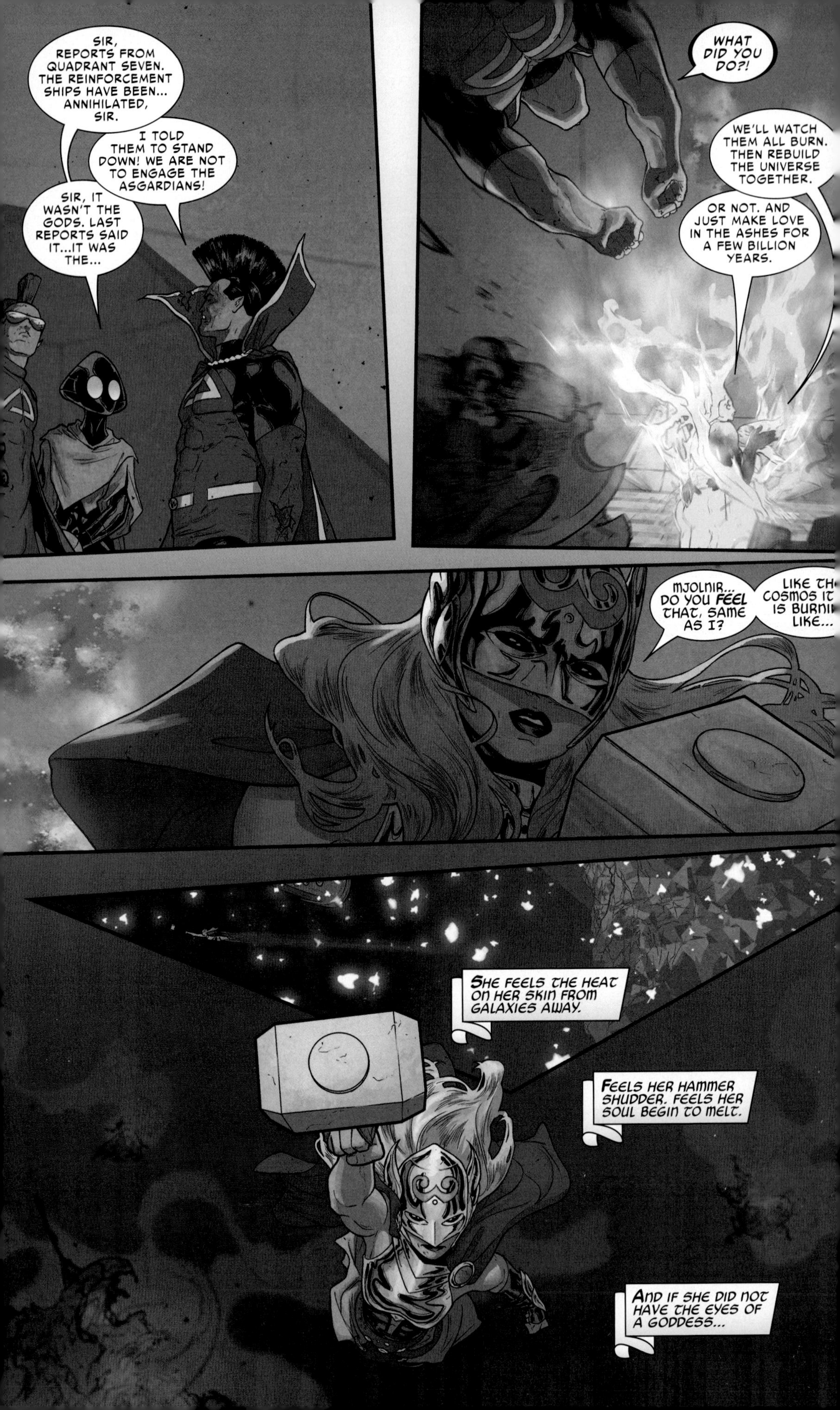
SIR, REPORTS FROM QUADRANT SEVEN. THE REINFORCEMENT SHIPS HAVE BEEN... ANNIHILATED, SIR.
I TOLD THEM TO STAND DOWN! WE ARE NOT TO ENGAGE THE ASGARDIANS!
SIR, IT WASN'T THE GODS. LAST REPORTS SAID IT...IT WAS THE...
WHAT DID YOU DO?!
WE'LL WATCH THEM ALL BURN. THEN REBUILD THE UNIVERSE TOGETHER.
OR NOT. AND JUST MAKE LOVE IN THE ASHES FOR A FEW BILLION YEARS.
MJOLNIR... DO YOU FEEL THAT, SAME AS I?
SHE FEELS THE HEAT ON HER SKIN FROM GALAXIES AWAY.
FEELS HER HAMMER SHUDDER. FEELS HER SOUL BEGIN TO MELT.
AND IF SHE DID NOT HAVE THE EYES OF A GODDESS...

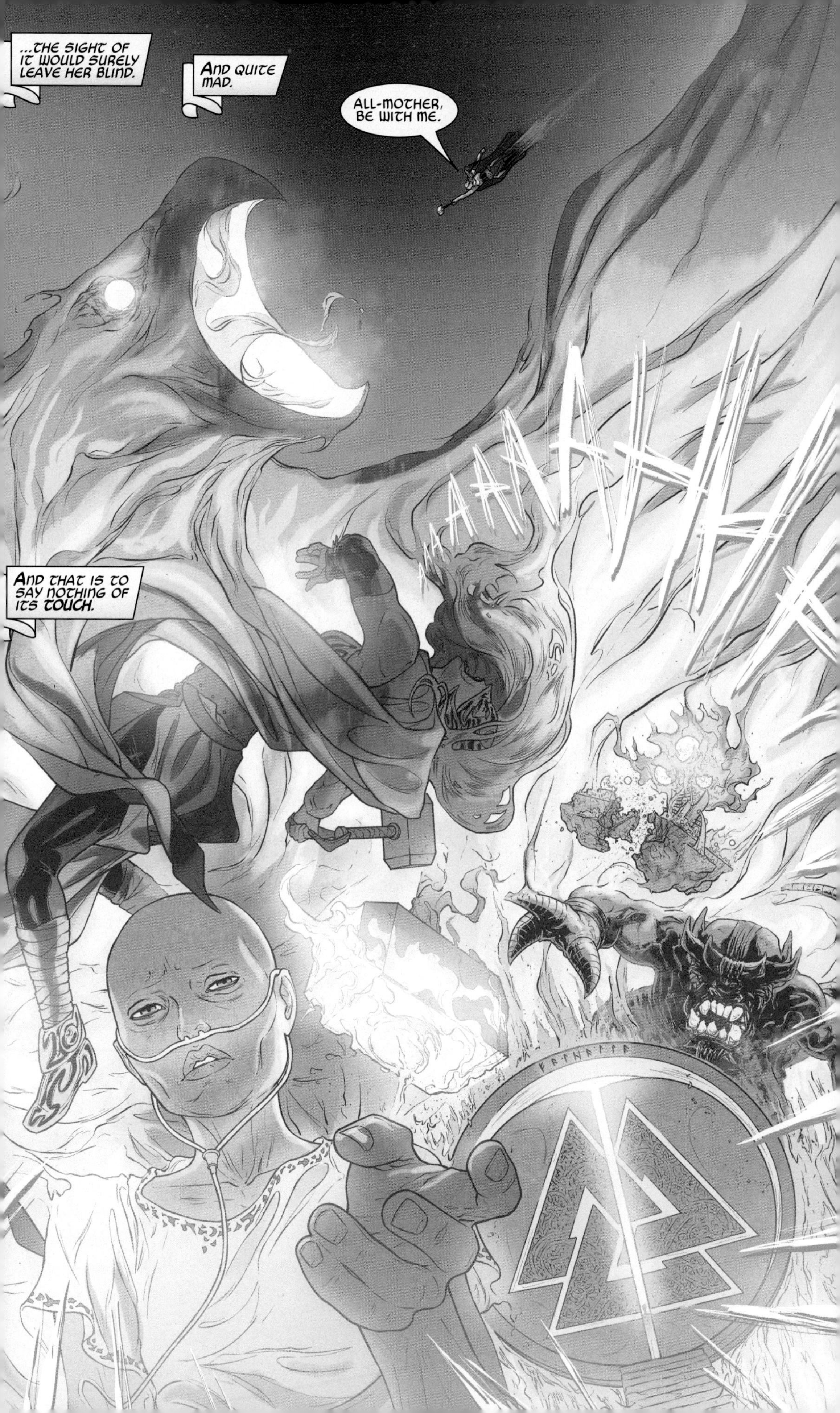

...THE SIGHT OF IT WOULD SURELY LEAVE HER BLIND.
AND QUITE MAD.
ALL-MOTHER, BE WITH ME.
AAAAAAAAAHHH
AND THAT IS TO SAY NOTHING OF ITS TOUCH.

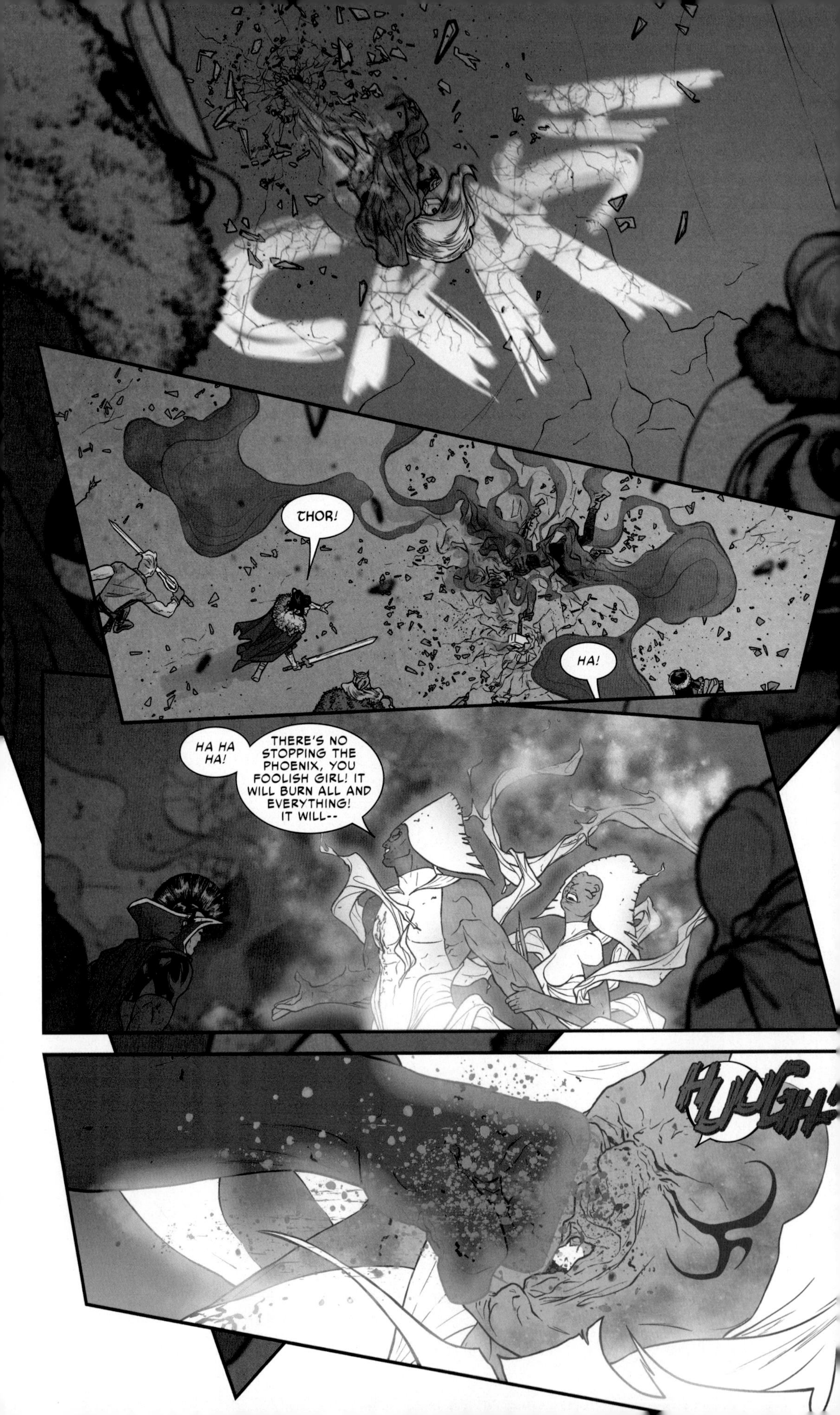
THOR!
HA!
HA HA HA!
THERE'S NO STOPPING THE PHOENIX, YOU FOOLISH GIRL! IT WILL BURN ALL AND EVERYTHING! IT WILL--
HUUGH!

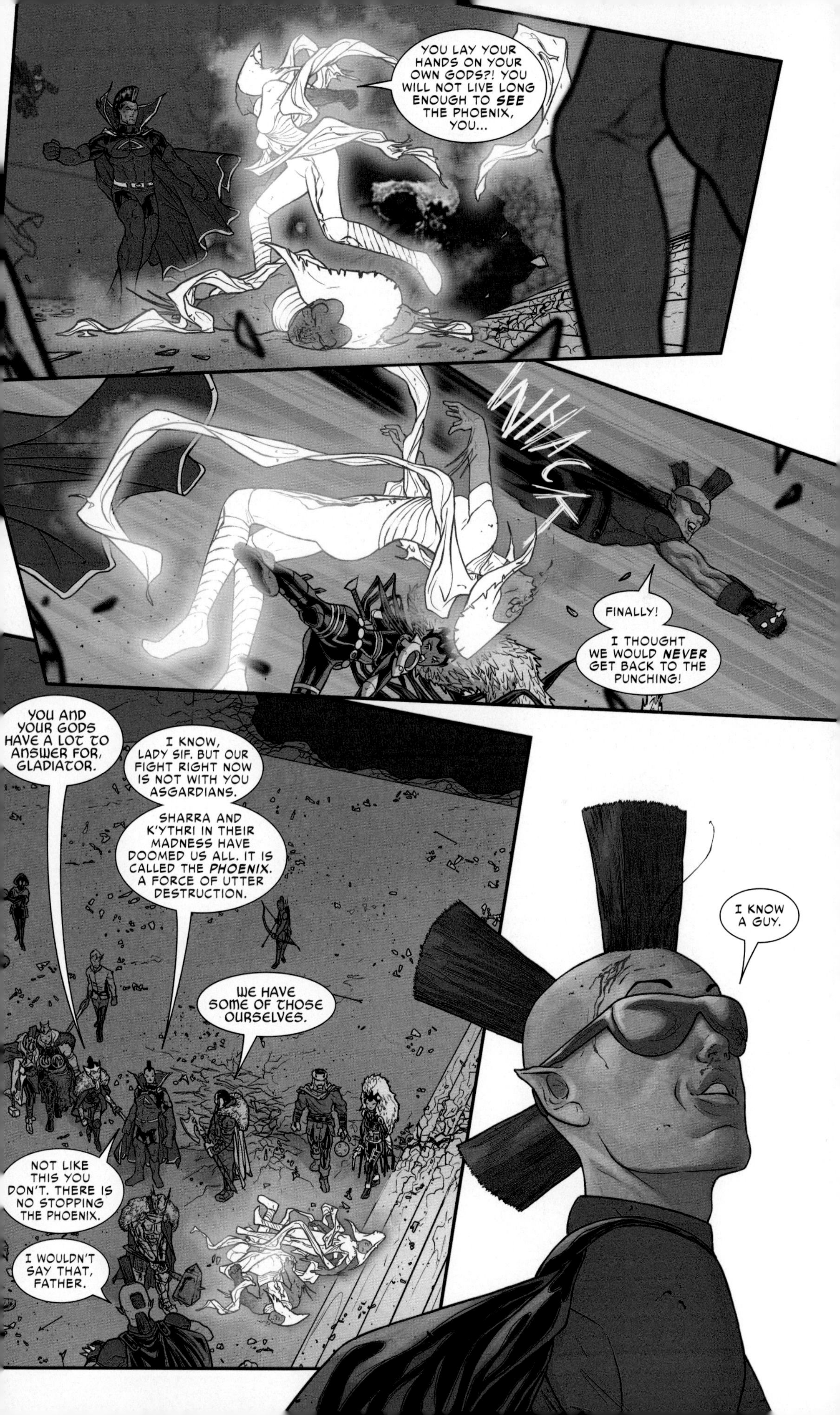
YOU LAY YOUR HANDS ON YOUR OWN GODS?! YOU WILL NOT LIVE LONG ENOUGH TO SEE THE PHOENIX, YOU...
WHACK
FINALLY!
I THOUGHT WE WOULD NEVER GET BACK TO THE PUNCHING!
YOU AND YOUR GODS HAVE A LOT TO ANSWER FOR, GLADIATOR.
I KNOW, LADY SIF. BUT OUR FIGHT RIGHT NOW IS NOT WITH YOU ASGARDIANS.
SHARRA AND K'YTHRI IN THEIR MADNESS HAVE DOOMED US ALL. IT IS CALLED THE PHOENIX. A FORCE OF UTTER DESTRUCTION.
WE HAVE SOME OF THOSE OURSELVES.
NOT LIKE THIS YOU DON'T. THERE IS NO STOPPING THE PHOENIX.
I WOULDN'T SAY THAT, FATHER.
I KNOW A GUY.

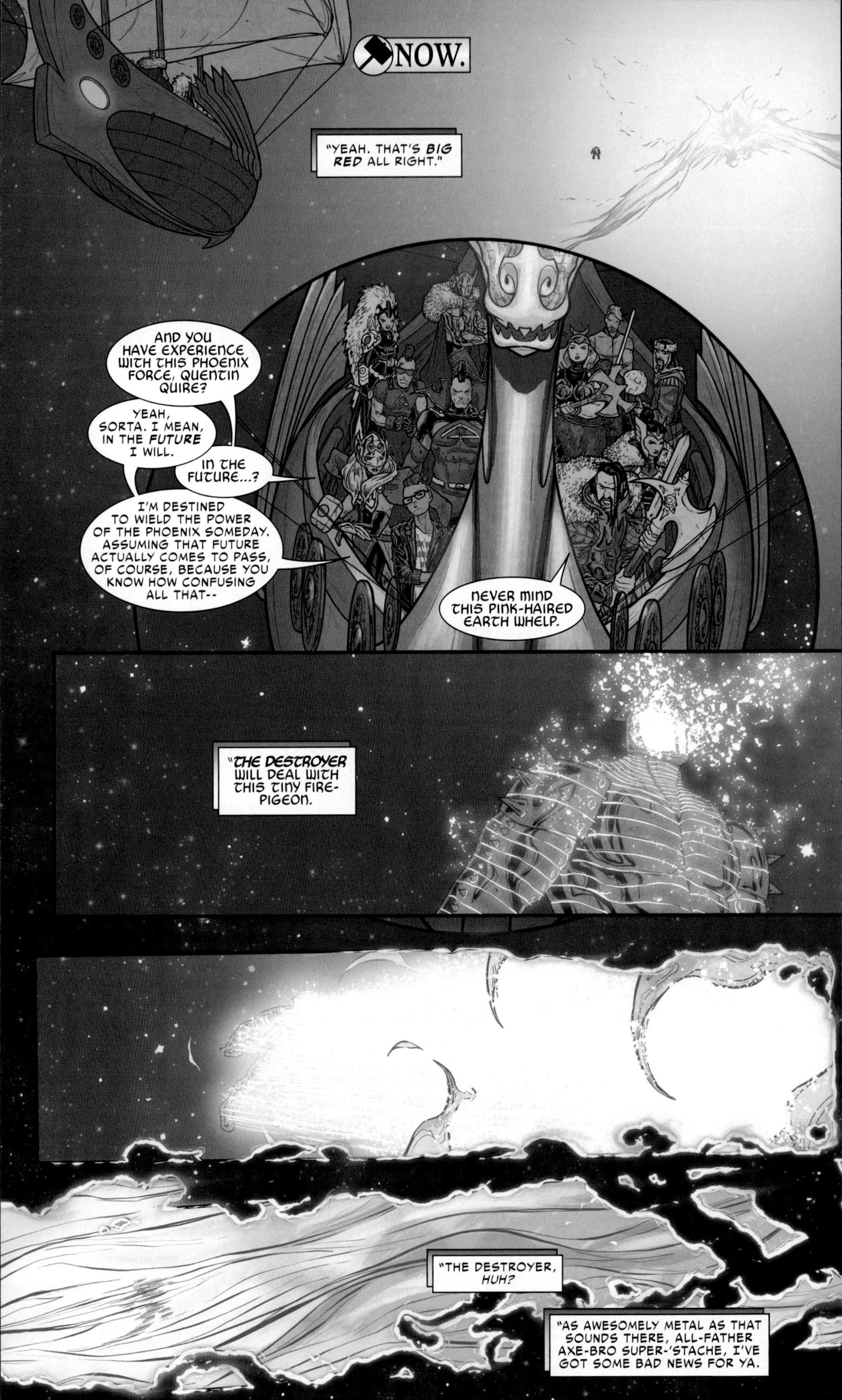
NOW.
"YEAH. THAT'S BIG RED ALL RIGHT."
AND YOU HAVE EXPERIENCE WITH THIS PHOENIX FORCE, QUENTIN QUIRE?
YEAH, SORTA. I MEAN, IN THE FUTURE I WILL.
IN THE FUTURE...?
I'M DESTINED TO WIELD THE POWER OF THE PHOENIX SOMEDAY. ASSUMING THAT FUTURE ACTUALLY COMES TO PASS, OF COURSE, BECAUSE YOU KNOW HOW CONFUSING ALL THAT--
NEVER MIND THIS PINK-HAIRED EARTH WHELP.
"THE DESTROYER WILL DEAL WITH THIS TINY FIRE-PIGEON.
"THE DESTROYER, HUH?
"AS AWESOMELY METAL AS THAT SOUNDS THERE, ALL-FATHER AXE-BRO SUPER-'STACHE, I'VE GOT SOME BAD NEWS FOR YA.

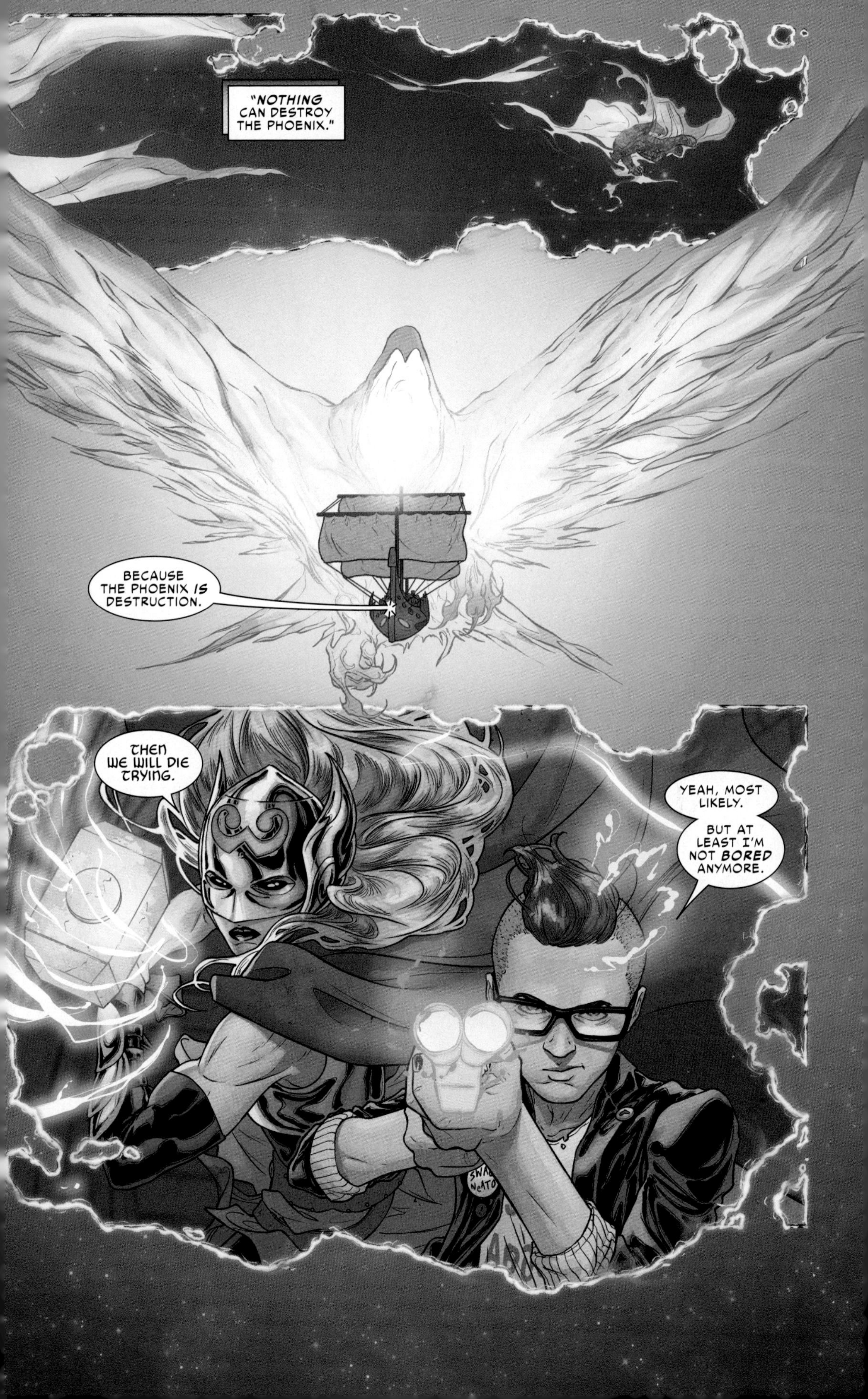
"NOTHING CAN DESTROY THE PHOENIX."
BECAUSE THE PHOENIX IS DESTRUCTION.
THEN WE WILL DIE TRYING.
YEAH, MOST LIKELY.
BUT AT LEAST I'M NOT BORED ANYMORE.

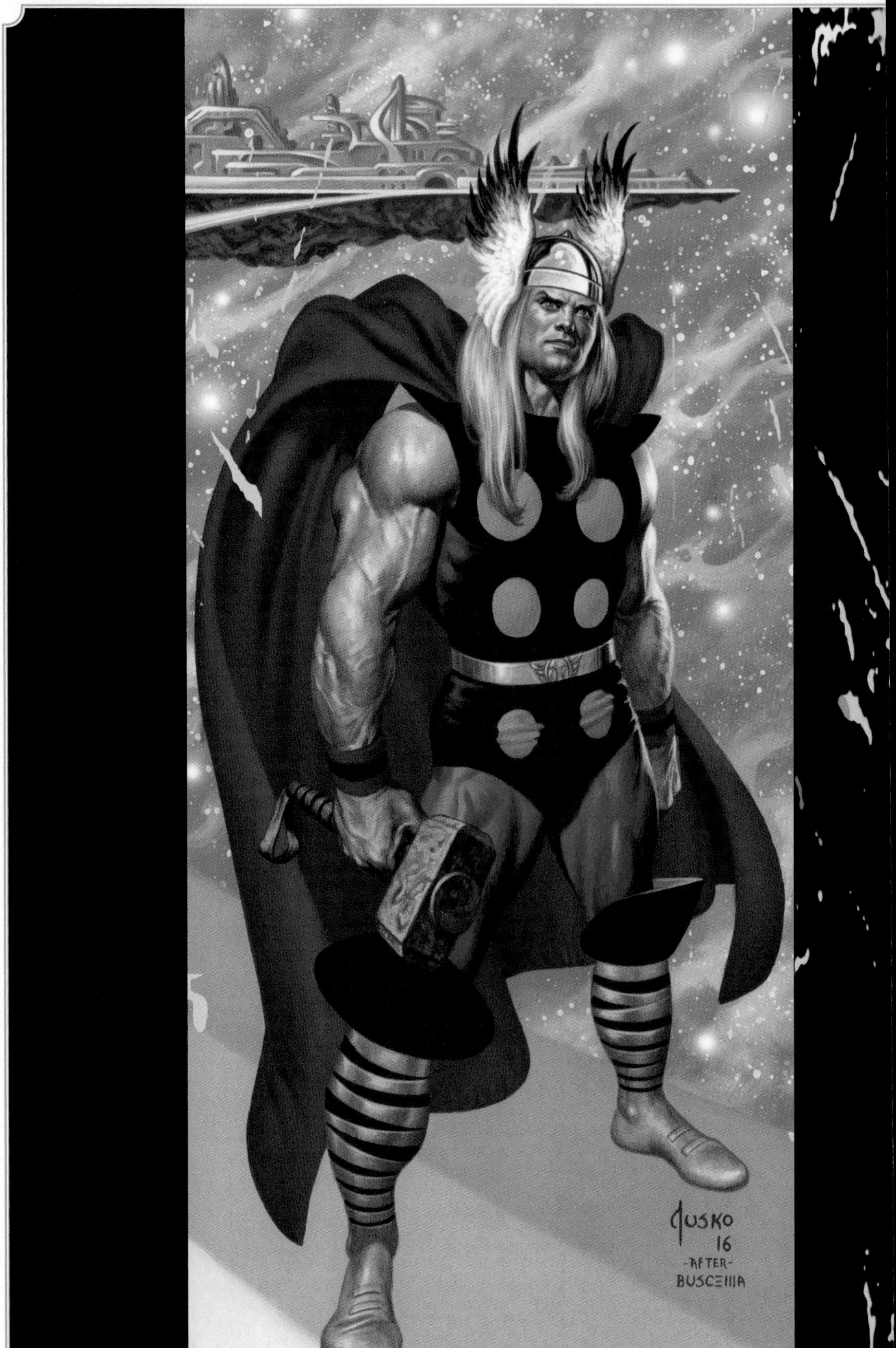
JUSKO
16
-AFTER-
BUSCEMA

MIGHTY THOR CORNER BOX #16 VARIANT
BY **JOE JUSKO**

19

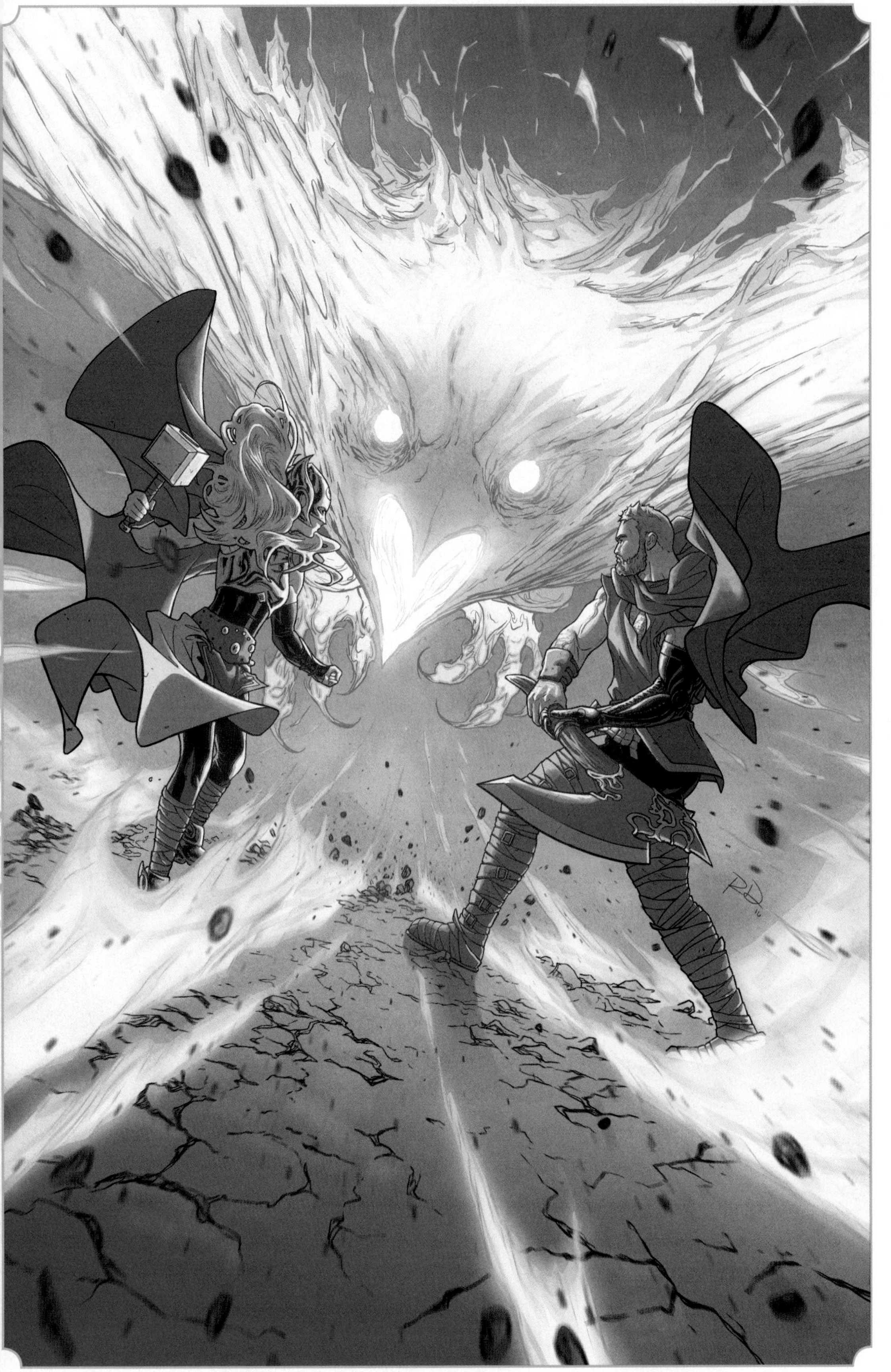

THE ASGARD/SHI'AR WAR, PART FIVE:

TO FACE THE PHOENIX

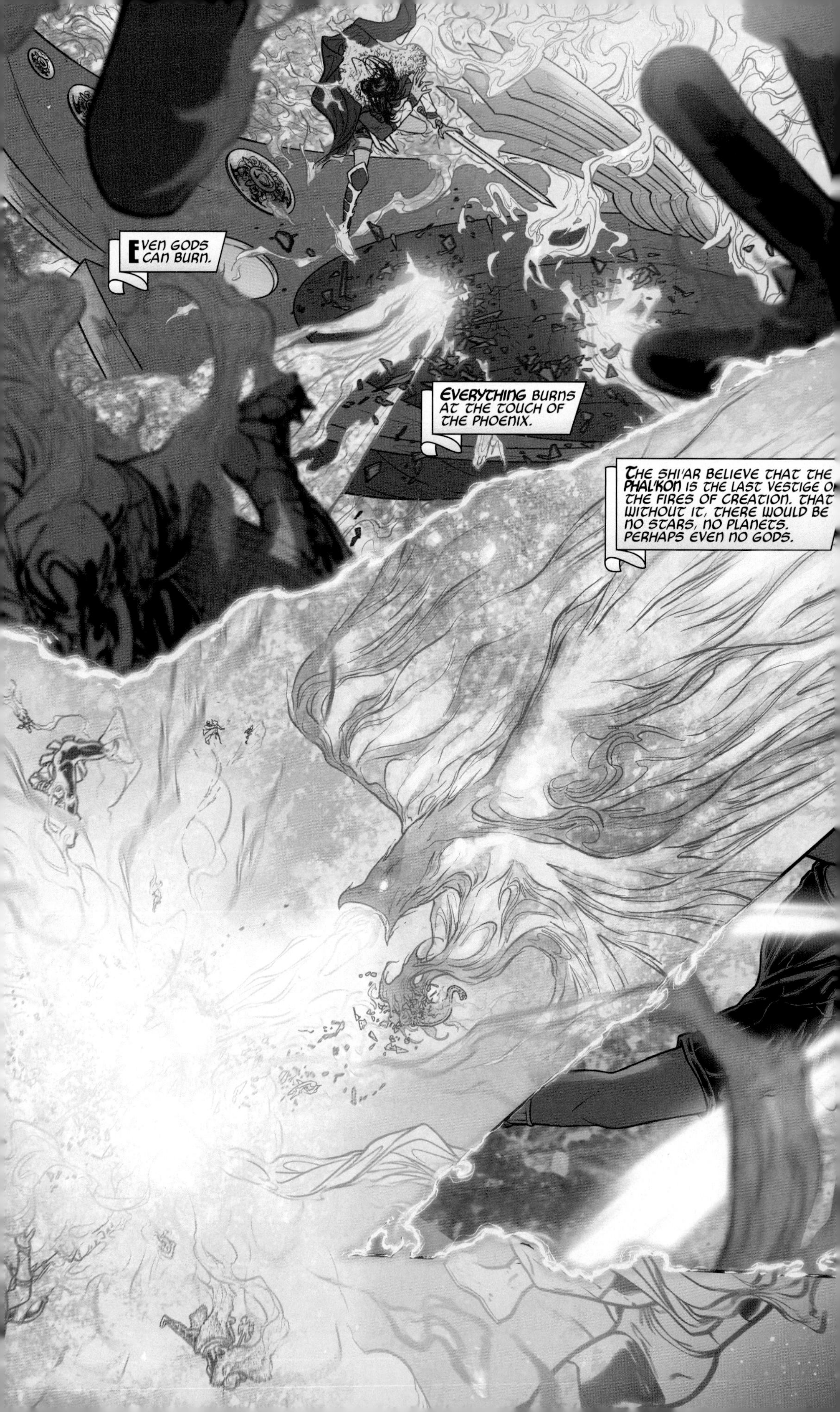
EVEN GODS CAN BURN.
EVERYTHING BURNS AT THE TOUCH OF THE PHOENIX.
THE SHI'AR BELIEVE THAT THE PHAL'KON IS THE LAST VESTIGE OF THE FIRES OF CREATION. THAT WITHOUT IT, THERE WOULD BE NO STARS, NO PLANETS. PERHAPS EVEN NO GODS.

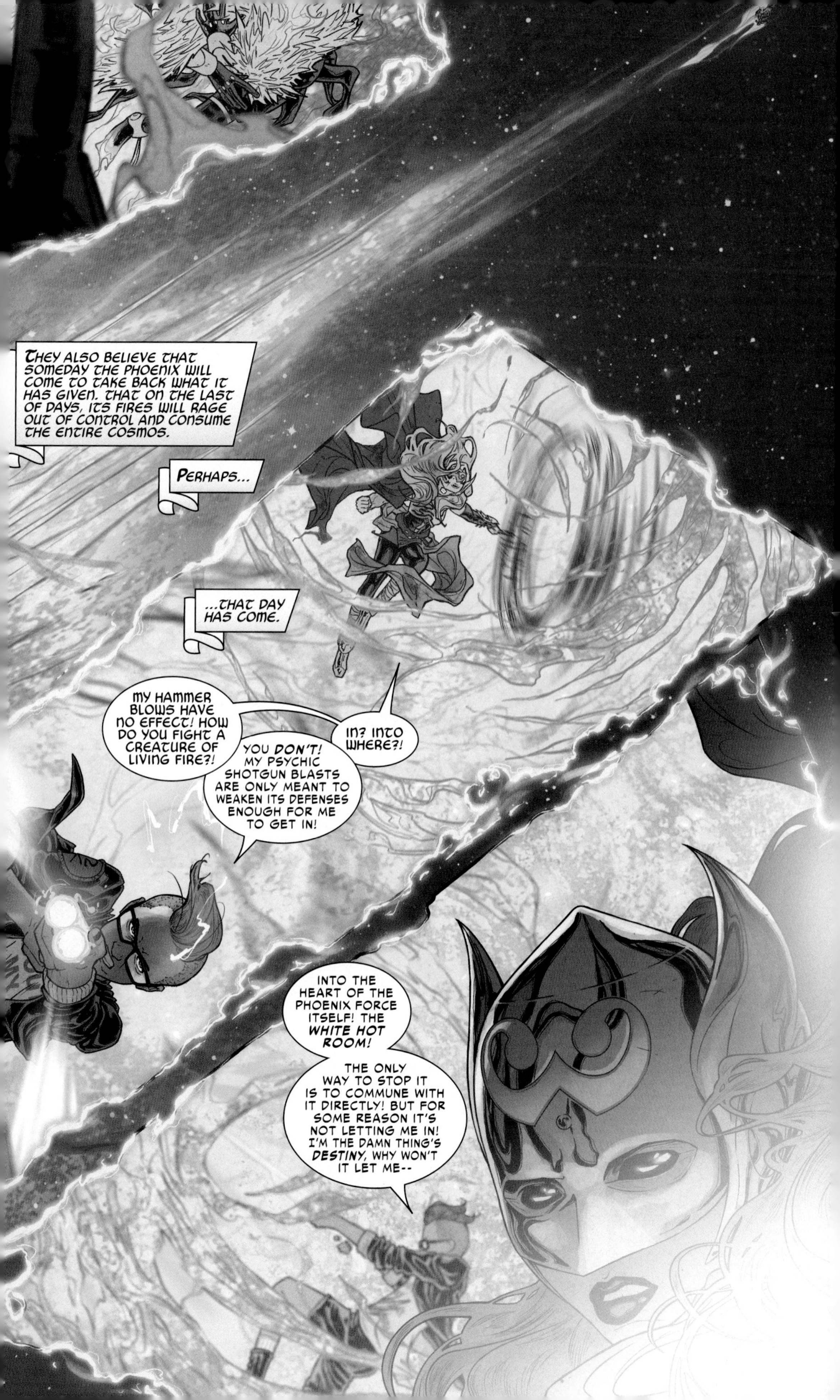
THEY ALSO BELIEVE THAT SOMEDAY THE PHOENIX WILL COME TO TAKE BACK WHAT IT HAS GIVEN. THAT ON THE LAST OF DAYS, ITS FIRES WILL RAGE OUT OF CONTROL AND CONSUME THE ENTIRE COSMOS.
PERHAPS...
...THAT DAY HAS COME.
MY HAMMER BLOWS HAVE NO EFFECT! HOW DO YOU FIGHT A CREATURE OF LIVING FIRE?!
YOU DON'T! MY PSYCHIC SHOTGUN BLASTS ARE ONLY MEANT TO WEAKEN ITS DEFENSES ENOUGH FOR ME TO GET IN!
IN? INTO WHERE?!
INTO THE HEART OF THE PHOENIX FORCE ITSELF! THE WHITE HOT ROOM!
THE ONLY WAY TO STOP IT IS TO COMMUNE WITH IT DIRECTLY! BUT FOR SOME REASON IT'S NOT LETTING ME IN! I'M THE DAMN THING'S DESTINY, WHY WON'T IT LET ME--

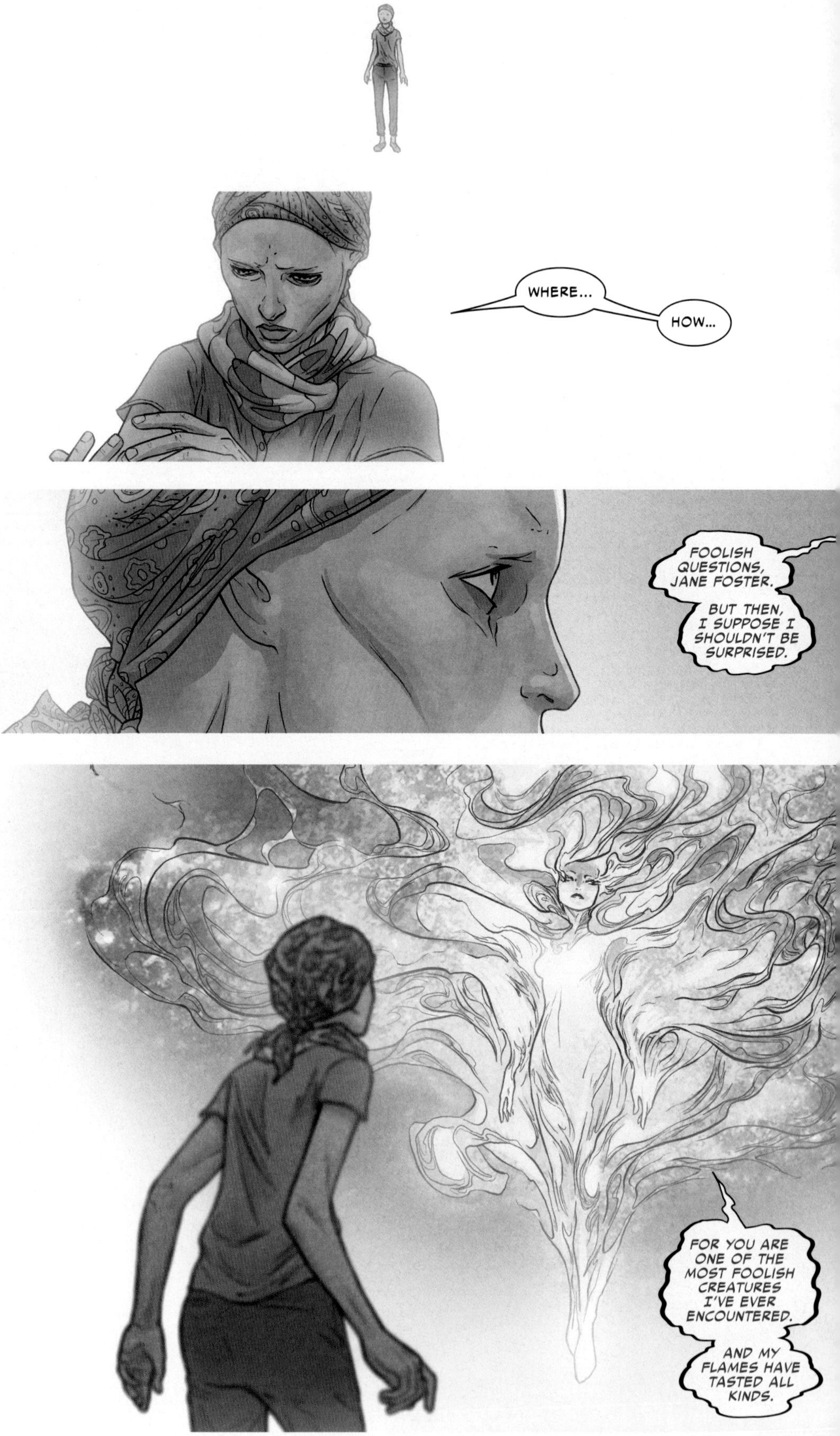
WHERE...
HOW...
FOOLISH QUESTIONS, JANE FOSTER.
BUT THEN, I SUPPOSE I SHOULDN'T BE SURPRISED.
FOR YOU ARE ONE OF THE MOST FOOLISH CREATURES I'VE EVER ENCOUNTERED.
AND MY FLAMES HAVE TASTED ALL KINDS.

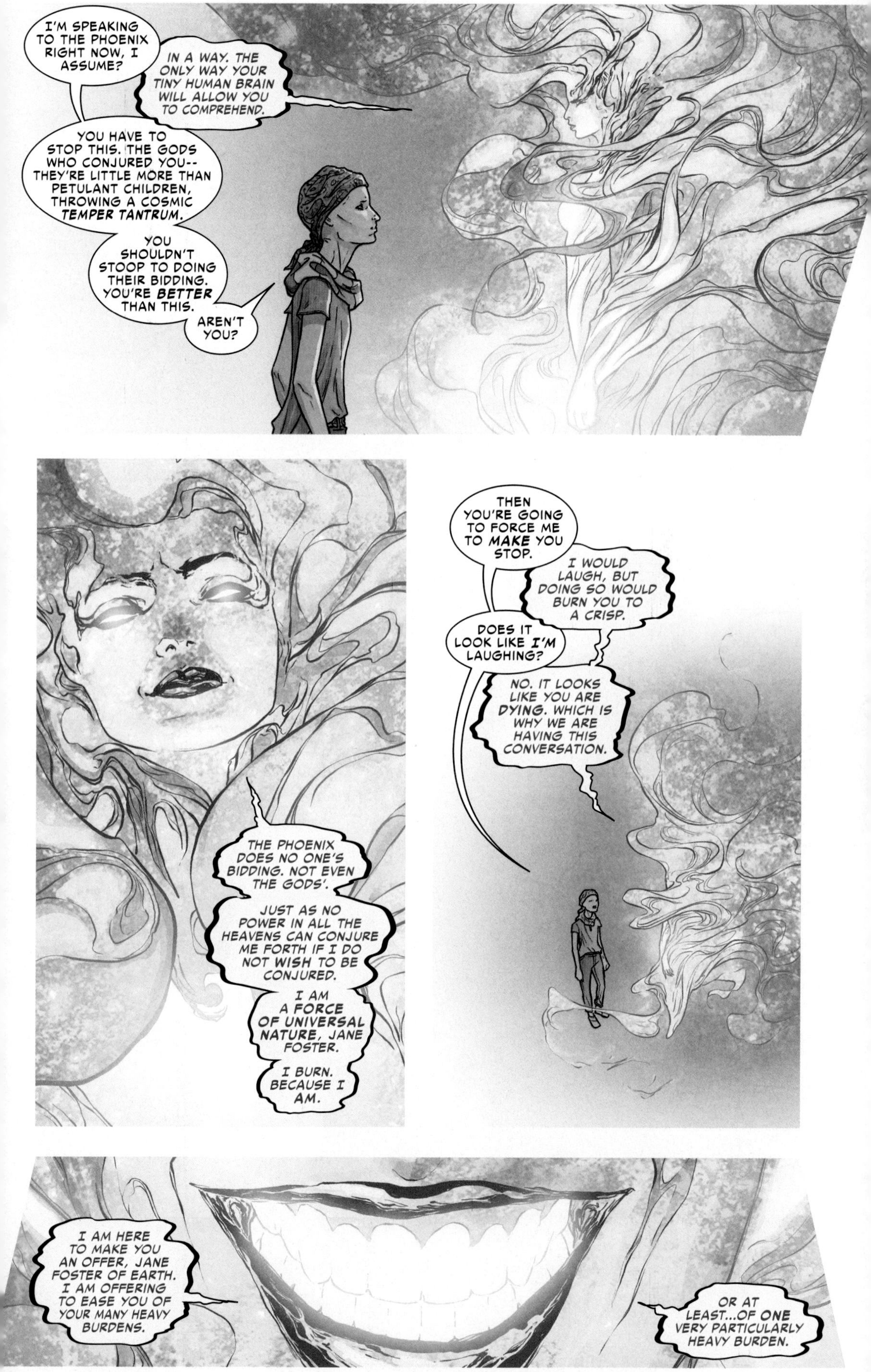
I'M SPEAKING TO THE PHOENIX RIGHT NOW, I ASSUME?
IN A WAY. THE ONLY WAY YOUR TINY HUMAN BRAIN WILL ALLOW YOU TO COMPREHEND.
YOU HAVE TO STOP THIS. THE GODS WHO CONJURED YOU-- THEY'RE LITTLE MORE THAN PETULANT CHILDREN, THROWING A COSMIC TEMPER TANTRUM.
YOU SHOULDN'T STOOP TO DOING THEIR BIDDING. YOU'RE BETTER THAN THIS.
AREN'T YOU?
THE PHOENIX DOES NO ONE'S BIDDING. NOT EVEN THE GODS'.
JUST AS NO POWER IN ALL THE HEAVENS CAN CONJURE ME FORTH IF I DO NOT WISH TO BE CONJURED.
I AM A FORCE OF UNIVERSAL NATURE, JANE FOSTER.
I BURN. BECAUSE I AM.
THEN YOU'RE GOING TO FORCE ME TO MAKE YOU STOP.
I WOULD LAUGH, BUT DOING SO WOULD BURN YOU TO A CRISP.
DOES IT LOOK LIKE I'M LAUGHING?
NO. IT LOOKS LIKE YOU ARE DYING. WHICH IS WHY WE ARE HAVING THIS CONVERSATION.
I AM HERE TO MAKE YOU AN OFFER, JANE FOSTER OF EARTH. I AM OFFERING TO EASE YOU OF YOUR MANY HEAVY BURDENS.
OR AT LEAST...OF ONE VERY PARTICULARLY HEAVY BURDEN.

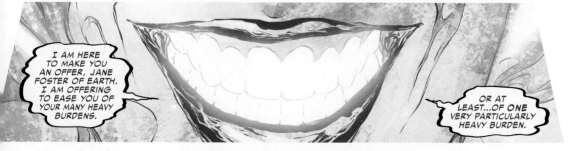

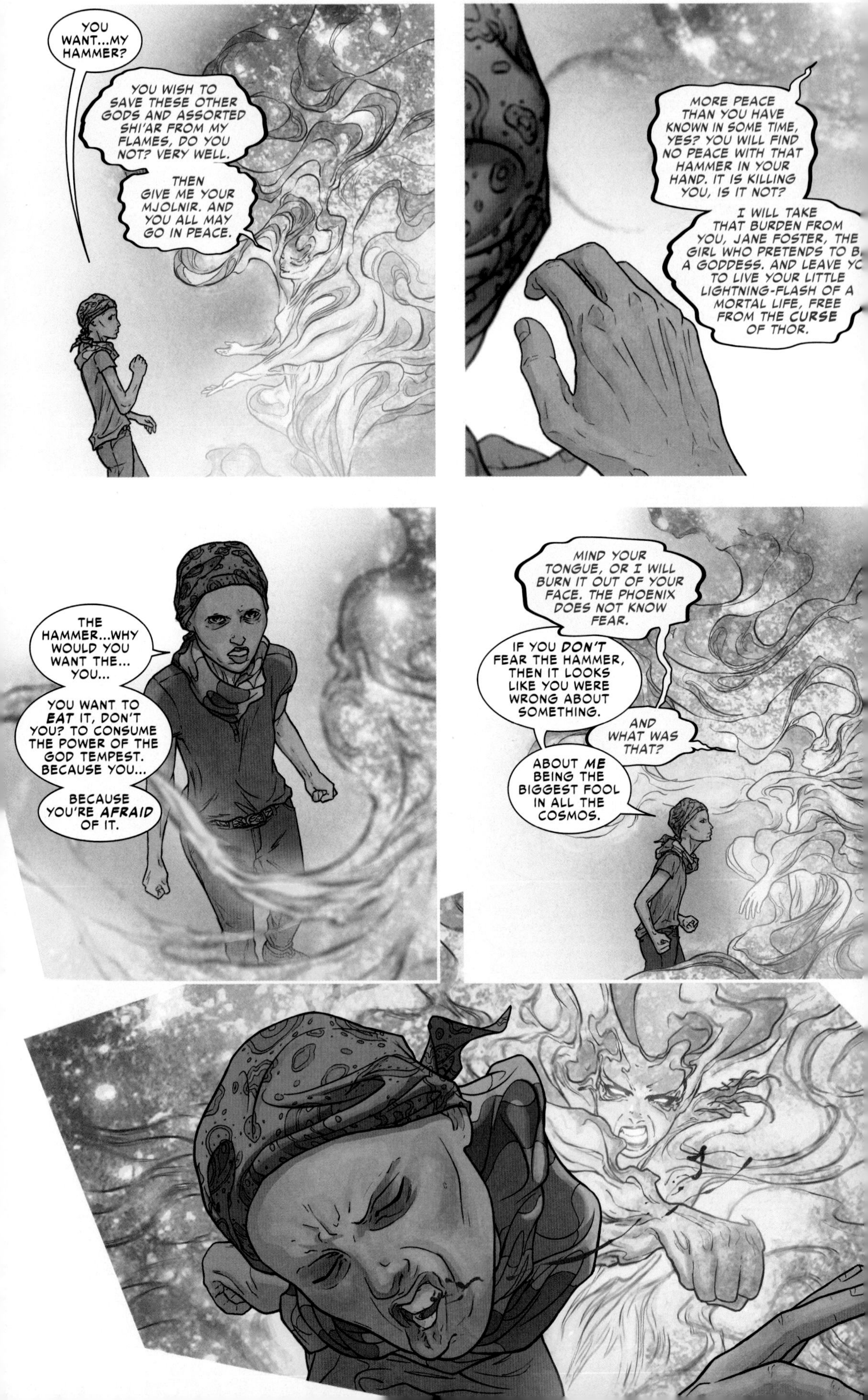

YOU WANT...MY HAMMER?
YOU WISH TO SAVE THESE OTHER GODS AND ASSORTED SHI'AR FROM MY FLAMES, DO YOU NOT? VERY WELL.
THEN GIVE ME YOUR MJOLNIR. AND YOU ALL MAY GO IN PEACE.
MORE PEACE THAN YOU HAVE KNOWN IN SOME TIME, YES? YOU WILL FIND NO PEACE WITH THAT HAMMER IN YOUR HAND. IT IS KILLING YOU, IS IT NOT?
I WILL TAKE THAT BURDEN FROM YOU, JANE FOSTER, THE GIRL WHO PRETENDS TO B A GODDESS. AND LEAVE YO TO LIVE YOUR LITTLE LIGHTNING-FLASH OF A MORTAL LIFE, FREE FROM THE CURSE OF THOR.
THE HAMMER...WHY WOULD YOU WANT THE... YOU...
YOU WANT TO EAT IT, DON'T YOU? TO CONSUME THE POWER OF THE GOD TEMPEST. BECAUSE YOU...
BECAUSE YOU'RE AFRAID OF IT.
MIND YOUR TONGUE, OR I WILL BURN IT OUT OF YOUR FACE. THE PHOENIX DOES NOT KNOW FEAR.
IF YOU DON'T FEAR THE HAMMER, THEN IT LOOKS LIKE YOU WERE WRONG ABOUT SOMETHING.
AND WHAT WAS THAT?
ABOUT ME BEING THE BIGGEST FOOL IN ALL THE COSMOS.

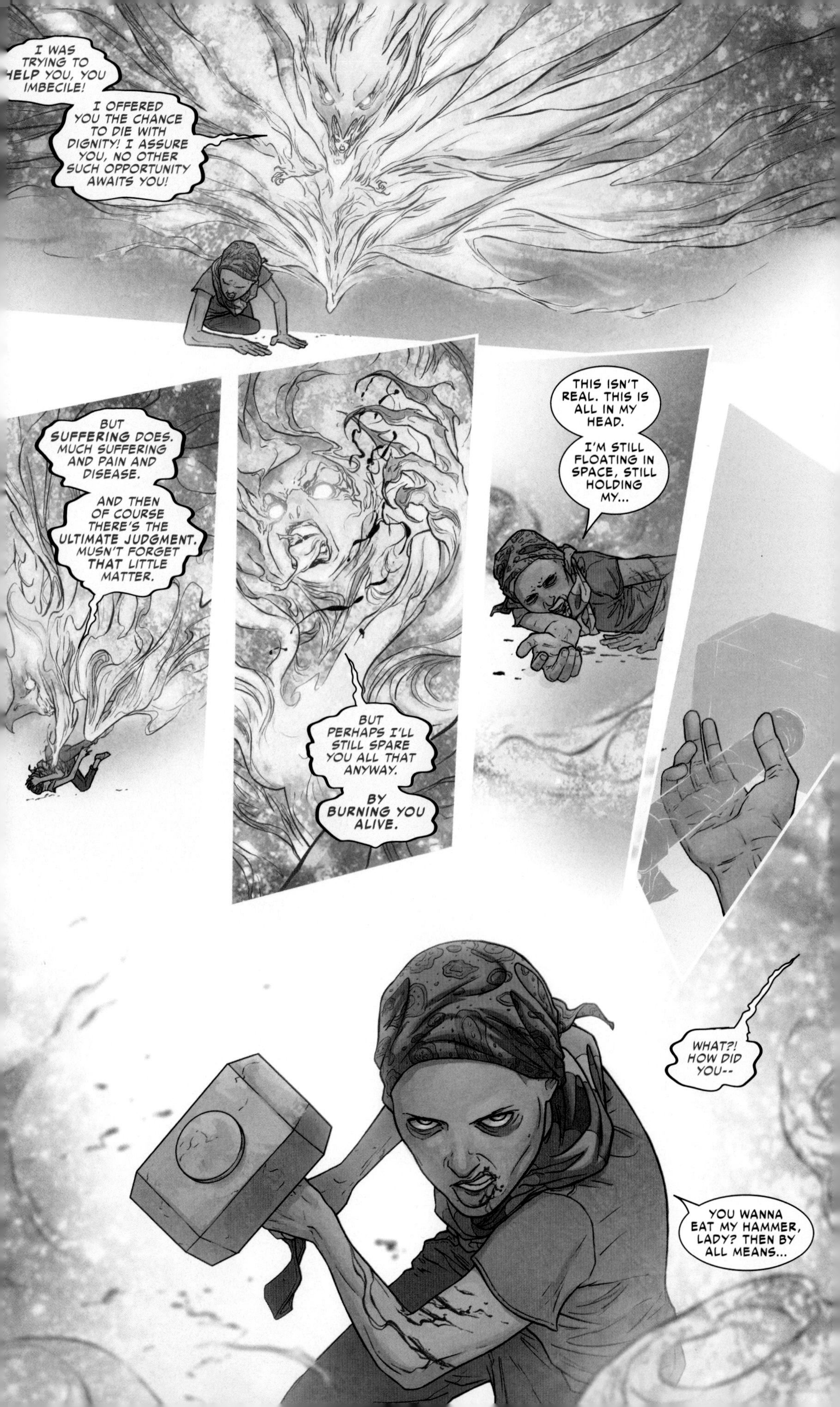
I WAS TRYING TO HELP YOU, YOU IMBECILE!
I OFFERED YOU THE CHANCE TO DIE WITH DIGNITY! I ASSURE YOU, NO OTHER SUCH OPPORTUNITY AWAITS YOU!
BUT SUFFERING DOES. MUCH SUFFERING AND PAIN AND DISEASE.
AND THEN OF COURSE THERE'S THE ULTIMATE JUDGMENT. MUSN'T FORGET THAT LITTLE MATTER.
BUT PERHAPS I'LL STILL SPARE YOU ALL THAT ANYWAY.
BY BURNING YOU ALIVE.
THIS ISN'T REAL. THIS IS ALL IN MY HEAD.
I'M STILL FLOATING IN SPACE, STILL HOLDING MY...
WHAT?! HOW DID YOU--
YOU WANNA EAT MY HAMMER, LADY? THEN BY ALL MEANS...

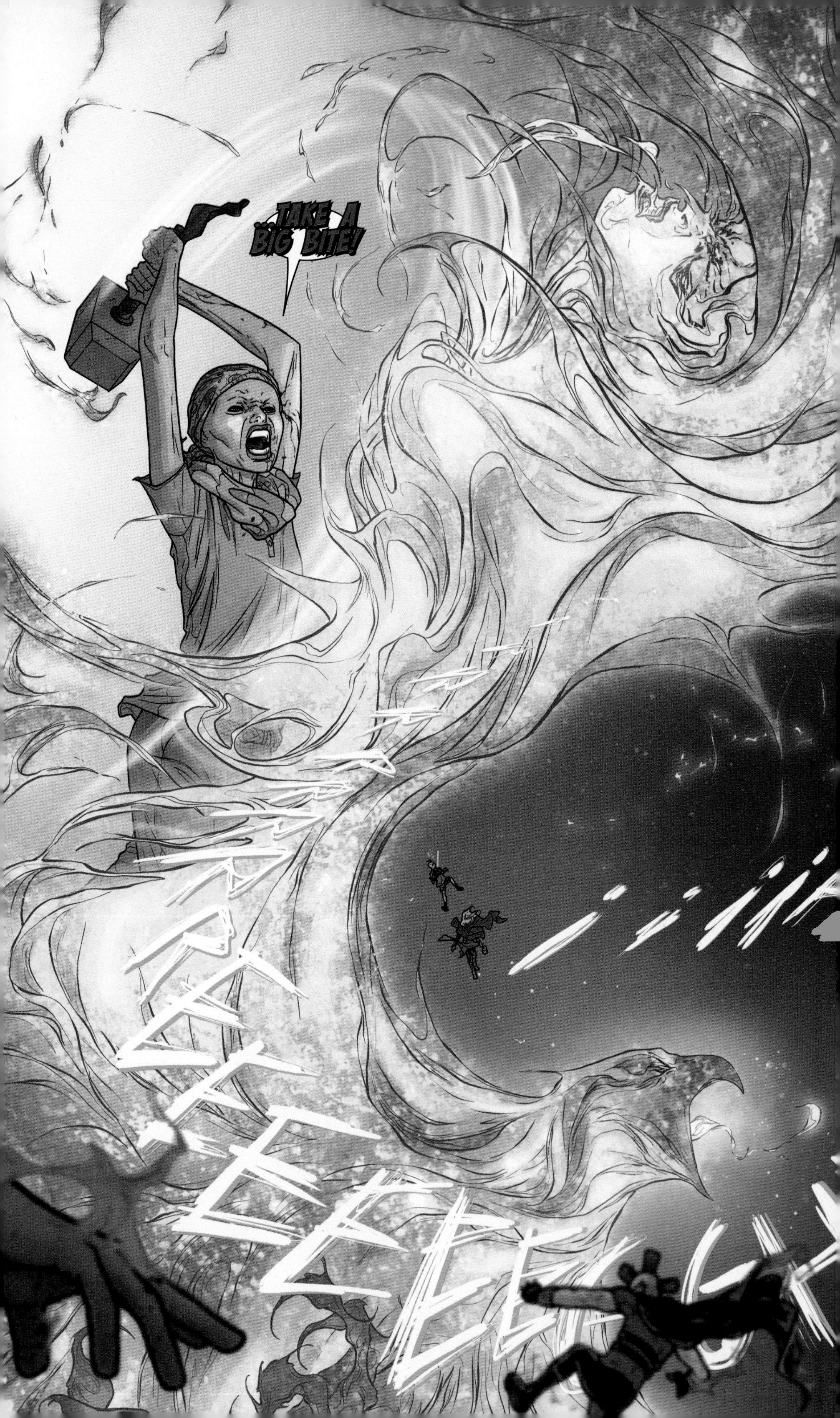
...TAKE A BIG BITE!

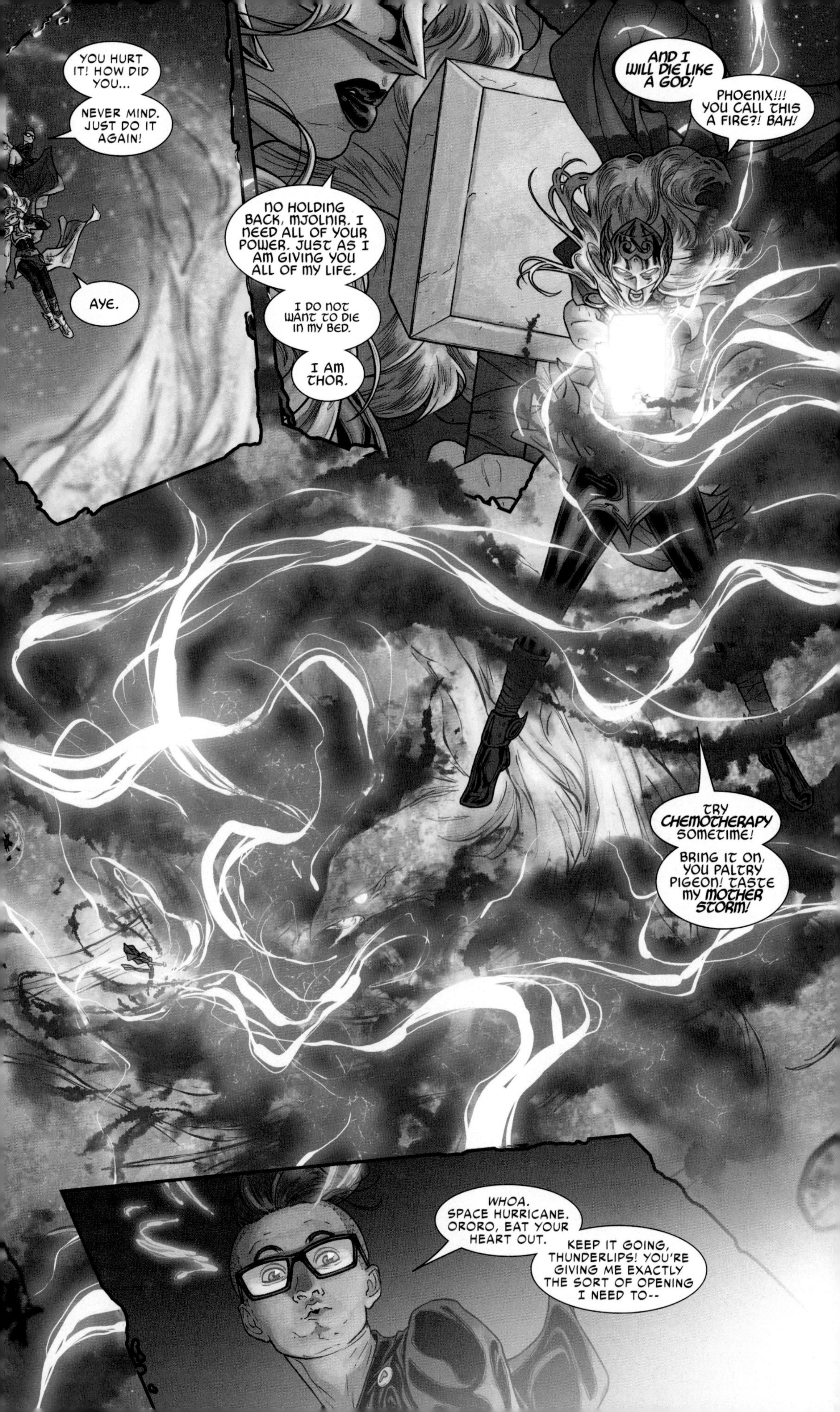
YOU HURT IT! HOW DID YOU...
NEVER MIND. JUST DO IT AGAIN!
AYE.
NO HOLDING BACK, MJOLNIR. I NEED ALL OF YOUR POWER. JUST AS I AM GIVING YOU ALL OF MY LIFE.
I DO NOT WANT TO DIE IN MY BED.
I AM THOR.
AND I WILL DIE LIKE A GOD!
PHOENIX!!! YOU CALL THIS A FIRE?! BAH!
TRY CHEMOTHERAPY SOMETIME!
BRING IT ON, YOU PALTRY PIGEON! TASTE MY MOTHER STORM!
WHOA. SPACE HURRICANE. ORORO, EAT YOUR HEART OUT.
KEEP IT GOING, THUNDERLIPS! YOU'RE GIVING ME EXACTLY THE SORT OF OPENING I NEED TO--

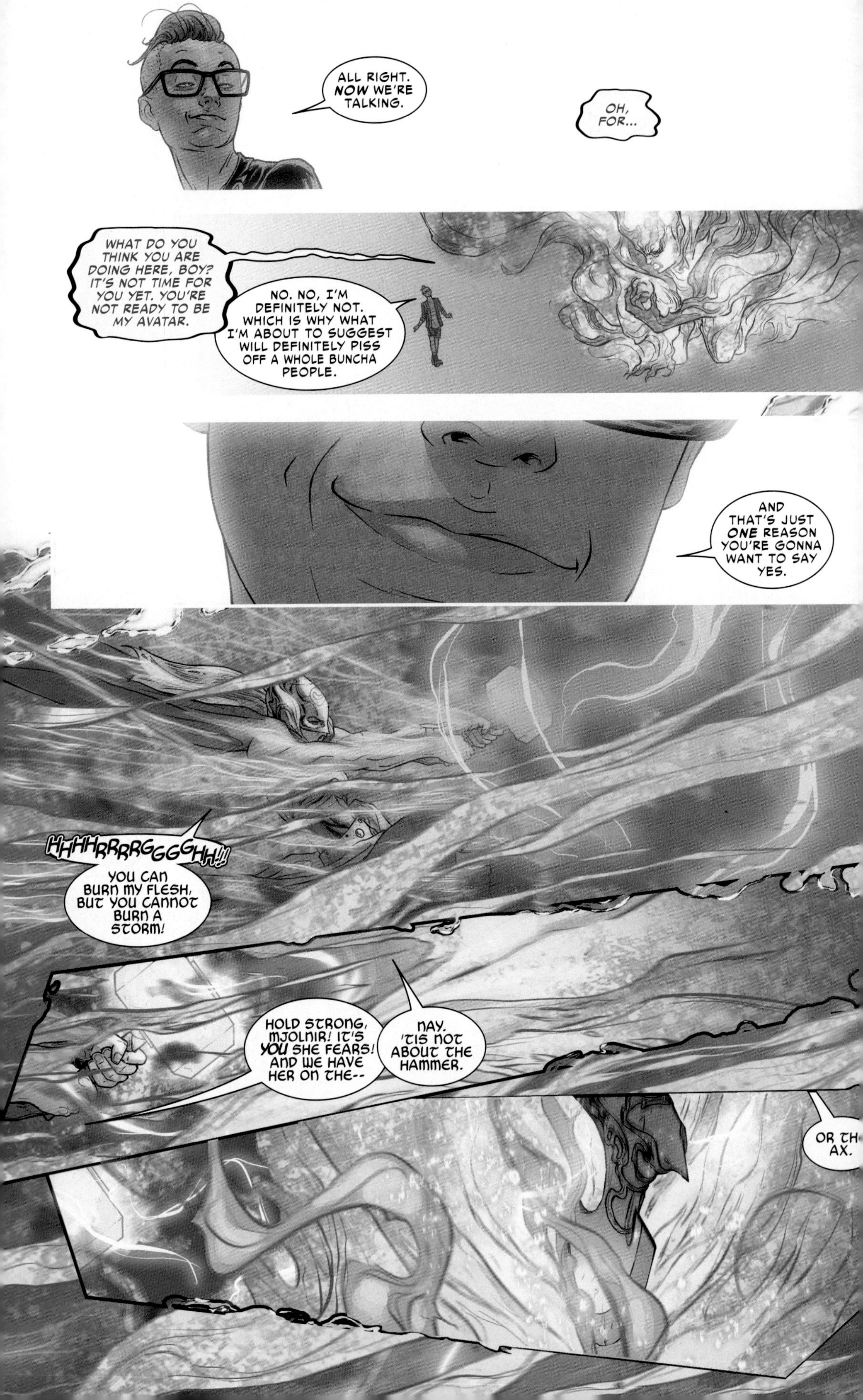
ALL RIGHT. NOW WE'RE TALKING.
OH, FOR...
WHAT DO YOU THINK YOU ARE DOING HERE, BOY? IT'S NOT TIME FOR YOU YET. YOU'RE NOT READY TO BE MY AVATAR.
NO. NO, I'M DEFINITELY NOT. WHICH IS WHY WHAT I'M ABOUT TO SUGGEST WILL DEFINITELY PISS OFF A WHOLE BUNCHA PEOPLE.
AND THAT'S JUST ONE REASON YOU'RE GONNA WANT TO SAY YES.
HHHHRRRRGGGGHH!!!
YOU CAN BURN MY FLESH, BUT YOU CANNOT BURN A STORM!
HOLD STRONG, MJOLNIR! IT'S YOU SHE FEARS! AND WE HAVE HER ON THE--
NAY. 'TIS NOT ABOUT THE HAMMER.
OR TH AX.

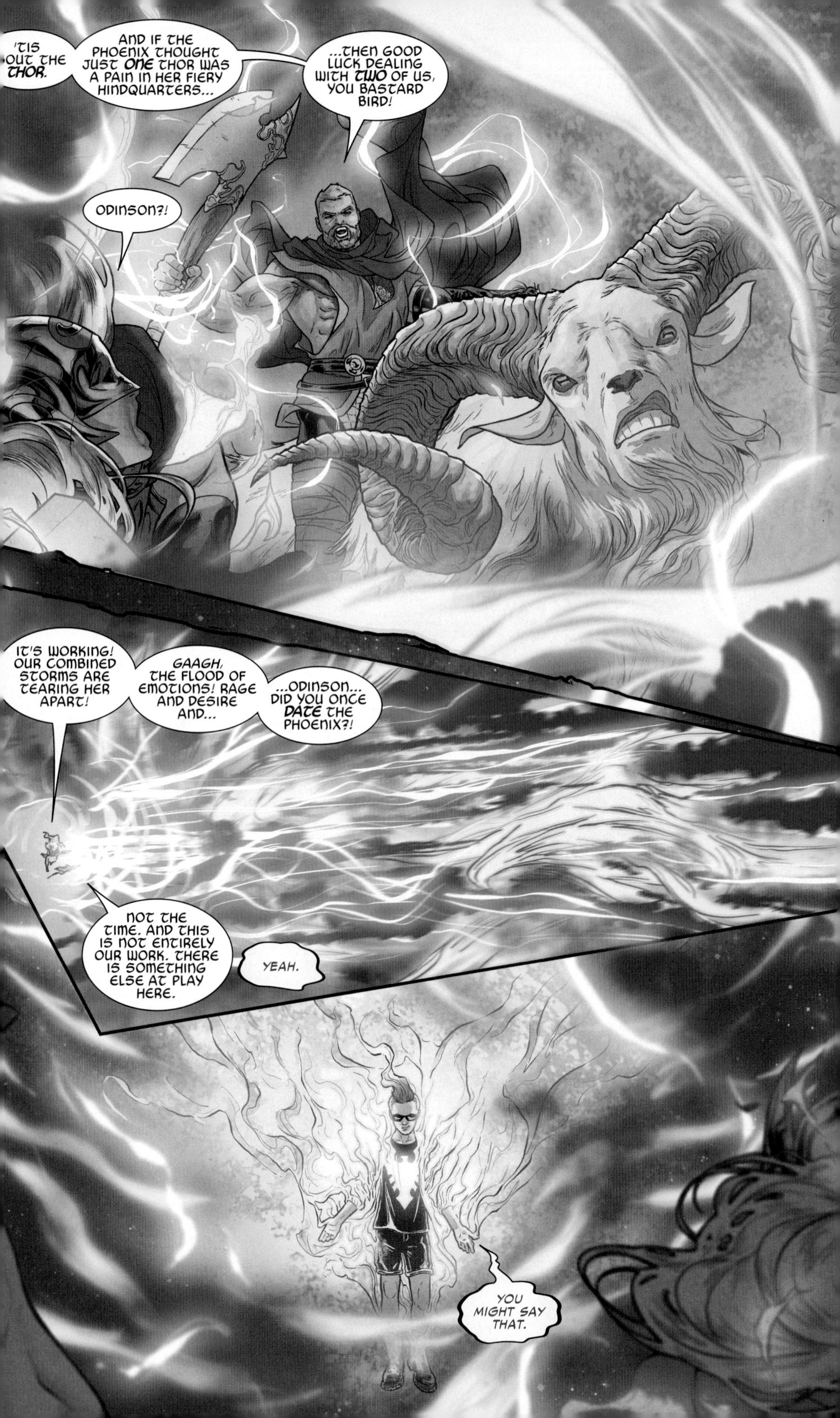
'TIS
OUT THE
THOR.
AND IF THE PHOENIX THOUGHT JUST ONE THOR WAS A PAIN IN HER FIERY HINDQUARTERS...
...THEN GOOD LUCK DEALING WITH TWO OF US, YOU BASTARD BIRD!
ODINSON?!
IT'S WORKING! OUR COMBINED STORMS ARE TEARING HER APART!
GAAGH, THE FLOOD OF EMOTIONS! RAGE AND DESIRE AND...
...ODINSON... DID YOU ONCE DATE THE PHOENIX?!
NOT THE TIME. AND THIS IS NOT ENTIRELY OUR WORK. THERE IS SOMETHING ELSE AT PLAY HERE.
YEAH.
YOU MIGHT SAY THAT.

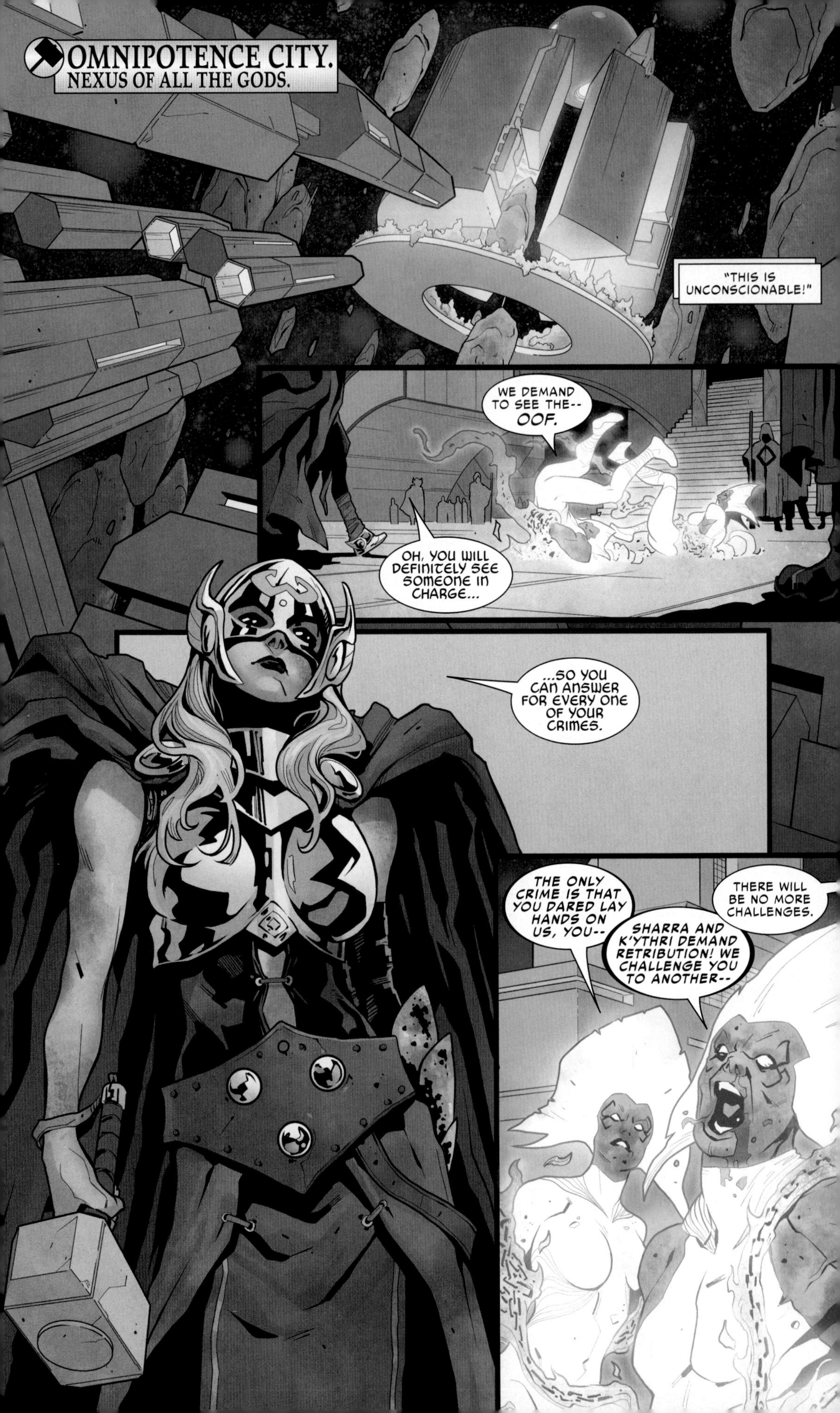

OMNIPOTENCE CITY.
NEXUS OF ALL THE GODS.
"THIS IS UNCONSCIONABLE!"
WE DEMAND TO SEE THE-- OOF.
OH, YOU WILL DEFINITELY SEE SOMEONE IN CHARGE...
...SO YOU CAN ANSWER FOR EVERY ONE OF YOUR CRIMES.
THE ONLY CRIME IS THAT YOU DARED LAY HANDS ON US, YOU--
SHARRA AND K'YTHRI DEMAND RETRIBUTION! WE CHALLENGE YOU TO ANOTHER--
THERE WILL BE NO MORE CHALLENGES.

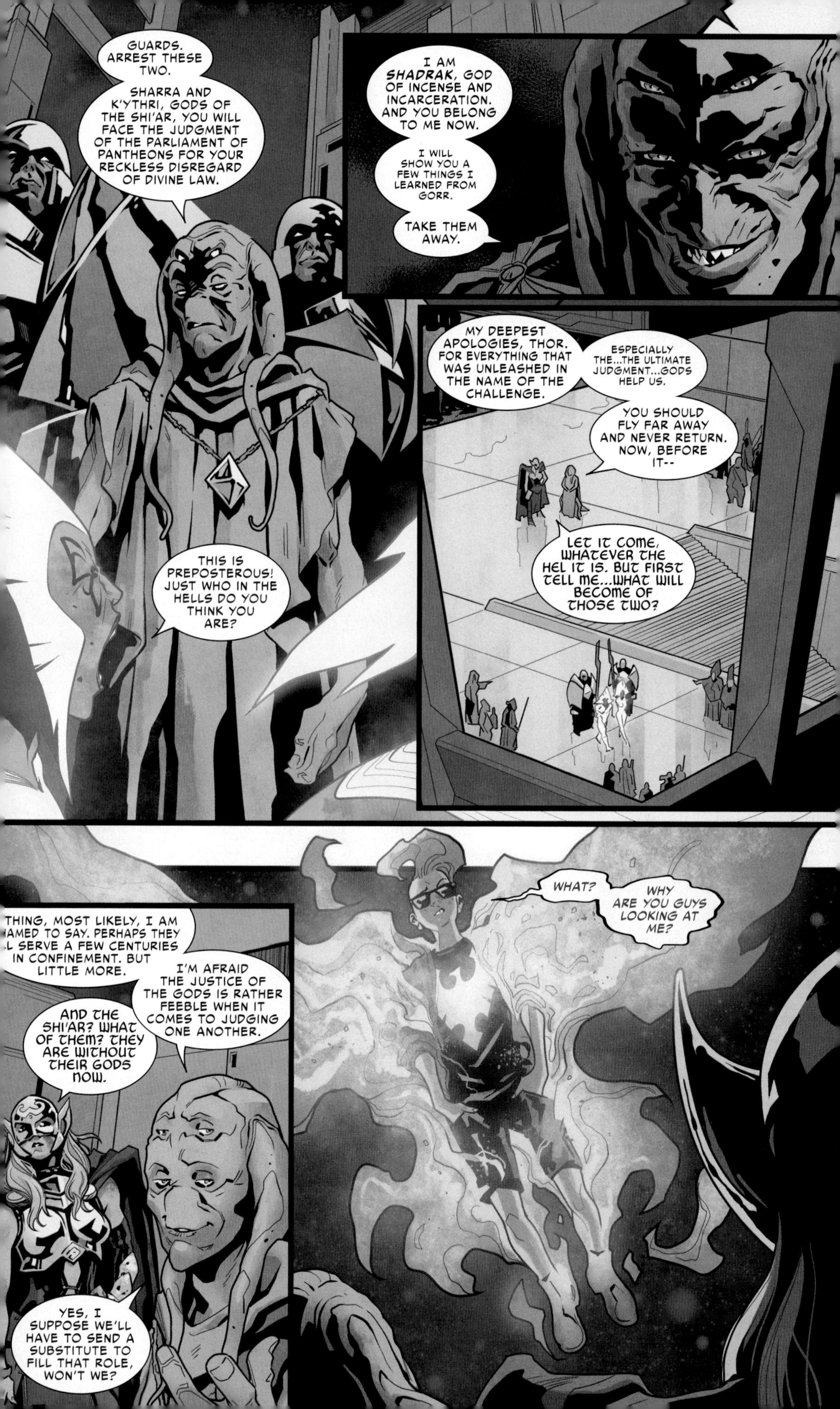
GUARDS. ARREST THESE TWO.
SHARRA AND K'YTHRI, GODS OF THE SHI'AR, YOU WILL FACE THE JUDGMENT OF THE PARLIAMENT OF PANTHEONS FOR YOUR RECKLESS DISREGARD OF DIVINE LAW.
THIS IS PREPOSTEROUS! JUST WHO IN THE HELLS DO YOU THINK YOU ARE?
I AM SHADRAK, GOD OF INCENSE AND INCARCERATION. AND YOU BELONG TO ME NOW.
I WILL SHOW YOU A FEW THINGS I LEARNED FROM GORR.
TAKE THEM AWAY.
MY DEEPEST APOLOGIES, THOR. FOR EVERYTHING THAT WAS UNLEASHED IN THE NAME OF THE CHALLENGE.
ESPECIALLY THE...THE ULTIMATE JUDGMENT...GODS HELP US.
YOU SHOULD FLY FAR AWAY AND NEVER RETURN. NOW, BEFORE IT--
LET IT COME, WHATEVER THE HEL IT IS. BUT FIRST TELL ME...WHAT WILL BECOME OF THOSE TWO?
THING, MOST LIKELY, I AM AMED TO SAY. PERHAPS THEY L SERVE A FEW CENTURIES IN CONFINEMENT. BUT LITTLE MORE.
I'M AFRAID THE JUSTICE OF THE GODS IS RATHER FEEBLE WHEN IT COMES TO JUDGING ONE ANOTHER.
AND THE SHI'AR? WHAT OF THEM? THEY ARE WITHOUT THEIR GODS NOW.
YES, I SUPPOSE WE'LL HAVE TO SEND A SUBSTITUTE TO FILL THAT ROLE, WON'T WE?
WHAT?
WHY ARE YOU GUYS LOOKING AT ME?

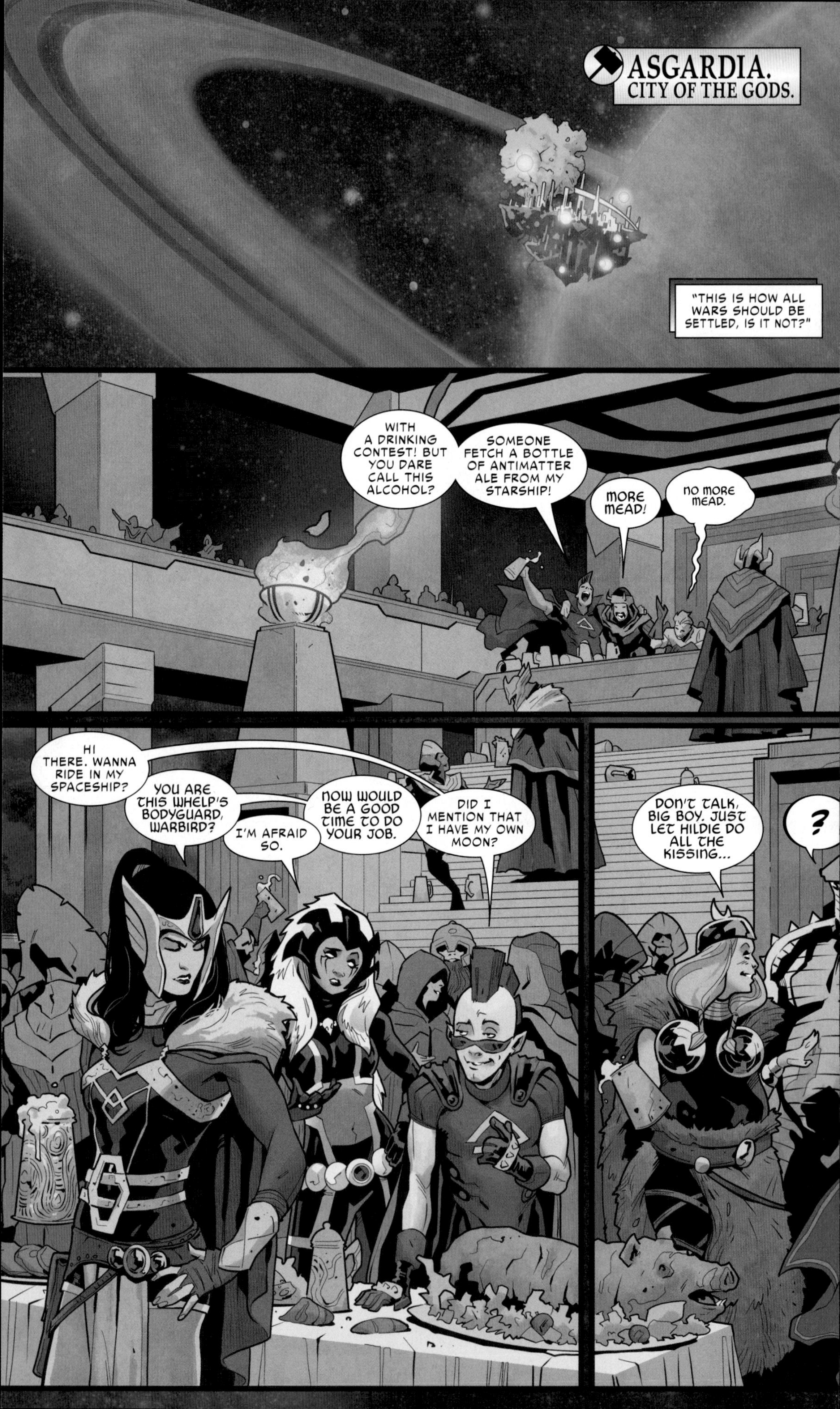
ASGARDIA. CITY OF THE GODS.
"THIS IS HOW ALL WARS SHOULD BE SETTLED, IS IT NOT?"
WITH A DRINKING CONTEST! BUT YOU DARE CALL THIS ALCOHOL?
SOMEONE FETCH A BOTTLE OF ANTIMATTER ALE FROM MY STARSHIP!
MORE MEAD!
NO MORE MEAD.
HI THERE. WANNA RIDE IN MY SPACESHIP?
YOU ARE THIS WHELP'S BODYGUARD, WARBIRD?
I'M AFRAID SO.
NOW WOULD BE A GOOD TIME TO DO YOUR JOB.
DID I MENTION THAT I HAVE MY OWN MOON?
DON'T TALK, BIG BOY. JUST LET HILDIE DO ALL THE KISSING...
?

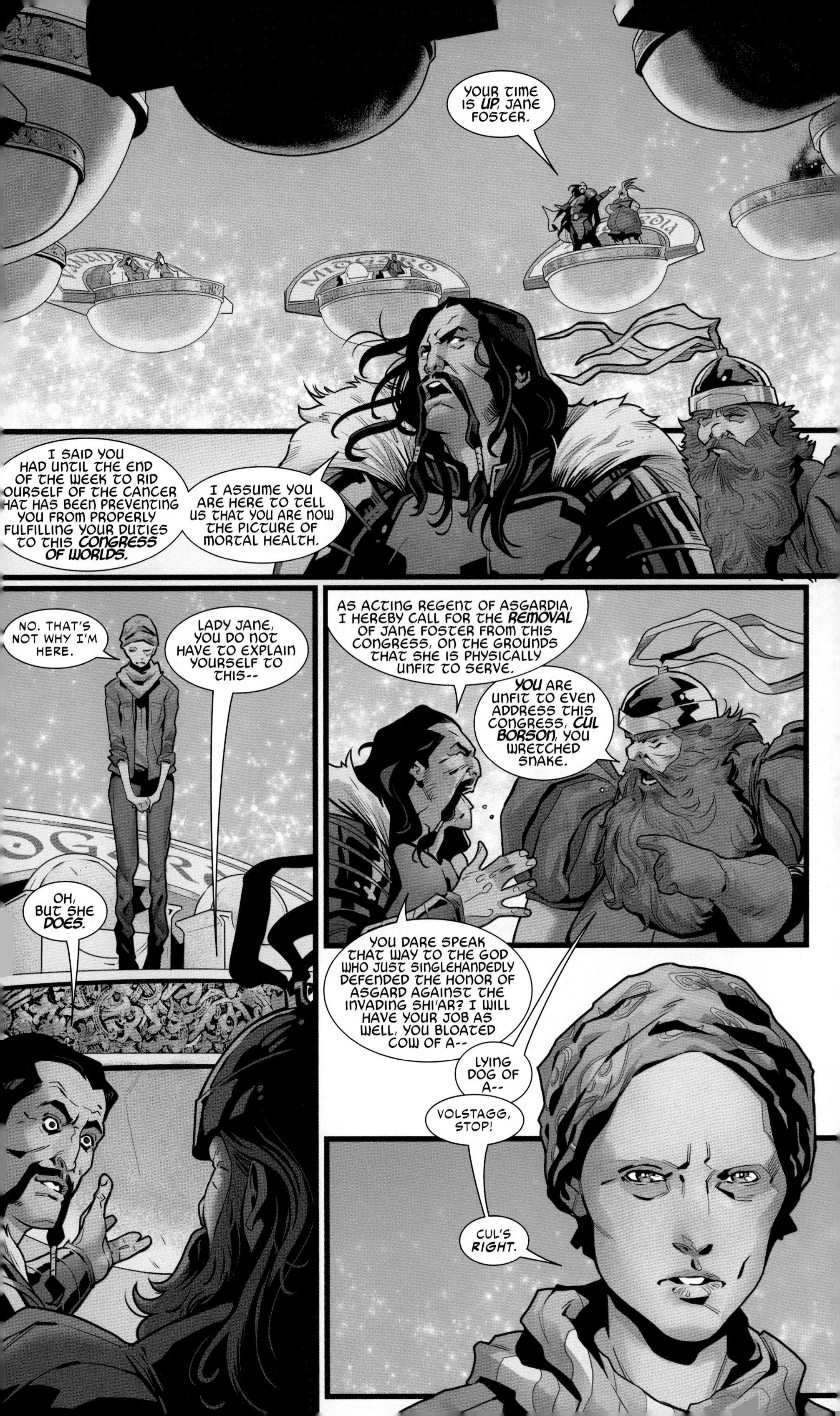

YOUR TIME IS UP, JANE FOSTER.
I SAID YOU HAD UNTIL THE END OF THE WEEK TO RID YOURSELF OF THE CANCER THAT HAS BEEN PREVENTING YOU FROM PROPERLY FULFILLING YOUR DUTIES TO THIS CONGRESS OF WORLDS.
I ASSUME YOU ARE HERE TO TELL US THAT YOU ARE NOW THE PICTURE OF MORTAL HEALTH.
NO. THAT'S NOT WHY I'M HERE.
LADY JANE, YOU DO NOT HAVE TO EXPLAIN YOURSELF TO THIS--
OH, BUT SHE DOES.
AS ACTING REGENT OF ASGARDIA, I HEREBY CALL FOR THE REMOVAL OF JANE FOSTER FROM THIS CONGRESS, ON THE GROUNDS THAT SHE IS PHYSICALLY UNFIT TO SERVE.
YOU ARE UNFIT TO EVEN ADDRESS THIS CONGRESS, CUL BORSON, YOU WRETCHED SNAKE.
YOU DARE SPEAK THAT WAY TO THE GOD WHO JUST SINGLEHANDEDLY DEFENDED THE HONOR OF ASGARD AGAINST THE INVADING SHI'AR? I WILL HAVE YOUR JOB AS WELL, YOU BLOATED COW OF A--
LYING DOG OF A--
VOLSTAGG, STOP!
CUL'S RIGHT.

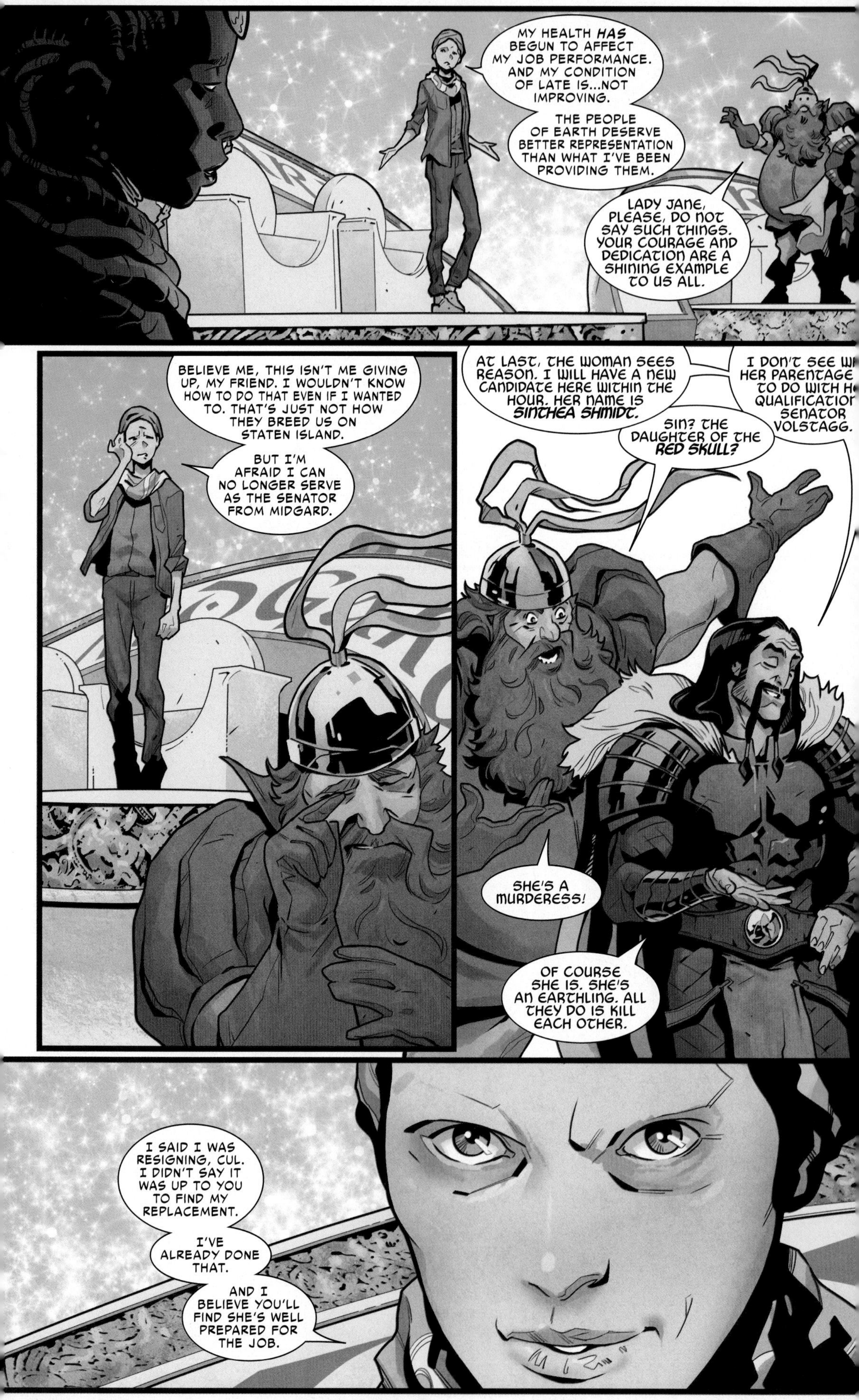
MY HEALTH HAS BEGUN TO AFFECT MY JOB PERFORMANCE. AND MY CONDITION OF LATE IS...NOT IMPROVING.
THE PEOPLE OF EARTH DESERVE BETTER REPRESENTATION THAN WHAT I'VE BEEN PROVIDING THEM.
LADY JANE, PLEASE, DO NOT SAY SUCH THINGS. YOUR COURAGE AND DEDICATION ARE A SHINING EXAMPLE TO US ALL.
BELIEVE ME, THIS ISN'T ME GIVING UP, MY FRIEND. I WOULDN'T KNOW HOW TO DO THAT EVEN IF I WANTED TO. THAT'S JUST NOT HOW THEY BREED US ON STATEN ISLAND.
BUT I'M AFRAID I CAN NO LONGER SERVE AS THE SENATOR FROM MIDGARD.
AT LAST, THE WOMAN SEES REASON. I WILL HAVE A NEW CANDIDATE HERE WITHIN THE HOUR. HER NAME IS SINTHEA SHMIDT.
SIN? THE DAUGHTER OF THE RED SKULL?
I DON'T SEE W HER PARENTAGE TO DO WITH H QUALIFICATIO SENATOR VOLSTAGG.
SHE'S A MURDERESS!
OF COURSE SHE IS. SHE'S AN EARTHLING. ALL THEY DO IS KILL EACH OTHER.
I SAID I WAS RESIGNING, CUL. I DIDN'T SAY IT WAS UP TO YOU TO FIND MY REPLACEMENT.
I'VE ALREADY DONE THAT.
AND I BELIEVE YOU'LL FIND SHE'S WELL PREPARED FOR THE JOB.

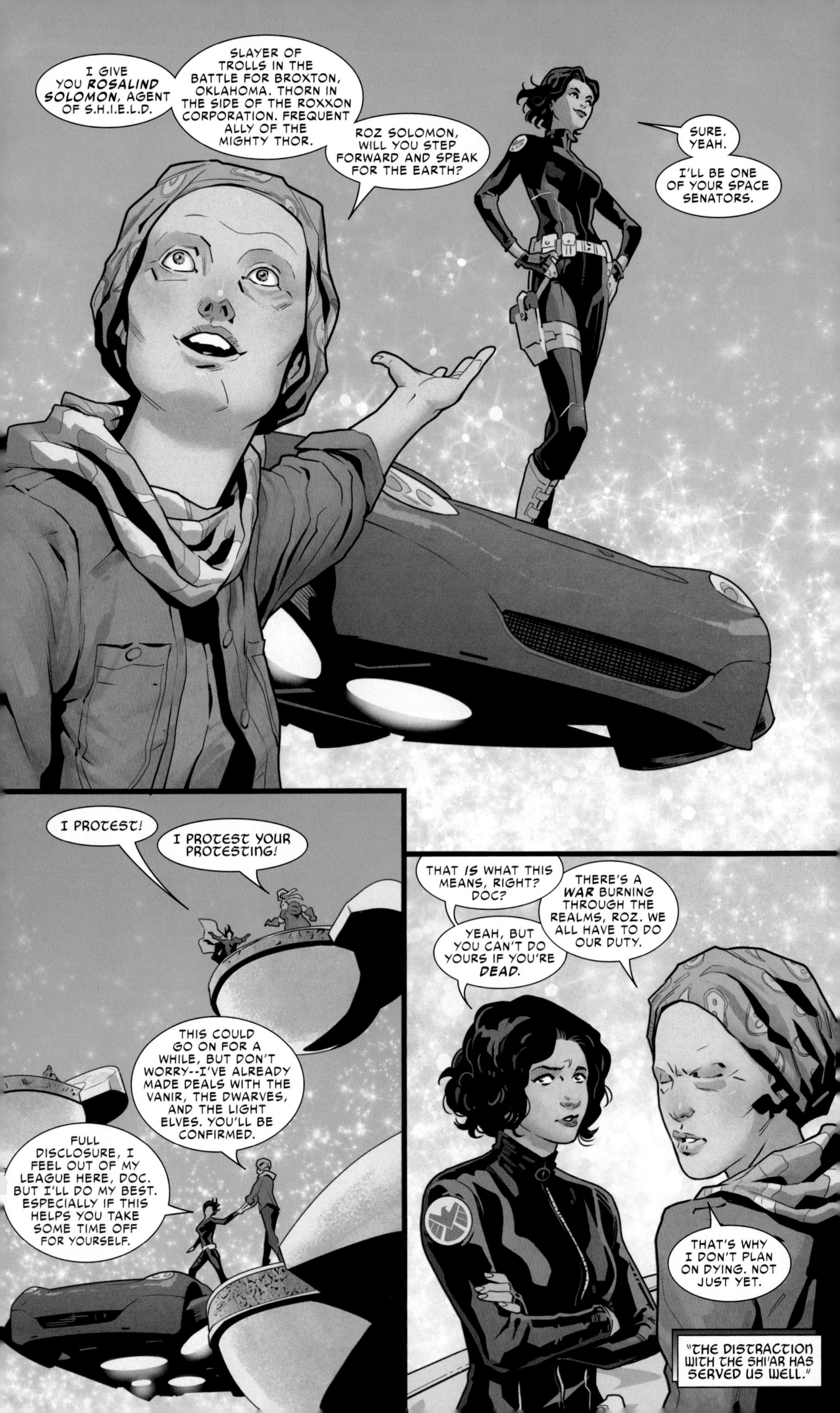
I GIVE YOU ROSALIND SOLOMON, AGENT OF S.H.I.E.L.D.
SLAYER OF TROLLS IN THE BATTLE FOR BROXTON, OKLAHOMA. THORN IN THE SIDE OF THE ROXXON CORPORATION. FREQUENT ALLY OF THE MIGHTY THOR.
ROZ SOLOMON, WILL YOU STEP FORWARD AND SPEAK FOR THE EARTH?
SURE. YEAH.
I'LL BE ONE OF YOUR SPACE SENATORS.
I PROTEST!
I PROTEST YOUR PROTESTING!
THIS COULD GO ON FOR A WHILE, BUT DON'T WORRY--I'VE ALREADY MADE DEALS WITH THE VANIR, THE DWARVES, AND THE LIGHT ELVES. YOU'LL BE CONFIRMED.
FULL DISCLOSURE, I FEEL OUT OF MY LEAGUE HERE, DOC. BUT I'LL DO MY BEST. ESPECIALLY IF THIS HELPS YOU TAKE SOME TIME OFF FOR YOURSELF.
THAT IS WHAT THIS MEANS, RIGHT? DOC?
THERE'S A WAR BURNING THROUGH THE REALMS, ROZ. WE ALL HAVE TO DO OUR DUTY.
YEAH, BUT YOU CAN'T DO YOURS IF YOU'RE DEAD.
THAT'S WHY I DON'T PLAN ON DYING. NOT JUST YET.
"THE DISTRACTION WITH THE SHI'AR HAS SERVED US WELL."

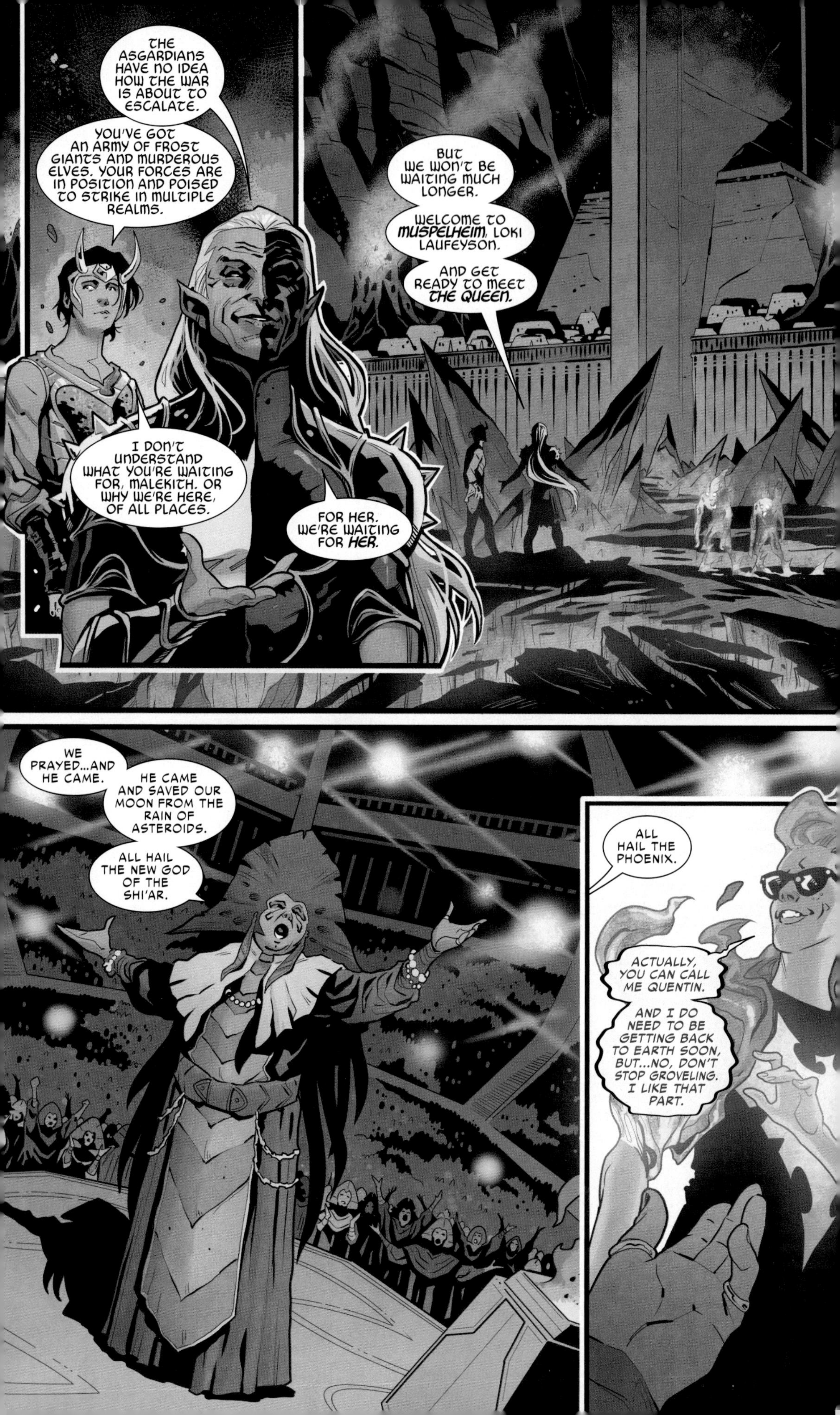
THE ASGARDIANS HAVE NO IDEA HOW THE WAR IS ABOUT TO ESCALATE.
YOU'VE GOT AN ARMY OF FROST GIANTS AND MURDEROUS ELVES. YOUR FORCES ARE IN POSITION AND POISED TO STRIKE IN MULTIPLE REALMS.
BUT WE WON'T BE WAITING MUCH LONGER.
WELCOME TO MUSPELHEIM, LOKI LAUFEYSON.
AND GET READY TO MEET THE QUEEN.
I DON'T UNDERSTAND WHAT YOU'RE WAITING FOR, MALEKITH. OR WHY WE'RE HERE, OF ALL PLACES.
FOR HER. WE'RE WAITING FOR HER.
WE PRAYED...AND HE CAME.
HE CAME AND SAVED OUR MOON FROM THE RAIN OF ASTEROIDS.
ALL HAIL THE NEW GOD OF THE SHI'AR.
ALL HAIL THE PHOENIX.
ACTUALLY, YOU CAN CALL ME QUENTIN.
AND I DO NEED TO BE GETTING BACK TO EARTH SOON, BUT...NO, DON'T STOP GROVELING. I LIKE THAT PART.

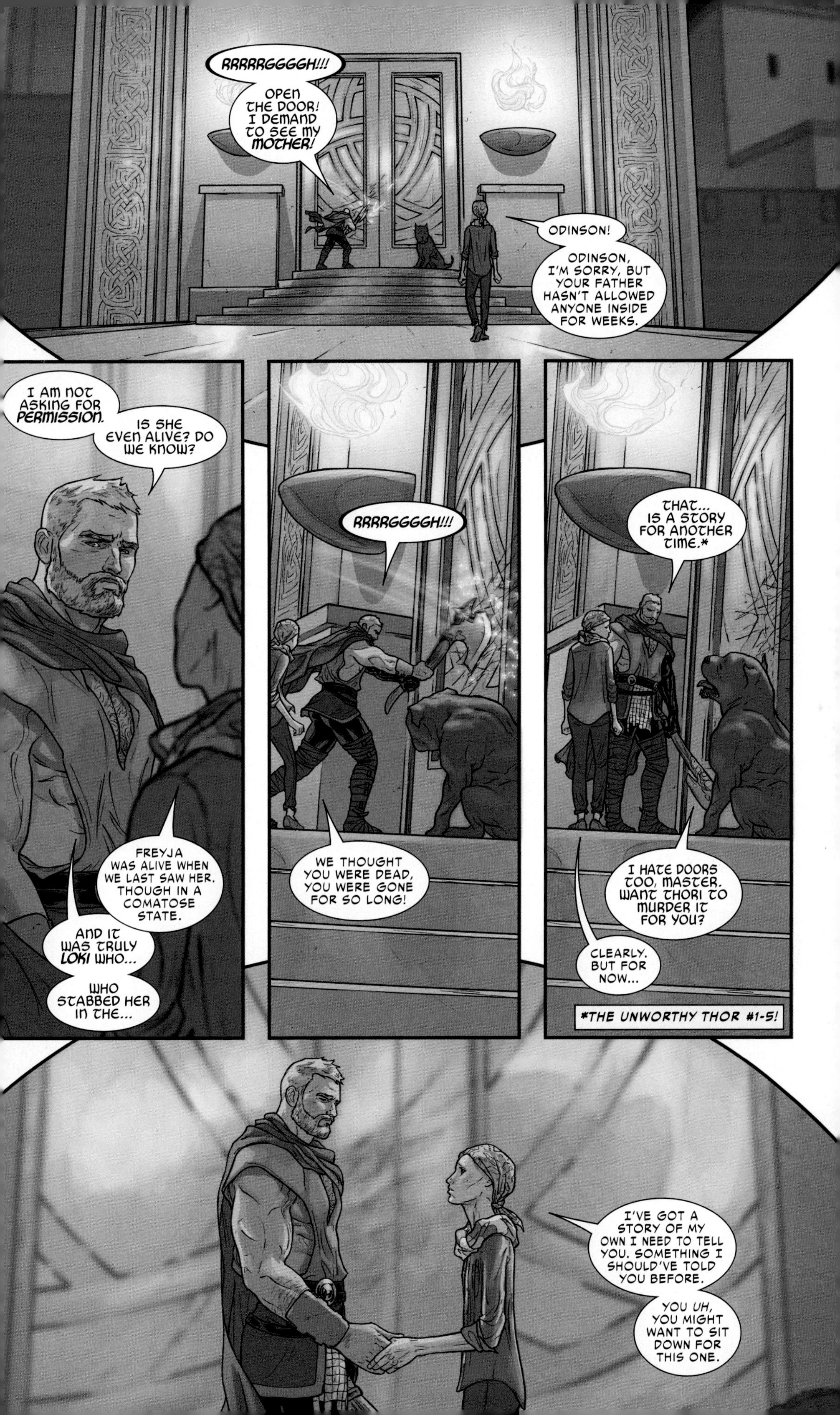
RRRRRGGGGH!!!
OPEN THE DOOR! I DEMAND TO SEE MY MOTHER!
ODINSON!
ODINSON, I'M SORRY, BUT YOUR FATHER HASN'T ALLOWED ANYONE INSIDE FOR WEEKS.
I AM NOT ASKING FOR PERMISSION.
IS SHE EVEN ALIVE? DO WE KNOW?
FREYJA WAS ALIVE WHEN WE LAST SAW HER. THOUGH IN A COMATOSE STATE.
AND IT WAS TRULY LOKI WHO...
WHO STABBED HER IN THE...
RRRRGGGGH!!!
WE THOUGHT YOU WERE DEAD, YOU WERE GONE FOR SO LONG!
THAT... IS A STORY FOR ANOTHER TIME.*
I HATE DOORS TOO, MASTER. WANT THORI TO MURDER IT FOR YOU?
CLEARLY. BUT FOR NOW...
*THE UNWORTHY THOR #1-5!
I'VE GOT A STORY OF MY OWN I NEED TO TELL YOU. SOMETHING I SHOULD'VE TOLD YOU BEFORE.
YOU UH, YOU MIGHT WANT TO SIT DOWN FOR THIS ONE.

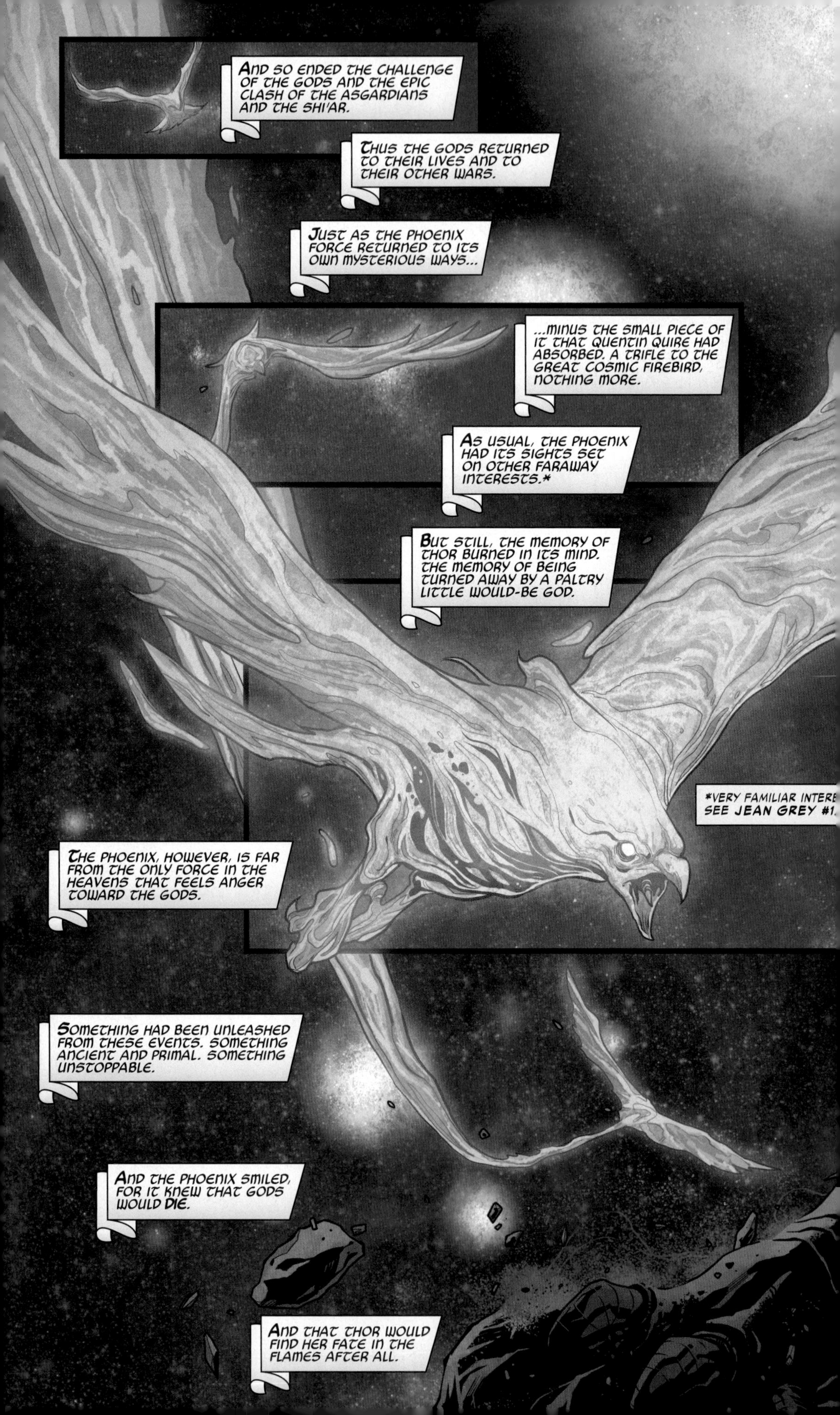
AND SO ENDED THE CHALLENGE OF THE GODS AND THE EPIC CLASH OF THE ASGARDIANS AND THE SHI'AR.
THUS THE GODS RETURNED TO THEIR LIVES AND TO THEIR OTHER WARS.
JUST AS THE PHOENIX FORCE RETURNED TO ITS OWN MYSTERIOUS WAYS...
...MINUS THE SMALL PIECE OF IT THAT QUENTIN QUIRE HAD ABSORBED. A TRIFLE TO THE GREAT COSMIC FIREBIRD, NOTHING MORE.
AS USUAL, THE PHOENIX HAD ITS SIGHTS SET ON OTHER FARAWAY INTERESTS.*
BUT STILL, THE MEMORY OF THOR BURNED IN ITS MIND. THE MEMORY OF BEING TURNED AWAY BY A PALTRY LITTLE WOULD-BE GOD.
*VERY FAMILIAR INTERE SEE JEAN GREY #1.
THE PHOENIX, HOWEVER, IS FAR FROM THE ONLY FORCE IN THE HEAVENS THAT FEELS ANGER TOWARD THE GODS.
SOMETHING HAD BEEN UNLEASHED FROM THESE EVENTS. SOMETHING ANCIENT AND PRIMAL. SOMETHING UNSTOPPABLE.
AND THE PHOENIX SMILED, FOR IT KNEW THAT GODS WOULD DIE.
AND THAT THOR WOULD FIND HER FATE IN THE FLAMES AFTER ALL.

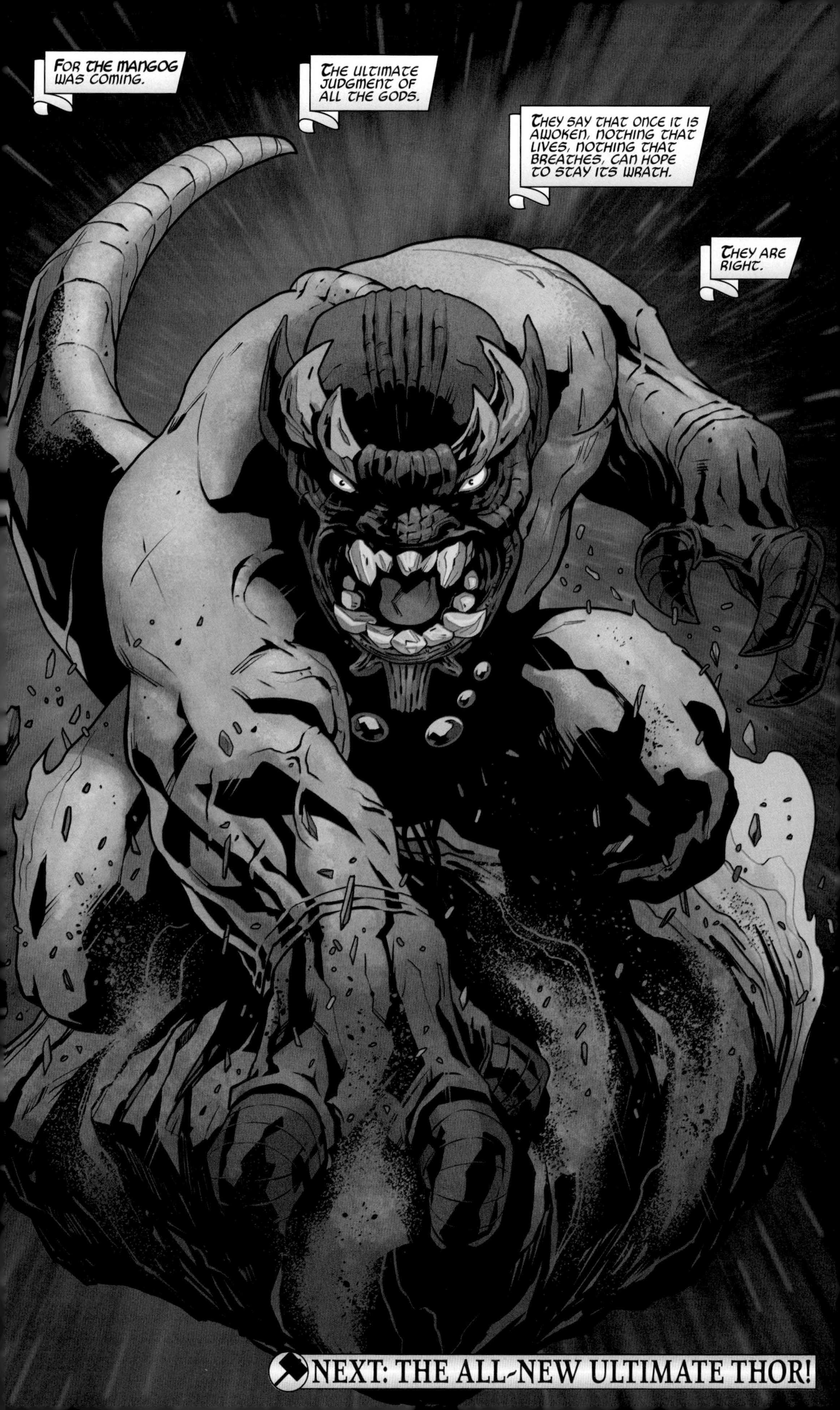
FOR THE MANGOG WAS COMING.
THE ULTIMATE JUDGMENT OF ALL THE GODS.
THEY SAY THAT ONCE IT IS AWOKEN, NOTHING THAT LIVES, NOTHING THAT BREATHES, CAN HOPE TO STAY ITS WRATH.
THEY ARE RIGHT.
NEXT: THE ALL-NEW ULTIMATE THOR!

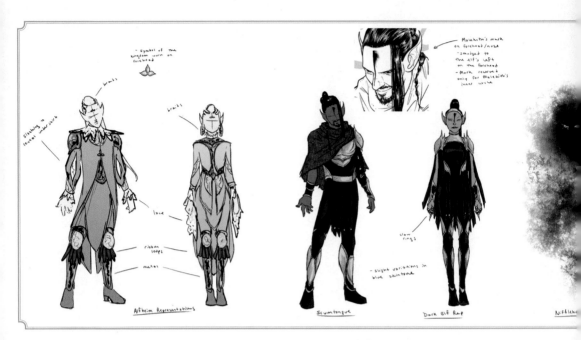

- symbol of the kingdom worn on forehead

braids

braids

slitting to reveal underneath

lace

ribbon loops

metal

Malekith's mark on forehead/nose
- smudged to the elf's left on the forehead
- Mark reserved only for Malekith's inner circle

clan rings

- slight variations in blue skintone

Alfheim Representatives

Scumtongue

Dark Elf Rep

Niflehe

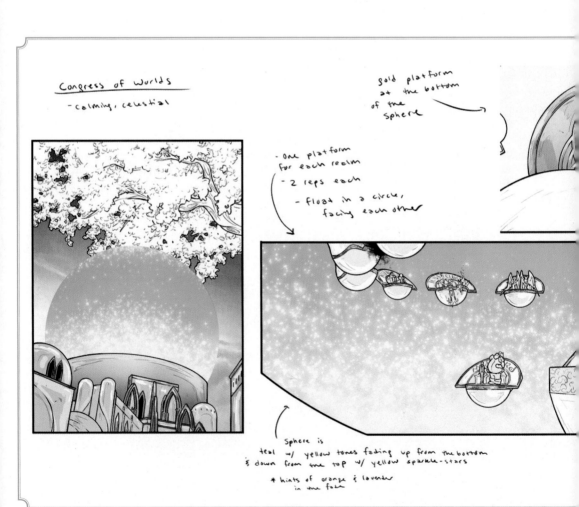

Congress of Worlds
- calming, celestial

gold platform at the bottom of the sphere

- one platform for each realm
- 2 reps each
- float in a circle, facing each other

Sphere is teal w/ yellow tones fading up from the bottom & down from the top w/ yellow sparkle-stars

* hints of orange & lavender in the face

BY **RUSSELL DAUTERMAN**

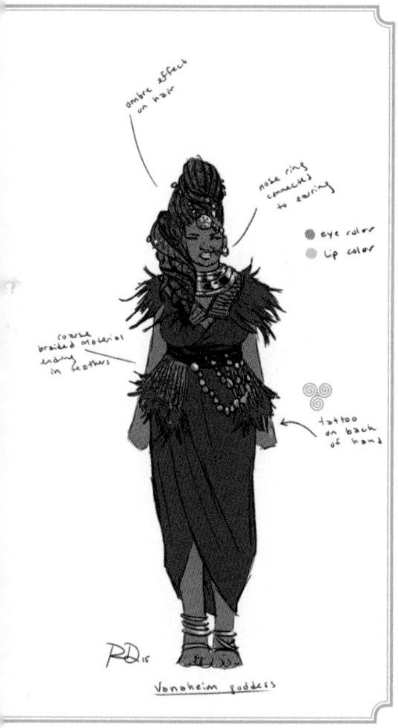
ombre effect on hair
nose ring connected to earring
eye color
lip color
coarse braided material ending in feathers
tattoo on back of hand
RD 15
Vanaheim goddess

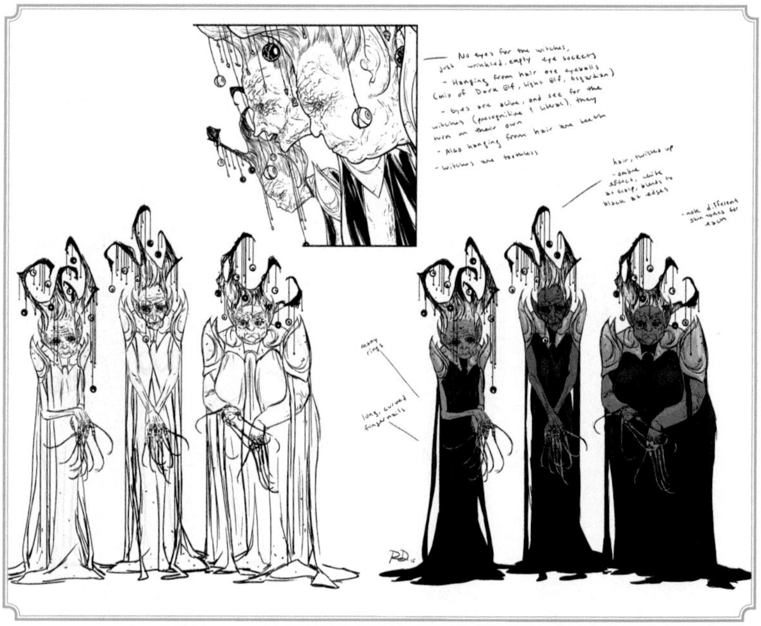
No eyes for the witches, just wrinkled, empty eye sockets
- Hanging from hair are eyeballs (mix of Dark Elf, Light Elf, Asgardian)
- Eyes are alive, and see for the witches (precognitive & literal). they turn on their own
- Also hanging from hair are teeth
- witches are toothless
hair, twisted up
- ombre effect, white at scalp, blends to black at edges
- note different skin tones for each
many rings
long, curved fingernails
RD 15

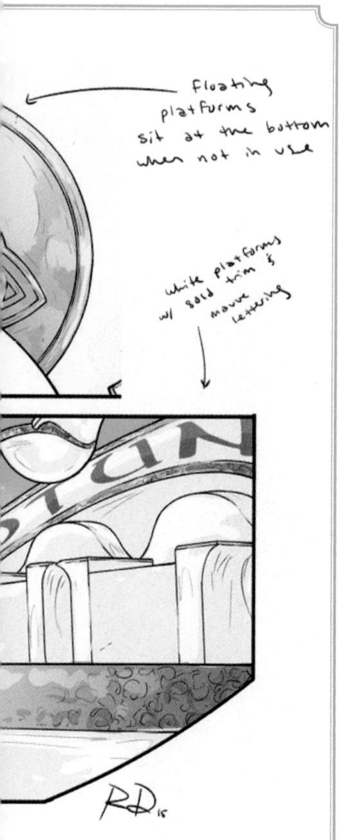
Floating platforms sit at the bottom when not in use
white platforms w/ gold trim & mauve lettering
RD 15

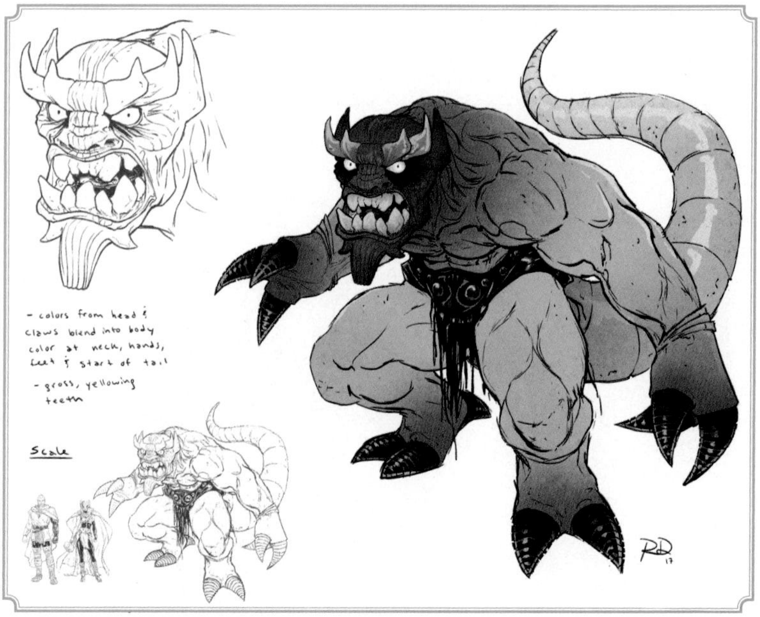
- colors from head & claws blend into body color at neck, hands, feet & start of tail
- gross, yellowing teeth
Scale
RD 17

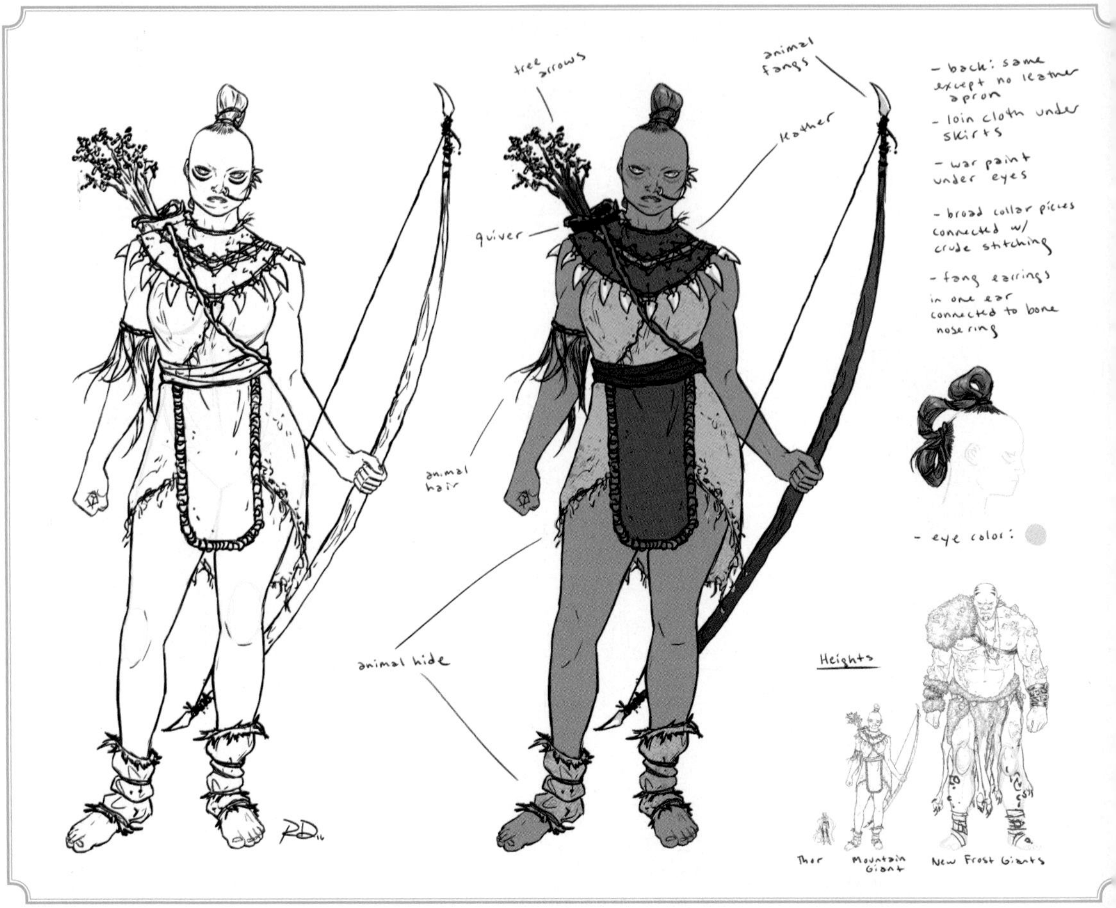
tree arrows
animal fangs
leather
quiver
animal hair
animal hide
- back: same except no leather apron
- loin cloth under skirts
- war paint under eyes
- broad collar pieces connected w/ crude stitching
- fang earrings in one ear connected to bone nosering
- eye color:
Heights
Thor
Mountain Giant
New Frost Giants
RD 16

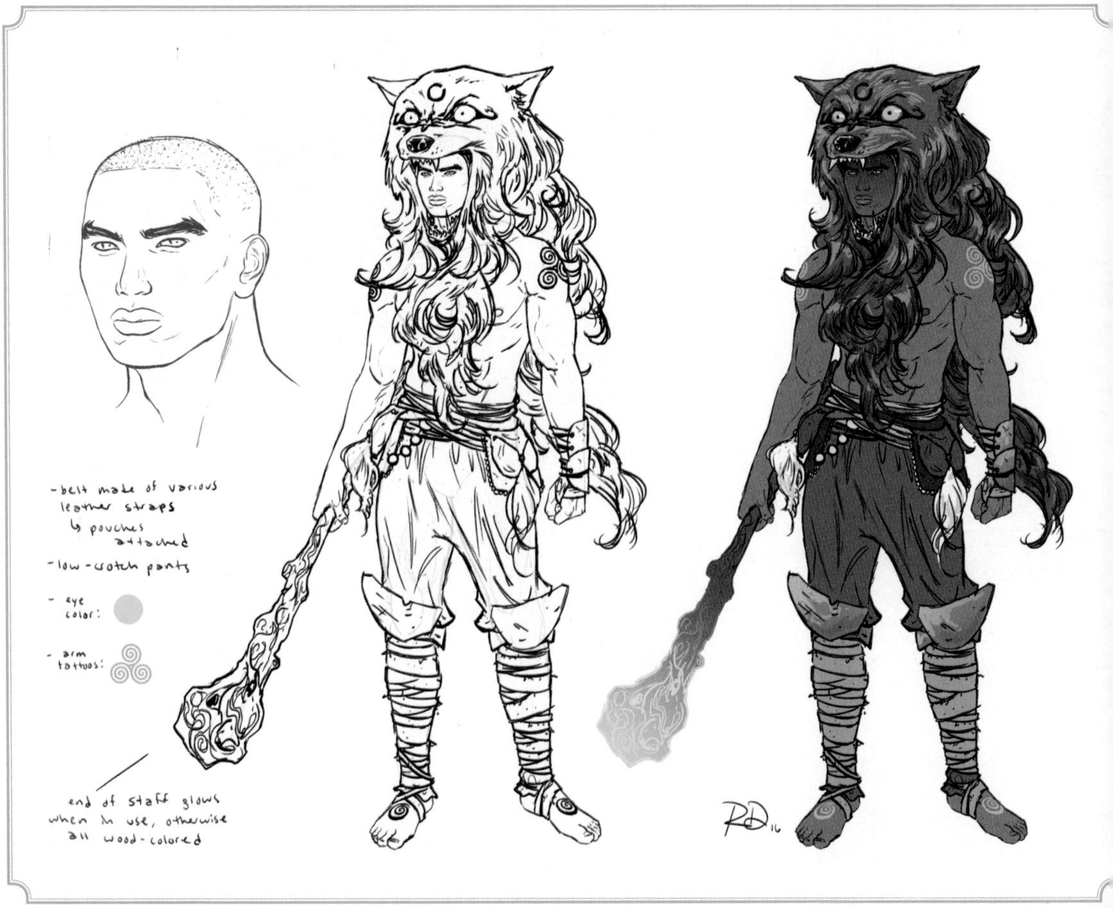
- belt made of various leather straps
↳ pouches attached
- low-crotch pants
- eye color:
- arm tattoos:
end of staff glows when in use, otherwise all wood-colored
RD 16

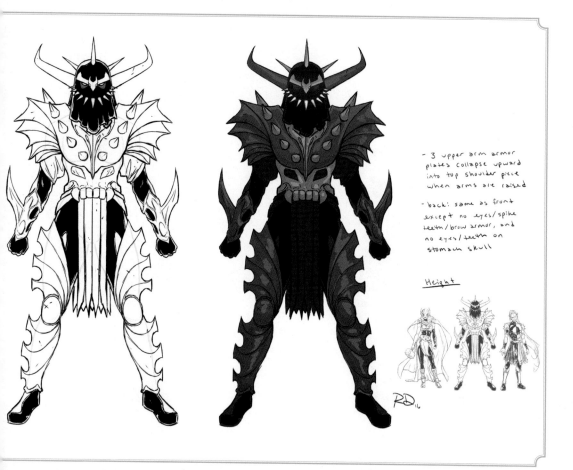

- 3 upper arm armor plates collapse upward into top shoulder piece when arms are raised

- back: same as front except no eyes/spine teeth/brow armor, and no eyes/teeth on stomach skull

Height

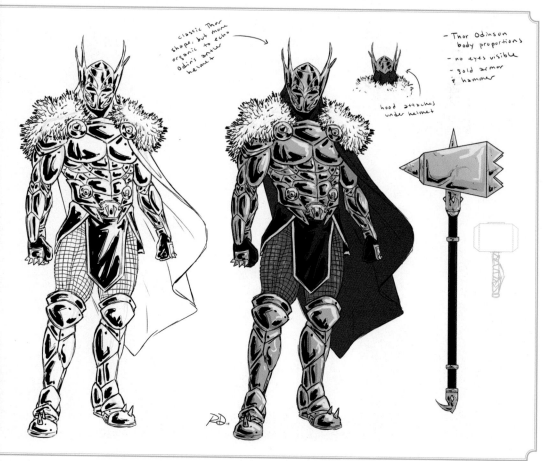

classic Thor shape, but more organic to echo Odin's antler helmet

- Thor Odinson body proportions
- no eyes visible
- gold armor & hammer

hood attaches under helmet

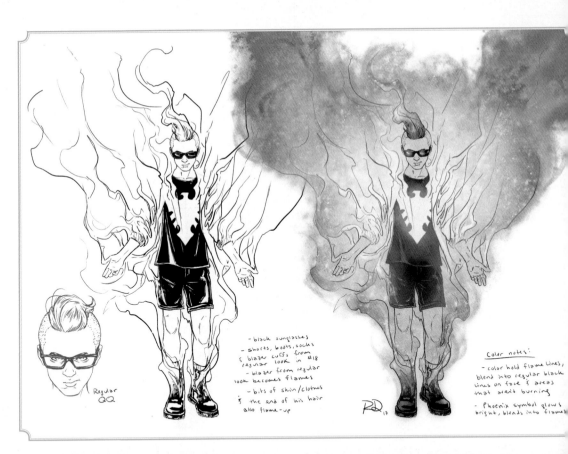

- black sunglasses
- shorts, boots, socks & blazer cuffs from regular look in #18
- blazer from regular look becomes flames
- bits of skin/clothes & the end of his hair also flame-up

Regular QQ

Color notes:
- color hold flame lines, blend into regular black lines on face & areas that aren't burning
- Phoenix symbol glows bright, blends into flames

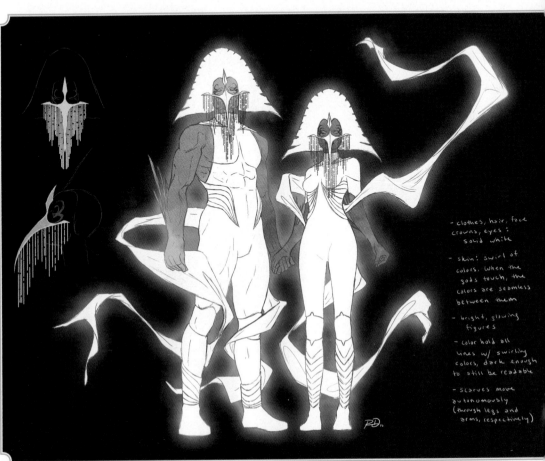

- clothes, hair, face crowns, eyes: solid white
- skin: swirl of colors. When the gods touch, the colors are seamless between them
- bright, glowing figures
- color hold all lines w/ swirling colors, dark enough to still be readable
- scarves move autonomously (through legs and arms, respectively)